Curating Revolution

Politics on Display in Mao's China

How did China's Communist revolution transform the nation's political culture? In this rich and vivid history of the Mao period (1949–1976), Denise Y. Ho examines the relationship between its exhibits and its political movements, arguing that exhibitions made revolution material. Case studies from Shanghai show how revolution was curated: museum workers collected cultural and revolutionary relics; neighborhoods, schools, and work units mounted and narrated local displays; and exhibits provided ritual space for both ideological lessons and political campaigns. Using archival sources, ephemera, interviews, and other historical materials, *Curating Revolution* traces the process by which exhibitions were developed, presented, and received. Its examples range from the First Party Congress Site and the Shanghai Museum to the "class education" and Red Guard exhibits that accompanied the Socialist Education Movement and the Cultural Revolution. With its socialist museums and new exhibitions, the exhibitionary culture of the Mao era operated in two modes: that of a state in power and that of a state in revolution. Both reflecting and making revolution, these forms remain part of China's revolutionary legacy today.

Denise Y. Ho is Assistant Professor of twentieth-century Chinese history at Yale University.

"A lucid and compelling history, *Curating Revolution* brings Mao-era exhibits to life in vivid, tangible, and deeply human detail. Ho's thoughtful analysis of these 'object lessons' and the purposes they served illuminates as never before the profound relationship between ideology and materiality in Mao-era political culture. In the process, the familiar categories of revolution, history, culture, propaganda, and participation all take on new and rich significance."

Sigrid Schmalzer, University of Massachusetts Amherst

"Exhibitionary culture was interwoven into the very fabric of daily life in Mao's China. Ho tells a fascinating story about the people who shaped that culture – curators, collectors, workers, teachers, schoolchildren, docents, and urban residents – and she does it with exceptional scholarship and rich use of archival sources."

Kirk A. Denton, The Ohio State University

"China under Mao tried harder than any state in history to inculcate a new consciousness in its citizens. *Curating Revolution* creatively bridges institutional studies of mass campaigns and oral histories to reveal how the use of objects and exhibitions narrated the past, explained the present, and awakened viewers to defend the revolution."

Karl Gerth, University of California, San Diego

"A wonderful study, chock full of new information gleaned from impressive archival, documentary, and interview sources. The theme of using exhibitions to 'make revolution' is clearly and convincingly developed. *Curating Revolution* is destined to be an important book."

Elizabeth J. Perry, Harvard University

Cambridge Studies in the History of the People's Republic of China

Series Editors

Jeremy Brown, Jacob Eyferth, Daniel Leese, Michael Schoenhals

Cambridge Studies in the History of the People's Republic of China is a major series of ambitious works in the social, political, and cultural history of socialist China. Aided by a wealth of new sources, recent research pays close attention to regional differences, to perspectives from the social and geographical margins, and to the unintended consequences of Communist Party rule. Books in the series contribute to this historical re-evaluation by presenting the most stimulating and rigorously researched works in the field to a broad audience. The series invites submissions from a variety of disciplines and approaches, based on written, material, or oral sources. Particularly welcome are those works that bridge the 1949 and 1978 divides, and those which seek to understand China in an international or global context.

Curating Revolution

Politics on Display in Mao's China

Denise Y. Ho

Yale University

CAMBRIDGE
UNIVERSITY PRESS

University Printing House, Cambridge CB2 8BS, United Kingdom

One Liberty Plaza, 20th Floor, New York, NY 10006, USA

477 Williamstown Road, Port Melbourne, VIC 3207, Australia

314-321, 3rd Floor, Plot 3, Splendor Forum, Jasola District Centre, New Delhi - 110025, India

79 Anson Road, #06-04/06, Singapore 079906

Cambridge University Press is part of the University of Cambridge.

It furthers the University's mission by disseminating knowledge in the pursuit of
education, learning and research at the highest international levels of excellence.

www.cambridge.org
Information on this title: www.cambridge.org/9781108417952
DOI: 10.1017/9781108283830

First published 2018

A catalogue record for this publication is available from the British Library

ISBN 978-1-108-41795-2 Hardback
ISBN 978-1-108-40614-7 Paperback

For my parents, Chee K. Ho and Chui-chu Lok

Contents

List of Illustrations   *page* x
List of Abbreviations   xiii
Acknowledgments   xiv

Introduction   1

1   Making a revolutionary monument: The First Party
    Congress Site   25

2   Exhibiting New China: "Fangua Lane Past and Present"   60

3   Curating belief: Superstition versus science for Young
    Pioneers   103

4   Cultivating consciousness: The class education exhibition   138

5   The Cultural Revolution's object lessons: The Exhibition
    of Red Guard Achievements   174

6   Antiquity in revolution: The Shanghai Museum   211

    Conclusion   248

Bibliography   267
Chinese Character List   287
Index   290

Illustrations

0.1 Depiction of the Shanghai Municipal Museum
(*Liangyou*, no. 120, 1936)   *page* 10

0.2 Depiction of the Shanghai Municipal Museum
(*Shaonian*, vol. 1, 1937)   11

0.3 Visitors at the Shanghai Municipal Museum, undated
(SMA H1-1-31-723)   12

0.4 Film still from *Haigang* (On the Docks), 1972   20

0.5 Stage design for *Haigang* (On the Docks), 1974   20

1.1 Exterior of the First Party Congress Site, undated
(SMA H1-22-1-1)   31

1.2 First Party Congress Site meeting room, undated
(SMA H1-22-1-2)   32

1.3 Soviet and Turkish peace delegations in the Shanghai
Revolutionary Memorial Hall, undated (SMA H1-27-1-56)   44

1.4 Chairman of the Malawi Workers' Movement visits the First
Party Congress Site, undated (SMA C1-2-5169)   45

1.5 *Paying Respects at the First Party Congress Site*, 1974 (Shanghai
renmin meishu chubanshe) (Collection of the Shanghai
Propaganda Poster Art Centre)   51

2.1 *Fangua Lane Has Changed*, Xu Yao, undated (Shanghai
renmin chubanshe)   62

2.2 Panorama of Fangua Lane, August 11, 1963 (SMA
H1-11-6-41)   69

2.3 Moving day in Fangua Lane, July 19, 1964 (SMA
H1-6-11-44)   70

2.4 Fangua Lane's first Spring Festival, February 2, 1964
(SMA H1-11-6-45)   72

2.5 Fangua Lane, Clifton Firth Collection (Sir George Grey
Special Collections, Auckland Libraries)   78

2.6 Women representatives from Chile tour Fangua Lane,
April 16, 1966 (SMA H1-13-8-86)   82

2.7 Women representatives from Chile tour the preserved
shantytown houses, April 18, 1966 (SMA H1-13-8-82) 85

2.8 Women representatives from Chile walk through the new
apartments, April 18, 1966 (SMA H1-13-8-84) 86

2.9 Wall hangings in an apartment in Fangua Lane, June 20,
2012 96

2.10 Diorama of the shantytown at the Shanghai City History
Exhibition Hall, June 12, 2013 99

2.11 Depiction of a 1978 home interior at the Shanghai Expo,
2010 100

2.12 Depiction of a 2008 home interior at the Shanghai Expo,
2010 101

3.1 Film still from *Yiguan hairen dao* (The Way of Persistently
Harming People), 1952 107

3.2 Illustration of a temple from "Love Science and Eliminate
Superstition," 1963 (SMA C27-1-51) 110

3.3 Poster from the exhibition "Eliminate Superstition"
(Kexue puji chubanshe, 1965) (Collection of the Shanghai
Propaganda Poster Art Centre) 113

3.4 Illustration of a natural disaster from "Love Science and
Eliminate Superstition," 1963 (SMA C27-1-51) 117

3.5 Illustration of a fortune-teller from "Love Science and
Eliminate Superstition," 1963 (SMA C27-1-51) 118

3.6 Illustration of a spirit medium from "Love Science and
Eliminate Superstition," 1963 (SMA C27-1-51) 119

3.7 Illustration of an exorcist from "Love Science and Eliminate
Superstition," 1963 (SMA C27-1-51) 120

3.8 *Take a shuttle and explore outer space*, by Zhang Ruiheng
(Hebei renmin chubanshe, 1979) (Collection of the Shanghai
Propaganda Poster Art Centre) 123

4.1 Prop design for the class education exhibition, *Haigang*
(On the Docks), 1974 139

4.2 Prop design for the class education exhibition, *Haigang*
(On the Docks), 1974 140

4.3 Scene from *Shouzuyuan* (Rent Collection Courtyard), 2016 141

4.4 Workers at an *yiku sitian* exhibition, undated
(SMA H1-23-24-8) 149

4.5 Photograph from the Shanghai Class Education Exhibition
showing a worker's scar, undated (SMA H1-23-29-18) 155

4.6 Photograph from the Shanghai Class Education Exhibition
of a worker from Shenxin Number Nine Mill, undated
(SMA H1-23-29-13) 160

5.1 Film still of a house search, undated (Cultural Revolution
    Video Collection: Decade in the Great Cultural Revolution,
    Fairbank Collection, Fung Library, Harvard University)   187
5.2 Film still of a house search, undated (Cultural Revolution
    Video Collection: Decade in the Great Cultural Revolution,
    Fairbank Collection, Fung Library, Harvard University)   188
5.3 Yan Jichang's fur coat from the Exhibition of Red Guard
    Achievements   192
6.1 Postcard of the Longhua Pagoda, René Antoine Nus, ca.
    1930s (Virtual Cities Project, Institut d'Asie Orientale)   212
6.2 Bronzes on display in the Shanghai Museum, ca. 1960s
    (SMA H1-14-3-23)   222
6.3 A Venezuelan women's delegation tours the Shanghai
    Museum, July 21, 1963 (SMA H1-13-2-84)   223
6.4 Group photo of the staff of the Shanghai Museum during
    acquisition of a placard from the Shanghai People's
    Commune, undated (Collection of Zheng Zhong)   233
6.5 Staff of the Shanghai Museum pose in the foyer of the
    Shanghai Museum, September 27, 1967 (Collection of
    Zheng Zhong)   238
6.6 Receipt from the Wenwu Small Group, August 14, 1968
    (Collection of Qu Yongfa)   239
6.7 Denouncing the Kong family's entrance tablet (Shanghai
    xinwen tupianshe, 1974) (Collection of Thomas H. Hahn
    Docu-Images)   241
6.8 Surveying the luxuries of the Kong family (Shanghai xinwen
    tupianshe, 1974) (Collection of Thomas H. Hahn
    Docu-Images)   242

Abbreviations

BMA	Beijing Municipal Archive
CCP	Chinese Communist Party
CPPCC	Chinese People's Political Consultative Conference
CCRG	Central Cultural Revolution Group
HPDA	Huangpu District Archive
PLA	People's Liberation Army
PSB	Public Security Bureau
SHWWBWGZ	Ma Chengyuan, Huang Xuanpei, and Li Junjie, eds., *Shanghai wenwu bowuguan zhi* (Gazetteer of Shanghai's cultural relics and museums)
SMA	Shanghai Municipal Archive
SZYWBLJ	Chen Qiuhui, ed., *Shen Zhiyu wenbo lunji* (Collected writings by Shen Zhiyu on cultural relics and museums)
WDGW	Song Yongyi, ed., *Zhongguo wenhua da geming wenku* (Chinese Cultural Revolution database)
ZBDA	Zhabei District Archive

Acknowledgments

I am fortunate to have had many teachers. As an undergraduate at Yale, I was first introduced to the Chinese language by William Zhou and George Krompacky, and was granted one of the first Light Fellowships to study in Beijing. To see Teachers Zhou and Su Wei in the audience at my alma mater in 2014, so many years later, brought joy to my heart. In History Department seminars, John Demos taught the historian's craft, John Gaddis encouraged us to *be* historians, and it was Jonathan Spence's masterful storytelling that inspired me to go to China. After graduation, a teaching fellowship from the Yale-China Association sent me to Changsha for two years; I continue to learn from its teachers and students.

I owe a great debt to my teachers and mentors at Harvard. First thanks go to Philip Kuhn, a model of teaching and scholarship. I wish he could have seen this book. William Kirby introduced me to local contacts in Shanghai, and he never fails to be a source of encouragement. Henrietta Harrison's thoughtful feedback and intellectual generosity continues to set a high bar. In addition to my thesis committee, my graduate education was enriched by outside fields with Sven Beckert, Peter Bol, and Akira Iriye, and it was an honor to begin my college teaching in the "rice paddies" course under Peter Bol and Mark Elliott. Rubie Watson read a chapter of my thesis with great care and pushed me to clarify my argument.

Numerous institutions and individuals facilitated the research for this book. At Harvard I would like to thank the Harvard-Yenching Library and the Fairbank Collection in the Fung Library, especially the incomparable Nancy Hearst. In Shanghai I did much of my archival work at the Shanghai Municipal Archive and the Shanghai Municipal Library. In addition to their staff, I am grateful to Shen Zuwei, at that time of the Huangpu People's Government, and Hu Yuanjie, at the Huangpu District Archive. At the Shanghai Academy of Social Sciences, Duan Lian, Jin Dalu, and Ma Jun always made me feel welcome and answered my many questions. Among the many people in Shanghai who so kindly shared their memories and ideas, most must remain anonymous, but I extend particular gratitude to Li Junjie and Zhong Yinlan of the Shanghai Museum, Yang Peiming of the Shanghai Propaganda Poster Art Centre, and Zheng Zhong of *Wenhui bao*. I would also like to thank Judy Fugate at the University of Kentucky Library, Louise Jones and Gao Qi at The Chinese University of Hong Kong Library and the Universities Service Centre respectively, and Michael Meng and Tang Li at the Yale University Library.

My many work units have generously supported this book, both intellectually and materially. In graduate school, my work was funded by a Foreign Languages and Area Studies Fellowship, grants from the Harvard History Department and the Fairbank Center for Chinese Studies, and the Fulbright U.S. Student Program. At the University of Kentucky (UK), research and conference grants allowed me to visit China each year. For scholarly community and friendship, I would like to thank my colleagues in the UK History Department, especially my chairs Francie Chassen-López and Karen Petrone, and my mentors Kathi Kern and Gretchen Starr-Lebeau. In Modern and Classical Languages, Liang Luo and Matt Wells of our "Gang of Three" exchanged work over coffee and supplied mutual encouragement. For completion of this book, I gratefully acknowledge my colleagues at the Chinese University of Hong Kong's Centre for China Studies, and funding from the Direct Grant for Research and the Research Grants Council of the Hong Kong Special Administrative Region (Project No. 14403714). At Yale, I thank the History Department, especially Glenda Gilmore and Naomi Lamoreaux, who arranged for a colloquium on this book in February 2016. The Frederick W. Hilles Publication Fund of Yale University provided resources for the cover art, editing, and images. Finally, I thank the students whose work has contributed to this book: Noah Fang, Guo Nianzhi, Liling Huang, Li Ying, Liu Xinyi, Liu Ying, Yawen Ludden, and Annemarelle van Schayik. The talented Sherril Wang created the artwork on the cover.

Over the years, my thinking has been shaped by careful readings and rigorous questions from many scholars. At the Association for Asian Studies annual meetings, I have benefited from the audiences, my co-panelists, and the following discussants: Tina Mai Chen, Xiaomei Chen, Gail Hershatter, Rebecca Nedostup, Elizabeth Perry, and Rubie Watson. Other scholars who have read portions of this book as conference papers include Julia Andrews, Susan Brownell, Neil Diamant, Delin Lai, Felicity Luftkin, Sigrid Schmalzer, Kuiyi Shen, Lisa Tran, and Eugene Wang. I am also grateful for comments from audiences at Berea College, Crane House: The Asia Institute, Indiana University, Ohio State University,

University of Hong Kong, University of Kentucky, and Washington University in St. Louis. I would like to extend special thanks to Deborah Davis, Kirk Denton, Valerie Hansen, Henrietta Harrison, Jie Li, Tobie Meyer-Fong, Peter Perdue, Elizabeth Perry, Sigrid Schmalzer, Rubie Watson, Yiching Wu, and two anonymous readers for Cambridge University Press for reading the full manuscript and providing detailed feedback. I am indebted to Nancy Hearst for her first-rate editorial work. Lucy Rhymer and her team at Cambridge brought this book to completion with professionalism and skill; I thank them and the editors of the series for their enthusiasm.

A previous version of Chapter 1 appeared in *Red Legacies in China: Cultural Afterlives of the Communist Revolution*, edited by Jie Li and Enhua Zhang © 2016 by Harvard University Asia Center. Parts of Chapter 6 come from "Revolutionizing Antiquity: The Shanghai Cultural Bureaucracy in the Cultural Revolution, 1966–1968," *The China Quarterly* 207 (September 2011): 687–705, © 2011 by Cambridge University Press. Many thanks to the original publishers for permission to use this material.

My classmates and friends continue to inspire me by their own scholarship and personal examples. To the history hens: Betsy More, Vernie Oliveiro, Harmony O'Rourke, and Juliet Wagner, may you write and make history. Kristin Poling spent a priceless week thinking with me by Kentucky's Lake Nolin and gave this book its title. I have also been inspired by friendship with a generation of students of China, including Jennifer Altehenger, Margaret Boittin, Sei Jeong Chin, Brooks Jessup, Loretta Kim, Chris Leighton, Jie Li, Silvia Lindtner, Minhua Ling, Kate Mason, Lü Pan, Ying Qian, Meg Rithmire, Cole Roskam, Priscilla Song, Tang Xiaobing, Jing Wang, Shellen Wu, and Lawrence Zhang. Michelle King is the *xuejie* par excellence, and I endeavor to express my gratitude by paying it forward. Finally, friends around the world—especially Argo Caminis, Angie Lai, and Areio Soltani—have shared tables and joys: I owe you a banquet.

My greatest fortune is my family. I wish to thank my sister Renee for standing with me and holding all of us to high standards. My sister Bonnie's curiosity and awareness has helped me to be true to myself. My brother Patrick follows his dreams and supports mine. I am so proud of the people my siblings have become and the good that they do in the world. Since 2010, Alex Ledin has made our every house a home; I thank him for hitching his star to mine.

This book is dedicated to my parents and my first teachers, Chee K. Ho and Chui-chu Lok.

Introduction

In Mao's China, to curate revolution was to make it material. To that end, a 1951 handbook—published for Shanghai neighborhood cadres two years after the establishment of the People's Republic of China in 1949—posed the following question: "How do you put on an exhibition?" This task was one of many for the local official charged with organizing the daily lives of those residents under his care. The slender string-bound volume explained all manner of practical responsibilities, from how to hold a meeting to how to register households. Among these tasks, it gave primacy to the work of propaganda. The handbook described techniques that would become ubiquitous symbols of everyday life in Communist China, including the neighborhood blackboard bulletin and the glass newspaper display case. But exhibition, the cadre learned, was a particularly powerful form of propaganda. Although people encountered many material objects in their daily lives, it was only when things were organized into a system that they might be used to illustrate the true face of an issue. "Every exhibition object," the handbook read, "has in and of itself a life and the ability to persuade."[1]

Making an exhibition was both mass education and mass mobilization. The Shanghai cadre was encouraged to put on displays because concrete objects were seen as appealing to people unaccustomed to abstraction, and because with narration an exhibit was accessible to all. The handbook suggested that viewers first encounter photographs, then artifacts, and finally diagrams. It was best if the cadre could gather items from neighborhood residents themselves, thus linking the exhibition to their personal experiences. He was advised on how to choose and arrange objects, and how to match exhibitions with political movements, including the campaigns to cherish public property, to Resist America

---

[1] *Jiedao lilong jumin shenghuo shouce* (A handbook for neighborhood residential life) (Shanghai: Xinwen ribao chubanshe, 1951), p. 42. For a more extensive guide to putting on exhibitions, see *Nongcun meishu shouce* (Handbook for rural art) (Shijiazhuang: Hebei renmin chubanshe, 1975), pp. 146–158.

and Support Korea, and to identify and attack counterrevolutionaries and spies. An exhibition allowed visitors to reflect on the past, awakening memories of their former lives in the so-called "old society" (*jiu shehui*), as pre-Communist China was known. A display juxtaposed this past with the contemporary "new society" (*xin shehui*), in which Chinese people had "stood up" (*fanshen*), the contrast between Old China and New China "stimulating the masses' patriotic feelings." But while the cadre sought to bring forth the "masses' emotions of love and hate," the ultimate goal was an understanding of the world and its systems.[2] What better way to reflect the truth of the world than through real things?

Almost a decade later, Shen Zhiyu, then a deputy director at the Shanghai Museum, similarly stressed the grassroots nature of museum activities. In a 1960 speech, he highlighted the transformation of museums in China since the 1949 "Liberation." Before Liberation, Shen stated, treaty-port Shanghai faced foreign incursions, and in British and French museums on Chinese soil, imperialism took cultural form. After Liberation and under the leadership of the Chinese Communist Party, he continued, the preservation of national cultural heritage was rightfully the task of the Chinese people. He cited the example of the staff of the Shanghai Museum working with neighborhood locals to locate and restore important historic sites, including the tenth-century Longhua Pagoda and the sixteenth-century Yu Garden. The masses, Shen claimed, made tens of thousands of donations to the museum, "reflecting a great transformation of consciousness and spirit." Emphasizing the role of the Shanghai Museum in mass education, he described the museum staff taking traveling exhibitions to the people. From classroom to cultural palace, from factory to village, in 1959 alone the museum reached an estimated 3.8 million people. Quoting Mao Zedong's seminal 1940 text, "On New Democracy," Shen Zhiyu explained how the Shanghai Museum's work would serve the socialist construction of the motherland.[3] To develop China's "new national culture" and increase "national self-confidence," Mao wrote, it is necessary to understand the development of ancient culture and to assimilate its democratic and revolutionary character. Hence, Mao concluded, respect for China's history would guide the masses to look to the future.[4]

---

[2] *Jiedao lilong jumin shenghuo shouce*, pp. 42–43.

[3] Shen Zhiyu, "Xuexi Mao Zedong sixiang, tigao wenwu, bowuguan gongzuo zhong de zhengcexing he sixiangxing" (Study Mao Zedong Thought and improve the adherence to the policy and ideological content of cultural relics and museum work), in Chen Qiuhui, ed., *Shen Zhiyu wenbo lunji* (Collected writings by Shen Zhiyu on cultural relics and museums) (Shanghai: Shanghai guji chubanshe, 2003), pp. 3–5 (cited hereafter as *SZYWBLJ*).

[4] Mao Zedong, "On New Democracy," in *Mao's Road to Power: Revolutionary Writings, 1912–1949, Vol. VII: New Democracy, 1939–1941*, edited by Stuart R. Schram (Armonk, NY: M.E. Sharpe, 2005), pp. 367–369.

Like the author of the neighborhood cadre's handbook, Shen outlined exhibition work and the importance of the material artifact. He was guided by Mao's essay "On Practice," in which Mao argued that perception is where knowledge begins, but that knowledge needs to be deepened into rational knowledge by understanding a thing's essence and its inherent laws.[5] Herein, Shen Zhiyu declared, lay the guiding principle for Chinese museology, and specifically, for the tasks of display (*chenlie*) and narration (*jiangjie*). Not only was the museum responsible for collecting artifacts and presenting them to viewers, it needed to interpret them in order to raise perception (*ganxing zhishi*) to the level of reason (*lixing zhishi*). This was the educative work of the museum, Shen explained, and moreover exhibition was to be ideological, scientific, and aesthetic. It should reflect Marxism-Leninism in the Chinese context, it should reveal developmental laws, and while it ought to be beautiful, aesthetics must serve ideology. In the same way that a viewer of the neighborhood exhibition was meant to return to everyday life with new eyes, a visitor to the Shanghai Museum was supposed to gain a new way of looking at the world. By attending an exhibition, Shen Zhiyu stressed, an audience would establish materialism as a world outlook.[6]

Both the neighborhood cadre and Shen Zhiyu used exhibitions to make revolution: the displays they curated were meant to spark political awakening, to create a revolutionary narrative that included the viewer, and to motivate him to participate in its realization. While a street-level exhibit presented everyday objects and the Shanghai Museum curated national treasures, both shared a number of assumptions. The curators of each believed that material artifacts were object lessons, capable of instilling correct understandings of history, of nation, and of revolution. For example, a neighborhood exhibition might display a beggar's rags, highlighting the poverty of a wartime refugee. At the museum, docents might present textiles to present-day weavers, linking their labor to workers throughout history. Both local cadre and museum director acknowledged that objects had to be supplemented with a narrative, whether it was because an illiterate resident required a young neighbor to read for him or because narration allowed a museum visitor to make the leap from perception to reason. Each curator assumed that exhibitions would cultivate New China's people to participate in socialist construction: the resident would understand "today's fortunate circumstances" and love "the new and the good," and the museum-goer would be educated in "patriotism,

---

[5] Mao Zedong, "On Practice," in *Mao's Road to Power: Revolutionary Writings, 1912–1949, Vol. VI: The New Stage, August 1937–1938*, edited by Stuart R. Schram (Armonk, NY: M.E. Sharpe, 2004), pp. 601–609.
[6] Shen Zhiyu, "Xuexi Mao Zedong," pp. 6–7.

socialism, and communism."[7] With his new worldview, the visitor would carry out the revolution. Curated in the present, an exhibition about the past would shape the future.

This book examines the exhibitionary culture of China's Mao era, a period beginning with the founding of the People's Republic in 1949 and ending with Mao's death in 1976. During the Mao years, also referred to as China's socialist period, exhibitions both reflected and made revolution.[8] For the state and the officials who created exhibitions, the purpose of collection and display was twofold: they determined the historical narrative and they projected state power. Exhibits reflected official history and politics, ordered and authorized knowledge, and created textbooks of and for revolution. For ordinary people like the neighborhood residents, display was a propaganda technique that made the revolution material and thereby intelligible. Like the adult literacy campaigns of the early 1950s, these basic exhibits taught individuals the vocabulary of the revolution; they provided templates to divide personal experiences into pre- and post-Liberation periods, and life histories between the "old society" and the "new society."[9] Although national and municipal museums were more elaborate and well-known than neighborhood and village displays, exhibitionary culture also served to localize the revolution, making propaganda at the grassroots.

Yet curating an exhibition in Mao's China was more than simply putting up a display. As propaganda officials wrote of factory exhibitions, "the opening marks half the work complete ... the work has only just begun."[10] In a tumultuous period of continuous revolution, exhibits played an indispensable role in political movements. Accompanying these campaigns, exhibits modeled participation, teaching a fount of words and creating a repertoire of action. Moreover, the ritual of visiting displays, as the cadre handbook suggested, encouraged the expression of emotions to spur mass action. As a tool of mobilization, an exhibition was not only revolution's textbook, it was also revolution's handbook. On the eve of the Cultural Revolution in 1966, exhibits about class showed visitors

---

[7] *Jiedao lilong jumin shenghuo shouce*, pp. 42–43; Shen Zhiyu, "Xuexi Mao Zedong," p. 6.

[8] Jeremy Brown and Matthew D. Johnson refer to the period from the mid-1950s to 1980 as "high socialism," marking the beginning and end of agricultural collectivization and state ownership of industry. See Jeremy Brown and Matthew D. Johnson, eds., *Maoism at the Grassroots: Everyday Life in China's Era of High Socialism* (Cambridge, MA: Harvard University Press, 2015), pp. 6–7.

[9] See Gail Hershatter, *The Gender of Memory: Rural Women and China's Collective Past* (Berkeley: University of California Press, 2011), p. 25.

[10] Shanghai Municipal Archive (cited hereafter as SMA), C1-2-3596-46, p. 50.

how to criticize and to denounce others, often by displaying the possessions of the accused. In this book I argue that curating revolution
taught people how to take part in revolution. Maoist exhibitionary
culture called on the masses to listen and to speak, to remember and
to weep, and to attack and to condemn. To curate revolution was to
make it.

Exhibitionary culture in China

In May 1949 the Shanghai Museum's first collection—2,853 objects—
arrived in two trucks that accompanied General Chen Yi's Third Field
Army. Chen, who would become Shanghai's first mayor after 1949 and
a backer of the Shanghai Museum during its early years, had ordered his
troops to preserve cultural relics (*wenwu*). These *wenwu*, some of which
had been unearthed while digging trenches, were collected "in preparation to use in building museums after the victory."[11] In his stewardship of
these objects of Chinese antiquity, Chen Yi was participating in a long
tradition of using art to symbolize political power. According to an early
Chinese myth, divine bronze tripods conferred the legitimacy of the
Mandate of Heaven.[12] This idea of rightful dynastic succession shaped
imperial collecting, whether of art or of canonical books.[13] Collection was
not limited to the court; in late imperial times local elites also established
a culture of connoisseurship and used the restoration and touring of
historic sites to reinforce a shared identity.[14] Into the twentieth century,
Chinese nationalists and revolutionaries continued to employ *wenwu*—
both objects and sites—as symbols of the nation. This took the form
of preserving collections as well as creating new monuments to the
revolution. With respect to the latter, historian Marc Andre Matten
applies Pierre Nora's concept of *lieux de mémoire* to suggest that Chinese
"places of memory"—from the mausoleum of founding father Sun
Yat-sen to Beijing's Tiananmen Square—shaped collective identity in

---

[11] Shen Zhiyu, "Huainian Chen Yi tongzhi dui wenbo shiye de juda guanhuai" (Cherishing
Comrade Chen Yi's great concern for museums and cultural relics work), in *SZYWBLJ*,
pp. 362–364.

[12] Hung Wu, *The Wu Liang Shrine: The Ideology of Early Chinese Pictorial Art* (Stanford, CA:
Stanford University Press, 1989), pp. 92–96.

[13] For a general history of imperial collecting, see Jeannette Shambaugh Elliot, with
David Shambaugh, *The Odyssey of China's Imperial Art Treasures* (Seattle: University of
Washington Press, 2005). On the classical canon, see R. Kent Guy, *The Emperor's Four
Treasures: Scholars and the State in the Late Ch'ien-Lung Era* (Cambridge, MA: Council on
East Asian Studies, Harvard University, 1987).

[14] See, for example, Craig Clunas, *Superfluous Things: Material Culture and Social Status in
Early Modern China* (Cambridge: Polity Press, 1991); Tobie Meyer-Fong, *Building
Culture in Early Qing Yangzhou* (Stanford, CA: Stanford University Press, 2003).

China.[15] By imagining "museums after the victory," Chen Yi envisioned the institutions of legitimate rule.

As Shen Zhiyu highlighted, the first museums in China were created by foreigners. The first was the Siccawei Museum, established in 1868 with the natural history collection of the French Jesuit Pierre Heude.[16] In 1874 the Royal Asiatic Society created its Shanghai Museum on land granted by the British Crown.[17] From the end of the Qing dynasty (1644–1911) and during the Republican era (1912–1949), these two museums were among the sights to see in Shanghai; travel guides described their "fantastic birds and curious beasts, the likes of which one does not often see."[18] At the outposts of empire, such foreign museums were extensions of what sociologist Tony Bennett calls the "exhibitionary complex," or a system of disciplinary relations and modern institutions in which knowledge projected power.[19] During this period, Chinese traveling overseas began to encounter the institution of the museum and the phenomenon of the World's Fair. While these travelers—like Arab visitors to Europe who saw imitation bazaars on display—witnessed Orientalism in the West, the Chinese also had the opportunity to curate, contributing to international expositions since London's Great Exhibition of 1851.[20] For Chinese reformers, however, a museum held

[15] Marc Andre Matten, ed., *Places of Memory in Modern China: History, Politics, and Identity* (Leiden: Brill, 2012); Pierre Nora, "Between Memory and History: *Les Lieux de Mémoire*," *Representations*, no. 26 (Spring 1989), pp. 7–24.

[16] A Republican-era source dates this museum to 1868, the year Heude first arrived in China, but other sources date it to 1883 at the mission compound, from whence it moved to L'Aurore University in 1930. See *Jiu Shanghai shiliao huibian* (Compilation of historical materials on old Shanghai) (Beijing: Beijing tushuguan chubanshe, 1998), reprint of *Shanghai yanjiu ziliao* (Materials on Shanghai research) (Shanghai: Zhonghua shuju, 1936, 1939), vol. 2, p. 365. Note that Siccawei is a transliteration for what today is referred to as Xujiahui.

[17] Arthur de C. Sowerby, "The History of the Shanghai Museum (R.A.S.)," *Journal of the North Branch of the Royal Asiatic Society*, vol. 65 (1934), pp. 3–10.

[18] See "Muchun you Xujiahui ji" (Record of travels to Xujiahui at the end of spring), *Shenbao* (Shanghai news), April 18, 1883. For the bamboo branch poem "Museum," see Gu Bingquan, ed., *Shanghai fengsu guji kao* (A study of Shanghai customs and historic sites) (Shanghai: Huadong shifan daxue chubanshe, 1993), p. 316. For a description from a travel guide, see Gu Guanying, comp., *Zhonghua quanguo mingsheng guji daguan* (China's famous places, historic sites, and grand vistas) (Shanghai: Dalu tushu gongsi, 1931), vol. 2, p. 53.

[19] Tony Bennett, "The Exhibitionary Complex," in *Culture/Power/History: A Reader in Contemporary Social Theory*, edited by Nicholas B. Dirks, Geoff Eley, and Sherry B. Ortner (Princeton, NJ: Princeton University Press, 1994), pp. 123–154.

[20] Timothy Mitchell, *Colonising Egypt* (Berkeley: University of California Press, 1988), especially ch. 1; Susan R. Fernsebner, "Objects, Spectacle, and a Nation on Display at the Nanyang Exposition of 1910," *Late Imperial China*, vol. 27, no. 2 (December 2006), p. 100. For Chinese observations, see Shanghai tushuguan (Shanghai Library), ed., *Zhongguo yu shibo: Lishi jilu, 1851–1940* (China and the world exposition: Historical records, 1851–1940) (Shanghai: Shanghai kexue jishu wenxian chubanshe, 2002).

more potential than either a cabinet of curiosities or a way of ordering the world. Instead, museums and exhibitions became associated with the machines of modernization. In 1895, for example, Kang Youwei's Shanghai Strengthening Society proposed opening a museum that would include the latest inventions and machines, explaining that neither words nor drawings were sufficient to understand an object.[21] By the waning years of the Qing dynasty, exhibitionary culture came to be increasingly linked to the nation. China began to host domestic expositions to advocate new national culture and native products. In 1905, the first Chinese museum was established in Jiangsu Province's Nantong by the reformer Zhang Jian.[22] Zhang was also a proponent of making public the imperial collection, which opened its doors as the Palace Museum on National Day in 1925.[23]

From the Qing dynasty to the Republican era, the Chinese term for museum underwent several transformations. At the end of the Qing, loan words from the Japanese included *bolanguan* (museum-library) and *bowuyuan* (museum-garden); Kang Youwei advocated for what he called *bowuyuan* and the Nantong Museum used these same characters.[24] Some museum-boosters during the Republican period even invented new characters. One proposal, for example, was a character made up of an object *wu* (物) within a box (囗). Other neographs include the character *bo* (博) for expansiveness, under a roof (宀) or a cover (冖).[25] Although *bowuyuan* continued to be used, the Chinese Museum Association (Zhongguo Bowuguan Xiehui) selected *bowuguan* for its title when it was established in 1935, the standard word for museum that remains to this day. In this book I will use the word "museum" for permanent institutions like the Shanghai Museum, which uses *bowuguan*

---

[21] Tang Zhijun, *Wuxu shiqi de xuehui he baokan* (Study societies and periodicals of the 1898 period) (Taibei: Taiwan shangwu yinshuguan, 1993), pp. 85–93.

[22] Fernsebner, "Objects, Spectacle, and a Nation," pp. 100–103; Qin Shao, "Exhibiting the Modern: The Creation of the First Chinese Museum, 1905–1930," *The China Quarterly*, no. 179 (September 2004), pp. 684–702.

[23] Cheng-hua Wang, "The Qing Imperial Collection, Circa 1905–1925: National Humiliation, Heritage Preservation, and Exhibition Culture," in *Reinventing the Past: Archaism and Antiquarianism in Chinese Art and Visual Culture*, edited by Hung Wu (Chicago: Center for the Art of East Asia, University of Chicago, 2010), pp. 320–341.

[24] Shen Zhiyu, "Bowuguanxue gailun" (Introduction to museology), in *SZJWBLJ*, p. 22; Qin Shao, "Exhibiting the Modern," pp. 691–692. Here I follow Qin Shao's translation of "museum-library" and "museum-garden."

[25] See, for example, in the *Journal of the Chinese Museum Association* the following articles: Yuan Tongli, "Kangzhan qizhong woguo bowuguan zhi dongtai yu qiantu" (The situation and future of our nation's museums during wartime), *Zhongguo bowuguan xiehui huibao* (Journal of the Chinese Museum Association), no. 1 (1941), pp. 2–4, and "Shanghai shibo zhenshi kaimu" (The formal opening of the Shanghai Municipal Museum), *Zhongguo bowuguan xiehui huibao*, vol. 2, no. 3 (1927), p. 15.

in its name. The First Party Congress Site, the place where the Chinese Communist Party (CCP) was founded, is more difficult to define: it includes a meeting site (*huizhi*) preserved as a monument, it is officially a *wenwu*, and it is also a memorial hall (*jinianguan*) that displays exhibitions (*zhanlan*). For simplicity, I will refer to the memorial hall with its exhibitions as a museum, bearing in mind that it was first intended to be a large museum of revolutionary history. Other words that refer to short-term exhibitions are *zhanlanguan* (exhibition hall), *zhanlanhui* (exhibition), and *chenlieguan* (display hall). One particular genre in Mao's China, the class education exhibition, even had its own short name, *jiezhan* (for *jieji jiaoyu zhanlan* [class education exhibition]).

Museums of revolutionary history originated with the Nationalist Party (Guomindang). Revolution in this context refers to the 1911 Revolution that ended imperial rule and the 1927 Northern Expedition that brought the Nationalist government to power. In exhibitions of the revolution, historical documents and martyrs' possessions figured prominently, meant to educate and to inspire. These exhibition halls also served as ritual spaces: they enshrined revolutionary relics and required visitors to perform three bows to a portrait of Sun Yat-sen.[26] Kirk Denton traces Communist exhibitionary culture on the revolution back to the Nationalist era. Examining the Revolutionary Memorial Hall at the 1929 West Lake Exposition, Denton observes a temporal narrative of progress; the importance of the Nationalist Party, ideology, and the founding father; the revolution as supported by the will of the people; and a revolutionary tradition inherited by current leaders.[27] Beyond narratives of revolution, Republican-era museum-boosters argued that exhibitions could be tools of mass education. In a 1936 text, Chen Duanzhi explained that New Culture intellectuals had misunderstood museums "as warehouses that preserved old tools, old objects, and old classes." The museum, Chen argued, was not a "decorative object" and, like the Soviet Union, China could use museums to spread ideology and to transform the people's consciousness.[28]

In Shanghai, the new Greater Shanghai Municipal Center included the Shanghai Municipal Museum. Housed in a modern concrete

---

[26] Chen Yunqian, "Local Exhibitions and the Molding of Revolutionary Memory (1927–1949)," *Chinese Studies in History*, vol. 47, no. 1 (Fall 2013), pp. 29–52.

[27] Kirk A. Denton, *Exhibiting the Past: Historical Memory and the Politics of Museums in Postsocialist China* (Honolulu: University of Hawai'i Press, 2014), especially pp. 46–52.

[28] Chen Duanzhi, *Bowuguanxue tonglun* (General survey of museum studies) (Shanghai: Shanghaishi bowuguan, 1936), p. 27; Chen Duanzhi, *Bowuguan* (Museums) (Shanghai: Shangwu yinshuguan, 1937), p. 22.

building with a grand Chinese roof, the Shanghai Municipal Museum focused on Shanghai and Chinese history, displaying local industries such as textile production and showcasing models of the city's new construction.[29] The museum was open for less than a year before the Sino-Japanese War broke out. After the war, in May of 1946, it re-opened in more modest quarters, displaying some of its collection that had been hidden during the Japanese Occupation.[30] In the context of the ongoing Chinese Civil War, special exhibition topics included Sun Yat-sen's life and letters, Shanghai's war of resistance, and the national revolution. By far the most popular was the three-day Sun Yat-sen exhibit, which was visited by 51,263 people.[31] Although the Shanghai Municipal Museum never returned to its original building, the edifice still stands today in Shanghai's Yangpu District. It is both a monument to Republican-era architecture and, together with a library cast in its mirror image, a representation of the contemporary vision of the museum and the library as two wings of cultural construction.[32]

Meanwhile, the CCP had plans of its own. As the story of Chen Yi's two trucks of relics demonstrates, the Party was also collecting objects of antiquity. In land reform, Communist cadres were ordered to preserve art and books seized from landlords, and as the People's Liberation Army (PLA) advanced, it took over collections and established local commissions for the protection of *wenwu*.[33] When the Communists took over Shanghai, the Shanghai Military Commission plastered large handwritten notices with instructions to gather up *wenwu* as "treasures of national culture and precious materials of national history."[34] As for artifacts of their own revolution, Tracey Lu explains that the CCP began planning for a museum as early as 1930 and decided in 1933 to

[29] "Shanghai shibo zhenshi kaimu," *Zhongguo bowuguan xiehui huibao*, vol. 2, no. 3 (1927), pp. 15–16.

[30] Li Chunkang, "Shanghai de bowuguan" (Shanghai's museums), *Lüxing zazhi* (Travel magazine), vol. 22, no. 7 (1948), p. 23; *Shanghai shili bowuguan yaolan* (Shanghai Municipal Museum exhibition), August 1948, pp. 2–3.

[31] *Shanghai shili bowuguan yaolan*, p. 13. Visitors during this month accounted for over half the annual total; later monthly figures never exceeded 19,000.

[32] Chen Duanzhi, *Bowuguanxue tonglun*, p. 23.

[33] "Zhongyang gongwei guanyu zuzhi huihuai gushu, guji de zhishi (Directive from the Central Construction Commission on preventing damage to ancient books and historic sites), July 10, 1947, in *Zhongguo gongchandang xuanchuan gongzuo wenxian xuanbian: 1937–1949* (Selected documents on the propaganda work of the Chinese Communist Party: 1937–1949) (Beijing: Xuexi chubanshe, 1996), p. 665. On the Shandong Commission on Cultural Relics and its exhibition, see "Jinan juxing gudai wenwu zhanlan" (Jinan mounts an ancient cultural relics exhibition), *Dongbei ribao* (Northeast daily news), February 5, 1949, p. 3.

[34] SMA B1-2-245, p. 10. This document is dated July 20, 1949.

Ill.0.1. Depiction of the Shanghai Municipal Museum, including its offices and rooms for reading, research, and assembly. *Liangyou*, no. 120 (1936), pp. 10–11

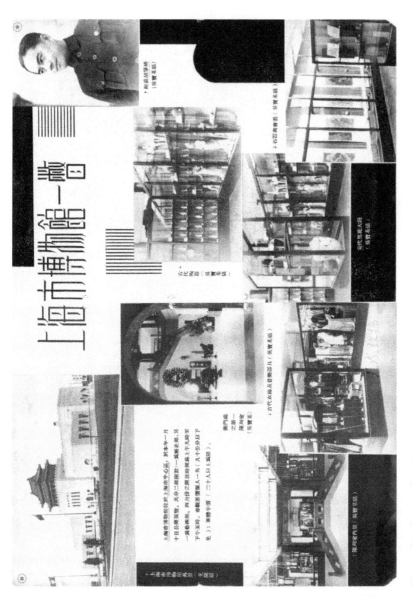

III.0.2. Depiction of the Shanghai Municipal Museum, its architecture, and the art and artifacts on display. *Shaomian,* vol. 1 (1937), pp. 8–9

Ill.0.3. Visitors at the Shanghai Municipal Museum, undated.
SMA H1-1-31-73

establish a central Museum of the Chinese Revolution.[35] In the base areas under Communist control, cadres put up public education displays, most often on topics of war or production.[36] On October 11, 1949, ten days after Mao stood on the Tiananmen rostrum and declared the founding of the People's Republic, the Museum of the Chinese Revolution was established in Beijing. Immediately thereafter, the Department of Propaganda issued a call to collect revolutionary cultural relics, *geming wenwu*.[37]

After 1949, Chinese museology followed the Soviet example. Chinese officials went on study tours to learn from Soviet museums, and the pages of the main museum trade journal, *Wenwu cankao ziliao* (Cultural relics reference materials), included many articles on Soviet museums and methods of display. In 1950, Wang Yeqiu of the State Bureau of

[35] Tracey L-D. Lu, *Museums in China: Materialized Power and Objectified Identities* (London: Routledge, 2014), p. 114.

[36] Zhongguo geming bowuguan (Museum of the Chinese Revolution), ed., *Jiefangqu zhanlanhui ziliao* (Materials on exhibitions in the liberated areas) (Beijing: Wenwu chubanshe, 1988).

[37] "Zhongyang xuanchuanbu guanyu shouji geming wenwu de tongzhi" (Central Department of Propaganda notice on the collection of revolutionary relics), October 11, 1949, in *Dangde xuanchuan gongzuo wenjian xuanbian, 1949–1966* (Selected documents on Party propaganda work) (Beijing: Zhonggong zhongyang dangxiao chubanshe, 1994), p. 34.

Cultural Relics wrote an admiring description of the Soviet Museum of the Revolution. Wang explained that a revolutionary museum was unfinished, to be continually added to until the arrival of communism.[38] The CCP adopted this perspective, and therefore collected not only historical materials but also artifacts from the present. During the Cultural Revolution, for example, institutions such as the First Party Congress Site and the Shanghai Museum collected materials in real time. Red Guard newspapers from this period include notices calling for the donation of documents for a Cultural Revolution collection.[39] In the course of revolution, new chapters were to be written and displays would teach the masses how to write the next.

Taking the Mao period as its focus, this book examines exhibitions as political, social, and cultural practice. It demonstrates that exhibits were a form of participatory propaganda: docents and visitors alike were part of their making and reception; they brought together other propaganda forms like local history and personal narrative; and they played an indispensable role in political campaigns. Such practices around exhibitions show that while the CCP inherited some exhibitionary techniques from its predecessor and from the Soviet model, others were particular to a revolution that was grassroots, materialist, and class-based. I propose that we think of socialist China's exhibitionary culture in two overlapping modes: one form is that of a state in power and the other is that of a revolutionary movement. Museums of antiquity or of revolution are examples of the former mode; like official textbooks, they legitimated the state that the revolution had brought to power and inscribed the revolution onto a national narrative. An exhibit that galvanized participation in a campaign, such as land reform or the Cultural Revolution, represents the latter mode; like a handbook, it identified political categories, taught vocabulary and slogans, and accused enemies of the revolution. One exhibition might partake of both modes, as in a showcase about modernization that could both affirm and mobilize. In Mao's China, politics on display legitimated and made revolution.

---

[38] Wang Yeqiu, "Sulian guoli geming bowuguan" (The Soviet Museum of the Revolution), *Wenwu cankao ziliao* (Cultural relics reference materials), no. 10 (1950), pp. 66–76.

[39] Hongweibing dianying zhipianchang yi geming qunzhong (One member of the revolutionary masses of the film studio Red Guards), "Shanghai hongweibing geming zaofan zhanlanhui zhengji wenhua da geming zhongyao wenxian" (The Shanghai Red Guards Revolutionary Rebels Exhibition is seeking important documents from the Cultural Revolution), *Wenyi zhanbao* (Newsletter from the cultural and artistic front), no. 36 (December 3, 1967), p. 4. From the collection of the History Department Library at Fudan University.

The politics of culture in Mao's China

The 1951 Shanghai neighborhood cadre's handbook ended its exhibition instructions with the following exhortation: an exhibit should be coordinated with other forms of propaganda, like the radio broadcast. Only in this way would a display be vivid and dramatic, "having sound and color."[40] With multi-media features, museums and exhibitions in Mao's China brought together many propaganda forms, including history and narrative as well as visual and material culture. As a space in which docents recited texts and in which audiences were encouraged to participate, an exhibition was most often a classroom and sometimes a theater. At the intersection of socialist education and propaganda, the history of exhibitionary culture contributes to recent work on the following questions: What was the culture of socialist China, and what did it do? How did culture influence politics, and what did it bring to China's Communist revolution? What was the political culture of the Mao period, and in what ways did it legitimize the regime and encourage participation in political movements?

Research on cultural production often refers to Mao's own writings on culture and on the relationship between art and politics. Mao's 1940 "On New Democracy" defined new democratic culture as a "national, scientific, and mass culture," an assimilation of the democratic and revolutionary characteristics of ancient and foreign culture with contemporary socialist culture.[41] Though at the time Mao wrote that this culture—as superstructure—would reflect contemporary politics and economics, in his later years and especially during the Cultural Revolution, culture was meant to transform the economic base. Two years after "On New Democracy," Mao's "Talks at the Yan'an Conference on Literature and Art" called on artists and writers to learn from the people, making explicit that literature and art were to be subordinate to politics.[42] Thus Mao's early texts and the political campaigns of the Mao years establish a tension: on the one hand, the former suggests that culture reflects politics and artists serve the Communist Party; on the other hand, the latter implies a leading role for culture in social transformation. Recent scholarship highlights the importance of cultural products. In 2008, Paul Clark's history of the Cultural Revolution argued that cultural practice was both central to the everyday life of ordinary people and part of

---

[40] *Jiedao lilong jumin shenghuo shouce*, p. 43.
[41] Mao Zedong, "On New Democracy," pp. 367–369.
[42] Bonnie S. McDougall, *Mao Zedong's "Talks at the Yan'an Conference on Literature and Art": A Translation of the 1943 Text with Commentary* (Ann Arbor: Center for Chinese Studies, University of Michigan, 1980).

a longer trajectory of modernization in literature and art.[43] Analyzing a wide range of propaganda art, historian Barbara Mittler demonstrates its pervasiveness and popularity, then and now.[44] The study of a particular genre allows scholars to trace its social influence, as in Yomi Braester's examination of cinema, which explains how films helped people envision the new socialist city.[45] On socialist visual culture, Xiaobing Tang writes that "it was centered on producing a new way of seeing ... both *how* and *what* to see."[46] To these works this book adds the example of the exhibition as a cultural product, one that taught people how to categorize objects in the world around them: remnants and relics of the past; products of the present and promises of the future; and proof of crimes and badges of class.

In addition to studies of cultural products, scholars have also examined the role of culture in politics. In his book on drama troupes before 1949 and in the early years of the People's Republic, Brian DeMare demonstrates how actors worked at the grassroots and on the front lines as propagandists, highlighting that art did more than serve politics—it was politics.[47] Elizabeth Perry's history of the coal mining town of Anyuan, a site central to early Communist Party mobilization, employs the concept of "cultural positioning" to suggest that the CCP owed much of its success to its deployment of culture, from religion and ritual to drama and art. Indeed, Perry argues that political legitimacy rests on both cultural and military power and that effective political mobilization relies on culture.[48] By going behind the scenes at exhibitions, this book reveals how one kind of grassroots propaganda was made. Like the troupe's actor, the curator tailored his message to the audience and the docent rehearsed a text to compel politically correct emotions. Like the organizer at Anyuan, both curator and docent taught a new revolutionary culture, one that combined elite traditions such as artistic

---

[43] Paul Clark, *The Chinese Cultural Revolution: A History* (Cambridge: Cambridge University Press, 2008).

[44] Barbara Mittler, *A Continuous Revolution: Making Sense of Cultural Revolution Culture* (Cambridge, MA: Asia Center, Harvard University, 2012). Mittler attributes both contemporary popularity and continued legacy to the ability of propaganda art to incorporate both traditional and foreign influences.

[45] Yomi Braester, *Painting the City Red: Chinese Cinema and the Urban Contract* (Durham, NC: Duke University Press, 2010).

[46] Xiaobing Tang, *Visual Culture in Contemporary China: Paradigms and Shifts* (Cambridge: Cambridge University Press, 2015), pp. 22–23.

[47] Brian James DeMare, *Mao's Cultural Army: Drama Troupes in China's Rural Revolution* (Cambridge: Cambridge University Press, 2015).

[48] Elizabeth J. Perry, *Anyuan: Mining China's Revolutionary Tradition* (Berkeley: University of California Press, 2012), especially pp. 4, 8–9, 287–288.

connoisseurship and writing history with popular rituals like storytelling and drama.

New cultural products together with cultural power created socialist China's political culture. Examining a range of state-sponsored projects from parades to oil paintings, historian Chang-tai Hung argues that these contributed to a political culture that legitimated Communist rule in the 1950s.[49] If culture is not only a product but also a practice, then political culture includes rituals, such as the Mao-era form of personal narrative, "recalling bitterness and reflecting on sweetness" (*yiku sitian*) and "comparing past and present" (*huiyi duibi*). Anthropologist Ann Anagnost links these forms—which asked individuals to think of past hardships and compare them with present good fortune—to the denunciation practice of "speaking bitterness" (*suku*) used during the land reform campaigns.[50] Focusing on the performance of *yiku sitian* in the Socialist Education Movement (1962–1966), historian Guo Wu argues that the practice aimed to transform individual and collective understandings of class.[51] While *yiku sitian* was primarily performed during political meetings, this book shows how local exhibits curated *yiku sitian* narratives—to be told by docents and through artifacts—and encouraged visitors to recall their own bitterness. Both the authority of the display and the ritual space of the exhibition hall lent credence to the narrative. Exhibitions thus played a part in political culture by showcasing official interpretations of history and politics and by making visitors students of its object lessons. In his analysis of the Mao cult, Daniel Leese highlights the power of rhetoric and ritual in both political mobilization and control.[52] Similarly, exhibition narratives and the ritual of attendance provided scripts of legitimacy and of revolution.

What made exhibition, as the 1951 Shanghai cadre was told, a powerful kind of propaganda? Unlike other forms, it relied on artifacts. To be sure, there were exhibits primarily of pictures or photographs, and indeed a pictorial exhibition was the easiest and cheapest type to mount. But ideally an exhibition emphasized objects above all, and indeed in exhibition records it was always the objects that most attracted the viewer; visitors often requested more objects and fewer texts. Exhibits and their

---

[49] Chang-tai Hung, *Mao's New World: Political Culture in the Early People's Republic* (Ithaca, NY: Cornell University Press, 2011).

[50] Ann Anagnost, *National Past-Times: Narrative, Representation, and Power in Modern China* (Durham, NC: Duke University Press, 1997), p. 38.

[51] Guo Wu, "Recalling Bitterness: Historiography, Memory, and Myth in Maoist China," *Twentieth-Century China*, vol. 39, no. 3 (October 2014), pp. 245–268.

[52] Daniel Leese, *Mao Cult: Rhetoric and Ritual in China's Cultural Revolution* (Cambridge: Cambridge University Press, 2011).

display items were well suited to the grassroots, materialist, and class-based revolution that was China's. Exhibitions were adapted to the locality and presented individual stories; the visitor could apply its lessons to his own life and to the material around him, no matter how quotidian. That Marxism was part of the triumvirate of Marxism-Leninism-Mao Zedong Thought meant that material artifacts were evidence of historical developments and relationships in production. Finally, objects offered a tangible authenticity that allowed possessions also to become proof. In Mao's continuous revolution, things could teach class lessons and identify class enemies. It was exhibitionary culture that gave material objects political power.

Sites of display

This book begins with the story of the Shanghai Museum's Shen Zhiyu and his search for the site of the 1921 First Communist Party Congress. Chapter 1, "Making a revolutionary monument," examines the First Party Congress Site as a revolutionary artifact and a museum of revolutionary history. Despite the imperative to create a definitive and authoritative textbook, the museum's archives demonstrate how curators wrote and revised, how the exhibition was modified to support contemporary politics, and how the First Party Congress Site cultivated a founding myth with Mao at the center. First Party Congress Site officials, responsible for curating the Communist revolution, endeavored to adhere to what was known as the "Red Line" (*hongxian*): interpreting history according to Mao Zedong's writings and portraying Mao as both founder and leader.

Turning from revolutionary history to narratives of the everyday, Chapter 2 studies a neighborhood called Fangua Lane, which was transformed from one of Shanghai's most impoverished slums to the five-story concrete apartment blocks of a workers' new village. The renovation of Fangua Lane symbolized the dramatic changes brought about by the Communist state, and just as the neighborhood became a metonym for New China, its people represented China's working class. Fangua Lane was displayed in two ways. First, it was the subject of exhibitions, either as a small part in a larger Shanghai history or as its own featured exhibit. Second, officials preserved a section of the shantytown houses to contrast the old and new societies. In this way, Fangua Lane became a showcase for visitors and foreign dignitaries to marvel at New China's accomplishments, or for Chinese schoolchildren to have a lesson on history and class. This chapter, "Exhibiting New China," analyzes the idea of the model (*dianxing*) in political culture and introduces the storytelling genre of *yiku sitian*. As a model and by telling an *yiku sitian* narrative, the workers' new village came to stand for linear progress towards a future of shared prosperity.

Exhibitionary culture—not limited to new lessons—also propagandized against traditional beliefs that did not suit the new society. Chapter 3 focuses on a small, local, and ad hoc exhibition designed for some of New China's youngest political subjects, the Communist Young Pioneers. Organizers of the Love Science and Eliminate Superstition Exhibition aimed to create modern subjects who rejected those beliefs and practices that the state labeled "superstition." However, the exhibition's texts against religion read as a question-and-answer catechism, and the teachers' observations after student visits suggest that traditional beliefs persisted. This case of an anti-superstition exhibition reads such displays as texts of not only what was promoted during the Mao period but also of how ideas and practices persisted despite repeated political campaigns against them. Though the Love Science and Eliminate Superstition Exhibition may not have fulfilled all of its organizers' claims, its example shows how display was part of the repertoire of grassroots propaganda.

The following two chapters consider how objects were linked to an individual's class status, how the display of personal possessions was part of Mao-era exhibitionary culture, and how exhibits explicitly served political campaigns. During the Socialist Education Movement, local officials throughout China, from the village level to the provincial capitals, curated class education exhibitions. Chapter 4 explores Shanghai's class education exhibition as an example of this genre. Here, extensive meeting notes and reports of visitor reactions—preserved in part because of later Red Guard denunciations—show that an exhibit was a site to learn the vocabulary of the latest political campaign. The class education exhibition also used display to make personal possessions proof of class status. As the Socialist Education Movement became the Cultural Revolution, attendees who had assiduously copied from the exhibition's bulletin boards mimicked both its format and its content to compose big-character posters (*dazibao*), searching for the kind of evidence that they had already seen on display.

Chapter 5, "The Cultural Revolution's object lessons," examines a showcase organized by the Red Guards from The East is Red Department Store, or what had been the famed Yong'an Department Store on Nanjing Road. Using objects and photographs that depicted items confiscated during Cultural Revolution house searches (*chaojia, chachao*), the Red Guards recycled formats, texts, and objects to argue that it was right to rebel. The technique of exhibition therefore became part of political rebellion against alleged class enemies, and the way Red

Guard exhibitions were viewed demonstrates how such spaces became ritualized: visitors shouted slogans, docents reenacted the house searches, and afterwards, some reflected that they had themselves not searched hard enough. Accounts by the Red Guards who served as docents reveal how they practiced "calling forth emotion"—emotion being a manifestation of ideological correctness—and how they saw narrating the Cultural Revolution as itself "making revolution."

The final chapter focuses on the Shanghai Museum, one of China's most prominent art collections. Established in 1952, the museum developed under experts trained before 1949, who in turn cultivated a new generation. From its beginnings, it exhibited Chinese art, organized by dynasty but superimposed with the Marxist stages of history. In addition, the museum hosted temporary exhibitions, curating revolutionary relics or class education exhibitions. But when the Cultural Revolution broke out, the Red Guards' "Attack on the Four Olds" threatened not only the museum but also *wenwu* throughout the city. Chapter 6, "Antiquity in revolution," uncovers how officials at the Shanghai Museum confronted the Red Guard attack on antiquity by arguing that *wenwu* were not part of the "Four Olds," or representative of the old thinking, old culture, old customs, and old habits. This defense drew on Mao's writings on Chinese history and culture, incorporating antiquity into revolution. Though Shanghai Museum officials shut its doors at the Cultural Revolution's height, it continued to collect and later to curate, in the name of the revolution.

Curating revolution

In the revolutionary model opera *On the Docks* (Haigang), which was made into a film in 1972, a moment of political awakening occurs in a class education exhibition. Standing in the middle of a museum display, a young dockworker named Han Xiaoqiang confronts the contrast between Shanghai's imperialist past and its socialist present. Against a backdrop that includes Mao quotations, oil paintings of labor's toil, and artifacts of imperialist oppression, an old dockworker sings a tale of past suffering. Holding a worker's identity card in his hand, the older worker compares this experience to young Han's role in New China. As Han Xiaoqiang listens, he is moved to tears, resolving not to forget his roots and committing himself anew to the revolution.[53] This

---

[53] Shanghai jingjutuan "Haigang" juzu ("On the Docks" crew of the Shanghai Opera Troupe), ed., *Haigang* (On the docks) (Beijing: Renmin wenxue chubanshe, 1974), pp. 48–58, 167–209.

Ill.0.4. Film still from *Haigang* (On the Docks), 1972

Ill.0.5. Stage design for *Haigang* (On the Docks), 1974, p. 282

dramatized exhibit has all the elements of a real one: artifacts, illustrations, and Mao Zedong Thought. The relationship between the old dockworker and the young one models an exhibit's ideal reception, perception becoming reason: past is linked to present, memory leads to awakening, and consciousness promises action. On the painted backdrop, the exhibition's walls open out onto a glittering nightscape. Red neon characters reading "Long Live Chairman Mao" are reflected in Shanghai's still harbor, the semi-circular arc suggestive of the next day's rising sun.

The goal of this book is to restore to history the Mao-era exhibitions that this *On the Docks* scene represents. To do so I trace the entire process of putting on an exhibition, from collection to exhibition, from narration to reception. I refer to all of these stages as curation, though in their own times each step might have borne different labels. The 1951 Shanghai neighborhood cadre was told how to run an exhibition, which incorporated display (*chenlie*) with arrangement, and narration with propagandizing (*xuanchuan*).[54] Shen Zhiyu's Mao-era writings use the term "exhibition work," highlighting the dual importance of both display and narration, and referring to a 1956 museology slogan that museums have three characteristics: collection, research, and propaganda.[55] Handbooks that museum workers carried into the reform period treat display and "mass work" as two tasks, defining the former as the preparation of an exhibit and the latter as the narration to fulfill its educative purpose.[56] This book's case studies demonstrate how museums and exhibitions in socialist China curated collections, curated narratives, and curated rituals. To take the fictive class education exhibition in *On the Docks* as an example, curating begins with collecting artifacts and commissioning illustrations, continues with the narrative young Han Xiaoqiang hears, and is complete when Han's consciousness is awakened and he carries his revolutionary resolve into the world beyond the stage.

To get at curation in each of its steps, I rely primarily on archival materials. While newspaper accounts of museums and exhibitions describe collection (celebrating archaeology or praising donations), the content of displays, and visitors' reactions, these stories were carefully selected and the writing was subject to approval, resulting in articles that present the ideal reception. In contrast, the Shanghai Municipal

[54] *Jiedao lilong jumin shenghuo shouce*, pp. 42–43.
[55] Shen Zhiyu, "Xuexi Mao Zedong," pp. 5–7; Shen Zhiyu, "Bowuguanxue gailun" (Outline of museology), in *SZYWBLJ*, p. 24.
[56] *Wenwu gongzuo shouce* (Handbook for cultural relics work) (Shanghai: Shanghaishi wenwu guanli weiyuanhui, n.d.), pp. 164–165.

Archive, the Huangpu District Archive, and the Zhabei District Archive offer general reports, meeting minutes, multiple drafts of exhibition texts, docent scripts with questions-and-answers, reports on visitors' feedback, and post-exhibition accounts ranging from school follow-up activities to the docents' self-criticisms. Relevant files come from the Shanghai Municipal Bureau of Culture, the Culture and Education Office of the Shanghai Municipal People's Committee, and the Shanghai Municipal Propaganda Department, among others.[57] Though these bureaucratic documents were also written for an audience, they reveal what went on behind the scenes at a museum: How did curators assess their viewers and how did they design the exhibit accordingly? What parts of an exhibition survived revision and what parts were removed? What kinds of visitor questions were the most difficult and how was the docent supposed to answer them? And how did officials evaluate an exhibit's success?

Ephemera and oral history are also important components of the research in this book. The lessons of the anti-superstition exhibition, for example, were replicated in pamphlets for children, giving a sense of how one form of propaganda mirrored another. As neither the class education exhibitions nor the Red Guard exhibits appeared in the official news media, docent handbooks and souvenir pamphlets purchased online from secondhand booksellers allow examples from Shanghai to be placed in the larger landscape. Oral accounts, including published oral histories, Internet memoirs, and my own interviews round out the archival and ephemeral materials. Individuals with an official capacity, such as curators or those whose memoirs have been published are named; otherwise the interviewees are identified only by age and background. Of the exhibition objects themselves, the First Party Congress Site and the Shanghai Museum continue to maintain their collections, and in Fangua Lane the apartment blocks remain while the once-preserved shantytown houses have long since vanished. Similarly, the artifacts of everyday life are extant only in the occasional archival photograph or in class education exhibition ephemera. Yet even without many of those objects whose perception was to become reason, this book restores the process by which they were curated, the better to understand the revolution they made.

The museums and exhibitions examined in this book are both exceptional and representative. The First Party Congress Site and the Shanghai Museum are respectively an icon of revolutionary history and a premier

---

[57] At the Huangpu District Archive I studied sites like the Shanghai City God Temple, but I was not allowed to search the index on my own. At the Zhabei District Archive, where Fangua Lane is located, I was permitted to look at the index and at photographs but not at the actual files. I did not find similar materials in the Beijing Municipal Archive.

collection of Chinese art and antiquities. The First Party Congress Site was Shanghai's most important official *wenwu* during the Mao period, and in national pilgrimages of revolutionary sites it was the place to begin one's journey.[58] The Shanghai Museum, as a steward of national treasures, illustrates how socialist China incorporated artistic tradition into its revolutionary narrative, serving as a model for other Chinese art museums.[59] These two sites, together with the workers' new village of Fangua Lane, were part of many a foreign delegation's itinerary, as exemplars of China and its revolution.[60] The remaining exhibitions, far more ephemeral, represent genres that were mounted throughout China. Though Fangua Lane was particular to Shanghai, the display of shanty-town or peasant housing as symbols of class suffering was found every-where. The Love Science and Eliminate Superstition Exhibition echoed other science dissemination displays.[61] The genre of class education exhibition was similarly ubiquitous, with curators and docents traveling to study from each other; Shanghai modeled itself after Shandong. Likewise, Shanghai's Red Guard curators imitated their counterparts in Beijing. Thus, even if the artifacts and narrative of Shanghai exhibitions were rooted in local history, the displays and rituals around them reflected broader practice.

Why curate revolution in Shanghai? After all, the Chinese Communist revolution was a rural and peasant one; when PLA troops and CCP cadres entered the cities they were warned of urban decadence and its corrupting influences. Yet against portrayals of capitalist and colonial Shanghai was an image of the revolutionary, proletarian city. Films in the 1950s included parades celebrating Shanghai's liberation, the reform of capitalists, and mobilization of neighborhoods during political campaigns.[62] Children's books and popular newspapers also reinscribed the city with revolution: Nanjing Road with its department stores was

---

[58] *Quanguo gesheng, zizhiqu, zhixiashi diyipi wenwu baohu danwei mingdan huibian* (The first group of national cultural relic protection units in each province, autonomous region, and special municipality) (Beijing: Wenwu chubanshe, 1958), p. 10; Nie Bing and Qian Yan, "Renmin zhanshi xin xiangdang" (The people's soldiers turn their hearts toward the Party), *Jiefangjun huabao* (PLA pictorial), July 1976, p. 2.

[59] Interview in Shanghai with Li Junjie, July 20, 2011.

[60] See "Jiating qiyi de Zhao Zongli zai Shanghai canguan" (Naval defector Zhao Zongli tours Shanghai), *Renmin ribao* (People's daily), October 26, 1964, p. 2; "Waishi wanglai" (Foreign dealings), *Renmin ribao*, April 7, 1978, p. 4.

[61] In 1964, for example, Zhejiang Province arranged for such a traveling exhibition to visit counties and cities. See *Xuanchuan dongtai 1983* (Propaganda trends 1983) (Beijing: Zhongguo shehui kexue chubanshe, 1984), pp. 19–20, 62–64.

[62] See Braester, *Painting the City Red*, pp. 59–72. Braester argues that in the 1950s Shanghai—through film—was successfully remade into a socialist city, and it was not until the mid-1960s that Shanghai was vilified during the Good Eighth Company Campaign.

depicted as the site where straw-sandaled soldiers entered Shanghai, and articles about the Bund described how the foreign buildings now housed socialist work units.[63] *Renmin ribao* (People's daily) explained that it was now the "People's Bund," and a poet for *Wenhui bao* (Wenhui daily) praised the two lions in front of the former Hong Kong and Shanghai Bank, once witnesses to imperialism but now belonging to the people.[64] Even in the dramatized exhibition in *On the Docks*, the setting of Shanghai is important: it encompasses the transformation of workers' lives, the threat of a counterrevolutionary to restore capitalism, and—because Han Xiaoqiang is responsible for loading seed bound for Africa—the connection between China and world revolution. Perhaps, in the same way that a greater contrast between past and present made a narrative more compelling, curating Shanghai made evident the difference between China old and new. If the process of curation started with collection, Shanghai was a city rich in artifacts as well as narratives. From the rare art treasures in the Shanghai Museum to the everyday possessions that became exhibits of class, the curator had access to all manner of objects to display. And it was with the collection of the First Party Congress Site, the icon of the CCP's founding, that curating revolution began.

[63] He Xiaoqian, "Women zou zai Nanjing lushang" (Let's go for a walk on Nanjing Road), in *Xin Shanghai gushi* (Stories of new Shanghai) (Shanghai: Shaonian ertong chubanshe, 1964); Cheng Qi, "Wushinianqian de waitan: Diguozhuyi yinhang de jizhongdi" (Fifty years ago on the Bund: Center of imperialist banking), *Xinwen bao* (News daily), August 20, 1959, p. 3.

[64] Cheng Shi, "Waitan: Diguozhuyi qinlüe zuixing de jianzheng" (The Bund: Evidence of the crimes of imperialism), *Renmin ribao*, March 12, 1965, p. 5; Lu Mang, "Waitan, meiguise de zaochen" (Rosy-colored morning on the Bund), *Wenhui bao* (Wenhui daily), May 28, 1963, p. 4.

1   Making a revolutionary monument: The First Party Congress Site

Shen Zhiyu was on a political mission. On a September day in 1950, the thirty-four-year-old cadre—vice Party secretary of the Art Workers' Association—was summoned by telephone to the Shanghai Party Committee Propaganda Department. Standing together with official Yang Zhongguang in the office on Huashan Road, Shen received marching orders from Yao Zhen of the Propaganda Department. The Shanghai Party Committee had decided to act on an idea suggested by Mayor Chen Yi. It would locate the site of the first CCP meeting, and there establish a memorial museum. Shen and Yang were tasked with locating the meeting site, if possible in time for the thirtieth anniversary of the Party's founding the following year. In his Subei accent, Yao declared, "As the Shanghai Party Committee, searching for the Party's birthplace is one of our important political responsibilities."[1]

For the narrative of New China, the preeminent revolutionary relic was the site where the Party was founded. Just as Shanghai residents collected artifacts of their personal histories, so too did the Party search for the material remains of the First Party Congress Site (*yida huizhi*). Found and restored, the First Party Congress Site would come to play a number of roles in the People's Republic. As the official birthplace of the Communist Party, it was protected as a cultural relic and became a venue for political pilgrimages. Shanghai officials also preserved the surrounding area and planned for a museum of revolutionary history. The buildings adjacent to the restored meeting room held exhibitions that told the story of Party founding. The First Party Congress Site, in

---

[1] This chapter's account of locating the First Party Congress Site is drawn from three sources. The first is a 1988 account by Shen Zhiyu entitled "Yida huizhi shi zenyang zhaodao de" (How the First Party Congress Site was found), in *SZYWBLJ*, pp. 353–357. The second is a 1991 interview with Shen Zhiyu by Ye Yonglie, entitled "Zhonggong zhichu de zhuixun: Fang Shen Zhiyu tongzhi" (Searching for the origins of the Communist Party: An interview with Comrade Shen Zhiyu), in *SZYWBLJ*, pp. 412–420. The third is a posthumous account that includes memories by Shen's widow. See Chen Zhiqiang, *Wenbo xianqu: Shen Zhiyu zhuan* (Museum pioneer: A biography of Shen Zhiyu) (Shanghai: Shanghai wenhua chubanshe, 2011), pp. 97–110.

addition to being a monument and an exhibition, was also a collection; in an era of continuous revolution, officials continued to gather contemporary artifacts. More than six decades after the founding of the People's Republic, it still plays these roles: a site of patriotic education, a museum with exhibitions, and a collection that sponsors scholarly research. The First Party Congress Site remains an icon, a *lieu de memoire* persisting among Shanghai's glittering skyscrapers, an architectural silhouette that graces lapel pins marked with July 1, 1921 as the date that Mao claimed for the Party's establishment.[2]

Today the First Party Congress Site is carefully distinguished by a brown street marker that is standard for Shanghai's historic sites. It directs visitors to a block of five residences located within the high-end entertainment area of Xintiandi. The two-story houses, typical of Shanghai lane housing, are a modest gray-and-red brick, with doorframes crowned by elaborate carving. The site has now been immaculately restored and it is adorned with identical shrubbery; a marble placard identifies it as a National Cultural Relic and the Chinese flag waves from one corner. But in 1950, when Shen Zhiyu set forth on his search under the shade of Shanghai's parasol trees, no one knew for certain where the First Party Congress Site was located. One can imagine his trepidation as he replied to Yao, "The task is indeed glorious, but it will be very difficult ... the French Concession is so huge, how can we even begin?"[3] Yet finding the site, as this chapter will show, was the easiest step. Far more politically fraught was how to use the revolutionary relic to tell Party history.

I begin with the excavation and authentication of the First Party Congress Site as a revolutionary relic. Memoirs by Shen Zhiyu and others, together with archival documents, reveal the role of material culture—here, revolutionary relics—in political legitimacy. I then turn to the problem of curating exhibitions at the First Party Congress Site, using materials from exhibition plans to official scripted answers to illustrate how difficult it was to do history in Mao's China. Even as an exhibition of revolutionary history was portrayed as the definitive textbook, against the backdrop of socialist China's tumultuous political campaigns First Party Congress Site officials struggled to remain in

---

[2] It has now been determined that the First Party Congress meeting took place on July 23, 1921. See, for example, Zhongguo gongchandang diyici quanguo daibiao dahui huizhi jinianguan (Memorial hall of the Chinese Communist Party's First Party Congress Site), ed., *Zhongguo gongchandang diyici quanguo daibiao dahui huizhi* (The Chinese Communist Party's First Party Congress Site) (Shanghai: Shanghai renmin meishu chubanshe, 2001), p. 103. Nevertheless, the Party still celebrates the anniversary on July 1.
[3] Shen Zhiyu, "Yida huizhi shi zenyang zhaodao de," p. 353.

accord with the Maoist "Red Line." Their curation of revolution in the early 1960s demonstrates the difficulties of doing history, both in researching Communist Party founding and in portraying it as an exhibition text and a docent script. During the Cultural Revolution the First Party Congress Site exhibition became a political broadside, and although its reform-era restoration called for a return to *wenwu* and to historical accuracy, it remains bound by the Party whose founding it tells.

Excavating and authenticating revolution

The search for the First Party Congress Site began with a counterrevolutionary document and the wife of a traitor. A member of the Shanghai's Public Security Bureau (PSB) named Zhou Zhiyou was the son of Zhou Fohai and Yang Shuhui; Zhou Zhiyou's late father had been one of the original participants at the First Party Congress, but he later joined the Wang Jingwei puppet government.[4] While the father threw in his lot with the collaborators, the son joined the Communist underground and eventually became a member of New China's security apparatus. Zhou Zhiyou reminded the Propaganda Department that his father had written memoirs, which included an account of the First Party Congress meeting.[5] Thus with this confluence of characters and with the Propaganda Department and the PSB working together, Shen Zhiyu began his search based on two leads. He had a letter of introduction that would allow him to read the classified memoirs and the PSB agreed to release from prison Zhou Fohai's widow, Ms. Yang Shuhui, to assist in Shen's revolutionary task.[6] Rushing to the library with his letter, Shen Zhiyu spent an entire day reading Zhou Fohai's memoirs, gleaning for his efforts one sentence: "Every night, we would meet at the home of Mr. Li Hanjun, on Beile Road."[7]

---

[4] As a delegate to the First Party Congress, Zhou Fohai represented the Chinese students in Japan. He left the Party in 1924 and joined the collaborators in 1938, rising to the positions of vice director of the Administrative Yuan under Wang Jingwei as well as minister of finance and mayor of Shanghai. After World War II, he was sentenced to life and he died in prison in 1948. Ye Yonglie, "Zhonggong zhichu de zhuixun," p. 413; Zhongguo gong-chandang diyici quanguo daibiao dahui huizhi jinianguan, ed., *Zhongguo gongchandang diyici quanguo daibiao dahui huizhi*, p. 98.

[5] Ye Yonglie, "Zhonggong zhichu de zhuixun," pp. 413–414.

[6] Shen Zhiyu, "Yida huizhi shi zenyang zhaodao de," p. 353; Ye Yonglie, "Zhonggong zhichu de zhuixun," pp. 413–414; Chen Zhiqiang, *Wenbo xianqu*, pp. 98–99.

[7] The relevant excerpt is reproduced in *Shanghai geming shi yanjiu ziliao: Jinian jiandang 70 zhou nian* (Research materials on Shanghai's revolutionary history: Commemorating the 70th anniversary of the founding of the Party) (Shanghai: Shanghai sanlian shudian, 1991), pp. 321–324; Chen Zhiqiang, *Wenbo xianqu*, pp. 98–99.

Two days later Shen Zhiyu and his colleague Yang Zhongguang met Yang Shuhui for the first time. Ms. Yang was then forty-nine years old, dressed in blue cotton clothing and wearing her hair short and straight, a world away from former elegant portraits dressed in flowered *qipao*.[8] Her first idea was to bring them to Chen Duxiu's house on Nanchang Road, which was both the home of the CCP's founder and the offices of *New Youth* magazine. She remembered the house because she and Zhou Fohai had lived in the pavilion room after they were first married. Beyond the main entrance, there was a salon used by Chen Duxiu as a meeting room, where she recalled that a blackboard read, "During meetings, speeches are limited to fifteen minutes," and that Chen's rocking chair had been in the room.[9] This site established, Shen Zhiyu and Yang Zhongguang decided to split their tasks; Shen would search for Li Hanjun's home, while Yang followed a thread in other materials that suggested that the First Party Congress meeting might have taken place at Bowen Girls' School.

On his own, Yang Zhongguang searched the archives of Shanghai's Bureau of Education and interviewed former residents who confirmed the address of the girls' school; he sent photographs to Mao and Dong Biwu, another original participant. Mao and Dong inspected the photos and reported that the school had provided dormitory space for the participants but—contrary to the information in Zhou Fohai's memoirs—the actual meeting took place at the home of Li Hanjun's brother, Li Shucheng. Yang then went to Beijing to visit Li Shucheng, then minister of agriculture, and was given the following address—Number 78, Wangzhi Road, in the French Concession. Though Bowen Girls' School was rejected as the site of the meeting, it was still deemed a revolutionary site (*geming yizhi*). After the Central Committee dispatched Li Da—yet another participant—to Shanghai for authentication, the Shanghai Municipal Government bought the property and invited the daughter of the former principal, herself a contemporary student, to oversee restoration of Bowen Girls' School.[10]

Meanwhile, Shen Zhiyu and Yang Shuhui took walks along Beile Road, which had been renamed Huangpi South Road in 1943. Shen

---

[8] Ye Yonglie, "Zhonggong zhichu de zhuixun," pp. 412–413. For a photo of Yang, see Chen Zhiqiang, *Wenbo xianqu*, p. 110.

[9] Shen Zhiyu, "Yida huizhi shi zenyang zhaodao de," p. 353; Ye Yonglie, "Zhonggong zhichu de zhuixun," pp. 415–416.

[10] Shen Zhiyu, "Yida huizhi shi zenyang zhaodao de," pp. 354–355.

Zhiyu, bespectacled and dressed in his blue cadre suit, followed half a meter behind Yang Shuhui. Over thirty years had passed since Yang Shuhui had delivered letters to the house for her husband. In the much-changed landscape, she would seize upon a house but then determine that it was not the Li residence. Then, on one of their walks she suddenly stopped near the intersection of Huangpi South Road and Xingye Road (formerly Wangzhi Road), arrested by the sight of a two-story white-washed building labeled "Hengfuchang Noodles." "This," she said to Shen, "seems a bit like the Li family's back door!" During subsequent days, Ms. Yang returned on her own to inspect the building, and Shen interviewed the neighbors. From Dong Zhengchang, the proprietor of a sauce-and-pickle shop, they learned that the house had been built in the 1920s by a woman surnamed Chen. The Li brothers had rented two of the units, knocking out the dividing wall to make one residence. In 1924 the woman Chen rented out the house to family members, who became secondary landlords. It later became a pawnshop, and when Shen and Yang Shuhui arrived in 1951, it was a small noodle factory with two families residing on the second floor.[11] In Shen Zhiyu's account, when the occupants learned that their building was the birthplace of the CCP, "everyone clapped their hands and smilingly exclaimed, 'So it turns out that the place where we live is on precious ground!'" Told that the site would become a memorial museum and that the families would have to relocate, Shen remembered that they gladly assented, stating, "that is as it should be!"[12]

As the next step, the First Party Congress Site had to be authenticated. At the time, it was by no means assured that it would become a monument. When the Shanghai Propaganda Department reported to its superiors in the Central Committee's Central Propaganda Department, the response was that *if* the sites—the *New Youth* office, Bowen Girls' School, and the First Party Congress Site—were indeed genuine, they could be preserved and made into monuments.[13] While still

---

[11] Ibid., p. 355; Ye Yonglie, "Zhonggong zhichu de zhuixun," pp. 417–418; Chen Zhiqiang, *Wenbo xianqu*, p. 102. For two photos of what the building looked like in 1951, see Zhonggong Shanghai shiwei dangshi yanjiushi and Shanghaishi wenwuju (Research Office of the Shanghai Communist Party Committee and the Shanghai Municipal Bureau of Cultural Relics), eds., *Zhongguo gongchandang zaoqi zai Shanghai shiji* (Historical vestiges in Shanghai from the Chinese Communist Party's early period) (Shanghai: Tongji daxue chubanshe, 2013), p. 12.
[12] Shen Zhiyu, "Yida huizhi shi zenyang zhaodao de," p. 355.
[13] "Zhongyang guanyu dang de diyici daibiao dahui de dizhi baocun wenti gei Shanghai shiwei de zhishi," July 3, 1951 (Central directive to the Shanghai Party Committee regarding preservation of the First Party Congress Site), in *Zhongguo gongchandang xuanchuan gongzuo wenxian xuanbian: 1946–1949* (Selected documents on the

verifying the site, the Shanghai Party Committee rented the houses in September 1951, bought the property in May of the following year, and began to submit it to inspection.

The Shanghai Party Committee initially decorated the rooms with paintings of Marx and Lenin and samples of Mao Zedong's calligraphy. In the winter of 1952, when Wang Yeqiu of the Cultural Relics Bureau inspected the site, he ordered that the rooms be restored to their original condition, explaining that "a memorial museum to revolutionary history should be decorated exactly as it was originally; in this way, you will allow visitors to imagine the original scene and will inspire feelings of deep veneration."[14] In 1953, three miniature replicas were sent to the Central Propaganda Department in Beijing. Mao inspected the models and dispatched Bao Huiseng, another participant and then an adviser to the State Council, to Shanghai. In March 1954 Bao Huiseng and Xue Wenchu (Mrs. Li Shucheng) confirmed the location of the meeting. Xue Wenchu provided instructions on how to restore the interior and later donated artifacts, including a tea service and a chair.[15]

Still, Shanghai officials were unable to complete the restoration, as researchers debated whether the meeting had taken place upstairs or downstairs. The arrangement of the house was finally settled in 1956, when Dong Biwu—then president of the Supreme People's Court—inspected the site. In those days, Dong explained, the delegates met downstairs because there were women in the family of the household, who remained upstairs. Officials thus placed a rectangular table on the first floor, as the meeting room remains arranged to this day.[16] Throughout the 1950s, Shanghai officials worked to follow Wang Yeqiu's directive on authenticity, which even extended to the neighborhood; the adjacent buildings were preserved in order to maintain

propaganda work of the Chinese Communist Party: 1946–1949) (Beijing: Xuexi chubanshe, 1996), p. 249.

[14] Ye Yonglie, "Zhonggong zhichu de zhuixun," p. 419.

[15] Shen Zhiyu, "Yida huizhi shi zenyang zhaodao de," p. 356. See also SMA B172-4-313, pp. 5–6.

[16] For an institutional account of some of the events here, see Chen Peicun and Ren Rui, "Jianguan sishinian zhi huigu" (Looking back on forty years since the establishment of the museum), Shanghai geming shiliao yu yanjiu (Materials and research on Shanghai's revolutionary history) (Beijing: Kaiming chubanshe, 1992), vol. 1, pp. 236–238. The archival record also reveals that careful accounts were made of these visits, the questions asked, and the answers. One such example exists for the visit by Dong Biwu's wife in 1964, which refers back to Dong's earlier comments and includes summaries of telephone conversations. SMA 172-1-477, pp. 95–97.

Ill.1.1. Exterior of the First Party Congress Site, undated.
SMA H1-22-1-1

the original atmosphere.[17] In his oral history Chen Peicun, who began working at the First Party Congress Site in 1958, remembers the meticulous care that went into restoration: carpenters replicated

[17] SMA B172-1-477, pp. 26–31.

Ill.1.2. First Party Congress Site meeting room, undated. SMA H1-22-1-2

furniture according to Xue Wenchu's memories, the tea service was specially commissioned at Jingdezhen and Yixing, and the state allocated gold to gild the rim of the vase on the table.[18]

Both in authenticating the site and restoring the interior, officials of the First Party Congress Site emphasized the paramount importance of accuracy. Memoirs and memories were not entirely reliable: Zhou Fohai's memoirs were off on the name of the street; some accounts claimed that Bowen Girls' School was the site of the congress; and Shen Zhiyu waited for Dong Biwu's visit before placing the meeting table on the first floor. From the beginning, Party history had to be presented in an authoritative and coherent way. After all, the Party's rise to power was attributed to its correct historical understanding.[19] Although the First Party Congress Site opened to limited internal visits in September 1952, in February 1954 the Central Propaganda Department ordered that the site could not be fully open to visitors until the interior had finally been decided upon.[20] The First Party Congress Site, as a revolutionary relic, was part of the Party's self-fashioning. Its claims of authenticity undergirded the Party's legitimacy.

The First Party Congress Site topped the list of national revolutionary relics, and also lent Shanghai its political and cultural cachet. In 1961, when the state issued its first list of national "cultural relic protection units" (*wenwu baohu danwei*), four such designations, all of them revolutionary sites, were in Shanghai.[21] Finding the First Party Congress Site was part of a broader attempt to mark revolutionary places within the city's landscape. Part of Chen Peicun's job was to survey traces of revolutionary sites, and the archival record includes many examples of attempts to find and preserve sites with Mao's revolutionary

---

[18] Duan Lian, Song Shijuan, and Chen Ling, eds., *Wangshi yu jiyi: Shanghai diqu bowuguan, jinianguan koushu fangtanlu* (Past and memory: A record of oral histories and interviews from Shanghai local museums and memorial halls) (Shanghai: Shanghai cishu chubanshe, 2010), p. 56. Chen Peicun's oral history also includes an account of the discovery, but it is not first-hand.

[19] For the Soviet case, Frederick Corney argues that "Istpart was born of a need for stability and coherence . . . An internally consistent history of the revolution and party would help provide a stable past to anchor the Soviet regime." Frederick C. Corney, *Telling October: Memory and the Making of the Bolshevik Revolution* (Ithaca, NY: Cornell University Press, 2004), pp. 111–125.

[20] Chen Peicun and Ren Rui, "Jianguan sishinian zhi huigu," p. 238.

[21] *Quanguo gesheng, zizhiqu, zhixiashi diyipi wenwu baohu danwei mingdan huibian* (The first group of national cultural relic protection units in each province, autonomous region, and special municipality) (Beijing: Wenwu chubanshe, 1958), p. 10. The other three were Sun Yat-sen's residence, the headquarters of Socialist Youth, and the tomb of Lu Xun. See Ma Chengyuan, Huang Xuanpei, Li Junjie, eds., *Shanghai wenwu bowuguan zhi* (Gazetteer of Shanghai's cultural relics and museums) (hereafter cited as *SHWWBWGZ*) (Shanghai: Shanghai shehui kexueyuan chubanshe, 1997), p. 387.

footprint.[22] In the 1960s, for example, officials interviewed old cadres and Mao's associates to determine where Mao had lived in Shanghai.[23] In another case, the Bureau of Culture convened a conference to determine whether or not Mao had ever visited a garden that was slated for destruction.[24] By 1964, the First Party Congress Site officials had logged over 4,600 interviews.[25] Thus the First Party Congress Site was responsible not only for the history of the meeting it commemorated but also for revolutionary relics in Shanghai writ large. These *geming wenwu* were collected, researched, and restored. Writing the Party's founding narrative would prove to be a task of no less political import.

A founding narrative for the Communist Party

In October 1950, just as Shen Zhiyu was beginning his search, Wang Yeqiu of the State Cultural Relics Bureau published an account of his visit to the Soviet Museum of the Revolution for the benefit of his colleagues in museum work. Wang illustrated display techniques that would be widely adopted in Chinese museums: large oil paintings, charts comparing past and present, artifacts, and the extensive use of historical documents. The experience of his visit was both didactic and affective. Particularly impressive to Wang was a set of torture instruments, including a leather whip that led him to recall his own imprisonment as a member of the Communist underground. "This was familiar to me, because I also survived the leather whip of China's reactionary rulers." Wang Yeqiu expressed his admiration for the Soviet Museum of the Revolution as a growing collection that depicted a contemporary narrative.[26] In the same way, to exhibit the revolution in China was to write history as it was being made.

Museums as educative, artifacts as triggers of memory, collections as works in progress—these characteristics also had antecedents in the Republican era (1912–1949). In 1928 the Nationalist Government established a committee to create a museum of the revolution in

[22] Duan Lian, Song Shijuan, and Chen Ling, eds., *Wangshi yu jiyi*, pp. 58–61.
[23] SMA B172-1-477, pp. 107–115.
[24] SMA B172-1-477, pp. 134–139. In this case, the Shanghai Bureau of Culture determined that Mao had never visited the garden, called *Shenjia huayuan*, and therefore the Shanghai Nanshi Power Plant was allowed to raze the grounds to provide an area for storage of oil tanks.
[25] SMA B172-1-477, pp. 9–11.
[26] Wang Yeqiu, "Sulian guoli geming bowuguan" (The Soviet Museum of the Revolution), *Wenwu cankao ziliao*, no. 10 (1950), pp. 66–76.

Nanjing.[27] As Kirk Denton shows, the Nationalists commemorated the revolution to display their political legitimacy. At the Revolutionary Memorial Hall at the 1929 West Lake Exposition, for example, visitors bowed before a statue of founding father Sun Yat-sen, they viewed artifacts of individual martyrs and of revolutionary history, and they followed a narrative of progress that featured the Nationalist Party—supported by the people—as China's guiding force.[28] It was through such symbols and rituals of nation and history, Henrietta Harrison argues, that the Republican citizen was made. The Communist Party inherited both the monuments and the practices that surrounded them. The Sun Yat-sen Mausoleum in Nanjing is perhaps the most prominent example, a site that the CCP incorporated into its own political rituals.[29] Similarly, one of Shanghai's national revolutionary relics was Sun Yat-sen's Shanghai residence, originally donated to the state in 1945 as a place where citizens might study his Three Principles of the People.[30]

As Nationalists and Communists contended for power, each simultaneously collected the artifacts of its own revolution. Concurrent with the 1929 West Lake Exposition, Nationalist local governments issued orders to collect revolutionary objects. Although Denton points out that the 1930s saw a downplaying of the discourse of revolution, the postwar Shanghai Municipal Museum explicitly curated shows of revolutionary relics.[31] For the Communists, archaeologist Tracey Lu dates the earliest plan to display "items with revolutionary significance" to 1930, and the decision to create a Central Museum of Revolution to 1933.[32] In its base areas, the Communist Party mounted small-scale exhibitions, not yet able to establish a museum of the revolution until after its military victory.[33] The Museum of the Chinese Revolution was established in Beijing in

[27] Henrietta Harrison, *The Making of the Republican Citizen: Political Ceremonies and Symbols in China, 1911–1929* (Oxford: Oxford University Press, 2000), p. 213.

[28] Kirk A. Denton, *Exhibiting the Past: Historical Memory and the Politics of Museums in Postsocialist China* (Honolulu: University of Hawai'i Press, 2014), pp. 46–52.

[29] Delin Lai, "Searching for a Modern Chinese Monument: The Design of the Sun Yat-sen Mausoleum in Nanjing," *Journal of the Society of Architectural Historians*, vol. 64, no. 1 (March 2005), pp. 22–54.

[30] SMA Q1-6-676.

[31] "Jiangsu geming bowuguan choubeichu zhengji xize" (Collection of regulations for the Jiangsu Revolutionary Museum Preparatory Committee), *Shanghai tebieshi jiaoyuju jiaoyu zhoubao* (Shanghai Municipal Bureau of Education education weekly), no. 4 (1929), pp. 7–8; Denton, *Exhibiting the Past*, p. 52; SMA Q235-2-3460, pp. 16–17; *Shanghai shili bowuguan yaolan* (Shanghai Municipal Museum exhibition), August 1948, p. 5.

[32] Tracey L-D. Lu, *Museums in China: Materialized Power and Objectified Identities* (London: Routledge, 2014), p. 114.

[33] Denton, *Exhibiting the Past*, p. 52.

1949, its edifice one of the "Ten Great Buildings" constructed to celebrate the tenth anniversary of the People's Republic in 1959. As historian Chang-tai Hung argues, Beijing's Museum of the Chinese Revolution was central to the Party's creation of a master narrative of revolution, part of a new political culture that helped to legitimize CCP rule in the 1950s.[34]

In writing this master narrative, historians at the Museum of the Chinese Revolution and the First Party Congress Site drew on the Soviet example. Chinese cultural officials like Wang Yeqiu went on study tours, the pages of the trade journal *Wenwu cankao ziliao* (Cultural relics reference materials) often included articles on Soviet exemplars, and handbooks of Soviet museology were translated into Chinese.[35] Soviet pamphlets and guidebooks from the 1930s describe the system of museums that Wang Yeqiu and others would visit and then later transplant to New China. In *Museums of the U.S.S.R.*, published in 1939 by Moscow's Foreign Languages Publishing House, Olga Leonova stressed how the Soviet government preserved historic sites and collections, crediting the Red Army for restoring a cottage on the Pushkin estate and safeguarding Tolstoy's Yasnaya Polyana as a neutral zone.[36] Leonova introduced the Lenin Museum as a monument to "the founder of new Russia" and wrote that "as the visitor passes from room to room he, as it were, turns the pages of a huge book devoted to the unparalleled life of the genius of the Great October Socialist Revolution."[37] The museum was a literal textbook, with rooms in the Lenin Museum paralleling chapters in Stalin's *History of the Communist Party of the Soviet Union (Bolsheviks): Short Course.*[38] Finally, as Wang Yeqiu noted in his report, the Soviet Museum of the Revolution continued into the present. Its final section, in Leonova's words, was "devoted to Socialist construction ... the exhibits here give the visitor a vivid picture of the progress of Socialist industry, collective

---

[34] Chang-tai Hung, *Mao's New World: Political Culture in the Early People's Republic* (Ithaca, NY: Cornell University Press, 2011), pp. 11–13, 21.

[35] In 1957, for example, *Wenwu cankao ziliao* (Cultural relics reference materials) featured several issues on Soviet museums to celebrate the October Revolution. In the same year, the Chinese translated a 1955 handbook entitled *Sulian bowuguanxue jichu* (Fundamentals of Soviet museology) (Beijing: Wenwu chubanshe, 1957).

[36] O. Leonova, *Museums of the U.S.S.R.* (Moscow: Foreign Languages Publishing House, 1939), p. 5.

[37] Ibid., p. 8.

[38] Marien van der Heijden, ed., *Museums in Revolution: Four Historical Museums in Moscow* (Amsterdam: IISG, 1998), p. 9. See Commission of the Central Committee of the C.P.S.U.(B), ed., *History of the Communist Party of the Soviet Union (Bolsheviks): Short Course* (New York: International Publishers, 1939).

farming, and education."[39] In borrowing from Soviet exhibitionary culture, Chinese museums were also fashioned as living textbooks. Like the Lenin Museum in paralleling Stalin's *Short Course History*, Chinese museums of the revolution followed Mao's periodization of history from his 1940 essay, "On New Democracy."[40]

Though Shanghai's First Party Congress Site would follow Beijing's Museum of the Chinese Revolution as its authority, Shanghai's site was not a *tabula rasa* on which to inscribe a living textbook. Both monument and museum, it centered around the meeting room as a revolutionary relic. Plans for the First Party Congress Site went through several transformations. The original plan of October 1951, proposed by the Shanghai Party Committee, was to create a revolutionary history museum with three branches: the meeting site would exhibit Party history and Mao Zedong's writings, the New Youth office would curate the history of the labor movement, and Bowen Girls' School would present Mao Zedong's personal effects.[41] In January 1952, the Shanghai Bureau of Culture officially established a preparatory office for the Shanghai Revolutionary History Memorial Museum, which began renovations in May. Three years later, the Memorial Museum Preparatory Committee began to draft plans to create an entire new museum. Its proposal to the Ministry of Culture in 1956 encompassed a huge block surrounding the First Party Congress Site, including a museum and a garden.[42] In Chen Peicun's oral history he explains that the committee issued a call in 1959 to collect revolutionary relics, and within half a year it had amassed over 20,000 objects. A national conference, in which architectural historian Liang Sicheng participated, discussed plans for the large museum complex, which were approved by the Shanghai Party Committee. Though building materials had already been delivered to the site, the Great Leap Forward and its subsequent austerity brought construction to a halt.[43] The exhibition attached to the First Party Congress Site remained in the original buildings and the plan for the Shanghai Revolutionary History Memorial Museum was eventually abandoned, though it leaves its footprint in the outlines of today's Xintiandi.

Despite the loss of funds to create a new expanded museum, First Party Congress Site staff continued to organize exhibitions, both for the site and for traveling displays. During holidays, museum workers visited cultural

---

[39] Leonova, *Museums of the U.S.S.R.*, pp. 14–15. See also *Guide to the City of Moscow, a Handbook for Tourists* (Moscow: Co-operative Publishing Society of Foreign Workers in the U.S.S.R., 1937), pp. 97–102.

[40] Hung, *Mao's New World*, pp. 119–122.

[41] Chen Peicun and Ren Rui, "Jianguan sishinian zhi huigu," p. 237.   [42] Ibid., p. 238.

[43] Duan Lian, Song Shijuan, and Chen Ling, eds., *Wangshi yu jiyi*, p. 57.

palaces, schools, and street committees to provide pictorial exhibitions. They verified dozens of other revolutionary sites and collected materials on their history. The First Party Congress Site designed research projects with names like "The Great Wall of the Working Class," "The Spread of Marxism-Leninism," "The May Fourth Movement," and "The Cultural Revolutionary Movement during the Second Revolutionary War."[44] In turn, these projects became exhibitions in the Shanghai Museum, youth palaces, and the Shanghai Workers' Palace.[45] Like the Soviet museum described by T. G. Koloskvoa, "understood as a 'new type of monument,' not as a passive depository of dead memory but as an active distributor of proletarian culture," the First Party Congress Site was more than a restored building and a collection of artifacts.[46] It was an active propaganda organ for Party and revolutionary history.

At the First Party Congress Site, the route through the exhibition began in the meeting room, followed by a three-room supplementary display, and it concluded in a reception room for discussion and for leaving comments.[47] Official Party history unfolded chronologically through the display, supported by pictures, photographs, and replicas of documents mounted on the walls or displayed in glass cases. Following standard periodization, the exhibition began with the Opium War, the Taiping Rebellion, and the 1911 Revolution, and then focused on New Democratic Revolution since the May Fourth Movement.[48] Three titles supported by Mao quotations marked the divisions of the display: The Great Wall of the Chinese Working Class, Marxism-Leninism Spreads to China, and The Establishment of the CCP.[49] Wherever possible, local Shanghai history was integrated into the larger national narrative. For example, curators took care to depict the Shanghai people opposing the Mixed Court of the foreign-run International Settlement and to show Shanghai workers participating in the patriotic May Fourth Movement.[50] But despite these straightforward titles and "On New Democracy" as the guiding text, constructing a narrative of Party founding remained difficult. The "three years of natural disaster" with its great famine (1959–1961) challenged the direction of the revolution, the Sino-Soviet split (1960) shook the Soviets from their leading role, and

[44] Chen Peicun and Ren Rui, "Jianguan sishinian zhi huigu," p. 241.
[45] Ibid., p. 253. Examples of these exhibitions include "The Life of Lenin," "A Pictorial Exhibition Commemorating 35 Years of the May Fourth Movement," and "An Exhibition on the Third Uprising of Shanghai Workers."
[46] T. G. Koloskvoa, "Central Museum of V.I. Lenin," in *Museums in Revolution: Four Historical Museums in Moscow*, edited by Marien van de Heijden (Amsterdam: IISG, 1998), p. 36.
[47] SMA B172-5-240, p. 20.   [48] SMA B1-2-770, p. 4; SMA B172-5-521, p. 17.
[49] SMA B172-5-240, pp. 5–9.   [50] SMA B172-1-477, pp. 72–75.

contemporary debates over theory and practice made curators of revolution uneasy. How should one follow the "Red Line" of Mao Zedong Thought during the rising cult of Mao? In this atmosphere, the First Party Congress Site was a living textbook in more ways than one, telling a tale that made Party founding a great turning point and that placed Mao at its center.

Telling revolution and the politics of the "Red Line"

Of the October Revolution, historian Frederick Corney suggests that its telling "was not a *description* of events but rather an *argument* for a particular representation of events." As the founding event of the Soviet Union, the history of October had to be uniform and stable. Exhibitions and museums on the October Revolution provided a "correct understanding" of revolution and Party, in visual and material form.[51] As shown in the studies of Beijing's Museum of the Chinese Revolution by Denton and Hung, so too was its narrative an argument for Mao's "Red Line," using his interpretation of history and politics to weave an authoritative, consistent exhibition. But despite championing the "Red Line" as a guiding principle, there was no clear definition of how to follow it.[52] What of the First Party Congress Site, which—as a central artifact on display—was at once monument, historic site, and museum?

Some of the dilemmas faced by First Party Congress officials were observed by the scholar Pierre Ryckmans when he visited the site during the Cultural Revolution. Though archival records of foreign visitors usually relate polite responses and the Chinese press reported great enthusiasm expressed by foreign friends, Ryckmans experienced a museum of the absurd, rife with confusion and contradictions. In his memoir he describes how disputed facts were glossed with authority, how the meeting room was displayed with twelve chairs, and how he was told that the First Party Congress met on July 1, 1921. Uncomfortable circumstances—the presence of foreigners, the participants who later defected, and the actual decisions of the meeting—were omitted. Ryckmans suggests that museum officials chose "arbitrarily from among various contradictory accounts of the event." His guide and the curator are portrayed as fools, the thinness of the short lecture is attributed to the guide's ignorance, and the

---

[51] Corney, *Telling October*, pp. 8–11, 111, 116–118.
[52] Denton, *Exhibiting the Past*, p. 55; Hung, *Mao's New World*, pp. 119–122.

stammering curator is unable to recommend a book on Party history.[53] But archival evidence shows that First Party Congress Site officials knew exactly what they were doing. Behind the scenes of the museum, officials were fully aware of contradictions, were often purposefully ambiguous, and were instructed to feign ignorance or to reply to certain questions with non-sequiturs. Beneath the "Red Line" narrative of revolutionary history lay uncertainties, contradictions, and uncomfortable truths.

At the First Party Congress Site, revolutionary history was told through two texts, a physical text on the walls and an oral script recited by docents. The physical text included narrative, illustrations, and captions—a literal textbook history. As visitors were guided through the site, docents recited an oral script, one prepared for Chinese guests and one delivered to foreign visitors. A third text supplemented the docent's narrative: a list of questions and approved answers. These three texts and their revisions reveal the difficulties of interpreting and following the "Red Line." In August 1960, First Party Congress officials wrote a report explaining that they had carefully studied Beijing's Museum of the Chinese Revolution's own "Red Line," and summarized the policy as using Mao's analysis of revolution to frame the exhibition's contents, emphasizing Mao's role in Party activities, and using Mao's writings to highlight the influence of his thought.[54]

To emphasize Mao's role in the revolution, the "Red Line" stressed action, ideology, and leadership. At the time of Party founding, the report by the First Party Congress officials explained, Mao represented the correct direction of the combination of Marxism-Leninism with the realities of the Chinese revolution. In order to highlight Mao's ideas and actions, museum officials elevated Mao's activities throughout, interpreting the May Fourth Movement according to his own analysis and emphasizing his organization of the Hunan workers' movement. Mao's writings were prominently displayed in order to demonstrate that he had recognized the importance of cultivating the workers' consciousness and that his stress on the peasant movement—as opposed to Party founder Chen Duxiu's emphasis on the importance of the cities—had been the correct strategy.[55] As Ren Wuxiong, formerly vice director and Party branch secretary of the First Party Congress, recalled, "if you mentioned the founders of the Party, there was only Mao Zedong and Li Dazhao. By the Cultural Revolution, you

[53] Simon Leys, *Chinese Shadows* (New York: Penguin Books, 1974), pp. 90–92.
[54] SMA B172-5-240, p. 104.   [55] SMA B172-5-240, pp. 98–100.

couldn't even speak of Li Dazhao."[56] The First Party Congress' adherence to the "Red Line" thus took place against the backdrop of what Elizabeth Perry calls the "construction of a revolutionary tradition," in which local histories were rewritten to burnish the credentials of the Communist Party's top leaders.[57] At the same time, Susanne Weigelin-Schwiedrzik explains, historical texts written in 1964 and 1965 were increasingly Mao-centric. As one of her Party historiography informants recalls, "How did we formulate [Party history] then? When studying the history of the Chinese Communist Party, its history constituted a 'red thread,' Mao Zedong Thought was the focus, and the works of Chairman Mao the 'basic teaching material.'"[58]

On historical events, First Party Congress Site officials criticized their past work for merely putting one event after another. In order to follow the "Red Line," each peasant movement had to be larger than the previous one, and also had to demonstrate some kind of ideological breakthrough. By touring the Museum of the Chinese Revolution in Beijing, the Shanghai officials explained, they had learned much. In portraying revolutionary history, each event should represent some aspect of Mao Zedong Thought, and critical historical events and issues were to embody Mao's correct policies. Later in their report, the authors suggested that events be ordered by importance, not necessarily by chronology.[59]

To follow the "Red Line" in the 1960s was also to explicitly serve the politics of the present. This could be done, the First Party Congress Site officials suggested, by integrating proper quotations, by referring to the present in the docents' narration, and by organizing the content in such a way as to allude to contemporary politics. For example, curators were to emphasize struggle when addressing the history of the United Front. In discussing "On New Democracy," one should refer to the idea of continuous revolution and the stages of the revolution to underscore that the revolution was still in progress. Proper quotations should serve "present-day socialist construction."[60] In a later revision in 1964,

[56] Duan Lian, Song Shijuan, and Chen Ling, eds., *Wangshi yu jiyi*, p. 65. For the pre-First Party Congress history of the CCP in both official and unofficial histories, see Vera Schwarcz, *Time for Telling Truth is Running Out: Conversations with Zhang Shenfu* (New Haven: Yale University Press, 1992), p. 97. Schwarcz writes that "Most Party historians before 1979 started with the July 1921 Communist Party Congress in Shanghai ... [which] was assumed to be the beginning of 'real' Party history."
[57] Elizabeth J. Perry, *Anyuan: Mining China's Revolutionary Tradition* (Berkeley: University of California Press, 2012), pp. 153–204.
[58] Susanne Weigelin-Schwiedrzik, "Party Historiography," in *Using the Past to Serve the Present: Historiography and Politics in Contemporary China*, edited by Jonathan Unger (Armonk, NY: M.E. Sharpe, 1993), pp. 166, 168.
[59] SMA B172-5-240, pp. 100–103.   [60] SMA B172-5-240, p. 102.

officials continued to accord with contemporary politics, highlighting the then "anti-imperialist, anti-revisionist struggle." In addition to including illustrations of Shanghai's Mixed Court and the May Fourth demonstrations, a new document, a 1920 Chinese gazette explaining Lenin's repeal of the unequal treaties, continued the anti-imperialist theme. To emphasize continuous struggle and warn against revisionism, the First Party Congress Site followed the Museum of the Chinese Revolution by including Li Dazhao's essay, "On Question and Theory," to explain the triumph of theory over Hu Shi's pragmatism.[61] In the years leading up to the Cultural Revolution, the First Party Congress Site was thus one of several living textbooks; as Xiaomei Chen has shown, another prominent textbook was the 1964 song-and-dance epic *The East is Red*, which similarly portrayed Mao as the founding father of the Communist Party and celebrated his "correct line" as a guide to revolution's victory.[62]

The First Party Congress Site exhibition was also a visual representation of the "Red Line": important images were physically enlarged, specific sections were highlighted in red, and quotations were literally decorated with red flags.[63] Visuals were revised continuously, and items included or excluded spoke to the exigencies of contemporary politics. In the 1964 revision, several pictures were replaced, including a drawing of Taiping soldiers, a small group of uninspired-looking men seen from behind. In its place, a new illustration was commissioned, with the Heavenly King Hong Xiuquan pumping his fist in the air and "leading the peasant masses." In the bright colors of propaganda art, the peasant masses have suitably fierce expressions, turning to rally around Hong Xiuquan with upturned faces and feet planted apart, surrounded by waving flags.[64] Rejected images, not unlike the iconic *Founding Ceremony of the Nation* by Dong Xiwen with its painted-over portraits of politically disgraced leaders, underscored the correct interpretation of historical figures.[65] For example, in 1962 the Propaganda Department rejected one of the oil paintings commissioned by the First Party

[61] SMA B172-1-477, p. 73.
[62] Xiaomei Chen, "Performing the 'Red Classics': From *The East is Red* to *The Road to Revival*," in *Red Legacies in China: Cultural Afterlives of the Communist Revolution*, edited by Jie Li and Enhua Zhang (Cambridge, MA: Asia Center, Harvard University, 2016), pp. 151–183.
[63] SMA B172-5-240, p. 103.   [64] SMA B172-1-477, p. 79.
[65] Hung, *Mao's New World*, pp. 127–129. As Hung explains, the oil painting *Founding Ceremony of the Nation* underwent multiple revisions after first being painted in 1953. In 1954 Dong Xiwen painted out the purged Gao Gang, in 1967 he removed Liu Shaoqi, and in 1972 his students made a replica that eliminated Lin Boqu. All three were repainted in 1978.

Congress Site. Depicting the meeting, in the painting a young Mao stands center-right in the scene, one arm outstretched as he addresses the participants listening raptly around the table. A simple light fixture illuminates Mao like a spotlight, and on the walls of the room are portraits of Lenin and Marx and a calendar dated July 1. In his comments, Wang Chaowen of the Propaganda Department criticized his Shanghai colleagues for portraying *all* of the delegates because some had later left the Party, and for portraying the two foreigners, one of whom became a Trotskyite and the other whose history was unknown. A painting of the meeting, Wang asserted, could only include Mao, Dong Biwu, Chen Tanqiu, He Shuheng, and Wang Jinmei "having a conversation during the meeting." A painting of all the delegates, he emphasized, would lead to "adverse side-effects," and circulation of the painting in the press or other media would raise unanswerable questions.[66] One way to resolve the problem of this mise-en-scène was not to portray any people at all, which is how the meeting room was re-created.

To accompany the physical text, First Party Congress Site officials wrote two scripts for the docents who accompanied the visitors through the museum. To introduce the meeting room, the docent explained that twelve representatives—naming only those permitted in the above-mentioned painting—convened the First Party Congress on July 1, 1921. The narrative continued with the meeting's interruption by the French Concession police, explaining that the delegates later reconvened on a boat on a lake in nearby Jiaxing County, interpreting this anecdote as evidence that from its inception the Party had struggled with counter-revolutionary forces. The views of the delegates were analyzed as "rightist" or "leftist" deviations, the former mistaken for thinking the Party should focus on encouraging the study of Marxism among intellectuals, and the latter incorrect for advocating a separate working-class struggle. By contrast, the docent explained, Mao and his supporters advocated fighting for the development of the proletarian class, and with that gave birth to the Party on its proper path. The meeting room, the docent told the visitors, was restored to its original condition, as the revolutionary vestige (*geming shiji*) of that moment.[67]

---

[66] SMA A22-1-66, pp. 36–39. Wang Chaowen warned that even portraying those five was potentially dangerous. The archival record does not show the fate of this painting, but the version with Mao at the center and five or six figures appears in both newspaper photos and books. See *Jiefang ribao* (Liberation daily), August 29, 1977, p. 2; Shanghaishi wenwu bowuguan weiyuanhui (Shanghai Cultural Relics Commission), ed., *Shanghai de guanghui geming shiji* (Shanghai's glorious revolutionary traces) (Shanghai: Shanghai jiaoyu chubanshe, 1978), unnumbered page (caption: Mao zhuxi zai zhonggong yida huiyi xishang). This second image also includes Deng Enming.

[67] SMA B172-5-240, pp. 18–19.

Ill.1.3. Soviet and Turkish Peace Delegations in the Shanghai
Revolutionary History Memorial Hall, undated. SMA H1-27-1-56

For a foreigner like Pierre Ryckmans, a different text was prepared.
This script was more complete, giving the historical context for the
introduction of Marxism into China, listing the origins of the delegates,
and including the presence of the two Comintern participants. However,
although it was created for foreign consumption, it adhered no less to the
"Red Line." Mao's activities in Hunan were highlighted, the encounter
with the French Concession police was still interpreted as baptism by
enemy struggle, and the First Party Congress was still a turning point in
the Chinese revolution.[68]

Many pages of the script for foreigners were devoted to questions
visitors might ask and the appropriate responses, showing how such
questions were anticipated and how their answers were scripted. In fact,
docents at the First Party Congress Site had a list of problematic
questions grouped into three categories: in whose house the meeting
took place, the identity of the Comintern delegates, and the unnamed
Chinese delegates. Ownership of the house was problematic because Li
Hanjun had left the Party in 1924. Originally the docents responded

[68] SMA B172-5-240, pp. 22–23.

Ill.1.4. Chairman of the Malawi Workers' Movement visits the First Party Congress Site, accompanied by Xing Yupei, Wang Zhenggui, Zhou Liangzuo, and Chen Huage, undated. SMA C1-2-5169

that the house had been borrowed from a delegate, but then their answer was amended to "borrowed from a resident," and finally the answer was reduced to "it is unclear." The names of the Comintern delegates, known as Maring and Nikolsky, underwent a similar process of alteration; first the docents mentioned the presence of two foreigners and gave their names, but later they did not mention them at all.[69] Finally, the docents concluded that since most foreigners already knew

[69] Maring was the pseudonym of Comintern member Hendricus Sneevliet, a Dutch activist. Nikolsky was Vladimir Neiman, an agent of the Comintern's Far Eastern Secretariat.

about the Comintern delegates, they would mention their presence. But if asked their names, the proper answer was "it is unclear." The most problematic of the questions had to do with the unnamed Chinese delegates. The first prescribed response was to list the five approved members, as in the oil painting. The docents also tried, "Those who are now Party and state leaders include Comrade Mao Zedong and Comrade Dong Biwu." If visitors pursued this line of questioning, asking if any other participants were still living or if the docent would talk about other delegates, the docent had two choices: "There is also Comrade Li Da, who is president of Wuhan University. Other participants died of illness, or some changed political affiliations," or "it is unclear."[70]

Officials at the First Party Congress Site were certainly aware that some foreign visitors were dissatisfied with the scripted answers. The docents reported that though some refrained from asking follow-up questions, their "facial expressions were unhappy."[71] However, although docents worried that *not* providing answers would hurt China's friendship with the foreigners—who, after all, were all socialist friends—they persisted in their subterfuge. In addition to the non-answers, the docents were instructed on how to change subjects swiftly. If asked who owned the house, the docent should respond quickly that the rooms were borrowed and then launch into the story of the French police, "turning the foreign visitors' attention in another direction." If the visitors persisted, the docent was ordered not to give any specific answer.[72] Another solution to the number-of-delegates problem was simply to put out *more* chairs than there were participants.[73] That the answer to every question eventually devolved into "it is unclear" suggests not the confusion or ignorance that Ryckmans indicated, but carefully calculated deflection.

These tensions between questions and answers and between historical facts and the "Red Line" were also mirrored behind the scenes in the First Party Congress Site's historical research. Both Chen Peicun and Ren Wuxiong conducted research—Chen surveying historic sites and Ren working through the collection of artifacts that grew to over 100,000 objects. Ren in particular had a passion for Party history. As a student at Shanghai's Hujiang University and then at Hangzhou's Zhejiang University, he had been a member of the Party underground.

See Alexander V. Pantsov, with Steven I. Levine, *Mao: The Real Story* (New York: Simon & Schuster, 2012), pp. 100–106.

[70] SMA B172-5-250, p. 24.   [71] Ibid.   [72] SMA B172-5-240, p. 23.

[73] In response to a Soviet trade delegation's questions about there being only twelve chairs, sixteen chairs were subsequently displayed. SMA B172-5-240, pp. 15–16.

From a position in the Shanghai Bureau of Culture, in 1957 he requested a transfer to the First Party Congress Site. But as his first year on the job coincided with the Anti-Rightist Movement, Ren ran into political restrictions. His first project, a chapter on museology for a book on Shanghai's cultural achievements, was not accepted for publication as the Shanghai Bureau of Culture came under attack as a "department of emperors, generals, and ministers," concerned only with piles of old paper and not with the lives and spirit of the working masses. In a recent oral history Ren explains his philosophy, "I have always thought that research on Party history must respect the historical facts. If the time is not yet right, then accumulate historical materials first and research them later."[74] The archival record shows that Ren and his colleagues indeed worked hard to gather information and trace original sources, carefully documenting their research. One particularly difficult question they faced was: what was Mao's actual role in the First Party Congress? The way museum officials sought to answer this question highlights a number of problems in following the "Red Line" and of doing history in general: contradictions between memoirs and official history, the ghostwriting of memoirs and missing official histories, and bureaucratic barriers between First Party Congress researchers and Central Archive authorities.

In November 1964 the First Party Congress Site set out to find the answer to a question that was sometimes posed by foreign visitors: "Comrade Dong Biwu recalls that Chairman Mao was elected a Central Committee member at the First Congress; this appears in 1961 in your media reports; can this [fact] be verified?" When Dong's secretary visited the museum, researchers questioned him about this issue. The secretary responded that Dong was not relying on his own memory but rather on documents from the Soviet Union in the Central Party Archives. But after Shanghai museum officials requested the materials from the Central Party Archives, the Beijing archivists replied that this matter had not yet been researched and hence they could not reach a conclusion. Shanghai's researchers persisted, going to Beijing to consult their colleagues at the Museum of the Chinese Revolution. There they received the same answer that the Central Party Archives had provided. So the First Party Congress Site scripted the following answer:

At the time, Chairman Mao was the leader of the Hunan small group. After the First Party Congress he did leadership work in the Hunan Party. In the early years of the Communist Party, Chairman Mao combined Marxism-Leninism

[74] Duan Lian, Song Shijuan, and Chen Ling, eds., *Wangshi yu jiyi*, pp. 62–63, 66.

with the practical realities of the Chinese revolution. He is the representative of the birth of the Party on the proper path.[75]

Like many of the other answers in the docent script, the uniform answer did not address the question. Despite the meticulously documented research—interviews, attempted access to Party archives, and a pilgrimage to the Museum of the Chinese Revolution—researchers' determination to seek truth from facts was thwarted. In addition to and complicating the issue of the availability of sources was the reliability of the accessible materials. First Party Congress Site officials eventually realized that Dong Biwu's memoir, whose content appeared in the press and had been cited by visitors, was not actually written by Dong.[76] When the researchers confronted the ghostwriter, they pointed out that there were discrepancies between the 1961 memoir and earlier Party histories. They also had no updated Party history upon which to rely; officials had either a ghostwritten memoir or out-of-date Party histories to serve as sources. The second problem of sources was that documentation on the First Party Congress was limited. Perhaps the scant documentation was embarrassing, or perhaps in the wake of the Sino-Soviet split in 1960 the Soviet-sponsored Comintern role in convening the First Congress was an undesirable detail; in either case, these reasons might have closed the doors in the faces of the researchers from the First Party Congress Site. There was no way to seek truth from facts.

In fact, only the highest-ranking Party historians—those writing interpretations for the Communist Party Central Committee—had access to archives; lower-ranking historians were only allowed to read propaganda materials.[77] But the reason the First Party Congress Site officials were denied archival access may have been more significant than a question of sources or the Soviet role. The uncomfortable silence came from the suggestion that Mao was less important at the First Party Congress than he had been made to appear. The document in the Comintern archives, which the Chinese held in the Central Party Archives, did not include any names.[78] There were no sources to affirm that Mao was made a Central

---

[75] SMA B172-1-477, p. 80. This answer was approved by the Propaganda Department in February 1965.

[76] SMA B172-1-477, p. 96.

[77] Weigelin-Schwiedrzik, "Party Historiography," pp. 159–160.

[78] van de Ven explains that the report to the Comintern stated that three men were elected to the Secretariat, and that other published sources and party histories agreed that these three men were Chen Duxiu (to head the Secretariat), Zhang Guotao (organization), and Li Da (propaganda). Hans J. van de Ven, *From Friend to Comrade: The Founding of the Chinese Communist Party, 1920–1927* (Berkeley: University of California Press, 1991), p. 88. The document from the Comintern Archives is reproduced in *Zhongguo gongchandang xuanchuan gongzuo wenxian xuanbian: 1915–1937* (Selected documents on the

Committee member at the First Party Congress Meeting. Beyond the embarrassment that Dong Biwu and the media had been wrong was the inconsistency about the early political influence of Mao Zedong at precisely a time when the exhibition had to follow the "Red Line" to highlight the role of the paramount leader and the influence of Mao Zedong Thought. The truth was that Mao was not central to the First Party Congress meeting, nor was the First Party Congress meeting a decisive moment in the history of the Communist Party. As historian Hans van de Ven has shown, the early years of the CCP were marked by weak central leadership, conflicts between central and local branches, and failed attempts to organize mass movements. The Party was organized along Leninist lines in 1925, became a mass political party with a centralized organization in 1925–1927, and absorbed a much larger and diverse membership in the wake of the 1925 May Thirtieth Movement.[79] At the moment of its founding and throughout the period of the First United Front, the CCP was subordinate to the Nationalists and subject to the factionalism in the Comintern.[80] Though Mao had immortalized the Party's founding as "a great event that opened the heavens and earth," the First Party Congress was not the turning point that the "Red Line" required.[81]

Perhaps, just as the First Party Congress Site researchers knew that Dong Biwu did not write his own memoir, they may also have surmised that the Central Party Archives were closed to them because they did not contain the right answer. Despite Ren Wuxiong's commitment to collect historical materials while waiting out the political storms, an exhibition still had to be mounted. Curators thus had to tiptoe around uncertainties and hope that "further research" would resolve the problem, while docents told visitors that Mao was "the representative of the birth of the Party" rather than actually answering their questions.[82] A seemingly

propaganda work of the Chinese Communist Party: 1915–1937) (Beijing: Xuexi chubanshe, 1996), pp. 323–326.

[79] van de Ven, *From Friend to Comrade*, pp. 240–241.

[80] Bruce A. Elleman, *Diplomacy and Deception: The Secret History of Sino-Soviet Diplomatic Relations, 1917–1927* (Armonk, NY: M.E. Sharpe, 1997) and *Moscow and the Emergence of Communist Power in China, 1925–30: The Nanchang Uprising and the Birth of the Red Army* (London: Routledge, 2009).

[81] This 1949 quotation is still included in recent popular histories. See, for example, Zhang Wenqing et al., *Mao Zedong zai Shanghai* (Mao Zedong in Shanghai) (Shanghai: Shanghai shudian chubanshe, 1993), p. 14.

[82] A reform-era Party School history explains, "Although Mao Zedong was not one of the CCP's initiators (*faqi ren*) ... in thinking and in organization he made a contribution to the founding of the Chinese Communist Party." See Hua Xing, "Mao Zedong he Zhongguo gongchandang de chuangli" (Mao Zedong and the founding of the Chinese Communist Party), in *Mao Zedong zai Shanghai*, edited by Zhonggong Shanghai shiwei dangshi yanjiushi (Party history office of the Shanghai Party Committee of the Chinese

trivial question posed at the First Party Congress Site brings the problem of telling revolution in the Mao years into sharp relief. History was supposed to be an authoritative master narrative. After all, the Communist Party's correct understanding of history was a reflection of both its legitimacy and its power. But behind the scenes of the museum, curating a stable narrative proved harder than collecting and restoring the revolution's material remains. The "Red Line" fashioned history into myth, even as the revolutionary narrative was revised yet again in the era of continuous revolution.

The Cultural Revolution and its aftermath

During the Cultural Revolution years, the "Red Line" made the First Party Congress Site a monument to Mao. Though it was closed for the first three years of the Cultural Revolution (1966–1969) and its display in the three exhibition rooms was removed, it reopened its doors in 1969 to a far greater number of visitors. In contrast to the 100,000 cadres and foreigners who were received from 1952 to 1965, the Shanghai Revolutionary Committee ordered that it be opened to worker-peasant-soldier groups, and over four million visitors were logged between 1966 and 1976.[83] Some pilgrims to the First Party Congress Site are depicted in a late Cultural Revolution propaganda poster by the Shanghai People's Art Publishing House (1974). There are workers in coveralls, men in blue cadre suits, military men in uniform, and even ethnic minorities in various costumes. During this period, the First Party Congress Site was portrayed as the first stop on a pilgrimage of revolutionary sites. Paired with poems like a traditional tourist itinerary of the eight vistas, one was to begin at the First Party Congress Site and end on Beijing's Tiananmen Square—from the First Congress to the ten great buildings that commemorated the tenth anniversary of the PRC founding in 1959.[84]

For visitors during the Cultural Revolution, the "Red Line" was already visible from the street. The eaves of the entire block were emblazoned with "Long Live the Communist Party! Long Live the

Communist Party) (Beijing: Zhonggong dangshi chubanshe, 1993), p. 256. A more recent history acknowledges that Mao Zedong was "an ordinary representative" at the meeting and that at the time he was not a great personage and was still a young student of Marxist-Leninism. Meng Xing, *Shui zhu chenfu: Zhonggong yida daibiao chenfulu* (Who is in control: The rise and fall of the delegates to the First Party Congress) (Beijing: Renmin chubanshe, 2009), pp. 150–151.

[83] SMA B172-3-127, p. 51; SMA B172-3-221, p. 30. Note that in 1966 the Shanghai Revolutionary History Memorial Museum Preparatory Office was renamed the First Party Congress Memorial Hall (*yida jinianguan*), SMA B172-3-85, p. 2.

[84] Nie Bing and Qiao Yan, "Renmin zhanshi xin xiangdang," p. 2.

Ill.1.5. *Paying Respects at the First Party Congress Site*, 1974. Shanghai renmin meishu chubanshe. Image courtesy of the Shanghai Propaganda Poster Art Centre

Great Leader Chairman Mao!" A central portrait of Mao recalled his position on the Tiananmen rostrum, and Mao quotations filled the spaces between the doors and spilled over onto a billboard gracing the adjacent street corner.[85] Outside the entrance to the First Party Congress Site, reported *Jiefang ribao* (Liberation daily), the sound of people reciting the *Quotations of Chairman Mao* filled the air.[86] In the meeting room, the narrative script was guided by Mao's actions and Mao's interpretation of revolutionary history. His words were woven into the text with "Chairman Mao says," or "Chairman Mao teaches us;" at times the Chairman was not attributed at all, suggesting both that the quotation was already known as his and that following the "Red Line" to its extreme erased any boundaries among Mao's words, the Party's, and the narrative of revolution. The Cultural Revolution text, like any other verbal

---

[85] Shanghaishi wenwu baoguan weiyuanhui, ed., *Shanghai de guanghui geming shiji*, p. 1; Zhonggong Shanghai shiwei dangshi yanjiushi and Shanghaishi wenwuju eds., *Zhongguo gongchandang zaoqi zai Shanghai shiji*, p. 14.

[86] Jin Dalu, *Feichang yu zhengchang: Shanghai "wenge" shiqi de shehui shenghuo* (Extraordinary and ordinary: Social life during Shanghai's "Cultural Revolution" period) (Shanghai: Shanghai cishu chubanshe, 2011), 2 vols., p. 77.

interchange during this period, ended with obligatory choruses of a long life to Chairman Mao.[87]

If the difference in the presentation of the "Red Line" was a matter of degree, the total experience of the visitor was much changed. Instead of being given a lecture by a docent, a carefully crafted tape-recording was played for the Chinese visitors. The recorded narrative began with a later historical event, the October Revolution instead of the Opium War. In its final few paragraphs it also extended its commentary to the present. In contrast to earlier exhibitions at the First Party Congress Site—which like the Beijing Museum of the Chinese Revolution avoided the socialist period—the tape-recording concluded with criticisms of all of Mao's perceived enemies within the Party, from Chen Duxiu to recent adversaries such as Peng Dehuai and Liu Shaoqi.

Archival memos suggest that the recording was frequently updated; though Lin Biao once featured prominently in the narrative, with his fall from grace he was swiftly added to the list of opportunists, and there was a special exhibit on his crimes.[88] The narrative text of the First Party Congress Site thus changed from revolutionary textbook to political broadside. Such political updates were not always limited to the final paragraphs; during the Criticize Confucius, Criticize Lin Biao Campaign, Mao's role at Party founding was rewritten to include his opposition to Confucius and Mencius.[89] The medium of the tape-recorder provided the First Party Congress Site with a technology suited to an era of tumultuous politics: one could make a new tape immediately, no individual docent could be faulted for misspeaking, and no one could ask any questions.[90]

Outside of the restored meeting room, the exhibition rooms remained shuttered. Over these years the leadership of the First Party Congress Site repeatedly proposed a new exhibition, but Zhang Chunqiao and Yao Wenyuan, members of the Shanghai Revolutionary Committee and later known as part of the notorious "Gang of Four," rejected such requests because they were too politically sensitive.[91] In the meantime, as the Cultural Revolution unfolded, the First Party Congress Site continued to collect revolutionary relics. Together with the Shanghai

---

[87] SMA B172-3-85, pp. 35–39.

[88] SMA B172-3-85, pp. 34, 38–39; SMA B172-3-127, p. 7. For earlier portrayals of Lin Biao, see SMA B244-3-143, p. 19.

[89] SMA B172-3-127, p. 29.

[90] Foreigners were still received in person, and an extensive list of appropriate answers was supplied to the docents, explaining the purpose of the Cultural Revolution, the meaning of revisionism, the nature of Liu Shaoqi's crimes, and so forth. SMA B244-3-143, pp. 22–30.

[91] SMA B172-3-127, p. 41.

Museum, the First Party Congress Site took in the *wenwu* of the Cultural Revolution—from documentary evidence to material detritus—even saving the cigarette cartons which Shanghai workers used to write notes to their wives during the Anting Incident.[92] Thus the idea of a revolutionary history museum that would continue to add to its collection persisted. As Ren Wuxiong's recollections suggest, researchers remained steadfast in collecting, even when the time to interpret and display was not yet right.[93]

In line with Cultural Revolution rhetoric, the First Party Congress Site used publications and traveling exhibitions to bring revolutionary relics to the masses. For example, Shanghai's People's Press published a book for young readers entitled *Kan geming wenwu, xue geming chuantong* (Look at revolutionary relics, study the revolutionary tradition). Filled with stories about revolutionary *wenwu*—from the seals of Hunan peasant associations to the personal effects of revolutionary martyrs— this genre was popular enough to inspire an entire series with the same title.[94] Beyond the museum, First Party Congress Site docents brought traveling exhibitions to various venues in Shanghai, including the Shanghai Museum, the Shanghai Youth Palace, and the Pudong Workers' Palace, reaching an estimated 360,000 visitors over eight months in 1975–1976. Not all visitors were part of organized groups; on one day, 1,000 of the 4,000 attendees at the Shanghai Youth Palace were individuals attending on their own.[95] In the countryside, the First Party Congress Site organized small portable displays that were carried to suburban factories and countryside communes, reaching many thousands who were unable to visit Shanghai.[96] Although the official reports of a universally glowing reception must be read with caution, it seems that the docents were freer to interact with visitors outside the confines of the museum. For example, in the weeks following Zhou Enlai's death when people in Shanghai donned black armbands in defiance of orders not to mourn the premier, exhibition viewers

[92] Interview with Shanghai Academy of Social Sciences historian Jin Dalu, July 2, 2013. See a photo of a collection team's official seal in *Shilin* (Historical review), no. 136 (2012), p. 31. For a report on such activities, see SMA B172-3-176. The Anting Incident occurred in Shanghai on November 10, 1966, when a train with worker rebels—attempting to reach Beijing to meet with central leaders—was halted by order of the State Council. See Elizabeth J. Perry and Li Xun, *Proletarian Power: Shanghai in the Cultural Revolution* (Boulder, CO: Westview Press, 1997), pp. 34–36.

[93] Duan Lian, Song Shijuan, and Chen Ling, eds., *Wangshi yu jiyi*, p. 66.

[94] *Kan geming wenwu, xue geming chuantong* (Look at revolutionary relics, study the revolutionary tradition) (Shanghai: Shanghai renmin chubanshe, 1976). Additional books in this series, on topics such as the Anyuan workers' movement and the soldiers of Huaihai, were published in subsequent years. They were written by local propaganda departments or Party history offices.

[95] SMA B172-3-221, pp. 25, 31.   [96] SMA B172-3-221, pp. 30–38.

requested that the display include photographs from Zhou's life. The inclusion of eight photographs, approved by the Shanghai Bureau of Culture, briefly acknowledged the masses' right to memorialize their own history.[97]

With Mao's death in 1976, the First Party Congress Site took on two new roles: a place of mourning and a site of political rectification. With both, visitors performed loyalty to Mao and to the Party. During the immediate days following Mao's death, waves of people made pilgrimages to Shanghai.[98] On the first anniversary of his death, national and local papers featured the First Party Congress Site, reiterating that this was the location where the Great Helmsman had personally raised the first red flag and that this was the sacred birthplace of the Party.[99] Media descriptions included accounts of exemplary pilgrims who made pledges of duty and sacrifice—sisters building the socialist countryside, students being sent off to Xinjiang Province, and soldiers being deployed. The newspapers depicted foreign visitors in the same manner of those making pilgrimages, going out of their way to visit the site, copying Mao quotations from the walls, and leaving in the guestbook hyperbolic comments about China being a revolutionary fortress for the world.[100]

During the early post-Mao years, the First Party Congress Site served as a stage to rectify the Cultural Revolution's excesses while continuing to affirm the memory of Mao and Party founding. Museum officials blamed the Gang of Four for obstructing their work and praised Zhou Enlai instead for encouraging the exhibition of revolutionary relics. Individuals used the site to perform their own rehabilitations. *Jiefang ribao* described one such example: upon his release, Huang Chibo, a veteran and a former public security official imprisoned during the Cultural Revolution, rushed to the First Party Congress Site. Gazing at

[97] SMA B172-3-221, pp. 2–3. On the black armbands, see John Kamm, "Shanghaied at the Feather and Down Minifair," in *My First Trip to China: Scholars, Diplomats and Journalists Reflect on their First Encounters with China*, edited by Kin-ming Liu (Hong Kong: East Slope Publishing Limited, 2012), pp. 220–227.

[98] Wang Jinyou, "Huainian Mao zhuxi jianchi xue Dazhai" (Remembering Chairman Mao, adhering to the study of Dazhai), *Zhejiang ribao* (Zhejiang daily), September 21, 1976, p. 3.

[99] "Hongqi juchu zhan zhengcheng" (Journey to the exhibition where the red flag was raised), *Jiefang ribao*, August 29, 1977, p. 2; "Guanghui qizhi zhi zhengcheng" (The glorious flag leads our journey), *Wenhui bao* (Wenhui daily), September 7, 1977, p. 2.

[100] "Mao zhuxi de guanghui zhao huanyu" (Chairman Mao's glory shines upon the whole world), *Jiefang ribao*, October 18, 1977, p. 3. For further discussion on the Cultural Revolution emphasis on China as a model for the world revolution, see Zachary A. Scarlett, "China after the Sino-Soviet Split: Maoist Politics, Global Narratives, and the Imagination of the World" (PhD diss., Northeastern University, 2013).

the chairs and tea service in the meeting room, Huang told the docent, "This is the place where Chairman Mao created the Party; it must be preserved!"[101] Insofar as the First Party Congress Site represented the Party and its origins, its preservation represented the restoration of the pre-Cultural Revolution revolutionary narrative, its materiality a relic in its religious sense.

In 1980, a new exhibition in a renovated First Party Congress Site provided an even more complete rectification of names. Though Mao was still listed as the first participant, the names of all thirteen participants were included.[102] Photographs and essays by Party founders Li Dazhao and Chen Duxiu were placed on display. Liu Shaoqi, who had been vilified in the tape-recording from the Cultural Revolution, was incorporated into a section on labor-organizing activities and depicted leading a strike at Anyuan. Museum officials stressed the use of historical materials, especially memoirs and essays by participants, and highlighted the need for a "scientific attitude that [seeks] truth from facts." To this end, they prominently displayed the documents passed at the meeting of the First Party Congress, materials to which museum officials had been denied access in 1964.[103] Remembering this period today, Yao Qingxiong—a retired director of the Lu Xun Memorial Hall—related how the First Party Congress Site removed the Mao quotations on its interior walls. "You could read [the quotations] or include them in the narration, but how could you put them in the rooms? How could you say people did not participate? This was not historically accurate!"[104]

The new exhibition reflected broad changes in attitudes toward historical research. As the curators of Beijing's Museum of the Chinese

---

[101] *Jiefang ribao*, August 29, 1977, p. 2.

[102] See Dong Tingzhi and Zhang Zurong, "Guanyu zhonggong 'yida' daibiao renshu de jizhong shuofa" (Several ways of explaining the number of delegates to the "First Party Congress"). In *Dangshi yanjiu ziliao* (Party history research materials), edited by Zhongguo geming bowuguan dangshi yanjiushi (Party history research office of the Museum of the Chinese Revolution) (Chengdu: Sichuan renmin chubanshe, no. 1, 1980), pp. 157–162.

[103] "Zhonggong yida huizhi jinianguan tiaozheng chenlie neirong" (The contents of the revised exhibition at the Memorial Museum of the First Party Congress Site), *Wenhui bao*, July 1, 1980, p. 1.

[104] Interview with Yao Qingxiong, July 25, 2013. Yao joined the Lu Xun Memorial Hall after completing his military service in 1955; he served as its vice Party secretary and retired as director. In 1982 he began working for the Shanghai Bureau of Culture and also served as interim director of the Shanghai History Museum. He remembers how during the Cultural Revolution all the walls of the Lu Xun Memorial Hall were painted red. In 1973 he approached Deng Yingchao, wife of Premier Zhou Enlai, regarding what to do with problematic people in the exhibition. He explained that people later became braver and slowly began to change the exhibition.

Revolution explained in 1979, "the *wenwu*, documents, and photographs that reflect historical reality cannot be purposely edited."[105] Using the example of a ballad from the Anyuan workers' movement that had been changed to include Mao's name, curators argued that one could not fabricate history. The Museum of the Chinese Revolution thus overturned the idea of the "Red Line." One could not write Party history from start to finish according to Mao Zedong Thought, portray Mao Zedong Thought as a completely formed ideology, or use Mao quotations to stand in for historical events. Further, the curators explained that one could not read the past according to the present, exaggerate the role of individuals—including Mao himself—or use the museum to judge individuals' mistakes without accounting for their overall contributions to history. Finally, one could not modify or fake artifacts or photographs.[106] The Museum of the Chinese Revolution thus enumerated the characteristics of the "Red Line" in practice, rejecting Mao-era museology as a negative example. To restore the revolutionary narrative to history was to rectify the Party's political legitimacy.

Conclusion: Red tourism and patriotic education

Today the First Party Congress Site and its displays bear few of the distinctive marks of the Mao era. Gone are the Soviet-style narrative and the epic paintings and gone is the Cultural Revolution–era billboard with Mao Zedong quotations. No longer does the exhibit elide names from the text nor do the curators remove chairs from the meeting room. Writing in 2009, curator Ni Xingxiang criticized the long neglect of objects. The latest expansion of the permanent exhibition follows the newest trends in global museology, "using objects to represent history." Curator Ni explained that the museum's duty is to use contextualization and new technologies to "bring the *wenwu* and the viewers closer together, to allow the viewers and the *wenwu* to have face-to-face conversations and interactions."[107] The principle of "using objects to represent history"

---

[105] Zhongguo geming bowuguan dangshi chenlie bu (Party History Exhibition Department of the Museum of the Chinese Revolution), "Dangshi chenlie de jige wenti" (Several issues regarding exhibiting Party history), *Dangshi yanjiu ziliao*, no. 6 (1979), p. 123.

[106] Ibid., pp. 122–129.

[107] Ni Xingxiang, "Chedi 'yiwu daishi' chenlie zhidao sixiang de tihui" (The experience of thoroughly carrying out the exhibition principle of "using objects to represent history"), *Zhongguo bowuguan tongxun* (Chinese museums newsletter), no. 9 (2000), pp. 6–8.

changes the Mao-era imperative; rather than use *wenwu* as props for the revolutionary narrative, today's First Party Congress Site exhibition centers on the objects themselves.

But this does not mean that the display of revolutionary history is no longer ideological. In the same way that the Mao-era First Party Congress Site was designated Shanghai's first and foremost revolutionary relic and the first stop on a PLA soldier's map of the revolution, today the monument is central to two reform-era phenomena: Red Tourism and patriotic education. Red Tourism, as Kirk Denton explains, is both a top-down and a locally sponsored program to use revolutionary sites to promote the tourist industry.[108] With its own Five-Year Plan (2005–2010), Red Tourism is part of a larger movement of "patriotic education" to stimulate not simply love of the nation but also love of the Party that styles itself as the nation's steward. The importance of such political indoctrination is underscored by the fact that it was at Beijing's Museum of the Chinese Revolution—one year after the Tiananmen student movement—that Jiang Zemin suggested that young people had no understanding of history; the task of the museum was therefore to "strengthen patriotic education, patriotism, and socialist education."[109] In 1997 the First Party Congress Site was named a national model for patriotic education and curators today continue to identify educating youth as their central mission.[110]

The architectural historian Samuel Liang argues that the ideology of the First Party Congress Site is now one of a "hegemonic power structure" and that the original revolutionary meaning of the site— underground, rebellious, and radical—has been erased. Liang suggests that this revolutionary history is now an anachronism, buried with the residential neighborhood that was destroyed to create the luxury entertainment and shopping complex of Xintiandi. He calls the First Party Congress Site and Xintiandi "a false preservation and a false revolution," in which neither the political revolution nor the consumer revolution are authentic.[111] Liang's analysis highlights one of the two

---

[108] Denton, *Exhibiting the Past*, pp. 219–225.

[109] "Jiang Zemin tongzhi canguan 'Zhongguo gemingshi chenlie' jieshushi de jianghua" (Speech by Comrade Jiang Zemin upon viewing the conclusion of the "Exhibition of Chinese revolutionary history"), *Dangshi yanjiu ziliao*, no. 9 (1990), pp. 2–3. Note that the "revolutionary tradition" is absent from this list of priorities.

[110] Zhonggong Shanghai shiwei dangshi yanjiushi and Shanghaishi wenwuju, eds., *Zhongguo gongchandang zaoqi zai Shanghai shiji*, p. 15; interview with Xin Honglin, vice director of exhibitions at the Memorial Museum of the First National Congress of the Communist Party of China, June 13, 2007.

[111] Samuel Y. Liang, "Amnesiac Monument, Nostalgic Fashion: Shanghai's New Heaven and Earth," *Wasafiri*, vol. 23, no. 3 (2008), pp. 47–55.

modes of socialist China's exhibitionary culture—that of a state in power rather than that of a revolutionary movement. Since the creation of the First Party Congress Site, its displays have been primarily in this state in power mode, creating a legitimizing narrative of Party history. But because the narrative is one of revolution, authenticity to revolution still has power.

The objects on display remain classified as revolutionary relics. Although they are sometimes referred to simply as *wenwu*, and some curators prefer the term "modern relics" (*jinxiandai wenwu*) as being more "scientific," it is the artifacts' association with the revolution that makes them worth preserving.[112] Now that "using objects to represent history" guides exhibitionary culture, authenticity is ever more important to legitimacy. As curator Ni has argued, if the exhibition does not make clear the authenticity and provenance of the revolutionary relic, then it "cannot truly move the hearts of the viewers and the audience will be suspicious of the authenticity of the revolutionary relic ... and this will seriously affect the social position of the revolutionary memorial museum, directly influencing the effectiveness of the revolutionary memorial museum on society."[113] If the *wenwu* are not authentic, then neither is the revolution.

Party historiography continues to shape how the First Party Congress Site is presented. Though the permanent exhibition focuses on objects, it is still structured by sections, for instance: "The Establishment of the Chinese Communist Party is the Inevitable Outcome of Chinese Historical Development," "The Establishment of the Chinese Communist Party is the Product of the Integration of Marxist-Leninist Thought and the Chinese Workers' Movement," and "The Establishment of the Chinese Communist Party is the Great Event that Opened a New Era."[114] Mao's shadow, too, remains long. Though the text of the exhibition corrects the date of the First Party Congress to July 23, 1921, Party founding is still celebrated in China on Mao's date of July 1, a fact that has not gone unremarked as

---

[112] Interview in Shanghai with Xin Honglin, June 13, 2007.

[113] Ni Xingxiang, "Chedi 'yiwu daishi' chenlie zhidao sixiang de tihui," p. 7. Sigrid Schmalzer documents a similar concern with authenticity. In one case, a docent in the 1950s used the fact that Peking Man's fossils were replicas to lambast imperialism. In a more recent example, local museums resent the fact that their own originals are exhibited in Beijing rather than on site. Sigrid Schmalzer, *The People's Peking Man: Popular Science and Human Identity in Twentieth-Century China* (Chicago: University of Chicago Press, 2008), pp. 102, 185.

[114] Zhongguo gongchandang diyici quanguo daibiao dahui huizhi jinianguan, ed., *Zhongguo gongchandang diyici quanguo daibiao dahui huizhi*, pp. 27, 63, and 91.

symptomatic of the Party's historical amnesia.[115] In a life-size diorama of wax statues depicting the meeting room and all of its participants, Mao remains the central, standing figure, with his right hand caught mid-gesture, illuminated by light.[116]

Critics of the persistence of July 1 notwithstanding, the First Party Congress Site in many ways escapes the dilemmas of exhibiting the revolution. Unlike Beijing's Museum of the Chinese Revolution—renamed the National Museum of China in 2003—it never had to display the longer arc of the revolution, nor grapple with exhibiting the tragedies of the Mao period. While the National Museum of China elides the politically sensitive past, the raison d'être of the First Party Congress Site is to curate only Party founding in all of its promise, not the future that was yet to come.[117] But elsewhere in Shanghai, another Mao-era exhibition once told the narrative of New China. In Chapter 2, we visit a different site that was also designated a revolutionary *wenwu*. In the workers' new village of Fangua Lane, the material of the "old society" and the "new society" was used to tell a story of transformation, of the lives and in the words of New China's people.

---

[115] Ye Sang, *China Candid: The People on the People's Republic*, ed. by Geremie R. Barmé, with Miriam Lang (Berkeley: University of California Press, 2006), p. 7. In 1980, an article in a propaganda newsletter informed readers that the dates of the First Party Congress had been determined to be July 23–31 and therefore the Party's birthday should be celebrated on July 23. But until a decision was made, newspapers were to maintain the previous formulation. See "Guanyu dang de danshengri de gongkai xuan-chuan" (On the open dissemination of the Party's birthday), in *Xuanchuan dongtai (xuanbian): 1980* (Propaganda trends [Selections]: 1980). (Beijing: Zhongguo shehui kexue chubanshe, 1981), pp. 291–292.

[116] See Zhongguo gongchandang diyici quanguo daibiao dahui huizhi jinianguan, ed., Zhongguo gongchandang diyici quanguo daibiao dahui huizhi, pp. 100–101.

[117] Denton, *Exhibiting the Past*, p. 73.

2   Exhibiting New China: "Fangua Lane Past and Present"

On a misty November morning in 1963, Félix Pita Rodríguez and Wang Lanhua must have appeared a strange pair. The Cuban poet, age fifty-four, was in Shanghai as part of a goodwill trip to China; perhaps he was dressed as he is in a photograph in contemporary Chinese translations of his work—dapper in a suit and tie, flower at his lapel. With an aquiline nose and his hair slicked back, he must have looked his role as vice president of Cuba's Association of Writers and Artists, a literary counterpart to Shen Zhiyu of the Shanghai Museum.[1] Wang Lanhua, seven years his junior, was the head of Fangua Lane's neighborhood committee and served as his guide. At five feet eight, she was tall for a Chinese woman of her generation, and she likely was wearing clothes that she reserved for such occasions—a padded cotton coat, black trousers, and cloth shoes—with her bobbed hair secured with two long hairpins.[2] Pita Rodríguez later wrote that he was drawn to China for its "revolutionary poems," and in Shanghai he found his poem in the neighborhood of Fangua Lane and in the person of Wang Lanhua.[3]

Pita Rodríguez had already written an ode to Shanghai, celebrating its factories' churn toward the future while memorializing as eternal the writer Lu Xun. But he set pen to paper again to write about a shantytown (*penghuqu*) of the past, the concrete apartment buildings going up in its place, and the neighborhood's unnamed storyteller. "In Fangua Lane,"

---

[1] Félix Pita Rodríguez, *Zhongguo renmin de shou* (Manos del pueblo Chino y otros poemas), trans. by Zhao Jinping (Beijing: Zuojia chubanshe, 1964). A biography and photograph of Pita Rodríguez are included on the enclosed bookmark. Special thanks to George Ledin, Jr. for his efforts in locating this poem.

[2] Wing-Chung Ho, *The Transition Study of Postsocialist China: An Ethnographic Study of a Model Community* (Singapore: World Scientific, 2010), p. 89. I am indebted to Wing-Chung Ho's ethnographic research on the neighborhood. Wang Lanhua, whom he refers to as Ms. Q, was one of his informants. I reached Ms. Wang's daughter by telephone in 2012 but by that time, at the age of ninety-five, she was deaf and could not receive visitors. I have retained the names used in published and publicly available sources, while citing those who spoke directly with me by age and occupation. For a roughly contemporaneous photo of Wang Lanhua, see Ho, *The Transition Study of Postsocialist China*, Ill.2.8.

[3] Pita Rodríguez, *Zhongguo renmin de shou*, pp. 1–3.

he wrote, "I witnessed the Chinese people burying a remnant of the old days." Explaining the past hunger and poverty in the thatched houses and describing the workers' new village (*gongren xincun*) was a woman "dignified and pure-faced, like a statue." A delegate to the local people's congress, she narrated her past sufferings as a beggar in the shantytown, but her sights were set on the future. Pita Rodríguez concluded his poem by likening the "steel-willed woman" to her own motherland, "using her own strength/she buries the old days/she constructs a New China."[4] Wang Lanhua, in life as in the poem, was a metonym for the Fangua Lane neighborhood, and its people synecdoche for China's working class.[5]

To get to Fangua Lane, a 1965 book of stories explained to its reader, one would arrive by train at Shanghai's North Station in Zhabei District and then follow Tianmu Road to the east. Next to the overpass a visitor would see "five-story apartment residences neatly in rows one after another, flooded with light. Around the flowerbeds of the residences, there are children bathed in sunshine. Some of them are playing Chinese jump rope, and some are sitting around an old grandfather who is telling them revolutionary stories."[6] The Fangua Lane neighborhood was a stop on the Cuban poet's itinerary and a feature in the book of stories for the same reason: the transformation from a notorious slum to a workers' new village was a material manifestation of the change in workers' lives. Construction on Fangua Lane, which had begun several months before Pita Rodríguez' visit, eventually came to house almost 2,000 families. Equipped with water, electricity, and gas, and including a nursery and primary school, bookstore, and food shop, Fangua Lane was Shanghai's showcase, one of two residential areas open to foreign visitors.[7] Its vista, shown below in an illustration for use in the

---

[4] Pita Rodríguez, *Zhongguo renmin de shou*, pp. 15–17. The two poems were also printed in *Jiefang ribao* (Liberation daily), November 13, 1963, p. 4. On November 26, 1963, Mao Zedong received Pita Rodríguez and his wife in Beijing at the Great Hall of the People; during the visit the two men discussed Lu Xun and his poetry. See Guangxi Zhuang Autonomous Region Archive, X1-33-125, pp. 114–119.

[5] Though the woman is unnamed, it was Wang Lanhua. According to the 1998 gazetteer, she was the only person so distinguished from Fangua Lane. See Guo Tiancheng, Cao Yiding, and Qian Xuezhong, eds., *Zhabei quzhi* (Zhabei District gazetteer) (Shanghai: Shanghai shehui kexueyuan chubanshe, 1998), pp. 725–729, 1292.

[6] Jin Bian, "Fangualong de jinxi" (Past and present in Fangua Lane), in *Shanghai de gushi* (Stories of Shanghai) (Shanghai: Shanghai renmin chubanshe, 1965), vol. 4, p. 61.

[7] Feng Meichun, "Fangualong de bianqian" (Historical changes in Fangua Lane), in *Shanghai wenshi ziliao wenji: Zhabei juan* (Collection of Shanghai historical materials: Zhabei volume) (Shanghai: Shanghaishi zhengxie wenshi ziliao bianjibu, 2004), pp. 239–242; Guo Tiancheng, Cao Yiding, and Qian Xuezhong, eds., *Zhabei quzhi*, p. 282. The other area open to foreigners was Caoyang New Village in Putuo District; Marie-Claire Bergère begins her book on Shanghai with her 1957 visit to a

Ill.2.1. *Fangua Lane Has Changed* by Xu Yao, undated (Shanghai renmin chubanshe). The caption reads, "After Liberation, the working people of Fangua Lane stood up and became their own masters. Under the care of the Party, they moved into bright and spacious workers' new housing." Ephemera in the author's personal collection

kindergarten classroom, was emblematic of the "new society," as life in post-1949 Communist China was called. Indeed, in Mao's China the year 1949 as a turning point was inscribed into everyday speech. The word "Liberation" and the use of temporal frames such as "before Liberation" and "after Liberation," Gail Hershatter explains, "meant organizing one's own memories into a personal and collective narrative of emancipatory progress."[8]

As the old grandfather—like Wang Lanhua—would surely tell, life in Fangua Lane's "new society" had to be understood in the context of its pre-1949 past, the "old society." Though Zhabei District had flourished in the late Qing and early Republican eras, wartime fighting and devastating fires left the area razed to the ground; after 1945, it was flooded with refugees from the civil war.[9] On the eve of the revolution, Fangua

shantytown. Marie-Claire Bergère, *Shanghai: China's Gateway to Modernity*, trans. by Janet Lloyd (Stanford, CA: Stanford University Press, 2009), p. 1.

[8] Gail Hershatter, *The Gender of Memory: Rural Women and China's Collective Past* (Berkeley: University of California Press, 2011), p. 25. I use "Liberation" as an actor's category.

[9] Christian Henriot, "A Neighbourhood under Storm: Zhabei and Shanghai Wars," *European Journal of East Asian Studies*, vol. 9, no. 2 (2010), pp. 292–296; Zhang Xiaochuan, *Jindai Shanghai Zhabei jumin shehui shenghuo* (Social life in modern Shanghai's Zhabei District) (Shanghai: Shanghai cishu chubanshe, 2009), pp. 271–273.

Lane consisted of between 3,000–4,000 shantytown houses inhabited by over 16,000 people, whose lives were so marked by suffering and privation that gazetteers today still describe it as a veritable hell on earth.[10] The old grandfather's "revolutionary stories" were made tangible by the backdrop against which he told them: eighteen shantytown houses preserved in 1966 by the Zhabei People's Committee and the Shanghai Cultural Relics Commission.[11] The old society was displayed for the new.

Fangua Lane was an exhibition in more ways than one. First and foremost, the neighborhood was a living display of Shanghai's past and present. Even before renovations began, the neighborhood received foreign visitors like Pita Rodríguez. The American journalist Edgar Snow, most famous for his 1937 biography of Mao, paid a visit during his 1960 return trip to China. Snow especially requested to visit Zhabei District's "jungle of bamboo huts," which he remembered as worse than the slums ringing Mexico City and not unlike the shantytowns of Kowloon in Hong Kong. Though Snow arrived too early to see the new apartment blocks, he dutifully reported that the streets were clean and the remaining houses improved. He noted new willow trees and public fountains, health stations and nurseries, and "the grinning kids [who] were no longer in rags and covered with sores." Wang Lanhua greeted Snow and his companion, and before he left he looked in on an elderly woman in her tidy home. While three grandchildren did their homework, music played on the radio and a fish simmered on the stove. Nothing was wanting, Snow later wrote, except perhaps a sewing machine.[12]

After the renovations, the living display continued to evoke the past through the preservation of a select few dwellings. Newspapers attributed the preservation of the eighteen houses to Wang Lanhua, who proposed their use to educate the next generation.[13] As a group, in December 1977 the houses were designated a revolutionary relic by the Shanghai Revolutionary Committee. According to the local gazetteer, from 1979 to 1985 visitors from sixty-eight countries (and Hong Kong, Macau, and

[10] Feng Meichun, "Fangualong de bianqian," pp. 240–241.   [11] SMA B3-2-199.

[12] Edgar Snow, *Red China Today: The Other Side of the River* (Harmondsworth: Penguin Books, 1970), pp. 515–516. Snow translates Fangua Lane as "Pumpkin Town." Although he does not name Wang Lanhua, the "businesslike woman" who calls herself the "lane committee chairman" could be no one else.

[13] Wang Lanhua, "Qian xinju, gan dang'en" (Moving into the new homes, feeling the Party's benevolence), *Wenhui bao* (Wenhui daily), July 17, 1964, p. 2. The only earlier suggestion I have located is an article that states that Shanghai followed local cadres from Guangdong's Hailingdao who preserved one fisherman's house for socialist education. Mei Yuan, "Chaiqian zhixi" (Congratulations on renovation), *Renmin ribao* (People's daily), October 20, 1963, p. 6.

Taiwan) numbered 7,353 people in 628 groups. Between 1990 and 1993, fifty-five school groups visited Fangua Lane, totaling 15,122 people.[14] On a visit to Fangua Lane, the juxtaposition of the "old society" and the "new society" was enlivened by the residents, who—in addition to serving as guides and telling their stories—posed with artifacts of the past, an old man with his tattered rickshaw.[15]

In addition to this living exhibition, Fangua Lane played a role in Shanghai's history exhibitions, a diorama in one section of Shanghai's Class Education Exhibition of 1965.[16] On the eve of the Cultural Revolution, the display of the neighborhood, entitled "Fangua Lane Past and Present, " took on its fullest elaboration in a stand-alone exhibition at the Zhabei Workers' Palace. Just as the 1951 *Handbook for Neighborhood Residential Life* suggested, curators used the "method of juxtaposition" to "make the old even more ugly, and the new even more worthy of love."[17] The contrast, the introduction to "Fangua Lane Past and Present" declared, would give rise to class consciousness.[18]

In this chapter I consider these intertwined exhibitions of Fangua Lane, the narrative supported—like the First Party Congress Site—by stories in newspapers, in children's books and school lessons, and even as a script in Shanghai's storytelling movement.[19] If the First Party Congress Site memorialized Party founding as revolution's origin story, Fangua Lane's revolutionary history was told in the juxtaposition of the shantytown with the workers' new village, the contrast between a begging gourd and a model worker's certificate, and in the tales of the people who had "stood up." The exhibitions show how Fangua Lane's narrative was molded by and for the political culture of the Mao era. Fangua Lane was the embodiment of *fanshen*. This chapter also reveals Fangua Lane's exhibition as participatory propaganda. Not only did its displays curate with objects and feature the stories of its residents, its living exhibition required taking

[14] Guo Tiancheng, Cao Yiding, and Qian Xuezhong, eds., *Zhabei quzhi*, p. 1293. Although these statistics are incomplete, they round out anecdotal accounts that report waves of students and workers visiting during the Cultural Revolution, sometimes three to five days per week, and organized school groups and foreign visitors during the reform era. http://wenda.google.com.hk/wenda/thread?tid=509bcae11597983b (accessed February 16, 2014).

[15] In a photo from the Zhabei District Archive (hereafter cited as ZBDA), an elderly man poses with his rickshaw in a shantytown house. I was not permitted to copy the citation, but the files are in the range of ZJ-30-E0##.

[16] SMA B3-2-199, p. 25.

[17] *Jiedao lilong jumin shenghuo shouce* (A handbook for neighborhood residential life) (Shanghai: Xinwen ribao chubanshe, 1951), pp. 42–43.

[18] SMA B3-2-199, p. 22.

[19] "Gushiyuan zhunbei chunjie jin chaguan" (Storytellers prepare to go to the teahouses during Spring Festival), *Renmin ribao*, January 26, 1965, p. 6. The script was called "Fangua Lane's Great Changes" ("Fangualong jubian").

active part: it was folded into the repertoire of class education campaigns, like "comparing past and present" and "recalling bitterness and reflecting on sweetness." Listening to "revolutionary stories" retold by those who had lived them, visitors considered the material of past and present, sometimes even swallowing a "bitterness meal" (*yikufan*) made from leaves and chaff. Finally, Fangua Lane was presented as a model, exceptional in all ways yet showcased as representative. In the Mao years, Fangua Lane was Shanghai's revolutionary object lesson, a socialist-realist portrayal of a future utopia.

Fangua Lane as a narrative

Fangua Lane was named after a legendary pumpkin that grew in the shape of a dragon, becoming uncommonly large with curling tendrils like the mythic creature's whiskers.[20] Today, residents of Shanghai remember Fangua Lane because of the poverty of the shantytown, explaining that in Shanghainese Fangua Lane is referred to as "wuzikok" (*xiazhijiao*), the "lower corner," as compared to the upscale neighborhoods, or "upper corners," like Xuhui District in the former French Concession. Though a bird's-eye view would encompass the kinds of thatched roof houses that were preserved, the neighborhood was synonymous with a makeshift dwelling called a "*gundilong*," or an earth-rolling dragon, a semi-circular frame thrust into the earth and covered with reed matting, mimicking the awnings of the modest boats on which many of its residents had come to Shanghai. One retired nurse (b. 1928) explained, "Fangua Lane is precisely a *gundilong*. At that time, it was very, very poor. [The people in the] *gundilong* were all poor, from the lowest rung of society."[21] Informants emphasize that the houses only reached the height of a grown man's chest, and they would stand up during interviews to gesture its dimensions or crouch down to show how one would get inside.[22] In Wang Lanhua's words, the *gundilong* was the symbol and the portrait of working people's lives in Old China, when, as a ditty suggested, even inside one had no

---

[20] Feng Meichun, "Fangualong de bianqian," p. 240; Guo Tiancheng, Cao Yiding, and Qian Xuezhong, eds., *Zhabei quzhi*, p. 1291; Cai Fengming and Zhang Lili, eds., *Minsu Shanghai: Zhabei juan* (Folk customs of Shanghai: Zhabei volume) (Shanghai: Shanghai wenhua chubanshe, 2007), p. 152. One of Wing-Chung Ho's informants claims that it was her father-in-law who grew the pumpkin. Ho, *The Transition Study of Postsocialist China*, pp. 235–236.

[21] Interview in Shanghai, July 6, 2013. Wing-Chung Ho's informants also frequently made such comments. Ho, *The Transition Study of Postsocialist China*, p. 57.

[22] Interview in Shanghai with a piano teacher (b. 1959, to a workers' family), July 3, 2013; interview in Shanghai with a former resident (b. 1948), July 5, 2013.

shelter from the rain.[23] Another saying had it that one could not take three steps in Fangua Lane without stooping, this supplicant posture the position of the pre-Liberation subject.[24] With Liberation, however, the *gundilong* came down and the workers could stand erect. Fangua Lane, *Renmin ribao* (People's daily) declared in 1960, was a microcosm of "old society" transformed into new.[25]

But Fangua Lane was not always a shantytown. In the late Qing and early Republican eras, Zhabei District flourished as a major area of Chinese residence and control. It was separated from the old Chinese walled city, bordered to the east and south by the International Settlement, with which it shared Suzhou Creek. At the terminus of a railway line that connected Shanghai to neighboring cities, it grew rapidly, light industry followed by larger factories in the late 1920s and the early 1930s. With industrial development came a population boom, making it one of the most densely populated areas in the city, attracting merchants and workers from neighboring provinces as well as sojourners from the southern province of Guangdong.[26] In 1921 a local gazetteer painted a portrait of a bustling local economy: "Factories and shops stand like trees in great numbers/boats with their cargo gather in a crowd/the most flourishing thoroughfare of land and water is at Zhabei."[27]

The geography that had advantaged Zhabei's economic rise, however, proved to be its wartime undoing. As historian Christian Henriot has documented, Zhabei was engulfed by fighting on three occasions in the decade between 1927 and 1937. The conflicts devastated homes and businesses, created a large refugee population, and inflicted on the civilian population a violence that Henriot argues was unknown in Europe.[28] War first struck Zhabei in 1927 when Chiang Kai-shek's Northern Expedition took Shanghai, establishing a pattern that included fighting over the train station, heavy combat in the residential areas, and great fires that left many people homeless. In 1932 a Japanese attack on Zhabei again trapped the civilian population in its crossfire. Cut off from the

---

[23] Wang Lanhua, "Fangualongli shuo jubian" (Speaking of the great changes in Fangua Lane), *Wenhui bao*, August 22, 1999, p. 1. The ditty on the *gundilong* goes: "Outside it pours/inside it drizzles/it ceases outside/inside it drip-drip-drops." The ditty appeared in 1965, in Jin Bian, "Fangualong de jinxi," p. 62.

[24] "Fangua Lane is a cave of sewers/go three steps and take a bow (*jugong*)," in Jin Bian, "Fangualong de jinxi," p. 63.

[25] Jin Zhonghua, "Renmin shengli de shidai" (The era of the people's victory), *Renmin ribao*, October 1, 1960, p. 8.

[26] Henriot, "A Neighbourhood under Storm," pp. 292–296.

[27] Guo Tiancheng, Cao Yiding, and Qian Xuezhong, eds., *Zhabei quzhi*, p. 83.

[28] Henriot, "A Neighbourhood under Storm," p. 318. Henriot argues that "civilian direct participation in the war effort [more so than in Europe] was probably a key feature of wars in modern East and Southeast Asia."

International Settlement, the area became a battle zone between Chinese and Japanese troops and a target for heavy bombardment by more than one-half of the Japanese air force. Fires set by incendiary bombs and Chinese troops in retreat leveled houses and factories, which were not rebuilt in the aftermath. The final wartime blow came in 1937, when three months of conflict, bombardment, and fire razed it to the ground, with 95 percent of its buildings destroyed.[29] It was to this Shanghai that Wang Lanhua and her husband fled as refugees, carrying with them one cotton blanket. Here she gathered vegetable peelings to keep her family from starvation and gave birth to her second child on the mud floor of a *gundilong*.[30]

The living conditions of war-ravaged Shanghai, as Edgar Snow's memories suggest, held a place in foreign imaginaries of China. In the 1930s, the new Soviet city of Magnitogorsk—built around an iron-ore mountain and envisioned as an exemplar of socialist construction—had neighborhoods of mud huts, the largest of which was called "Shanghai." As Stephen Kotkin explains, Shanghai "was synonymous in the early part of the twentieth century with all the evils of a capitalist city: dark, narrow streets littered with trash, drenched in soot, teeming with huddled masses, and generally overcome by squalor and reputed moral decadence." Whether in popular parlance or in novels, Magnitogorsk's Shanghai was represented by mud huts, dark and backward. Despite attempts to eliminate "Shanghai" through decrees against the mud huts and provisions for alternate housing, the buildings—officially renamed "Workers' Settlement" by the local authorities—persisted.[31]

Conditions in the real Shanghai, its socialist city still some years into the future, became worse. Over Zhabei's scorched earth, a second wave of refugees washed up, fleeing the Chinese Civil War. From 1945 to 1948, the population of Zhabei grew from 216,000 to 548,000, primarily composed of unskilled migrants who built shantytown houses on the abandoned no-man's land after the barbed wire cordons came down.[32] Historian Hanchao Lu explains that Fangua Lane was one of Shanghai's biggest shantytowns, "typical of slums created as a result of wars," and inhabited by people who were effectively homeless.[33] Recent gazetteers illustrate the density of the shantytown and the precariousness of the

---

[29] I am indebted to Henriot's "A Neighbourhood under Storm," pp. 298–315.

[30] SMA B3-2-199-18, pp. 28–29.

[31] Stephen Kotkin, *Magnetic Mountain: Stalinism as a Civilization* (Berkeley: University of California Press, 1995), pp. 176–178.

[32] Henriot, "A Neighbourhood under Storm," p. 316; Guo Tiancheng, Cao Yiding, and Qian Xuezhong, eds., *Zhabei quzhi*, p. 83.

[33] Hanchao Lu, *Beyond the Neon Lights: Everyday Shanghai in the Early Twentieth Century* (Berkeley: University of California Press, 1999), pp. 122–123.

lives of its residents: on an area of less than 100 *mu* (17 acres) lived an estimated 16,000 people.[34] This population was mostly unemployed or underemployed; in one survey of 202 households, 45 percent had no means of employment, and of the 404 people between the ages of sixteen and forty-five only 19 percent were employed.[35] Such unskilled labor included dockworkers and pedicab drivers. Others, like Wang Lanhua, begged or picked over garbage to survive. As anthropologist Wing-Chung Ho shows in his 2000–2001 ethnography, elderly residents still remembered—over half a century later—how they were preyed upon by local bosses and Nationalist soldiers, terrorized by conscription and bullying, and forced to give gifts and pay bribes.[36] When the dragon-shaped pumpkin appeared on the eve of Liberation, the local boss built a temple around it and people burned incense and ingested both the ashes and the dragon's whiskers for their alleged healing powers.[37]

Despite the official narrative division between the pre-1949 "old society" and the post-Liberation "new society," Fangua Lane in the early 1950s was slow to recover. In the realm of politics, the CCP organized meetings at which the people of Fangua Lane denounced the local bosses as counterrevolutionaries, and Wang Lanhua's participation on the neighborhood committee was part of a city-wide mobilization of residents from the bottom-up.[38] In terms of the economy, the state began to address the problem of labor, establishing a registration office to allocate work to the unemployed. Fangua Lane's residents were sent out to work in steel, textiles, handicrafts, and transportation, while others were given service jobs and worked in stores. By November 1954, a survey revealed that 1,001 people in 889 families had found employment, and the state also provided cash and grain subsidies.[39] Public works—including water taps, public toilets, and trash bins—improved basic living conditions, and though an estimated 3,800 houses remained, many

[34] Feng Meichun, "Fangualong de bianqian," p. 241.
[35] Guo Tiancheng, Cao Yiding, and Qian Xuezhong, eds., *Zhabei quzhi*, p. 1291. This was a study of Lane 425 on Datong Road, a branch of Fangua Lane.
[36] Ho, *The Transition Study of Postsocialist China*, pp. 70–76.
[37] According to Cai Fengming and Zhang Lili, eds., *Minsu Shanghai*, p. 152, locals began praying to the pumpkin and collecting nearby water before the temple was built. Wing-Chung Ho's informants remember that the local boss, who built the temple in about 1947, spread rumors about the pumpkin's alimentary effects and forced people to buy medicine made of the incense ash. Ho, *The Transition Study of Postsocialist China*, p. 73.
[38] SMA B3-2-199-18, p. 34. See also Frederic Wakeman, Jr., "'Cleanup': The New Order in Shanghai," in *Dilemmas of Victory: The Early Years of the People's Republic of China*, edited by Jeremy Brown and Paul G. Pickowicz (Cambridge, MA: Harvard University Press, 2007), p. 44.
[39] Guo Tiancheng, Cao Yiding, and Qian Xuezhong, eds., *Zhabei quzhi*, p. 1291. In 1953–54 subsidies totaling 6,891 yuan were given to 999 people; during the same period 283 people were provided with 6,400 *jin* of grain.

Ill.2.2. Panorama of Fangua Lane, August 11, 1963. SMA H1-11-6-41

families rebuilt their straw-thatched houses or started to build anew with wood and bamboo.[40] But despite the improvements in employment and sanitation that Edgar Snow observed, living standards remained basic. Writing in 1964, *Jianzhu xuebao* (Journal of Architecture) described Fangua Lane as a typical shantytown inhabited by textile and transport workers, with three generations living under one roof and owning only modest furniture. As the architects explained, building materials were poor and living conditions crowded.[41]

In the 1950s, Fangua Lane was one of many neighborhoods slated for renewal. However, for the same reasons that a large-scale revolutionary history museum was never built on the First Party Congress Site, plans did not proceed until the post–Great Leap Forward economic recovery.[42] In 1961 Shanghai Vice Mayors Cao Diqiu and Li Gancheng inspected Fangua Lane, and in January 1963 the Shanghai Party Committee passed a directive to renovate the neighborhood. Construction began in October of that year, with a first group of forty-five families moving into new apartments in July of 1964. After two years, construction of the workers' new village was complete: thirty-one five-story buildings provided housing and utilities to 1,818 households.[43] Shanghai's *Jiefang ribao* reported

---

[40] Feng Meichun, "Fangualong de bianqian," p. 242. By 1963 most people were living in new dwellings, the majority (63 percent) in new thatched houses and the rest in wood and bamboo houses. A very small number (.81 percent) had tile houses.

[41] Xu Hanhui, Huang Fuxiang, and Hong Birong, "Shanghaishi Zhabeiqu Fangualong gaijian guihua sheji jieshao" (An introduction to the reconstruction plan for Fangua Lane in Zhabei District of Shanghai), *Jianzhu xuebao* (Journal of architecture), no. 2 (1964), p. 20.

[42] Chen Yingfang, ed., *Penghuqu: Jiyi zhong de shenghuo shi* (Shantytown district: Memories of life histories) (Shanghai: Shanghai guji chubanshe, 2006), p. 20; Chen Yingfang, "Shehui kongjian jiegou yu chengshi pinkun: 1949 nian hou de Shanghai penghuqu" (The structure of social space and urban poverty: Shanghai's shantytowns after 1949) (Hong Kong: Centre for China Urban and Regional Studies, Hong Kong Baptist University Occasional Paper no. 80, February 2008), pp. 13–14.

[43] Feng Meichun, "Fangualong de bianqian," p. 242; Guo Tiancheng, Cao Yiding, and Qian Xuezhong, eds., *Zhabei quzhi*, p. 282. In the 1970s, West Tianmu Road residential

Ill.2.3. Moving day in Fangua Lane, July 19, 1964. SMA H1-6-11-44

on the residents' en-masse return to Fangua Lane, with photographs
showing residents bearing their possessions, parade-like, on wooden
carts.[44] Lining the streets for the spectacle were other residents awaiting
their turn, witnesses to history in the making.[45]

district built an additional thirteen-story residence and twenty-three five-story
residences.

[44] "Fangualong jumin xiqiyangyang qianru xinju" (The residents of Fangua Lane happily
move into their new homes), *Jiefang ribao*, July 17, 1964, p. 2.

[45] Wang Lanhua, "Qian xinju, gan dang'en," p. 2; "Zai nanwang de xinfu shikeli" (In the
unforgettable moment of good fortune), *Wenhui bao*, April 26, 1969, p. 4. Christian Hess
describes the "spectacle of 'moving day'" in Dalian, 1946, when Chinese workers moved
into former Japanese colonial housing. See Christian Hess, "Revolutionary Real Estate:
Envisioning Space in Communist Dalian," in *Visualizing Modern China: Image, History,*

The story of Fangua Lane's dramatic transformation was told and retold in local Shanghai papers; indeed, today's Shanghai residents recall that they knew about Fangua Lane in their youth because of the media. In 1960, in the wake of the Great Leap Forward, Shanghai papers began to illustrate the story of Zhabei District and Fangua Lane's physical changes.[46] One article on Zhabei's construction projects, for example, included photographs of new concrete apartment blocks and a grand theater, juxtaposing these pictures with two images of "old thatched houses." In an inset on the same page a cartoon depicts a resident standing on her top-floor balcony in the sunshine, offering flowers to returning swallows. A short poem by one Bian Qi describes the thatched dwellings becoming tiled houses, the returning spring swallows unable to recognize their new homes.[47] In other articles, the material changes to Fangua Lane as well as the very process of construction were understood as a teachable moment for all who took part: social scientists who researched living conditions were transformed and Fangua Lane's own architects declared their work a kind of class education.[48]

No lives were more transformed than those of its residents, and the most typical newspaper coverage of Fangua Lane was the narrative of the neighborhood paired with the stories of the residents. Spring Festival provided an opportunity for reporters to portray family reunions and celebrations during which the joy of the present called to mind the bitterness of the past. In 1965, for example, both *Wenhui bao* and *Jiefang ribao* ran articles depicting Fangua Lane families celebrating the new year. The *Jiefang ribao* article took the form of a door-to-door visit, showing relatives reunited, elders telling tales of the past, and entire families breaking into the song "Fangua Lane Has Changed." Each family vignette had its own moral. Before a painting of the old Fangua Lane and a portrait of Chairman Mao, Sun Xiuzhen explained that she had cast aside her paper gods and now sang of the revolution. "Revolutionary Mother" Xie Xiuying described the sacrifice of her son

---

and *Memory, 1750–Present*, edited by James A. Cook, Joshua Goldstein, Matthew D. Johnson, and Sigrid Schmalzer (Lanham, MD: Lexington Books, 2014), pp. 185–202.

[46] Karen Petrone, noting that Soviet institutions in 1936 organized exhibitions on the past twenty years of construction, writes, "Soviet cadres used these changes in physical environment as a stand-in for improvements in the lives of Soviet citizens." See Karen Petrone, *Life Has Become More Joyous, Comrades: Celebrations in the Time of Stalin* (Bloomington: Indiana University Press, 2000), p. 155.

[47] Bian Qi, "Bu ren jiushi fang" (Not recognizing the houses of former times), *Xinwen ribao* (News daily), January 5, 1960, p. 2.

[48] "Bianxie jieji douzheng lishi jiaoyu nianqing yidai" (Compiling class education history to teach the young generation), *Guangming ribao* (Guangming daily), August 16, 1963; "Fangualong zhuzhai sheji zuodao bijiao qiehe shiji" (The design of the residences in Fangua Lane fit the reality), *Wenhui bao*, April 10, 1964, p. 2.

Ill.2.4. Fangua Lane's first Spring Festival, February 2, 1964. SMA H1-11-6-45

in the Korean War, attributing her living conditions to the "blood of the revolutionary martyrs." Wang Lanhua, ever-present, appeared to comfort Xie in her grief.[49] On the fifteenth anniversary of the People's Republic, a similar story, entitled "Every Family in Fangua Lane,"

---

[49] "Xiaoying xinju diyichun: Fangualong jumin huandu chuxi" (Smilingly welcoming the first spring at a new residence: The residents of Fangua Lane welcome Spring Festival), *Jiefang ribao*, February 2, 1965; "Fangualong ying chunjie" (Fangua Lane welcomes Spring Festival), *Wenhui bao*, January 31, 1965.

mirrored a tour of model homes: a soldier's family, a mother reunited with her daughter after being separated "before Liberation," and Wang Lanhua teaching her son a revolutionary lesson. Explaining that taken together these families stood for workers who had experienced *fanshen*, *Wenhui bao* argued that the families of Fangua Lane represented the "laboring people of the entire nation!" With "every family a window," private life was on public display, and Fangua Lane's residents were China's working class.[50]

In the newspaper montages of Fangua Lane, *yiku sitian* was portrayed as a primary and unifying activity. This practice was the personal, oral remembrance of past suffering in light of the present, a narration that demonstrated the teller's awareness and served to enlighten his or her listeners. It was primarily through *yiku sitian* that Fangua Lane's history was told, whether by Wang Lanhua and other guides to visitors, or by elderly residents to their children and grandchildren. The ritual of *yiku sitian* was reported on at move-in and during the new year. The *Wenhui bao* explained how the old mothers of Fangua Lane "passed Spring Festival by remembering the old society, making this an important job for themselves during this time." Sun Lindi, the mother once separated from her daughter, remarked that she told her story wherever she could, visiting schools, allowing teachers to come to her home, and bringing guests to see the *gundilong*.[51] Sun Xiuzhen specifically asked for a water-color of the old Fangua Lane to *yiku sitian* with her children, saying in front of a portrait of Chairman Mao, "Now I understand ... in the past I was not fated to bitterness. It was because of the oppression of the exploiting classes. If I have *fanshen*'ed and now live a happy life, it is not because my fate has somehow changed, but because of the leadership of the Communist Party and Chairman Mao."[52] With *yiku sitian*, the dual narratives of transformation—of the built environment and in working lives—gained a third overlay: the individual testimony of political consciousness.

Yiku sitian as a form of political repertoire had its origins in the practice of "speaking bitterness." As Gail Hershatter explains, "speaking bitterness was most often elicited by Party-state cadres from poor peasants and women in a public forum designed to break the power of

---

[50] Shao Weiqian, Peng Ji'an, and Xu Kailei, "Fangualong jiajiahuhu" (Every family in Fangua Lane), *Wenhui bao*, September 28, 1964.

[51] "Fangualong ying chunjie" (Fangua Lane welcomes Spring Festival), *Wenhui bao*, January 31, 1965.

[52] "Xiaoying xinju diyichun: Fangualong jumin huandu chuxi" (Smilingly welcoming the first spring at the new residence: The residents of Fangua Lane welcome Spring Festival), *Jiefang ribao*, February 2, 1965.

local elites and to build support for the new state." In the process of land reform and into Liberation, as the Communists consolidated their power, speaking bitterness denounced both the oppression of the old society and the individuals who had profited from it. Hershatter argues that speaking bitterness provided a matrix and a language for people to tell their stories, and within these were "encode[d] a powerful explanation and [with Liberation] an end point for the terrible suffering of the early twentieth century."[53] The residents of Fangua Lane had their first encounter with speaking bitterness shortly after the Communists took over Shanghai, when police began to arrest local bosses as counter-revolutionaries. In subsequent public denunciation meetings, Wing-Chung Ho argues, the people of Fangua Lane learned their political vocabulary. For the first time, they spoke of themselves as proletarians and as workers.[54]

Though speaking bitterness no doubt influenced *yiku sitian*, its goals were to *recall* bitterness and to think of the present, a form dedicated less to justify a revolutionary change and more to legitimize the regime it brought to power.[55] This shift from speaking to remembering began in 1960. As Daniel Leese notes in his study of the Mao cult, remembering originated in the military, as soldiers from the countryside learned of starvation and violence in letters from home. In response, the PLA launched a campaign called "two remembrances, three investigations" (*liangyi sancha*), during which participants "compared their present situation with the bitterness of the past . . . feel[ing] gratitude toward the party, despite the present hardships." By 1961 a three-step campaign was deployed in all army units, culminating in the acknowledgment of the present's "source of sweetness in the correct leadership of the CCP and Mao Zedong."[56]

The renewal of Fangua Lane, the only shantytown to be so favored after the "three hard years," occurred just when Shanghai officials were launching a *huiyi duibi* campaign and when *yiku sitian* exhibitions were being organized. Beginning in mid-June 1963, the Shanghai Party Committee instructed factories to hold *huiyi duibi*, and by December of the same year, 500 bureau offices, over 3,000 work units, and almost one

---

[53] Hershatter, *The Gender of Memory*, pp. 34–37.

[54] Ho, *The Transition Study of Postsocialist China*, pp. 77–78.

[55] Guo Wu explains that recalling bitterness was different from speaking bitterness because whereas the latter was a mobilization technique, "the 'recalling bitterness' campaign in the 1960s aimed at reenacting class struggle and reinforcing class awareness by invoking collective memory." Guo Wu, "Recalling Bitterness: Historiography, Memory, and Myth in Maoist China," *Twentieth-Century China*, vol. 39, no. 3 (October 2014), p. 247.

[56] Daniel Leese, *Mao Cult: Rhetoric and Ritual in China's Cultural Revolution* (Cambridge: Cambridge University Press, 2011), pp. 99, 101.

million people were reported to have participated. Organizing a good *huiyi duibi*, as was explained in the newsletter *Neibu cankao* (Internal reference)—whose circulation was limited to cadres—included training activists to make model speeches, cultivating old workers to tell their stories, and using objects and pictures to create exhibitions within factories. By the end of 1963, all of Shanghai's youth palaces and workers' cultural palaces were organizing *yiku sitian* exhibitions.[57] As the shantytown came down and the workers' new village went up, Fangua Lane became an ideal *yiku sitian*, with the significance of its narrative amplified in its retelling.

In the same way that the First Party Congress Site exhibited the Chinese revolution according to Mao's "Red Line," Fangua Lane displayed the story of China's working people, linking their contemporary fortunes to the benevolence of the Party and Chairman Mao. Ann Anagnost asks, "In what way are nations 'like' narrations?" Referring to speaking bitterness, she suggests that it "represented for the party the process of merging the consciousness of the party with that of the 'the people,' which legitimated its claim to represent the voice of the masses."[58] Curating Fangua Lane's workers' new village thus required that those permitted to move back to the lane have personal histories that matched the narrative of the people as represented by the Party.

One of Wang Lanhua's contemporaries, a former textile worker (b. 1919) remembers that when she received foreign visitors, she "spoke from her own experience." The daughter of peasants from Qingpu County, she became a child laborer at age thirteen, married a dockworker at age nineteen, and eventually raised eight children on vegetable peels in a *gundilong*. All eight joined the Party and two daughters became local judges. Recalling that a Japanese guest had once suggested that new society was neither that good nor old society that bad, she replied, "What kind of life did we live in the old society? We lived a life not even worthy of cattle and horses. In the new society, we eat our fill and dress warmly; is it not obvious which society is better?"[59] In the person

---

[57] "Shanghaishi gongchang qiye dajiang jieji douzheng xingshi, renren canjia huiyi duibi" (Shanghai Municipality's factories and industries speak of class struggle, everyone participates in comparing past and present), *Neibu cankao* (Internal reference), August 20, 1963; "Shanghaishi gehang geye dagao huiyi duibi jinxing jieji jiaoyu" (Every industry in Shanghai Municipality compares past and present to carry out class education), *Neibu cankao*, December 6, 1963.

[58] Ann Anagnost, *National Past-Times: Narrative, Representation, and Power in Modern China* (Durham, NC: Duke University Press, 1997), pp. 2, 32.

[59] Interview in Fangua Lane, June 20, 2012. On the trope of "cattle and horses," see S. A. Smith, *Like Cattle and Horses: Nationalism and Labor in Shanghai, 1895–1927* (Durham, NC: Duke University Press, 2002). Tracing the phrase through workers' journals, leaflets, and speeches, Smith argues that it was used to articulate the human dignity of

of this textile worker was a life that traced the official arc of Liberation, and in her voice the narrative was an argument, made material through Fangua Lane's exhibition.

If the five-story apartment blocks were to showcase a socialist present and future, the eighteen shantytown houses were to preserve the past life "of cattle and horses." Unlike other public works projects in Shanghai—including Zhaojiabang Road and Yaoshui Lane—Fangua Lane retained its artifacts for *yiku sitian*. Its transformation was perhaps a sequel to Zhaojiabang Road and its Beijing antecedent, Dragon Whisker Creek. The drainage and repair of what was essentially an open sewer in an impoverished Beijing neighborhood was immortalized in a play by Lao She, who explained that he first "thought out the characters" and then "made them agree with the material in the [sociological] reports, so that, from being merely characters in a play, they became real people living on the banks of the ditch."[60] Yomi Braester argues that *Dragon Whisker Creek*, as a play (1951) and a film (1952), "bridged the material city and its allegorical visualization ... they retooled the audiences' vision" toward a new socialist city remade by the Communist Party.[61] Similarly, the narrative of Fangua Lane and its display cultivated a way of seeing the old and new society. Whereas Niangzi, the progressive middle-aged woman character in *Dragon Whisker Creek*, suggests putting up a stone marker where the new people's government made a fine road of a "stinking ditch," in another neighborhood that was named after a dragon, Wang Lanhua proposed an exhibition, a museum as a monument.[62]

Fangua Lane as exhibition

A folksong about Fangua Lane vividly illustrates the most basic conditions for life. Each rhyming phrase starts with a verb—to shelter oneself, to cover oneself, to eat, to dress—and ends with an object: a shack, a tattered quilt, an earthen bowl, and a few shredded rags. The subject of the phrases is startlingly absent, and we only catch a glimpse in the last line, which breaks the previous pattern to reveal heels escaping from a worn pair of shoes. The folksong, incorporated into the text of the exhibition "Fangua Lane Past and Present," served to mark the material

---

workers as well as to link the treatment of the Chinese nation by foreign powers with the treatment of workers by capitalists.

[60] Lao Sheh, *Dragon Beard Ditch: A Play in Three Acts*, trans. by Liao Hung-ying (Peking: Foreign Languages Press, 1956), p. 96.

[61] Yomi Braester, *Painting the City Red: Chinese Cinema and the Urban Contract* (Durham, NC: Duke University Press, 2010), pp. 27–29.

[62] Lao Sheh, *Dragon Beard Ditch*, p. 89; Wang Lanhua, "Qian xinju, gan dang'en," p. 2.

elements of life in the "old society," objects that in turn became part of a display of the past.[63] In contrast to the time when the folksong's subject was so insignificant that he had only his voice to lend to its singing, in the "new society" he became the docent of his personal past.

Fangua Lane was both a traditional display and a showcase. As the former, it was the subject of formal exhibitions curated in a hall, with themed sections of images and objects supported with texts. The fullest such exhibit, entitled "Fangua Lane Past and Present," went up in the spring of 1966 in the Zhabei Workers' Palace. As the latter, a visit to Fangua Lane was to attend a living exhibition. It included a tour of the eighteen shantytown houses—two of which were decorated as period rooms—followed by stops in the new apartments of selected residents. Visits by foreign guests were unlike those arranged for schoolchildren. The latter were likely there for "class education" and would hear the "old grandfather telling revolutionary stories," whereas the former might interview a chosen family in their home. If the traditional display in the Zhabei Workers' Palace, curated for Shanghai workers, made explicit the difference between "past and present," the living exhibition was meant to be less obvious but equally didactic. For example, in 1965 when the Shanghai People's Committee's Office of Cultural Exchange prepared a visit for New Zealand photographer Clifton Firth, it instructed, "[W]hen propagandizing our successes, allow him to look around. Use the method of comparing old and new (*xinjiu duibi*) and explain the differences in order to allow him to come to conclusions on his own." Perhaps the best measure of a successful tour of the living exhibition was whether the photographer trained his camera on the same vantages as those on display at the Workers' Palace.[64] The lone extant print of Fangua Lane in Clifton Firth's photography collection demonstrates that he did indeed capture the old and the new in one frame.[65]

"Fangua Lane Past and Present" was presented as a textbook, with local history integrated into a national revolutionary narrative. The preface to the display explained that Fangua Lane was a microcosm of the lives of workers before Liberation and that the purpose of the exhibition

---

[63] SMA B3-2-199-18, pp. 25–26. The folksong goes, "Living, living in a straw shack/ Covering, covering [oneself] in a ratty quilt/Eating, eating from an earthen bowl/ Wearing, wearing a few shreds of rags/Shoes exposing the heels."

[64] SMA C37-2-1223, pp. 2–7.

[65] Clifton Firth (1904–1980) donated his collection to the Auckland Libraries. Although photographs of Fangua Lane are neither in the digital collection nor among the negatives in cold storage, one A3-sized display print has been located. Special thanks to Keith Giles, Photograph Librarian of the Sir George Grey Special Collections, Central City Library, Auckland.

Ill.2.5. Fangua Lane. Clifton Firth Collection 34-697. Image courtesy of
the Sir George Grey Special Collections, Auckland Libraries

was to awaken the people's class consciousness.[66] The first half of the
exhibition, "Fangua Lane before Liberation," began with Chinese history
since 1840, following the "Red Line" of Mao Zedong Thought. A series
of photos portrayed Shanghai as the nexus of feudalism and imperialism's

[66] SMA B3-2-199, p. 22.

oppression; peasants exploited in the countryside fled to cities where in foreign factories they were once again oppressed, living lives not even worthy of "cattle and horses." As if buildings themselves could speak bitterness, the images juxtaposed the shantytown with extravagant foreign villas, and the captions explained that the contrast was a powerful denunciation, an accusation against semi-colonial and semi-feudal society.[67] The photographs were contextualized with a model of Fangua Lane, maps of the shantytown areas, and charts with employment data. Direct quotes from Fangua Lane residents provided narratives of suffering under contract labor, the wartime puppet government, and rampant inflation. Among the objects on display were items from the folksong referred to above as well as ragged blankets and clothing, the bran husks and vegetable skins on which beggars subsisted, and even a bucket and a sample of polluted water from Suzhou Creek.[68]

Like the montages that appeared in Shanghai newspapers, a section of "Past" was devoted to individual stories. The exhibition visitor first met Wang Lanhua, introduced as a typical portrait of a landless peasant in the "old society." The text explained that Wang came from a family of beggars; though her father sometimes found work as a hired hand, she and her siblings had to beg each winter, and on one occasion she was beaten by a landlord for scavenging kindling. When she and her husband arrived in Shanghai in 1937, they became shantytown people, putting up a shelter each night and taking it down each morning in order to avoid the International Settlement police.[69] On display were two artifacts—a begging gourd and a cotton blanket—and the text, describing a dark sky with crows, asked rhetorically, "The poor in the old society ate bitterness in the countryside and suffered in Shanghai. When would they be able to lift their heads?"[70]

Similar narratives followed Wang Lanhua's story. Liu Xiangzi was a refugee from the civil war whose family lived in the shell of a broken boat in Fangua Lane. Although the family eventually scraped together enough to build a *gundilong*, their home was finally destroyed when they could not afford to pay protection money to local gangs. Another refugee, You Yuelian, built a *gundilong* along a wastewater ditch, gleaning hemp and

---

[67] SMA B3-2-199, pp. 24–25.

[68] SMA B3-2-199, pp. 26–27. Hanchao Lu notes that in the 1960s people continued to use polluted water from Suzhou Creek for drinking, washing, and cleaning chamber pots. Lu, *Beyond the Neon Lights*, p. 121.

[69] For the shantytown policy of the International Settlement, see Janet Y. Chen, *Guilty of Indigence: The Urban Poor in China, 1900–1953* (Princeton, NJ: Princeton University Press, 2012), pp. 120–124.

[70] SMA B3-2-199, pp. 28–29.

scavenging garbage with her husband to survive. Unable to buy medicine for her two sons, You Yuelian lost them both to illness and eventually was forced to sell her two daughters. Zhang Jinxiu was a child laborer in a silk-reeling factory, beaten by the general supervisor, called the "Number One."[71] Liu Rifu was a rickshaw-puller, abused by an American soldier and fined by corrupt policemen. Gong Zhaodi, an old textile worker, lost all but one of her eleven children and was fired by a factory owner who fled to Hong Kong at the end of the civil war. Like that of Wang Lanhua, each vignette was illustrated with a montage and supplemented with artifacts: food substitutes, such as "*guanyin* flour" and grass roots, a piece of Liu Xiangzi's boat, and Zhang Jinxiu's one possession—a wooden box. Also on display was the way in which one might use the old society's objects for *yiku sitian*. Liu Xiangzi, for example, was depicted using her husband's old patched pants as an object lesson, saying to her eldest son, "If one of my children forgets the bitterness of the past and does not heed the Party, just tell him to wear this pair of pants!" To understand the old society, one had to don its clothing.[72]

Embedded in the second half of the display, "Great Changes after Liberation," was the answer to Wang Lanhua's plaintive question. This section began with a quotation from Chairman Mao in which he declared that China's fate was in the hands of its own people. It drew the viewer's eye to a photo of Mao atop Tiananmen Gate, then to the five-starred flag atop the Shanghai Bund, and finally to Zhabei District.[73] The characters of Fangua Lane's past reappeared in the workers' new village; the first artifact to be displayed was a speech by Wang Lanhua, now a delegate to the Shanghai People's Congress.[74] In the "Present," Wang was identified as Comrade Wang, the leader of her neighborhood committee and Party secretary of Fangua Lane. If Lei Feng, the orphan adopted by the Party and made into its good soldier, was the model son of the revolution, Party Secretary Wang was the personification of Party-as-mother: she guarded a fallen electricity line in a storm until dawn and

---

[71] For the employment structure in Shanghai cotton mills, see Emily Honig, *Sisters and Strangers: Women in the Shanghai Cotton Mills, 1919–1949* (Stanford, CA: Stanford University Press, 1986), especially ch. 2.

[72] SMA B3-2-199, pp. 29–33. For examples of using such artifacts to compare past and present, see "Shanghaishi gehang geye dagao huiyi duibi jinxing jieji jiaoyu," *Neibu cankao*, December 6, 1963, p. 1.

[73] SMA B3-2-199, p. 34. This quote comes from a speech by Mao at the preparatory meeting of the National Committee of the Chinese People's Political Consultative Conference (CPPCC), June 15, 1949.

[74] SMA B3-2-199, p. 36. Current residents spoke admiringly of the fact that because Wang Lanhua was illiterate, she had to memorize all of her speeches, thus making her all the more effective as a public speaker. Interview in Fangua Lane, June 20, 2012.

she adopted two orphan brothers.[75] In the exhibition's display cases, the begging gourd and the cotton blanket of the past were replaced by certificates and medals of the present, awarded by the state.

Similarly, other awards—for model workers, women pacesetters, and five-good-soldiers—were used to reintroduce the residents of the new Fangua Lane.[76] Rickshaw puller Liu Rifu was now a steelworker, Zhang Jinxiu a cotton-mill worker, and Gong Zhaodi returned to her job in the textile mill and was now happily retired on a state pension, passing her days with other retirees in *yiku sitian*. In the same way that the characters who reappeared in newspaper reports embodied a certain type, so too did the people in the exhibition represent particular stories; in the case of the child worker Zhang Jinxiu, her story preceded her name like an epithet. Likewise, as in the newspaper stories, Spring Festival was part of the exhibition's narrative, with new families—and more children—to better illustrate the largess of the state.[77] Following a traditional custom, multiple generations and many children were shown celebrating the new year, and in accordance with a revolutionary ideal, the young were employed in factories and honored as model workers, motivated by *yiku sitian*.

Furthermore, the model residents were presented doing exemplary things. Cadres offered free services like hair-cuts, and residents demonstrated their economy by saving water; one particularly thrifty resident, Shen Zhiyou, not only turned off his own lights but also turned off other people's lights as well.[78] Under the "new morality of communism," residents helped one another and pitched in to clean up the lane; people turned in lost money and missing ration coupons. Fangua Lane's young people volunteered to build socialism, with Zhang Jinxiu using *yiku sitian* to convince her daughter to settle in Xinjiang Province to develop China's far-western interior.[79] Perhaps the most explicit model behavior was

---

[75] SMA B3-2-199, pp. 37–38. This story also appeared in newspapers. See Chi Wen, "Wang Lanhua shouye" (Wang Lanhua stands guard through the night), *Wenhui bao*, March 8, 1964, p. 4.

[76] "Five-good-soldiers" refers to soldiers who were judged in the categories of political ideology, military skill, work style, completing assignments, and physical exercise.

[77] SMA B3-2-199, pp. 36–37, 40–41.

[78] SMA B3-2-199, p. 43. Contemporary handbooks reveal what services cadres were to offer residents. See, for example, Shanghaishi Xuhuiqu zuzhi renmin jingji shenghuo gongzuo zu (Work group on the economic life of the people in Xuhui District of Shanghai Municipality), ed., *Jumin shenghuo fuwu shouce* (Handbook for serving residential life) (Shanghai: Shanghai wenhua chubanshe, 1960).

[79] SMA B3-2-199, p. 44. Wang Lanhua also publicly urged educated youth to go to the countryside, using two of her own children as an example. See "Zai nanwang de xinfu shikeli" (In the unforgettable moment of good fortune), *Wenhui bao*, April 26, 1969, p. 4; Wang Lanhua, "Mao zhuxi enqing nuan wandai" (Chairman Mao's kindness warms 10,000 generations), *Wenhui bao*, September 28, 1976, p. 3.

Ill.2.6. Women representatives from Chile tour Fangua Lane, April 18, 1966. SMA H1-13-8-86

the display of a dialogue between Gong Zhaodi and an anonymous foreign visitor. Questioned about America, the retired cotton-mill worker demonstrated the effects of her newspaper reading group, declaring, "American imperialists are now invading Vietnam, killing the people of Vietnam. We support the Vietnamese people in their struggle." Asked further whether she too would fight in Vietnam, Grandma Gong replied, "Yes, I'd go! Just for the future of my grandchildren, I'd go!" In answer to her thoughts on the Party and Mao Zedong, Gong used her own story as an illustration of *fanshen*: "I've moved from a straw shack to a new apartment. This is all due to the prosperity brought about by the Communist Party and Chairman Mao!" Concluding her dialogue, Grandma Gong announced her goal to live until the arrival of communism, when all workers of the world would enjoy her privileged standard of living.[80] The exhibition text, arranged in a question-and-answer format, thus functioned as a political catechism, a model of what to say.

---

[80] SMA B3-2-199, p. 45. On the Chinese representation of the war in Vietnam, see Zachary A. Scarlett, "China after the Sino-Soviet Split: Maoist Politics, Global Narratives, and the Imagination of the World" (PhD diss., Northeastern University, 2013), especially ch. 2.

The exhibition "Fangua Lane Past and Present" demonstrates how Fangua Lane's narrative used individual stories to construct a symbolic tale of workers as a class. Preserving and retelling this narrative was central to Mao-era political culture, and the artifacts on display used material to represent class and liberation. The begging gourd and the worker's certificate were both badges of class, and likewise the *gundilong*'s transformation into the concrete apartment block was evidence of the correct leadership of the Party. Writing on the rise of exhibitions in nineteenth-century Europe, Tony Bennett suggests that museums were institutions that broadcast both knowledge and power. What Bennett terms the "exhibitionary complex" placed its viewers on the side of power, spectators as part of the spectacle, ultimately creating a self-regulating society that was formed according to the ideals of the exhibition.[81] In a similar way, the Mao-era exhibitionary complex projected an ordering of past and present, the ideal visitor a worker who shared in the narrative on display. Bennett further stresses that exhibitions "located their preferred audiences at the very pinnacle of the exhibitionary order of things they constructed. They also installed them at the threshold of greater things to come."[82] Likewise, the exhibition in Maoist China situated itself in New China, in the midst of socialist construction and on the cusp of a future utopia. Fangua Lane residents were the revolutionary vanguard, with Grandma Gong ever-vigilant until the day her good fortune would be shared by all.

The second form of display of Fangua Lane—the living exhibition on site—is an example of the exhibitionary complex taken even further. In a visit to the showcase of Fangua Lane, residents were the display and the visitors also part of the scene. Fangua Lane became so emblematic of Shanghai that a visit by a typical dignitary included both the neighborhood and the First Party Congress Site, with perhaps a factory or hospital along the way. Sometimes Fangua Lane was one of the only sites reported in the media, as if a visit was sufficient to have seen Shanghai. For example, in 1964 when Corporal Zhao Zongli defected from Taiwan, he was feted by Lin Biao and then given a tour of Shanghai's Industrial Exhibition and Fangua Lane.[83] Or, in 1978 when a delegation that included the Minister of Health from Bangladesh visited China, its stay in Shanghai was mentioned by way of a tour of

---

[81] Tony Bennett, "The Exhibitionary Complex," in *Culture/Power/History: A Reader in Contemporary Social Theory*, edited by Nicholas B. Dirks, Geoff Eley, and Sherry B. Ortner (Princeton, NJ: Princeton University Press, 1994), pp. 123–154.

[82] Ibid., p. 147.

[83] "Jiating qiyi de Zhao Zongli zai Shanghai canguan" (Naval defector Zhao Zongli tours Shanghai), *Renmin ribao*, October 26, 1964, p. 2.

Fangua Lane.[84] These foreigners' visits, as the notes for New Zealand photographer Clifton Firth show, were carefully choreographed. The itinerary was mapped, the individual encounters pre-planned, and the visitors' questions and comments were recorded.[85] In both of these forms of display—a formal exhibit and a living exhibit—Fangua Lane was like the First Party Congress Site, presenting a legitimizing narrative for a state in power, regardless of whether the visitors were Chinese or foreign.

Residents today remember how they were asked to prepare for foreign visits. As in Chen Ruoxi's short story, "Nixon's Press Corps," a grandmother from the residents' committee went door-to-door beforehand to tell everyone to take down their laundry.[86] Families were selected to host, and as one resident (b. 1930) explained, only better-off families with fewer people were chosen. A retired barber (b. 1943) remembered how the residents' committee would come for an inspection in advance, instructing people to clean up and wear nice clothes.[87] The former textile worker (b. 1919) said, "only those with good class status, who were politically reliable and with clean historical backgrounds, could receive guests."[88] Like "Fangua Lane Past and Present," a visit to the living exhibition was equally planned, its display carefully curated.

For foreign and domestic visitors alike, a tour of the living exhibition was ritualized, participatory propaganda. The foreigners were given a study of contrasts, and their interactions with Shanghai people were often scripted, like Grandma Gong's dialogue about Vietnam. Schoolchildren, already familiar with *yiku sitian* from the classroom, sat on little stools in front of the *gundilong*, hearing Fangua Lane's elderly residents tell tales of *fanshen*. During the Cultural Revolution, Shanghai students marched to Fangua Lane with their backpacks, going to a revolutionary site as part of their military training.[89] In addition to students, workers of all kinds also made

[84] "Waishi wanglai" (News of foreign dealings), *Renmin ribao*, April 7, 1978, p. 4.
[85] The archival records, in particular those of the Shanghai Federation of Trade Unions (which coordinated trips for foreign workers) and the Shanghai People's Committee in the Office of Cultural Contacts (which was responsible for foreign photographers and filmmakers), are among the most relevant. See, for example, SMA C1-2-5177, p. 18b; SMA C37-3-367, p. 4; SMA C37-2-584, p. 4; SMA C37-2-1223, pp. 2–7.
[86] Yan Baokang, "Linjie de chuang" (Window overlooking the street), *Guangming ribao*, September 7, 1985; Chen Ruoxi, *The Execution of Mayor Yin and Other Stories from the Great Proletarian Cultural Revolution*, trans. by Nancy Ing and Howard Goldblatt (Bloomington: Indiana University Press, rvsd. ed., 2004), pp. 191–202.
[87] Interview in Fangua Lane, June 17, 2012.
[88] Interview in Fangua Lane, June 20, 2012.
[89] Interview in Shanghai with a retired department store worker (b. 1957), July 24, 2013. See also "Zai Mao zhuxi '7–21 zhishi' de guanghui zhaoyao xia shengli qianjin" (March

Ill.2.7. Women representatives from Chile tour the preserved shantytown houses, April 18, 1966. SMA H1-13-8-82

forward under the brilliant victory of Chairman Mao's July 21 directive), *Guangming ribao*, June 22, 1975; and "Zhabeiqu liyong geming yizhi he jiniandi, dui qingshaonian jinxing geming chuantong jiaoyu" (Zhabei District uses revolutionary sites and memorial places to carry out traditional revolutionary education among the youth), *Wenhui bao*, January 15, 1990, p. 2.

Ill.2.8. Women representatives from Chile walk through the new apartments, April 18, 1966. Wang Lanhua is on the far left. SMA H1-13-8-84

the trip to Fangua Lane. Shanghai Museum staff, for example, used their visit to fire up their singing of patriotic songs.[90] In another account published in Shanghai's *Wenhui bao*, workers first toured an exhibition of

[90] "Chang geming ge, zuo geming ren: Bowuguanli chuanchu liaoliang gesheng" (Sing revolutionary songs and be revolutionary people: The museum spreads the sound of resonant music), *Wenhui bao*, January 25, 1966, p. 2.

"Comparing Fangua Lane Past and Present," listened to old workers make *huiyi duibi* speeches, and then together ate a "remembering bitterness meal" of steamed buns made of chaff. The 280 workers tearfully ate their bitterness meals in unison, "thinking of their parents' generation living in the shantytown, eating food fit for animals, and leading lives of cattle and horses."[91] A living exhibition in Mao's China was thus participatory propaganda. All had a ritualized part, and narratives were enlivened with artifacts not only to be beheld, but also—as *yikufan*—to be choked down with tears.

How was Fangua Lane received? It is difficult for present-day interviewees to step outside of their current selves and to remember the lessons of which Fangua Lane was a part; more often, remembrances turn into lectures on Fangua Lane as a form of propaganda, as a showcase for foreigners, and as representative of the shantytowns that were so widely prevalent that there was no need to make a special visit. One retired cadre (b. 1954) recalls that after his primary school teacher took him to Zhaojiabang Road, Shanghai's Dragon Whisker Creek, he wrote an essay for literature class—"Once upon a time, there was a stinking ditch . . . "[92]

Another interviewee, born in 1952 into a workers' family of eight children, remembers hearing stories of Fangua Lane and thinking "Socialism is great! It is better than other systems."[93] Another retired cadre (b. 1950) speaks of listening to speeches by model workers at school. "It was all about the old society, how bitter it was, and the new society, how wonderful it is . . . and so I would walk on the streets and think about how lucky I was to live in the new society."[94] With a few exceptions, members of the generation that had heard *yiku sitian* and that had come of age during the Cultural Revolution dismissed Fangua Lane as propaganda and changed the subject to talk instead of their own bitterness, their childhood hunger after the Great Leap Forward or the hardships of life as sent-down youths in the countryside.

As for the foreign visitors, their reactions, as reported in the official media, were predictably incredulous and admiring. In 1960, *Renmin ribao* described foreigners as particularly interested in Shanghai because the buildings constructed by the imperialists had given way to workers' new villages: "New China in a few short years has leapt over a hundred

---

[91] "Chi yikufan, si xinfuyuan" (Eating a bitterness meal, reflecting on the origins of good fortune), *Wenhui bao*, February 11, 1977, p. 3.

[92] Interview in Shanghai, July 20, 2013. He mainly remembered that he was one of two students to receive a score of 90 percent.

[93] Interview in Shanghai, July 21, 2013.

[94] Interview in Shanghai, July 2, 2013. Though his parents were a worker and a teacher, his grandfather had opened a shop, so the family was labeled "capitalist."

years ... The [foreign] friends say to us, if the Chinese people can do this, why can't we do it?"[95] Even archival reports of foreign visits veer little from the script. A Dutch photographer visiting the Shanghai suburb of Minhang in 1959 declared that the workers' housing was as beautiful as residences in France or Italy, stating that visiting Minhang was just like visiting America.[96] And Clifton Firth's handlers reported that he was suitably impressed by Fangua Lane's kitchens, and even though his camera accidentally caught a streetlight repairman dressed in shabby clothes, they concluded that the man's appearance overall was still acceptable.[97]

One particular case, however, demonstrates how ways of seeing could evade control. The Italian filmmaker Antonioni, in his documentary *Cina*, included a clip that allegedly paid less attention to the workers' new housing and more attention to the exhibition, calling the preserved shantytown a "museum of the horrors of the colonial period."[98] His camera lingering on the old houses was vilified as a counterrevolutionary act, and in a public criticism session held by the Fangua Lane Party Branch and Revolutionary Committee, seventy-one-year-old Wang Fuqing demanded that Antonioni return, hear his explanation of the old and new societies, and then properly film the *gundilong* and the new residences.[99] Despite the fact that Antonioni's camera lens did briefly encompass the workers' apartment blocks, the image had clearly departed from the script.

Wang Fuqing's indignation—prefaced with a narrative about his past life as a beggar and a rickshaw puller—calls our attention to another perspective, that of Fangua Lane's own residents. Maoist China's exhibitionary complex made them into historians and narrators, docents and hosts. But people like Wang Fuqing and Wang Lanhua continued to tell Fangua Lane's story well into the reform period because they, like so

[95] Jin Zhonghua, "Renmin shengli de shidai" (The era of the people's victory), *Renmin ribao*, October 1, 1960, p. 8.
[96] SMA C37-2-584, p. 4. See also Luo Bingguang, "Cong shejitushang kan xin Fangualong" (Looking at the new Fangua Lane through its designs), *Xinmin wanbao* (New people's evening news), October 12, 1964.
[97] SMA C37-2-1223, pp. 2–7.
[98] Michelangelo Antonioni, *Cina* (Rome: Rai Trade, 2007). "In this working class neighborhood in Shanghai a curious relic of the past is preserved, like a museum of horrors from the colonial period. These are the mud and straw huts in which millions of people lived until a quarter-century ago." Special thanks to Maria Sibau for the translation.
[99] "Fangualong de juda bianhua burong mosha" (The great changes in Fangua Lane are not easily wiped away), *Jiefang ribao*, February 8, 1974 and *Renmin ribao*, February 15, 1974, p. 3. Wang Fuqing had been a rickshaw-puller for twenty-seven years and was a frequent narrator at the exhibition. In 1977 he was appointed to the Shanghai People's Political Consultative Conference. Guo Tiancheng, Cao Yiding, and Qian Xuezhong, eds., *Zhabei quzhi*, p. 1292.

many of the residents who were chosen to live in the new apartment blocks, had experienced *fanshen* in New China. As Wing-Chung Ho and Petrus Ng show, Fangua Lane's elderly residents "had a strong sense of glory" to live there as it "implied that one possessed a revolutionary background."[100] Fangua Lane, curated as an artifact of social transformation, both derived and bestowed class status on its inhabitants. The neighborhood was termed a model and filled with residents who were literally new society's models, with the certificates to show it. In this way, Fangua Lane's exhibition over time contains an unintended lesson on the use of the model in socialist and postsocialist China.

Fangua Lane as a model

In its time, Fangua Lane was described as a "model," or even, in the words of a former resident, as a "model among models."[101] To be a model in Mao's China was to occupy a particular place in the political firmament. Haiyan Lee likens such models to imperial literati: "In the socialist cosmology, it was believed that the moral charisma of the paragons, once made public, would prove irresistible to all, summoning all to bask in their luminescence and follow their shining example."[102] Donald Munro traces models as a teaching device to both the Confucian tradition and the Chinese interpretation of Marxism, suggesting that although China is not unique in employing models, "there is a unique character to the functions that models serve in their society, to the status they receive, to the number chosen, and the seriousness with which they are regarded."[103] Beginning in the 1930s, the Party began using and rewarding models, and Mao himself argued that only through comparison with models could revolutionary people be transformed, proposing a dialectic between the model and the emulator.[104] From model workers to model villages and from the revolutionary soldier Lei Feng to the socialist commune Dazhai, the model was a central feature of political campaigns. Fangua Lane, as a model neighborhood par excellence, was filled with individual models (*mofan*, or *bangyang*) who were portrayed both as and following examples.

---

[100] Wing-Chung Ho and Petrus Ng, "Public Amnesia and Multiple Modernities in Shanghai: Narrating the Postsocialist Future in a Former Socialist 'Model Community,'" *Journal of Contemporary Ethnography*, vol. 27, no. 4 (2008), pp. 401–403.

[101] Interview in Shanghai with a former resident (b. 1948), July 5, 2013.

[102] Haiyan Lee, *The Stranger and the Chinese Moral Imagination* (Stanford, CA: Stanford University Press, 2014), p. 18.

[103] Donald J. Munro, *The Concept of Man in Contemporary China* (Ann Arbor: Center for Chinese Studies, University of Michigan, 2000), p. 135.

[104] Norma Diamond, "Model Villages and Village Realities," *Modern China*, vol. 9, no. 2 (April 1983), p. 163; Munro, *The Concept of Man*, p. 139.

But in the dialectic between model and emulator, the exceptional was exemplary. Munro points out that while the model is called typical, its qualities may be so far out of reach that it deters rather than motivates the emulator. As he shows in a study of the Mao-era educational system, the existence of models created an elevated class apart, contradicting the notion of egalitarianism.[105] Other scholars have shown how model villages were given additional resources and were enmeshed in webs of political networks dependent on their success.[106] Gail Hershatter's study of the woman labor model confirms a similar pattern for individuals, showing how personal narratives and speaking skills were cultivated.[107] A model could owe its status to a highly placed patron, as Jeremy Brown reveals in his case of Xiaojinzhuang, a village north of Tianjin that came to symbolize a cultural utopia at the behest of Mao's wife, Jiang Qing. Brown shows how urban officials staged Xiaojinzhuang for political purposes, transforming it into a national model toured by 100,000 visitors in 1975.[108] But despite their exceptional status and their cultivation, as Hershatter rightly reminds us, we should not dismiss either the authenticity of the models or the process by which they were created.[109] They were intended to be both representative and real.

What kind of model was Fangua Lane? It was not a model in the way that labor models were models—examples of work, innovation, and production. And if model villages were praised for their accomplishments without acknowledging the state's contributions, the investment in Fangua Lane in the 1960s was openly attributed to the state; newspapers explained that it was the work of the People's Government, its residents thanked the Party and Chairman Mao, and publications for overseas Chinese credited Shanghai Municipality or simply the "authorities."[110] Rather, Fangua Lane was to be taken as a model society with a model

[105] Munro, *The Concept of Man*, pp. 156–157; Donald J. Munro, "Egalitarian Ideal and Educational Fact in Communist China," in *China: Management of a Revolutionary Society*, edited by John M. H. Lindbeck (Seattle: University of Washington Press, 1971), pp. 256–301.
[106] Diamond, "Model Villages," p. 177; Edward Friedman, Paul G. Pickowicz, and Mark Selden, *Revolution, Resistance, and Reform in Village China* (New Haven: Yale University Press, 2005).
[107] Hershatter, *The Gender of Memory*, p. 220.
[108] Jeremy Brown, *City versus Countryside in Mao's China: Negotiating the Divide* (Cambridge: Cambridge University Press, 2012), pp. 200–228.
[109] Hershatter, *The Gender of Memory*, p. 216.
[110] "Zhubu xiaochu caopeng aifang, gaishan renmin juzhu tiaojian: Shanghai chaiqian gaijian Fangualong" (Eliminate straw shacks step-by-step, improve the people's living conditions: Shanghai renovates Fangua Lane), *Renmin ribao*, October 16, 1963, p. 2; A Li, ed., *Shanghai de gushi* (Hong Kong: Zhonghua shuju, Xianggang fenju, 1973), pp. 27–40. In 1999 Wang Lanhua attributed the investment to the Zhabei District

narrative. As a microcosm of New China, Fangua Lane boasted a literacy banner with words by Mayor Chen Yi, it earned rafts of certificates for art and culture, and it was named a model sanitation unit multiple years in a row.[111] Fangua Lane's residents themselves, as its exhibition demonstrated, represented a disproportionate number of models. Most importantly, as Munro outlines, models were "examples of virtues or attitudes that the rulers wish the masses to learn," and understood "the meaning of [their] work," or in the case of Fangua Lane's residents, what the neighborhood's new mien and their own status entailed.[112] Neighborhood and residents were showcase and spokespeople, their legitimacy derived from being ideal types.

However, beginning even with its pre-1949 history, Fangua Lane was exceptional. The wartime experience was singularly devastating, creating a massive shantytown settlement on razed earth, populated by unskilled laborers and refugees. With Zhabei District chosen as an experimental district in 1953 and Fangua Lane as the only neighborhood in the wake of the Great Leap Forward to be allotted funds for renewal, it remained unique both in the past and in its own present—a great study in contrasts.[113] Fangua Lane's new residents were also purposely chosen. One retired gas company worker (b. 1933) who was among the first group to enter the new apartment blocks noted that his family's privileged position came from the fact that his mother was a leader on the residents' committee, as "only cadres and model workers could be allotted a place in Fangua Lane."[114] That there was not enough room for everyone was hinted at in the newspaper accounts in which individuals were praised for sacrificing their places for more needy families. Though the local histories suggest that the number of households living in the old and new Fangua Lane were roughly equal, Wing-Chung Ho finds that only 502 of the original 1,964 households were able to stay, excluding the very poor who could not afford the rent, the disabled, and the mentally ill. In this way, Ho argues, "a 'revolutionary people' was actively 'created.'"[115]

Government: "Fangualongli shuo jubian" (Speaking of the great transformation in Fangua Lane), *Wenhui bao*, August 22, 1999, p. 1.

[111] SMA B3-2-199, pp. 41–42.   [112] Munro, *The Concept of Man*, pp. 140–142.

[113] SMA B3-2-199, p. 34; Chen Yingfang, ed., *Penghuqu*, p. 20; Chen Yingfang, "Shehui kongjian," pp. 13–14. Emily Honig makes a similar observation about a 1963 exhibition at the Shanghai Number Two Textile Mill, in which the most impoverished women during the most difficult period—the Japanese Occupation—were taken to represent the experience of all working women prior to Liberation. See Honig, *Sisters and Strangers*, pp. 132–135.

[114] Interview in Fangua Lane, June 20, 2012.

[115] For example, the local history (*wenshi ziliao*) account of Fangua Lane notes that in 1963 there were 1,965 households and in 1965 there were 1,818 households. See Feng

As a curated community of New China's models, the people of Fangua Lane were called upon to be spokespeople for the working class. Individually and collectively, they spoke out during political movements. Wang Lanhua was a critic of everything from theater to Japanese militarism. At the height of the Cultural Revolution, she attacked Deng Tuo and Liu Shaoqi; at its conclusion, she was Fangua Lane's chief mourner for Mao Zedong. Likewise, Fangua Lane residents as a group denounced whoever was the political enemy of the day, accusing targets from Liu Shaoqi to Antonioni for wishing to return them to the darkness of the past. Children at Fangua Lane Elementary School learned from "worker uncles" and critiqued poetry during the Criticize Lin Biao, Criticize Confucius campaign.[116] In addition to being spokespersons, residents were also the model audience, portrayed watching and responding to theater and films with spontaneous discussions on the old society.[117] In this capacity, the display of Fangua Lane also partook of the exhibitionary culture of a revolutionary movement, as the revolution's beneficiaries mobilized for political campaigns. At a time when the corollary to the threat of revisionism was an attendant slide into the past, no one was better at *yiku sitian* than those who had the artifacts to speak its bitterness.

But neither the construction of Fangua Lane nor the assembly of its residents made it any less a symbol of New China. Here it is useful to consider Michael David-Fox's study of Western visitors to the Soviet Union from 1921 to 1941. David-Fox describes an elaborate system that was developed to receive visitors, including the presentation of intentionally exceptional models and exhibitions that contrasted the tsarist past and the Soviet present. Yet this kind of showcase, he explains, brought "life as it should be closer to reality," as did other forms of literature and cultural production.[118] David-Fox argues against seeing model sites as Potemkin villages crafted only to cheat visiting foreigners, suggesting instead that such visits were part of making an argument, "inculcat[ing] a mode of looking at the heritage of the past and the

Meichun, "Fangualong de bianqian," pp. 239–242. Wing-Chung Ho uses sources from the Zhabei Archive. See Ho, *The Transition Study of Postsocialist China*, p. 43.

[116] "Yi pi Lin pi Kong wei zhongxin guohao shuqi shenghuo" (Spend your summer with Criticize Lin Biao, Criticize Confucius as the center), *Guangming ribao*, August 9, 1974; "Fangualong de juda bianhua burong mosha" (The great changes in Fangua Lane are not easily wiped away), *Renmin ribao*, February 15, 1974, p. 3.

[117] Li Cun, "Zai xinjuzhong yijiuhen: Fangualong jumin kan dianpian 'Bu wang jiejiku, yongji xuehaihen'" (Remembering an old hatred in the new residences: Fangua Lane residents watch the film, 'Never forget class bitterness, always remember the hatred of the bloody sea'), *Wenhui bao*, November 13, 1965, p. 2.

[118] Michael David-Fox, *Showcasing the Great Experiment: Cultural Diplomacy and Western Visitors to the Soviet Union, 1921–1941* (Oxford: Oxford University Press, 2011), pp. 113–114, 155, 172, 203.

promise of the future that became relevant, even decisive, for Communist and Soviet citizens too."[119] The idea that Chinese sites were Potemkin villages was not uncommon first in McCarthy-era America and then in the early 1970s when scientific delegations began to visit China.[120] But as Sigrid Schmalzer shows, many visitors understood that they were seeing models and did not claim that those places represented average or all conditions.[121] Like the Soviet showcases, Fangua Lane was meant to show Chinese reality as it was coming into being.

The example of Fangua Lane underscores the way models worked in time. If the neighborhood was a piece of the future in the present, it could only function as a promise for so long. While its residents acknowledged that "there are still many class brothers who do not yet live here," there was no way another community could raise the 5,000,000 yuan—never mentioned in Mao-era accounts—required for a Fangua Lane-like renovation.[122] No other shantytown would have the same fate. As sociologist Chen Yingfang finds, during this same period officials were instructed to clamp down on individuals who were building new shanty-town houses; cadres might only improve fire safety and sanitation or aid individuals in reinforcing existing structures.[123] Today, one former fac-tory worker (b. 1947) explains that there was never any reason to take notice of the propaganda surrounding Fangua Lane:

How many people could really enjoy that kind of treatment? It was for progressive people, labor models, people like that. As for ordinary people, they couldn't even dream of enjoying that kind of place. That would be completely irrelevant. If it wasn't for you, then you shouldn't pay it any mind. If you didn't have the proper political background, then you couldn't be so lucky."[124]

In fact, Christian Henriot has shown that the absolute number of shantytown settlements actually grew in the 1960s, and that by 1979 there were more shantytown houses in Shanghai than there had been in

---

[119] Ibid., p. 26. On the management of foreign visitors to China, see Anne-Marie Brady, *Making the Foreign Serve China: Managing Foreigners in the People's Republic* (Lanham, MD: Rowman & Littlefield, 2003), p. 120.

[120] For the former, see Robert Loh, "How the Chinese Reds Hoodwink Visiting Foreigners," U.S. Congress, House of Representatives, Committee on Un-American Activities, Eighty-Sixth Congress, Second Session, April 21, 1960.

[121] Sigrid Schmalzer, "Speaking about China, Learning from China: Amateur China Experts in 1970s America," *Journal of American–East Asian Relations*, vol. 16, no. 4 (Winter 2009), pp. 342–343.

[122] "Fangualong ying chunjie" (Fangua Lane welcomes Spring Festival), *Wenhui bao*, January 31, 1965.

[123] SMA B11-2-81, cited in Chen Yingfang, ed., *Penghuqu*, p. 14.

[124] Interview in Shanghai, July 21, 2013.

1949.[125] Asked about Fangua Lane as a showcase for foreigners, one former worker (b. 1957) laughed and said, "of course, they couldn't show you houses with people still living there!"[126] The eighteen shantytown houses were therefore unique as an empty, past, and museumified space.

Compared to the rest of Shanghai and China, Fangua Lane's was an exemplary narrative. However, within Fangua Lane it was clear that not everyone acted in model ways. Hints of discontent were even revealed in the text of the "Fangua Lane Past and Present" exhibition. It described, for instance, Wang Lanhua's struggles as an organizer, stating that "she encountered difficulties, even to the extent that people talked about her behind her back, and her heart was troubled." There were other signs of less-than-model behavior, with persuasion required to convince residents to live on less-desirable floors or to convince youth to volunteer to develop China's interior. That Liu Xiangzi had to threaten her son with his father's tattered pants suggests that some had indeed forgotten the past.[127] If contemporary reports in *Neibu cankao* are any indication, there were in fact many Shanghai youths who—from watching Hong Kong films to refusing to go to Xinjiang Province—needed such an object lesson.[128] Finally, as inhabitants of a showcase, not all of the residents wished to take part, with one informant saying that she purposely stayed indoors during visits, and others remembering that when groups of students came pouring in they would rush to shut their doors.[129]

In actuality, there were also classes within the model society of Fangua Lane. Those who were able to move into the new apartment blocks had to have good political backgrounds and to be able to afford them; informants suggested that those who yielded their places may not have been able to pay the rent. Such differences also affected apartment allocations; although the apartments were distributed in part based on the number of people in one's family, there were discrepancies in size, the desirability of certain floors, and the spatial layout of the neighborhood itself.[130] Within the neighborhood, there was even fragmentation. In one example, the families of former soldiers of the Shanghai Garrison Command were clustered around Number 41, Fangua Lane. As one blogger recalls, the military children only played with each other and seldom spoke

[125] Christian Henriot, "Slums, Squats, or Hutments? Constructing and Deconstructing an In-Between Space in Modern Shanghai (1926–65)," *Frontiers of History in China*, vol. 7, no. 4 (2012), pp. 520–524; Chen Yingfang, ed., *Penghuqu*, p. 21.
[126] Interview in Shanghai, July 15, 2013.   [127] SMA B3-2-199, pp. 29–30, 37, 44, 47.
[128] *Neibu cankao*, January 22, 1963, March 22, 1963, May 12, 1964, and July 22, 1964.
[129] Interview in Fangua Lane, June 17, 2012; http://wenda.google.com.hk/wenda/thread?tid=509bcae11597983b (accessed February 16, 2014).
[130] Ho, *The Transition Study of Postsocialist China*, p. 124.

Shanghainese: "They were mostly tall Northerners, speaking Northern dialects. There seemed to be a barrier between us. They had a superiority complex ... perhaps they didn't know that we could sense it."[131] The shared kitchens and bathrooms also gave rise to problems not depicted in the propaganda. Though residents of Fangua Lane were extolled in the exhibition for being careful not to waste water and electricity, common meters led to so much fighting that eventually each family had to have its own meter.[132] During the Cultural Revolution, Fangua Lane also saw its share of conflicts: it is rumored that young people living in Fangua Lane and those living outside did battle with each other, the haves against the have-nots.[133]

In the post-Mao era, Fangua Lane has gone from projecting the future to portraying the past. Zhabei District is now a place for Shanghai's poor people, either the sent-down youth generation left behind by the economic takeoff or migrant laborers from the countryside. Today, the five-story apartment blocks are a quaint socialist relic, dwarfed by skyscrapers and superceded by private apartment complexes. Though the outside of the buildings, which face the Zhabei District Government, has been maintained, the interiors of the apartments I visited were falling into disrepair, greasy walls still decorated with framed certificates. One middle-aged woman whom I encountered cooking in a common kitchen complained bitterly about her living conditions. Marrying into Fangua Lane in 1981, she said that it was like "living in the old society," and she suggested that I write to the government to insist that it be torn down.[134] Fangua Lane, once a model society populated with socialism's all-stars, is now the address for post-socialism's castoffs. Li Cunrong, a fifty-three-year-old railway maintenance worker, describing a household of eight living in an area of 51 square meters, explained that all of the apartments in Fangua Lane are "disorderly, crowded, and dirty." Despite this, Li and others—unlike the woman in the common kitchen—prefer to remain, uncertain where else they could afford to live. Li said that it would be impossible to buy an apartment, "even if we were to sell our blood, we couldn't buy an apartment that goes for 20,000 yuan a square meter!"[135] That Fangua Lane has once again become synonymous with poverty is evident in the pages of comments that followed one woman's 2012

[131] Lu Jianyun, "Linju juhui" (Neighbors reunite), February 25, 2012, http://blog.sina.com.cn/s/blog_6027a6cc01011dqp.html (accessed March 9, 2014).
[132] SMA B3-2-199, p. 43.
[133] Interview in Shanghai with historian Jin Dalu, July 2, 2013.
[134] Interview in Fangua Lane, June 17, 2012.
[135] Ding Yuguo, "Shanghai pinfu chaju diaocha baogao" (Report on Shanghai's disparities between the rich and the poor), August 29, 2011, http://blog.sciencenet.cn/blog-3100–480892.html (accessed March 9, 2014).

Ill.2.9. Wall hangings in an apartment in Fangua Lane. At left, a photograph and at right, a certificate for "retirement with honor." June 20, 2012. Photo by the author

Internet query. Answering her question about whether she should marry into Fangua Lane—partner good-looking, with an average salary and one ailing parent—her readers counseled her against such a move. The place is totally run-down, they wrote, and she should wait for a more equal match.[136] With the reemergence of poverty and insecurity among its residents, the workers' new village has become an anachronism, an obsolete relic of an old China dream.

One person, however, continued to tell the narrative of Fangua Lane well into the period of reform. Wang Lanhua's last article appeared on the front page of *Wenhui bao* in 1999, more than thirty-five years after she guided Félix Pita Rodríguez on his visit. Though the contours of the narrative and the description of the *gundilong* remained the same, Wang's self-description had changed dramatically from Pita Rodríguez' "steel-willed statue," the exemplary "revolutionary soldier" of the 1966 exhibition "managing the great affairs of state," and member of the

[136] www.douban.com/group/topic/29877528 (accessed February 16, 2014).

neighborhood's Cultural Revolution "Red Fighting Force."[137] In 1999, Wang Lanhua's self-portrayal was as one of many housewives just lending a hand, one of the "elder sisters" working on behalf of the lane. She said little about her own suffering, describing only the inadequacy of her husband's wages as a street sweeper. Wang admitted that compared with the new private apartments, the residences of Fangua Lane might seem to be lacking. But she declared that despite her children's urging, she could not bear to leave, still wanting to lead tours of the neighborhood, "letting everyone know all of the good things that New China did for us working people!" Her memories remained with the Fangua Lane of 1964, the most evocative passage a scene where she walks on its newly paved roads and admires the trees and flowers, hearing the songs of children wafting from Fangua Lane Primary School.[138] Construction not yet complete, it was a time when the model workers' new village still held out the promise of a future perfect.

Conclusion: Lessons from Fangua Lane

Where the eighteen shantytown houses once stood, there is now a budget chain hotel and an administrative building. Although the site was named an official cultural relic in 1977, the preserved houses and the three *gundilong* came down in 1992. Four of the thatched houses were relocated to a locked exhibition hall, but these final remnants too were removed in 1996; when I visited in 2012 no one could really remember when the exhibition ended, saying only that it no longer suited the times.[139] Elsewhere also, the Fangua Lane narrative has faded. On real-estate webpages, marketers do not mention either its socialist past or its shantytown history, choosing instead to describe at length its early Republican-era prosperity.[140] In books, the shantytown is referred to in academic terms rather than in political ones. A volume of images from old Shanghai, for example, describes the shantytown as a type of "residential

---

[137] See, for example, Wang Lanhua, "Zhujin xingongfang, buwang gundilong" (Moving into the workers' new housing, don't forget the *gundilong*), *Wenhui bao*, September 24, 1967, p. 6.

[138] Wang Lanhua, "Fangualongli shuo jubian" (Speaking of the great changes in Fangua Lane), *Wenhui bao*, August 22, 1999, p. 1.

[139] Guo Tiancheng, Cao Yiding, and Qian Xuezhong, eds., *Zhabei quzhi*, p. 1029; interview in Shanghai with a former resident, July 5, 2013. See also Ho, *The Transition Study of Postsocialist China*, pp. 116–117. Note that *Zhabei quzhi* dates the intermediary step to 1992, whereas Ho documents it as 1995–1996.

[140] Shanghai fangjiawang (Shanghai real estate net), http://sh.fangjia.com/xiaoqu/%E9%9 7%B8%E5%8C%97/%E7%95%AA%E7%93%9C%E5%BC%84 (accessed February 16, 2014).

architecture," though the text still retains the Mao-era practice of con-
trasting its houses with the "residences of Shanghai's upper- and middle-
class society."[141] In official texts, Fangua Lane's narrative has also been
elided; though local histories and the Zhabei District Gazetteer included
descriptions of Fangua Lane into the 1990s, the Zhabei volume in a set of
books celebrating twenty years of reform and opening in Shanghai makes
no mention of the past. The only reference to any shantytown is a photograph of former Shanghai mayor and later Chinese premier Zhu Rongji
visiting residents in an unnamed neighborhood, the honor of such a visit
outweighing the negative image of a concrete apartment block as a latter-
day slum.[142]

The exhibition of the shantytown does persist in one place. At the base
of the Pearl TV Tower, itself part of Shanghai's iconic landscape, in the
wax museum of the Shanghai City History Exhibition Hall, there is a
diorama of thatched houses and *gundilong*. A figure of a man dressed in
rags crouches underneath reed-matting half-a-man high, and other wax
statues carry children, gather kindling, and bear heavy loads on their
shoulders. The diorama has neither a marker nor an explanation, bizar-
rely wedged between a depiction of the Great China Hotel with its
swirling ballroom dancers and the Hardoon Gardens in miniature. Only
by reading the souvenir booklet might a visitor realize that these are all
meant to be old vistas and spaces, "past footprints." The booklet goes on
to explain that Shanghai is a city of migrants chasing the "Shanghai
Dream," providing the numbers of shantytowns in 1949 and concluding
that within the last ten years they have all been eliminated, replaced by tall
buildings and greenery. The ballroom scene is introduced as the grand
location of Chiang Kai-shek's wedding to Song Meiling and the gardens
as the site where Silas Hardoon invited Chinese scholars to study oracle
bones.[143] In the Mao-era exhibition of Fangua Lane, similar scenes were
captioned differently; the former would have been called a scene of the
reactionary Chiang Kai-shek, the latter an imperialist pleasure garden.
And in their juxtaposition with the shantytown, such images of opulence
would have been an accusation of the "old society."[144] Nonetheless, a

---

[141] Shanghai tushuguan (Shanghai Library), ed., *Lao Shanghai fengqing lu: Jianzhu xunmeng juan* (Old Shanghai's vistas: Architectural volume) (Shanghai: Shanghai wenhua chu-banshe, 1998).

[142] *Shanghai gaige kaifang ershinian: Zhabei juan* (Twenty years of Shanghai's reform and opening: Zhabei volume) (Shanghai: Shanghai yuandong chubanshe, 1998).

[143] Niu Weiping, *Bainian huiwei: Shanghai chengshi lishi fazhan chenlieguan xunli* (Recalling one hundred years: The exhibition hall on the history of Shanghai's urban development) (Shanghai: Shanghai yuandong chubanshe, 2003), pp. 108–111.

[144] SMA B3-2-199, p. 24. Elizabeth Perry also comments on the absence of politics in this exhibition. See her " Shanghai's Politicized Skyline," in *Shanghai: Architecture and*

Ill.2.10. Diorama of the shantytown in the Shanghai City History
Exhibition Hall, June 12, 2013. Photo by the author

Mao-era legacy still remains: though the living rickshaw-puller has been
replaced by a wax figure of a porter, the shantytown is, and must be,
portrayed as a relic of the past.

A second Mao-era legacy lies in the exhibition of home interiors,
using their material changes over time as a way to display the march
toward modernity. Beginning in the reform era, the idea that life will
continue to improve has been central to the state's legitimacy.
Although no longer framed in the stark contrast between past and
present, divided by pre- and post-Liberation, and now measured in
terms of consumer goods rather than housing and employment, a
narrative that looks toward a prosperous future persists. At the 2010
Shanghai Expo, the first display encountered by a visitor to the China
Pavilion was a series of dioramas showing a family's private space in
1978, 1988, 1998, and 2008. The 1978 and 1988 homes still displayed

Urbanism for Modern China, edited by Peter G. Rowe and Seng Kuan (Munich: Prestel,
2004), p. 107.

red-flag certificates of merit and showed the evolution of products from thermoses and wicker steamers to refrigerators and television sets. By 2008, however, tourists were shown a spacious family living room, complete with a modern IKEA-type sofa and replica Ming chairs, decorated with an abstract art poster and a fake bronze vessel. Thus, even though the exhibition at the China Pavilion only began in 1978, the material of everyday life was still shown as evidence of social transformation, and present exceptions—like Fangua Lane in its times—can still be considered representative.

An artifact that would have linked the China Pavilion's 1978 home to the Fangua Lane workers' new village is a poster of Chairman Mao, ubiquitous in the Zhabei District Archives' photographs of Fangua Lane interiors.[145] Putting up a Chairman Mao portrait was model behavior. As *Jiefang ribao* reported on move-in day in 1964, the couple Hua Zaifu and Chen Dongying first hung up a Chairman Mao portrait, purchased by their model-worker daughter with her own prize money.

Ill.2.11. Depiction of a 1978 home interior at the Shanghai Expo, 2010. Photo by the author

[145] ZBDA ZJ-30-E0##.

Ill.2.12. Depiction of a 2008 home interior at the Shanghai Expo, 2010. Photo by the author

Previously, Chen had pasted paper gods on her walls, but she now declared, "Let the paper gods and the old houses be taken down together!"[146] On Spring Festival in 1965, Sun Xiuzhen did *yiku sitian*

---

[146] "Fangualong jumin xiqiyangyang qianru xinju" (The residents of Fangua Lane happily move into their new homes), *Jiefang ribao*, July 17, 1964, p. 2.

before her Chairman Mao portrait, vowing never again to be superstitious, to beseech the gods, or to burn incense.[147] But while these portrayals presented what residents did and said, the "Fangua Lane Past and Present" display presented only physical proof of such changes in faith. Stories of the worship of Fangua Lane's eponymous dragon god reappeared in the post-Mao era of reform. What of the immaterial and supernatural world of belief? In Chapter 3 we explore how Shanghai officials attempted to use the technology of display to mold faith, to inculcate those "born under the red flag" to love science and cast out superstition.

---

[147] "Xiaoying xinju diyichun: Fangualong jumin huandu chuxi" (Smilingly welcoming the first spring at the new residence: The residents of Fangua Lane welcome New Year's eve), *Jiefang ribao*, February 2, 1965.

3   Curating belief: Superstition versus science for Young Pioneers

The visions of little Luo Genmei's grandmother formed the basis of a cautionary tale. In 1963 Luo was an eighth-grade student with otherwise impeccable credentials: she was from a workers' family and a member of Shanghai's Communist Young Pioneers, a model among her classmates. Yet her home life was filled with ghost stories, the stuff of "superstitions" that could be used to oppose Communist Party policies and that threatened her generation, "born under the red flag" of New China.[1] One day when Luo Genmei was in primary school, as she was doing her homework her grandmother suddenly had some kind of fit. The grandmother frothed at the mouth, her eyes rolled back in her head, and she spoke in the voice of a deceased landlord from her neighboring village. The ghost of the landlord reproached the villagers for not burning paper money for him to use in the afterlife. In another example, based on Luo's speech to her fellow Young Pioneers, the previous year her grandmother had dreamed of being pulled between her village's temple god and Shanghai's city god. The village god wanted her to return home, but Shanghai's city god insisted that he relied on Grandma Luo's offerings. If she were to return to the village, all of the ghosts of Shanghai's netherworld would wander without money to spend. When Luo's science teacher explained that there were no such things as ghosts or gods, Luo Genmei protested, "There are too, and I have seen them."[2]

From the mouth of one of the Communist Party's littlest agents, Luo Genmei's account was highlighted for several reasons. Her grandmother's visions were interpreted as opposition to Party policies; the adult who recorded Luo's story commented that Grandma Luo had an

---

[1] In this chapter and throughout the book I use the word "superstition" as an actor's category, recognizing that this was a negative label imposed by the state, even though the practices might be more accurately described as part of local religion. On the use of actor's categories, see Sigrid Schmalzer, *The People's Peking Man: Popular Science and Human Identity in Twentieth-Century China* (Chicago: University of Chicago Press, 2008), p. xviii.
[2] SMA C27-1-51, p. 144. On paper money, see C. Fred Blake, *Burning Money: The Material Spirit of the Chinese Lifeworld* (Honolulu: University of Hawai'i Press, 2011).

agricultural residence permit but did not want to return to the country-side. Therefore, her dream was an example of using superstition to resist the resettlement policy of the state, which at that time was transferring people back to a countryside that had recently known famine. At the same time, little Luo's stubborn insistence on the existence of ghosts was a case of the elder generation's superstitions corrupting the revolutionary youth. Although left unsaid, Luo's speech and the content of the dream indi-cated a number of troublesome behaviors and ideas: Grandma Luo continued to burn spirit money despite the state's attempts to prohibit the practice, she channeled ghosts, and through her, the spirit of the landlord reached beyond his grave to encourage the "feudal" practice of burning offerings. Unwittingly giving credence to the landlord's ghost, the report on Luo Genmei's speech concluded that there was a class enemy using superstition to threaten the new society.[3] Even the ghosts of landlords past could menace the revolution.

To measure young people's beliefs about superstitions, ghosts, and gods, the Shanghai Youth Science and Technology Education Station (Shanghaishi Shaonian Kexue Jishu Zhidaozhan) collected narratives like this one from Luo Genmei and from fellow Young Pioneers. The intent was to produce an exhibition to teach elementary and middle-school students to "Love Science and Eliminate Superstition" (re'ai kexue, po mixin). By conducting a survey, the organizers were following the pre-scribed pattern for mounting a directed propaganda display in China in the 1960s. First go to the masses and analyze their thinking, then collect materials and rework them to target that thinking; next use an exhibition as a classroom; and finally study the visitors' responses to determine its effectiveness.[4] Following this progression, the Science and Technology Education Station used its research to create an exhibit that ran from December 5, 1963 to January 11, 1964. Every afternoon from Wednesday through Saturday and on Sunday mornings, teachers led students—eventually numbering 13,405—to the exhibition on Yueyang Road in the former French Concession, an area chosen because of its high concentration of believers.[5] Docents led visitors through five rooms decorated with posters and other exhibition materials, and the students explored three activity rooms that included lessons on astronomy, a game

[3] SMA C27-1-51, p. 144.
[4] SMA C1-2-3596, pp. 46–53. The name of the author of this report is partly illegible, but what remains indicates that it was written on December 9, 1961, by the Propaganda Department of the CCP Commission on Textile Factories.
[5] SMA C27-1-51, pp. 1, 156. Here it is only specified that they were believers, but since Xuhui District was a wealthy area with foreign schools and many churches, it is likely referring to Christians.

demonstrating the workings of electricity, and a miniature telephone office.[6] The goal of these science lessons was to refute superstitious beliefs and to create revolutionary subjects of Luo Genmei and other members of her generation.

"Love Science and Eliminate Superstition" was just one of many science dissemination (*kepu*) activities held in Shanghai in 1963–1964. The exhibit later traveled to other schools in Jing'an, Huangpu, and Nanshi districts, and was viewed by a total of 31,700 visitors.[7] But in the context of science exhibitions in general and the Science and Technology Education Station's activities in particular, it was still extremely small. It never registered in the press like the displays featured in the magazine *Kexue dazhong* (Mass science), it was only one of hundreds of exhibitions available to Shanghai youth, and in terms of the number of attendees, it represented only about 16 percent of the students reached by the Science and Technology Education Station in 1963.[8] Compared to the First Party Congress Site or Fangua Lane, it was a temporary exhibition and known to relatively few. What does "Love Science and Eliminate Superstition" indicate about exhibitionary culture in the Mao period?

Though modest in scope, the exhibition is representative of the local and ad hoc displays that—from the neighborhood to the school to the factory—were a feature of everyday life in Mao's China. In the context of science education or health campaigns, Miriam Gross points out that exhibitions were regarded as one of the most popular and effective techniques.[9] As a propaganda exhibition that included research beforehand and follow-up afterwards, the process of making the Love Science and Eliminate Superstition Exhibition reveals both the kinds of beliefs that persisted in New China and the difficulties of replacing them with scientific understanding. Although in official reports the Science and Technology Education Station declared that students who believed in ghosts and gods now understood any imaginings to be a product of the brain, and that those who had thought spirits could make mischief now knew the "scientific logic" of such phenomena, work behind the scenes shows that the exhibition was not immediately effective. The text of the Love Science and Eliminate Superstition Exhibition demonstrates not only those beliefs propagandists wished people to adopt but also those

[6] SMA C27-1-51, pp. 123–125.   [7] SMA C27-1-58, p. 1.
[8] *Kexue dazhong* (Mass science) (October 1950), p. 51, (June 1952), pp. 172–174; *Kexue dazhong* (November 1952), pp. 350–353; SMA C42-1-140, pp. 18a–20b; SMA C27-1-58, p. 1.
[9] Miriam Gross, *Farewell to the God of Plague: Chairman Mao's Campaign to Deworm China* (Berkeley: University of California Press, 2016), pp. 95–96. Sigrid Schmalzer also notes the popularity of exhibitions on human evolution. See Schmalzer, *The People's Peking Man*, p. 68.

people continued to hold. Its format, a question-and-answer catechism that made science the only correct answer, suggests the limits of such an exhibition and why some students may have, in the end, only mouthed its lessons.

Campaigns against superstition

From the establishment of the People's Republic in 1949, the state attempted to curtail what it deemed superstition in two ways: by limiting practices and by propaganda. The latter task of persuasion worked to warn of the dangers of superstition as well as to convince people of the truth and superiority of science. This propaganda was often accompanied by exhibitions. An exhibit denouncing superstition was dramatized in the 1952 film *Yiguan hairen dao*, which attacked Yiguandao (Way of Pervading Unity), the largest redemptive society in post-1949 China.[10] Beijingers in the film are shown filing past displays enumerating the evils of the practice "wearing the overcoat of superstition" to commit acts of counterrevolution. Afterwards, visitors sit before a stage on which three women demonstrate Yiguandao rituals before one takes the microphone to "expose" and "accuse" the organization responsible for her father's death. The exhibit thus serves as a frame for a story told in flashback; the ending returns to the woman thanking the Communist Party and Chairman Mao and then concludes with a scene of three Yiguandao members brought to justice, the crowd of exhibition visitors becoming the masses at the sentencing.[11] The filmic exhibition underscores the legitimacy of the new regime while also warning of enemies of the revolution.

The other form of anti-superstition exhibition refuted popular beliefs with science. For example, in 1951 the Association for the Dissemination of Science in Shanghai marked the Mid-Autumn Festival with an exhibit for workers on the subject of the moon. In addition to discouraging people from praying to the moon for good fortune, or from thinking that a lunar eclipse was due to a heavenly dog eating the moon, a political lesson was

[10] *Yiguan hairen dao* (The Way of Persistently Harming People), directed by Li Enjie and Wang Guangyan (Beijing: Zhongyang dianyingju Beijing dianying zhipianchang, 1952). Special thanks to Kirk Denton for recommending this source. On the history of Yiguandao, see S. A. Smith, "Redemptive Religious Societies and the Communist State, 1949 to the 1980s," in *Maoism at the Grassroots: Everyday Life in China's Era of High Socialism*, edited by Jeremy Brown and Matthew D. Johnson (Cambridge, MA: Harvard University Press, 2015), pp. 340–364.

[11] Note that the confiscated objects in the story—American and Guomindang flags, handguns, badges, and so forth—make a reappearance in the courtroom, recalling the display objects at the beginning of the film.

Ill.3.1. Film still from *Yiguan hairen dao* (The Way of Persistently Harming People), 1952

emphasized: enlightened about the science of the moon and understanding that their former superstition was a form of class oppression, workers would better love the People's Government and the Communist Party.[12] An ad hoc exhibit might also be established on the site of a superstitious incident. In the example of holy water that Stephen Smith has studied, Communist Party work teams hastened to the sites of purported curative springs to explain to pilgrims why holy water was dangerous. Smith describes the 1953 Xinjing case near Shanghai as "the best-coordinated official intervention in a holy water episode" and the response of officials as "a textbook operation to suppress it." When an attempt to fill the spring led to violence, the work team turned to exhortation. An exhibit about bacteria was set up next to the holy water, with magnifying glasses to allow people to view the organisms teeming within.[13]

[12] Luo Dingjiang, "Jieshao yueliang zhanlanhui" (An exhibition to explain the moon), *Kexue dazhong* (June 1952), p. 173.
[13] Steve A. Smith, "Local Cadres Confront the Supernatural: The Politics of Holy Water (*Shenshui*) in the PRC, 1949–1966," in *The History of the PRC (1949–1976)*, edited by Julia Strauss (Cambridge: Cambridge University Press, 2007), pp. 155, 157, 163–164.

But a decade later, the organizers of the Love Science, Eliminate Superstition Exhibition noted that the superstitious beliefs of the old society continued to influence thinking among young people. Therefore, the targets of the propaganda were manifold, alternately referred to as superstition (*mixin*), "feudal superstition," "legends and sayings," and sometimes "religious superstition." As one Gu Jingqing— the only named exhibition organizer—stressed, youth lacked scientific knowledge, and this caused them to believe in souls, the premonition of dreams, and the existence of ghosts and gods. Without science, Gu argued, children would persist in the practices of their families, whether it was praying to the gods or attending Mass. To that end, the exhibition propagated scientific knowledge, promoted atheism, and established a materialist and class-struggle view of the world. The display consisted of three parts: the first rejected the existence of a spirit world, the second highlighted the dangers of superstitious thinking, and the third celebrated science and its role in socialist construction.[14]

Such opposition between science and superstition, or between modernity and religion, was not a new phenomenon. In a recent survey, Vincent Goossaert and David Palmer show how the categories of religion and superstition were integral to modernizing and revolutionary projects. They write that beginning in the 1900s, during the late Qing dynasty, a campaign to "reform the customs" separated religion from so-called superstition.[15] This understanding of superstition as a hindrance to modernity was inherited by the Nationalist regime. Examining the writings of political reformer Liang Qichao, Rebecca Nedostup argues that the idea that religion could be cleansed of superstition was central to the cultural reforms of the twentieth century.[16] Nationalist modernizing projects, however, created what Nedostup calls an "affective regime," replacing religion with the Nationalist Party's own versions of time, ritual practice, and commemoration.[17] The CCP also opposed superstition, which it explained via a narrative of class: in the old society superstition was used as a tool of oppression and therefore its remnants had to be cast off to make way for the new egalitarianism. Further, as Sigrid Schmalzer writes, the Communist Party not only disseminated science as knowledge and against superstition, it used science to support its political ideology:

Smith explains that although some were turned off by the bacteria, others concluded that they were "celestial insects," and some simply chose to boil the water before drinking it.

[14] SMA C27-1-51, p. 12.

[15] Vincent Goossaert and David A. Palmer, *The Religious Question in Modern China* (Chicago: University of Chicago Press, 2011), p. 52.

[16] Rebecca Nedostup, *Superstitious Regimes: Religion and the Politics of Chinese Modernity* (Cambridge, MA: Asia Center, Harvard University, 2009), p. 8.

[17] Ibid., p. 23 and especially ch. 7.

"Propagandists cared about science because it was useful as a means of turning political truths into 'natural' ones."[18]

Even before the Communist Party came to power in 1949, it had worked to limit what it deemed to be superstitious practices. In the Communist base areas, officials engaged in propaganda campaigns, encouraged the confiscation of temples, disrupted and secularized festivals, and converted workshops that had previously manufactured ritual goods.[19] Although the newly established state recognized and institutionalized five official religions—Buddhism, Islam, Catholicism, Protestantism, and Daoism—it continued to strictly limit the scope of religious activity. One primary way to do this was to control the material culture of religious practices, for example by monitoring and regulating the market for "superstitious products," or ritual goods like incense and paper money. Officials also modified the built environment of religion, reinscribing and preserving certain temples as historic and cultural sites. In 1954, one of the first sites to be restored in Shanghai was the Song dynasty pagoda at Longhua Temple, with reports explaining that repairing historic monuments was an achievement also celebrated in the Soviet Union.[20] The Shanghai Bureau of Culture and the Shanghai Cultural Relics Commission also restored the City God Temple, which re-opened to great popularity in 1961.[21] Though there was some debate about the meaning of the Xujiahui Cathedral, the Party Committee of the Shanghai Bureau of Culture eventually defended it as simultaneously a site of culture and a testament to foreign imperialism.[22]

Despite an official reinterpretation as cultural sites, temples and churches remained popular with the faithful as places of worship. Luo Genmei's account shows that her grandmother continued to burn paper money and to dream of the Shanghai city god. Today informants in Shanghai remember following their grandparents to temple or church in the 1950s and 1960s: the son (b. 1949) of a Nationalist official recalls having his fortune told at the City God Temple at age four or five, the daughter (b. 1949) in a workers' family went with her grandmother to the same temple at age eight or nine, and the daughter (b. 1957) of a factory head remembers the beauty of the music in her grandmother's church on Sundays.[23] Even those who did not go to temple or attend church

---

[18] Schmalzer, *The People's Peking Man*, p. 57.
[19] Goossaert and Palmer, *The Religious Question in Modern China*, pp. 149–151.
[20] Huang Bi, "Longhua guta de qingchun" (Spring at Longhua Pagoda), *Lüxing jia* (Traveler), no. 3 (1956), pp. 20–21.
[21] Huangpu District Archive (hereafter cited as HPDA), N92-8-868; Han Yingjie, "Shanghai lao chenghuang miao" (Shanghai's old City God Temple), *Lüxing jia*, no. 11 (1959), pp. 34–35.
[22] SMA B172-1-363, pp. 26–33.   [23] Interviews in Shanghai, July 9 and July 15, 2013.

Ill.3.2. Illustration of a temple from "Love Science and Eliminate Superstition," 1963. SMA C27-1-51

remember the trappings of religious practices at home: the family altar, the surreptitious burning of incense at night, monks in an upstairs apartment performing exorcisms, and a grandmother quietly reciting prayers *sotto voce*.[24] District archives attest to the popularity of religious sites. In 1956, for example, Nanshi District officials reported that the City God Temple was the second most visited temple in Shanghai, with over 50,000 people arriving every Sunday.[25] The impressions of the worker's daughter also refer to the crowds: "At that time, I was really scared. The sculptures were about as big as I was, and when you entered, there was incense and the temple was full of smoke. All those people were praying, so seriously ... it was completely different from all other places."[26]

Political campaigns that targeted religious leaders and later superstition writ large had their effect. During the Great Leap Forward, when

[24] Interviews in Shanghai, July 9, July 10, July 21, and July 24, 2013.
[25] HPDA N41-1-45.   [26] Interview in Shanghai, July 9, 2013.

ministers were sent to engage in manual labor, the number of churches in Shanghai declined from two hundred to eight.[27] Though religious practice rebounded in the wake of the Great Leap, in 1964—coterminous with the Love Science, Eliminate Superstition Exhibition—the Shanghai People's Committee ordered the Nanshi District People's Committee to "reduce the influence of the City God Temple on the masses." To discourage visitors, it was obscured from the street. An archway leading to the temple was removed, the main gate to the south boarded up, and the gate to the west was covered with bricks. Only a small side door to the east was allowed to remain open.[28] Not content to simply erase the temple from the external landscape of the district, the People's Committee carefully examined the items within. With the help of the Shanghai Cultural Relics Commission, it recommended that the Hall of the Ten Kings of Hell and the Constellation Hall be removed, a few bodhisattvas excised and stored elsewhere by the temple management association, and the remainder preserved only through photographs. Also slated for removal were the statues of the *yamen* runners, "as many as possible" of the temple's tablets, anything with "feudal and superstitious" writing, and a gate painted with pictures of gods and ghosts.[29] The archival record shows that these directions were indeed carried out, and that a similar process was applied to neighboring temples.[30]

At the same time, the Nanshi District Party Committee closed fifty of the seventy-two religious places in the district, and children were prevented from entering the remaining places, where the sale of incense and candles was prohibited and the opening hours were reduced—sometimes the temples were entirely shut down during holidays.[31] To the limiting of practice was added propaganda. The Nanshi District Party Committee organized the telling of revolutionary stories, and as it reordered the City God Temple, it simultaneously provided thought reform for people who lived nearby. Local residents were "educated" by the neighborhood Party Committee, and the Shanghai Bureau of Religious Affairs provided "thought education" to temple workers and religious leaders.[32] To illustrate the efficacy of such policies, the Party Committee recorded examples of both behavior and thought. Although Spring Festival of 1963

---

[27] Goossaert and Palmer, *The Religious Question in Modern China*, p. 162.
[28] HPDA N92-1-235, pp. 22–25.   [29] Ibid.
[30] SMA B3-2-139, pp. 28–30; HPDA N92-1-194, p. 9. It was also at this time that all government offices with names such as "City God Temple" or "Confucius Temple" were changed. See SMA B3-2-139, pp. 27–29; HPDA N92-1-194, p. 1.
[31] HPDA N92-1-235, p. 24. The City God Temple was officially closed in April 1966. See HPDA N92-1-266, p. 2.
[32] HPDA N92-1-235, pp. 22–25. The content of such thought reform is not included.

brought 47,975 people to the City God Temple, during the same period in 1964 only 13,746 were in attendance.[33] After thought reform, officials quoted residents approving of the anti-superstition campaign: "These kinds of feudal superstitious things are indeed harmful and have no benefit; they should be taken down as soon as possible," and "Such a quality building, to be covered in sculptures, what a pity!" Yet in the same breath that officials reported their success, they also spoke of the forthcoming 1965 campaign, which would include a "smash superstition exhibition."[34]

With such measures to restrict temple access and propagandize against religion, Shanghai local officials were participating in a larger campaign, the Socialist Education Movement. This political campaign, largely an attack on cadre corruption and an intensification of ideological education, also intersected with Mao's 1963 definition of "Three Great Revolutionary Movements." With scientific experimentation as part of a revolutionary triumvirate of class struggle and production, the dissemination of science—and attacks on superstition—increased.[35] In Zhejiang Province to the south of Shanghai, officials embarked on a year of exhibitions all entitled "Oppose Feudal Superstition." In October 1964, the main exhibit opened in Hangzhou and reproductions traveled throughout the province; the former attracted over 50,000 people and the latter reached an estimated ten million. While the display explained scientific phenomena, it also aimed to criticize and refute superstitious practices, using actual people—fortune-tellers, *fengshui* masters, and the like—and adapting the exhibit to include "real people and real events" from each locality. Zhejiang's Oppose Feudal Superstition Exhibition was hailed a great success: visitors denounced feudal practices on site, handing over their Buddhist icons and leaving comments thanking the Party for liberating them from their superstitious thinking.[36] In these reported responses, exhibition visitors echoed the protagonist in the film *Yiguan hairen dao* and the residents in the vicinity of Shanghai's City God Temple after having undergone thought reform. Beyond Zhejiang, even the most modest location could mount an Oppose Feudal Superstition Exhibition; in 1965, a set of thirty-five colored posters was circulated for display,

---

[33] HPDA N92-1-194, p. 22.   [34] HPDA N92-1-235, p. 24.

[35] Sigrid Schmalzer, *Red Revolution, Green Revolution: Scientific Farming in Socialist China* (Chicago: University of Chicago Press, 2016), pp. 39–40.

[36] *Xuanchuan dongtai 1983* (Propaganda trends 1983) (Beijing: Zhongguo shehui kexue chubanshe, 1984), pp. 62–64. Note that this report was written almost twenty years later in the context of the campaign against "spiritual pollution" in response to a 1982 directive by Hu Qiaomu to learn from such exhibitions. Hu was one of three leaders to personally oversee the original 1964–65 exhibit.

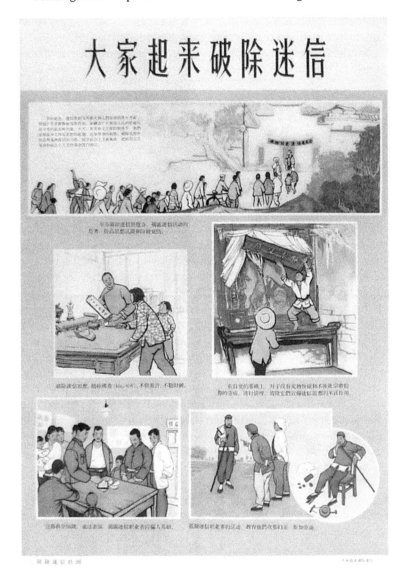

Ill.3.3. Poster from the exhibition "Eliminate Superstition" (Keji puji chubanshe, 1965). This poster illustrates how everyone can oppose superstition; note the top image of people attending an exhibition. The paper envelope containing the posters warns that they should not be exhibited, sold, or given to foreigners. Image courtesy of the Shanghai Propaganda Poster Art Centre

containing lessons from "the origins of superstition" to "study scientific knowledge to eliminate superstitious thinking."[37]

But what exactly was superstition and how did exhibition officials evaluate local beliefs? One way to get at the process of propaganda is to examine the Love Science and Eliminate Superstition Exhibition as a text. After all, in its making organizers went to the masses—in this case, remarkably frank children—and came up with a whole host of what they deemed to be superstitious beliefs. Students had innumerable questions. Some stemmed from curiosity about nature. How do orchids reproduce? Why do cacti have thorns? Why do mimosas curl up their leaves when touched?[38] On the supernatural, students asked why water goblins stuffed mud into the ears of those who had drowned, why people dream, and why—if there truly were no gods—were there still so many temples?[39] Among the list of youth views on gods and ghosts, recorders included not only their ideas but also the solutions they proffered. On the former, fourth grader Cui Ziying explained how the neglected dead would interfere with the living; another student reported that water goblins had to catch new bodies every three years in order to be reincarnated; and yet another insisted that one heard midnight chains rattling when the city god released his black and white monks to chase the living. To assuage their fears, the students prescribed responses to spirit encounters. If you hear your name called in the night, you should not answer; if you run into a vampire, you should flee in a straight line; and if you meet a ghost, you should buy him a hat but never buy him shoes.[40] From the experiences of Young Pioneers like Luo Genmei came the context for their worldviews: grandparents' and parents' beliefs and practices influenced their families, children delighted in telling each other's fortunes and relating ghost stories, and some students prayed with their parents or observed Sunday as a day of rest.[41] Having gone to the masses, the Love Science and Eliminate Superstition Exhibition operated on multiple fronts: it addressed questions and beliefs, it offered a narrative that explained superstition's origins in class and presented science as its antidote, and it replaced superstition with an ideology of science. Science was what superstition was not.

Rhetoric and narrative

As a display of science, the Love Science and Eliminate Superstition Exhibition included two experiments. The first was a response to

[37] *Pochu mixin guatu* (Posters from the exhibition "Eliminate superstition") (Beijing: Kexue puji chubanshe, 1965).
[38] SMA C27-1-51, p. 120b.   [39] SMA C27-1-51, p. 148.
[40] SMA C27-1-51, pp. 146–148.   [41] SMA C27-1-51, pp. 150–155.

students' questions about what happens to people after they die: Do they have souls? What happens to bodies after death? Why will people's hands and feet still move after they die? To answer these questions, the exhibition presented a freshly-killed frog, stimulating its brain to move its limbs and declaring that its movements were neither because of ghosts and gods nor because its soul was making mischief.[42] The second experiment set out to refute the idea of heavenly fire, or a fire lit by an invisible fire god. To demonstrate spontaneous combustion, the exhibition's narrator held up a piece of paper, dipped it in a solution of white phosphorous and vulcanizing carbon, and then pulled it out—the paper caught on fire. This was, the narrator stressed, a natural phenomenon.[43] Thus to an exhibition's repertoire of artifacts, drawings, and text, "Love Science and Eliminate Superstition" added the experiment as evidence.

The Science and Technology Education Station emphasized objects, regarding words as supplementary. This was in keeping with the idea of an exhibition using material evidence to bring perception to reason. But to the contrary, the exhibition relied primarily on rhetoric and narrative. It asked and answered questions, it made arguments for science and against superstition, and in evaluating the students' facility with the lessons, it relied on their ability to repeat them back. Moreover, behind the exhibition's narrative was a historical trajectory that followed superstition from antiquity to class society to socialist New China. The story went something like this: in ancient times, people knew little and attributed phenomena that they did not understand to the supernatural. They believed that eclipses were omens and that gods were responsible for disasters and disease; they submitted to fate and prayed for their next lives. Thereafter, the ruling classes used such superstitions as instruments of control. On the one hand, oppressors used ideas about heaven to elevate themselves as so ordained and on the other, they bent the people to their will by reinforcing faith in predestination. The persistence of superstitious beliefs was therefore a class threat to the revolution and to the Young Pioneers as revolutionary successors.[44] Like the anti-superstition pamphlets of the 1960s, the Love Science and Eliminate Superstition Exhibition began with this overarching narrative.[45] A history of class conflict was the exhibit's first lesson.

[42] SMA C27-1-51, p. 77.   [43] SMA C27-1-51, p. 90.   [44] SMA C27-1-51, pp. 6–7, 19.
[45] See, for example, *Pochu mixin wenda* (Questions and answers for eliminating superstition) (Shanghai: Shanghai renmin chubanshe, 1963), pp. 3–6; Sun Wu, ed., *Tantian shuodi po mixin* (Talk of everything and smash superstition) (Tianjin: Tianjin renmin chubanshe, 1964), p. 1; Xiao Ming, Xin De, and Bao Yuan, eds., *Jiang kexue po mixin* (Discussing science and smashing superstition) (Jinan: Shandong renmin chubanshe, 1963), pp. 1–3; Zhang Geng, *Jiang kexue po mixin* (Discussing science and smashing superstition) (Shanghai: Shanghai keji chubanshe, 1964), pp. 1–2.

The first third of the display was devoted to refuting any notion of gods or ghosts, a string of lessons on examples of superstitious thinking presented alternately as statements of fact or as questions. The docent began by refuting the existence of souls, explaining that people's actions are the result of activity in the brain and that people are made up of materials, not a body and a soul. Using a model of a brain, an illustration of the nervous system on a light-up board, and the unfortunate frog, the exhibit explained how dreams were a function of the brain (not a manifestation of the soul), why sleepwalking occurred when part of the brain failed to come to rest, and how fevers interfered with the brain (and delirium was not an encounter with a ghost). Answering the question about what happens after death, the docent declared that people had no souls, were not created by gods, and that the material that made them would decompose after death.[46]

A significant portion of the first third of the display was devoted to superstitions about ghosts, a topic that dominated the reports on student beliefs. These lessons were often framed as questions: "Are there really 'ghost wanderings'?" "Are there underwater ghosts?" To the former question, the docent answered that in darkness one walked in circles because one's legs were not quite the same length; to the latter question, he explained that people drowned not because of water goblins but because of whirlpools, leg cramps, or becoming tangled up in seaweed. One display board was devoted to the phenomenon of the will-o'-wisp, or "ghost fire," illustrating that it was neither ghosts lighting fires nor ghosts lighting their lanterns but rather phosphorescence created by decay; it was the lightness of such gas that resulted in it blowing around the ankles of passersby, not the presence of ghosts in pursuit. Indeed, the will-o'-wisp seems to be the classic example of science over superstition, with one retired cadre (b. 1954) able to recall the lesson half a century later.[47] Addressing other questions, the exhibition declared that dogs could not see ghosts, foxes could not become spirits, and owls were not inauspicious birds. The docent's narrative gave the young visitors a vocabulary for dismissing their fears; suspecting the presence of gods or ghosts was merely the result of superstitious thinking.[48]

The first third of the exhibit also included several lessons on natural phenomena. It explained that earthquakes were not mountain gods flying into a rage but the result of natural movement in the earth's crust. Likewise, floods and droughts were not due to manifestations of the Dragon King, and they could now be predicted and controlled by science.

---

[46] SMA C27-1-51, pp. 73–78.   [47] Interview in Shanghai, July 20, 2013.
[48] SMA C27-1-51, pp. 79–85.

Ill.3.4. Illustration of a natural disaster from "Love Science and Eliminate Superstition," 1963. SMA C27-1-51

The text mocked the people of antiquity and their fears of solar and lunar eclipses, beating drums and lighting firecrackers to scare the "heavenly dog" into releasing the sun. Nor were epidemics the workings of the god of plagues, nor tornados the work of the Dragon God, nor death caused by lightning heaven's retribution for sin. Throughout, the world was explained by natural phenomena, and the docent concluded that the earth was part of a greater universe that encompassed neither heaven nor hell, and it was not created by gods or by a lord in heaven.[49] As a transition to the second part of the exhibit, the text dismissed the power of fortune-tellers and spirit mediums. And perhaps in response to the continued popularity of elixirs and holy water, the docent dismissed claims to heal one hundred illnesses as schemes to fool and swindle the people.[50]

The second third of the exhibition elaborated on the "dangers of superstitious thinking" as not only foolish and wasteful but also as an actual

[49] SMA C27-1-51, pp. 86–93.
[50] SMA C27-1-51, p. 95. Steve A. Smith suggests that cases of holy or sacred water were "one of the most pervasive forms of what the communist authorities called 'feudal superstitious activity' in this period." Smith, "Local Cadres Confront the Supernatural," p. 146.

Ill.3.5, Ill.3.6, and Ill.3.7. Illustrations of a fortune-teller, a spirit medium, and an exorcist from "Love Science and Eliminate Superstition," 1963. SMA C27-1-51

threat to the revolution. From the abstract questions and answers to refute ghosts and gods, the text presented a series of vignettes, case studies from the past and the present. In the three stories presented to the students, superstition—including religion—was linked with imperialism and counterrevolution. This section of the exhibition began with the case of Bishop Gong Pinmei, who was accused of carrying out counterrevolution for the American imperialists and the Catholic Church. Displayed like an history exhibit, the case against Bishop Gong was supported by documents threatening excommunication for Catholics who praised the Party, instruments for working out a spy code, and guns and bullets supposedly hidden by Bishop Gong in order to sabotage the regime.[51] To a child knowing of Bishop Gong from the news and growing up hearing spy stories, the

[51] SMA C27-1-51, p. 98; Paul P. Mariani, *Church Militant: Bishop Kung and Catholic Resistance in Communist Shanghai* (Cambridge, MA: Harvard University Press, 2011), pp. 192, 196. Bishop Gong's 1960 trial at the Shanghai Intermediate People's Court displayed title deeds, gold, 62 Guomindang flags, 6 rifles, 1,382 bullets, and 2 radio

Ill.3.5, Ill.3.6, and Ill.3.7. (cont.)

exhibition's artifacts must have made a convincing case. At a church exhibition on counterrevolution in the 1950s, one retired cadre (b. 1950) remembers his fear of descending into the church basement, the gold bars and guns on tables and in glass cases, and the emphasis that such things had been hidden, "At that time, we wouldn't have been able to see American dollars normally, and once we saw them, we would think that they were definitely bad things ... I was really scared."[52]

As an example of contemporary counterrevolution, the docent warned of "bad elements" by telling a story about a commune in Rugao County, where after the death of one Yao Sheng, rumors began to circulate that the weeping ghost of the dead man wandered from village to village.

---

transmitters. In his 1979 letter of appeal, Gong explained that there were neither radios nor firearms at his residence.

[52] Interview in Shanghai, July 2, 2013.

Ill.3.5, Ill.3.6, and Ill.3.7. (cont.)

Sounds of his crying in the fields and the midnight creaking of his pushcart so frightened the villagers that they would hide in their houses at night, refusing to follow the orders of the production team leader to come out and guard the ripening wheat. Skeptical of the idea that this was a ghost, Song Guanglin, a member of the people's militia, took matters into his own hands, seizing on a shadow one night and discovering one Yao Jin, a "bad element" who had been a soldier for the Japanese puppet regime in the 1940s. According to the "real story" as told by the docent, Yao Jin had been pretending to be a ghost in order to steal young lima beans—a class enemy taking advantage of superstition in order to engage in sabotage.[53] In his skepticism and in uncovering the "ghost," Song Guanglin mirrored a textbook lesson about the writer Lu Xun, a connection that visiting students made in their post-exhibition reflections.[54]

[53] SMA C27-1-51, p. 99.
[54] SMA C27-1-51, p. 151. The anti-superstition lesson, in "Lu Xun Kicks the Ghost," is still remembered today. In the story, Lu Xun—a writer and a man of science—takes

The third story reached into the pre-1949 past, presenting the case of a French school in Shanghai's Xuhui District as "wearing the overcoat of religion to carry out cultural aggression." At the Xuhui School, the docent explained, foreign languages were used to make Chinese students forget that they were Chinese, religious organizations were actually counterrevolutionary organizations, and the school's system of discipline—which barred participation in patriotic activities—was reactionary. Connected to the missionaries was a final example of religion shielding infamy—the Chinese children who died in foreign orphanages. Among the photos on display were depictions of the morgue of Shanghai's Xujiahui Orphanage and a post-1949 photo of parents seeking revenge for those who had been entrusted there. To explain the photos on display, the docent intoned, "Fellow students, everyone have a look! This is the evidence that imperialism, borrowing religion and charity as names, killed countless numbers of our young children."[55] In these examples, the lines between religion and superstition, past and present enemies, and historic injuries and present threats were all blurred, linked only in belief's portrayal as a tool against the revolution and its people.

Under the category of the "dangers of superstitious thinking," the exhibition's second third also included contemporary threats to body and mind. In yet another case involving holy water, in 1958 a local shepherd boy in Baoshan County noticed a spring with bubbly water at the entrance to a cave. It was said that the words "holy peach" had appeared at the mouth of the cave, that a divine peach girl had descended to earth, that a magic horse had passed by the spring, and that its waters could cure one hundred illnesses. People from Shanghai's suburbs flocked to the site to burn incense and paper money, but the water reportedly made them sick.[56] In another example on display, one worker with tuberculosis enlisted a spirit medium to beseech the Buddha to cure him. He traded 120 yuan, a chicken, and three *jin* of vegetables for the offering, but the elixir made him worse; only a doctor at the Longhua

a short cut by a cemetery. Seeing what appears to be a ghost, Lu Xun begins to have doubts. But he approaches the ghost and shouts, and his flying kick lands on what turns out to be a grave robber. Interview in Shanghai, July 20, 2013.

[55] SMA C27-1-51, p. 101. Henrietta Harrison explains that anti-missionary campaigns in the People's Republic included demonstrations around the bones of dead children. The photograph she includes from the Wuchang orphanage, which was one of the orphanages listed at the exhibition, may be the very photograph on display. See Henrietta Harrison, "A Penny for the Little Chinese: The French Holy Childhood Association in China, 1843–1951," *American Historical Review*, vol. 113, no. 1 (February 2008), p. 91.

[56] SMA C27-1-51, p. 102. The docents explained that the bubbles were marsh gas, or methane.

sanatorium was finally able to cure him.[57] But even more dangerous than the threat of superstition to one's health was its threat to one's thinking and revolutionary will. Recapitulating the history of superstition, the docent reminded the students that it had been a tool of the ruling classes to make the poor believe that their lot was fated. The students were therefore enjoined to "believe in science, believe in truth, and cultivate [their] spirits so that [they] dare to think, dare to speak, and dare to struggle."[58]

The last third of the exhibition was entitled "Master Science, Conquer Nature," reflecting what Judith Shapiro has described as a "Maoist ideology [that] pitted the people against the natural environment in a fierce struggle," a discourse that promoted a "war against nature."[59] Sigrid Schmalzer further argues that science in Mao's China—as elsewhere— was inseparable from its political context, and that in popular science education superstition "referred unproblematically to any idea or practice that appeared unscientific or otherwise impeded China's entry into the modern world."[60] The exhibit's text thus attributed the mastery of science to the leadership of Chairman Mao and the Communist Party. Following Mao's directive to tame the Huai River, great irrigation works were built and the people's communes gave "free rein to collective power." Personifying nature, the docent called for a "struggle against floods and droughts" and asserted that "only by relying on our own labor will we be able to conquer nature." The lessons that followed, illustrated by contemporary photographs and even objects from a weather station run by Young Pioneers, heralded the leadership of the Party that had made agricultural oases of undeveloped land, had developed atmospheric science to anticipate weather patterns, and could even send PLA men into the sky to make rain. Alluding to Mao's words, science even made it possible to explore the earth's vast deposits, using labor to "open the mountains and split the earth, calling upon the high mountain to lower its head ... [and] the rivers [to] yield the way."[61]

The final lessons of "Love Science, Eliminate Superstition" argued that in mastering science one could fulfill, or even exceed, the imaginations of antiquity. While superstitious beliefs posited that the King of Hell caused

[57] SMA C27-1-51, p. 103.   [58] SMA C27-1-51, pp. 104–105.
[59] Judith Shapiro, *Mao's War Against Nature: Politics and the Environment in Revolutionary China* (Cambridge: Cambridge University Press, 2001), pp. 3–4.
[60] Schmalzer, *The People's Peking Man*, p. 28.
[61] SMA C27-1-51, pp. 109–112. The quotation is from 1958, "'Make the high mountain bow its head; make the river yield the way.' It is an excellent sentence. When we ask the high mountain to bow its head, it has to do so! When we ask the river to yield the way, it must yield!" Cited in Shapiro, *Mao's War Against Nature*, p. 68.

Ill.3.8. *Take a shuttle and explore outer space*, by Zhang Ruiheng (Hebei renmin chubanshe, 1979). Image courtesy of the Shanghai Propaganda Poster Art Centre

death, modern medicine was capable of even greater miracles: it could make new hearts and lungs as well as reattach broken hands. Though human ancestors had imagined an eye that could see for 1,000 *li* and a magical ear, telescopes and microphones made such dreams possible. Even the fortune-teller's claims about the future were exceeded by a computer's ability to calculate hundreds of operations, an "amazing foresight" electronic calculator. Finally, science would enable humanity to access the worlds that the ancients had only dreamed of: the "palace of the dragon" would be explored by deep-sea scientists and the "lunar palace" would be discovered via rocket and satellite expeditions. The text concluded by suggesting that hardworking students might one day fly into space, the docent gesturing to posters of children hard at work studying math (with the motherland and the four modernizations in the background) and of children spreading scientific knowledge (against a backdrop of science pictorials and the *Selected Works of Chairman Mao*).[62]

"Love Science, Eliminate Superstition" was literally a textbook come to life; it mirrored contemporary anti-superstition handbooks with lists of questions and answers.[63] The narrative also delivered an historical and class lesson, attributing superstition to ignorance and class oppression, twin evils from which the Party had liberated the people. It was an argument against superstition and for science, refuting each superstitious belief with a scientific explanation. But despite being about science, there was much about the exhibition that was not scientific. Statements of science were presented as already true because they were scientific, and superstitious beliefs were therefore false because they were not. Lessons were structured to begin with a "scientific" claim, like "foxes cannot become spirits," then the superstition was dismissed as "fabricated rubbish," concluding that a belief in a "thousand-year fox spirit" was nonsense.[64] Likewise, a first principle held that superstition was a product and tool of counterrevolution, and therefore anything associated with superstition or a bad element was counterrevolutionary. That commune member Yao Jin—who had pretended to be a ghost to steal lima beans—was already known to be a collaborator and a bad

---

[62] SMA C27-1-51, pp. 113–117, 122.

[63] In addition to such anti-superstition handbooks, a set of children's books called *Shiwange weishenme* (10,000 "Whys?") (Shanghai: Shaonian ertong chubanshe) began publication in 1962. These books are organized as questions and answers, with some themes overlapping with those in the anti-superstition handbooks. Particularly relevant are those that deal with animals (no. 10, 1974), dreams (no. 13, 1974), astronomy (no. 20, 1977), and the earth sciences (no. 21, 1978). However, the questions are not presented as superstitious beliefs.

[64] SMA C27-1-51, p. 83.

element meant that his exploitation of superstition was of necessity counterrevolutionary. With only a few exceptions, like the explanations of the will-o'-wisp or the formation of tornados, the docent's text relied more on a rhetoric of science *qua* science than on scientific inquiry.

In the end, the exhibition substituted an ideology of science for an ideology of superstition, rather than presenting science as a way of knowing or questioning. In this way, the Communist Party was following the path that Rebecca Nedostup argues was set by the Nationalists, i.e., offering a new state ideology in place of old superstitions. As psychiatrist Robert Jay Lifton wrote in 1963, the same year as "Love Science and Eliminate Superstition," science in Maoist China was part of an "ideological totalism" and alternate beliefs were rejected "first by exposing ... [them] as 'unscientific,' then by demonstrating that they [were] no longer necessary in a truly 'scientific environment.'"[65] The idea that science was in itself an unassailable truth—a concept not unique to China—was also later critiqued by Chinese observers. Writing of museums and science dissemination in 1995, Zhang Xing cited Party and State Council documents to stress that "past scientific dissemination mostly spread scientific knowledge and neglected the scientific *method* and scientific *thinking*."[66] In Mao-era exhibitions, students were told to "believe in science," with science as a set of incontrovertible facts and fixed first principles. Nowhere was it more evident that science and superstition were mutually exclusive than in the final section of the exhibition: because there is a nervous system, there is no soul; because there is an atmosphere, there is no heaven. That the rhetoric of science was not scientific may help explain why teachers struggled to impart its messages, and why they reported that some students "obeyed with their mouths rather than with their hearts." In the same way that students were to believe in revolution, they were asked to place their faith in science.

Post-exhibition and the persistence of belief

The students of Hufei School for Children of Boat People were mostly from families who lived on the water. Having seen cases of drowning, reported the school's Young Pioneers, many of the children believed in water goblins. Proletarian in origin but likely influenced by such stories, they were ideal visitors for the Love Science and Eliminate Superstition

---

[65] Robert Jay Lifton, *Thought Reform and the Psychology of Totalism: A Study of "Brainwashing" in China* (New York: W.W. Norton., 1963), pp. 459–460.

[66] Zhang Xing, "Bowuguan kepu jiaoyu gongneng tantao" (An exploration into the functions of museums in science dissemination education), *Sichou zhi lu* (The silk road), no. 6 (December 1995), pp. 54–55. Italics added.

Exhibition. For two weeks, the entire school curriculum was mobilized around the exhibition. From March 20 to April 4, 1964—at precisely the time of the Qingming tomb-sweeping festival—the school visited the exhibition, read newspapers and anti-superstition booklets, heard lectures at morning assemblies, asked and answered questions, told stories, engaged in experiments, and held discussions. Both teachers and students led the way. To dispel a school legend about a fox spirit living in a little thatched hut by the school, the teachers explained that foxes were animals just like any other animal and brought the students to examine the hut; as a result, the students purportedly no longer believed in the fox spirit. In response to student propagandizing, the Young Pioneers reported back to the Science and Technology Education Station, even the families of the teachers hastily got rid of their home incense burners.[67]

The comments on the exhibition made immediately after the visit were mostly pro-forma statements of approval.[68] Reports written later, like the contemporary responses to Zhejiang's Oppose Feudal Superstition Exhibition, demonstrate the lessons learned. On the historical lesson on superstition as a tool of class oppression, students at Hufei School reportedly reacted with fury at the "reactionary feudal rulers in the old society." Some fourth- and sixth-grade students declared that due to superstitious thinking in the past, rowers and scullers did not even dare to look at the water, covering their heads with their quilts. But "from this day forward, we will never again believe those ghost stories ... we won't believe in superstition and we won't be fooled by enemies and bad eggs. We'll be the brave successors to communism!"[69] On the nonexistence of gods and ghosts, the children of the boat people could recite the lessons on why there were no water goblins, on the phenomena of the will-o'-the-wisp and solar and lunar eclipses, and on why the barking of dogs was *not* because they had seen a ghost. With their thinking enlightened, their behavior changed. A Young Pioneer student leader declared that whereas in the past students would tell ghost stories at night, "now nobody tells such stories ... when I was on duty at night I [used to be] afraid of the sound of light bulbs and of walking in dark corridors, but now I have courage." Student Guo Laishun chimed in on the dangers of superstition, relating how he propagandized to his parents: "When I went home I told Mom and Dad not to believe in ghosts and gods, not to burn paper money, and not to waste any more money." One fifth grader named Liu Maoguang asserted that "scientific principles are truly correct; from now

[67] SMA C27-1-51, pp. 150–152.
[68] For exhibition comments, see SMA C27-1-51, pp. 139–142.
[69] SMA C27-1-51, p. 151.

on I will ardently love science."[70] The Hufei students' responses were echoed by other children as well, whose comments—perhaps selected by the Science and Technology Education Station to serve as models—often quoted verbatim from the texts of the exhibition.[71]

The correctness of the reported student answers are reflected in the memories of Shanghai people today. Many claim that superstition in their childhood referred to religion and they define superstition as "reciting scriptures," "burning incense and praying to the Buddha," or "believing in ghosts."[72] One retired English professor (b. 1945) recalls that "when we were students, religion was a taboo topic ... if you believed in the Communist Party, you couldn't also believe in religion. Marx said that religion was the opiate of the people ... if you were a young person and went into a temple, then people would watch you ... it was dangerous and it was bad. Nobody wanted to do this."[73] A present-day cadre born in 1957 into a workers' family, who would have been slightly younger than the Young Pioneers in the report, explained how one was supposed to turn in one's incense burners. "In school, you wouldn't dare talk about religion! Why, you'd be a little counterrevolutionary ... if this was discovered, there would be hell to pay!"[74] Yet even if some students did not dare talk about religion, the Hufei teachers suggested that some students only pretended to be convinced by the anti-superstition lessons, that among some of the students there remained the idea that one could not help but believe, and that the teachers themselves lacked the scientific knowledge to discredit the superstitions. They concluded that superstitious thinking was truly deep-rooted, and its eradication—like class struggle itself—would be "long term and complicated."[75]

The text of the Love Science, Eliminate Superstition Exhibition documented the kinds of behaviors and beliefs that persisted in Mao's China despite the state's anti-superstition campaigns. As the reports to and by the Science and Technology Education Station both before and after the exhibition indicate, "superstitious thinking" continued to shape how people saw the world around them. It did not matter whether or not they were Young Pioneers, or whether they were city children in

[70] SMA C27-1-51, pp. 150–152.   [71] SMA C27-1-51, p. 156.
[72] Interviews in Shanghai, July 9, July 10, July 20, and July 21, 2013.
[73] Interview in Shanghai, July 8, 2013.
[74] Interview in Shanghai, July 24, 2013. This informant was proud to explain that he was a descendant of workers and therefore he was a member of the five categories of red elements. In fact, his father had been doubly oppressed—first as a hired hand for a landlord in the Jiangsu countryside and then as a worker in a factory in Shanghai. Although his family had lived in a *gundilong*, he stated that he was "born under the red flag" and therefore he could not have lived in a *gundilong*.
[75] SMA C27-1-51, p. 152.

Xuhui District or boat children living on the margins: the ideas condemned by the exhibit remained, though perhaps for different reasons. Students were inclined to believe in souls and in the presence of ghosts among the living, perhaps because their teachers could not quite explain them away but also because ghost stories and other superstitions were simply fun. A daughter in a workers' family (b. 1949) remembers, "Of course, the grannies would tell ghost stories, and we children would love to listen to them … the scarier, the better! This telling of stories, no one could really control it."[76] The students surveyed by the Science and Technology Education Station could name all kinds of ghosts: hanging suicide ghosts, water goblins, vampires, big-headed ghosts, small-headed ghosts, and headless ghosts. They had vivid stories at the ready: wearing a green hat and covering his face with a fan, a ghost of a suicide victim haunted the elevator at Wukang Mansion; students from three schools claimed that the Red Star Theatre flashed red and green lights at night to the strains of opera-singing; and children living by the City God Temple said that they could hear the midnight clanking of chains and the sounding of gongs.[77]

Superstitious stories also appealed to students because of their explanatory power. Fourth-grader Cui Ziying from Yangpu District's Number Two Elementary School asserted that the failure to put out food offerings or to perform rituals for a deceased neighbor—i.e., not being superstitious—led to "ghosts making mischief" and to relatives falling ill. "After making up for the food offerings," Cui said stoutly, "a father quickly recovered from illness; this proves that there are ghosts."[78] To the distress of their teachers who read superstitious belief properly as fatalism, students also found fortune-telling appealing. At the same meeting with Luo Genmei, Young Pioneer leader Zhang Ruyu described her father's predictive powers. He had divined when an old person would die, when a patient with esophageal cancer would succumb to illness—to the month and day!—and he was so accurate that she asked her father to tell her own fortune. In answering the all-important question about the middle-school entrance examinations, Zhang Ruyu's father declared that she would succeed and so she did, testing into West Shanghai Middle School.[79] As the Science and Technology Education Station reported, a "minority" of students still prayed to the Buddha at the City God Temple, seeking blessings for their school entrance exams.[80]

---

[76] Interview in Shanghai, July 9, 2013.   [77] SMA C27-1-51, p. 153.   [78] Ibid.
[79] SMA C27-1-51, p. 144.
[80] SMA C27-1-51, p. 154. Competition to advance through the academic system was intense. As Andrew Walder calculates, only 9 percent of students who entered primary

Such beliefs persisted, school officials acknowledged, because of the faith of the students' families. Thus while the official line—and indeed the premise of "Love Science and Eliminate Superstition"—was that the revolutionary generation would not be so sullied, the Science and Technology Education Station reported that children "were deeply influenced by their families' feudal superstitious thinking; young people's beliefs in ghosts and gods were directly linked to their parents' faith in religion." From a family with devout Buddhist parents, student Yang Wanli dealt with his own adversities by chanting scriptures and praying. Xiangyang Middle School Junior 2 student Lin Deyuan maintained his Christian faith and practice, refusing to go to school on the Sabbath despite his teachers' repeated urgings. At Xuhui Middle School, Junior 1 student Zhou Deguo frequently went to mass at the Xujiahui Cathedral; devout in his beliefs, he was intent upon becoming a priest when he grew up.[81] The Science and Technology Education Station's reports, likely written to portray such students as minority outliers, nevertheless reflect a failure to completely eradicate "superstition."

Superstitious and religious practices were frequently reported in the classified *Neibu cankao* (Internal reference). These reports indicate that people in Shanghai continued to engage in such activities. In the 1950s the PSB apprehended fortune-tellers who were still active in New China. In a "certain area" on Yan'an East Road, the PSB cracked down on four fortune-tellers and two fortune-telling shops that employed a total of twenty-four people. Though they blamed them for being "bad elements," keeping people from working or seeing doctors, they admitted that the fortune-tellers did a good business, even making enough money to hire servants.[82] Officials also tracked superstitious practices by following the market for temple goods. During Spring Festival in 1956, the sale of incense and candles rose 45 percent over the previous year, with candles completely sold out and people lining up at dawn to buy tin foil to make offerings; the Shanghai market even attracted buyers from Anhui, Jilin, and Dalian. The City God Temple staff anticipated an even bigger year

school in 1965 could expect to enter junior high school, and 15 percent of those could expect to enter senior high school. "Overall, the odds of attending an academic high school for a student entering primary school in 1965 were 1.2 percent, and the odds of attending university less than 0.5 percent." Andrew G. Walder, *Fractured Rebellion: The Beijing Red Guard Movement* (Cambridge, MA: Harvard University Press, 2009), p. 20.

[81] SMA C27-1-51, p. 155.

[82] "Shanghaishi mingxiangguan cezitan: Xuanyang mixin weihai shehui shengchan he renmin shengming de xianxiang yanzhong" (Shanghai's fortune-telling booths: The serious phenomenon of propagating superstition harms social production and the people's lives), *Neibu cankao* (Internal reference), May 18, 1955.

in 1957, planning an additional 30,000 strings of paper ingots, 500 extra *jin* (550 pounds) of candles, and hiring twenty extra temporary workers. Among the pilgrims who crowded the City God Temple, there were not only many old women and housewives but also cadres and workers. Officials attributed the change either to a rise in salaries or to relaxed vigilance because of the Hundred Flowers Movement. But no matter the cause, Shanghai's temples and monasteries were said to be constantly crowded with people, "dense with incense smoke drifting toward the ceiling."[83]

If a moment of increased prosperity and political openness led to increased temple attendance, a period of heightened political campaigns and a devastating famine could also lead to the same. Documents published by historian Xun Zhou show that while collectivization led to attacks on religion as a "feudal superstition," the years of "natural disasters" that followed led to a religious revival in parts of the countryside, as peasants—failed by Party policies and local cadres—turned instead to faith. Acts of resistance took on a religious cast, whether it was the True Jesus Church praying for miracles or a millenarian revolt against local authorities. In the wake of the Great Leap Forward, Christians in Yunnan continued to secretly attend church; Catholics in Sichuan prayed quietly, "Life is so hard these days, let's prepare our souls and wait on God"; and elsewhere in both provinces cadres reported a resurgence of supernatural healing and requests to the Dragon God for rain. In this final case, peasants in the Xichang region of Sichuan even criticized local officials for their failure to provide religious succor. "In the old days, the local governor would make offerings outside the local government office to ask for rain. Nowadays the county heads do nothing."[84]

But in other instances officials *did* stand with the people, and one subtext in the reports on superstition was discomfort that the state's own agents—the cadres who appeared at the Shanghai City God Temple or the Young Pioneers interviewed for the exhibition—were believers. In the 1953 Xinjing holy water case, *Neibu cankao* reported, those who rushed to the site carrying bottles to fill with holy water included Party members, Youth League members, and cadres.[85] Cadres in Shanghai and elsewhere went to

[83] "Shanghaishi mixinpin xiaolu dazeng" (The Shanghai market for superstitious products increases greatly), *Neibu cankao*, January 29, 1957; "Jinnian Shanghaishi mixinpin he shouyi shoucai xiaolu dazeng" (This year the Shanghai market for superstitious products, funeral clothing, and coffins increases greatly), *Neibu cankao*, October 25, 1957.
[84] Xun Zhou, ed., *The Great Famine in China, 1958–1962: A Documentary History* (New Haven: Yale University Press, 2012), pp. 90–113.
[85] "Jiangsu gedi liuchuanzhe qu xianshui zhi baibing de mixin fengqi" (The superstitious practice of collecting holy water to cure all ills circulates in Jiangsu), *Neibu cankao*, May 26, 1953.

the City God Temple with their families and they even held elaborate funerals for their parents, drawing criticism for hypocrisy—"Party members also speak of superstition!"[86] After the early 1960s famine, when the economy took a turn for the better, some officials allowed or even joined in offerings for thanks. In 1962, production teams near Nanjing built altars and held religious festivals to pray for a plentiful harvest.[87] Later that year, peasants in villages in Guangdong Province pooled money to renovate temples and to build altars, communes took up collections to make offerings after a good harvest, and hundreds of people crossed county and commune lines to sweep their ancestral graves. Though some cadres did try to prevent such superstitious behavior, the masses insisted that they had "freedom of belief and there should be no interference." In one commune, both cadres and the masses attributed the successful harvest to the blessings of the gods.[88]

Why did anti-superstition campaigns, whether aimed at practice or belief, make such little headway? In a recent interview, a retired PSB officer in Shanghai (b. 1942) explained, "The old-hundred-names have had these beliefs for several thousand years! From the state's point of view, even if they wanted to eliminate them, they wouldn't be able to do so. These ideas were just in people's heads. Individuals could believe what they wanted."[89] Beliefs persisted and were much more complex than propaganda defined them to be. In the summer of 1963, the year of the Love Science and Eliminate Superstition Exhibition, one report from Jilin Province showed peasants scoffing at the bluntness of the official attacks. Forced to dig up their small temples and smash their own gods, the masses—"discontented"—replied by saying, "You go ahead and root them out. After you root them out, we'll rebuild them." This case was taken as an example of officials "not understanding the complexity of the

[86] "Beijingshi caiqu cuoshi zhizhi binzang de mixin huodong" (Beijing Municipality adopts measures to stop superstitious practices during funerals), *Neibu cankao*, December 10, 1963. As a way of preventing such funerals, the Beijing Municipal Government created a funeral services company. The PSB was mobilized to address the so-called fake monks who were making money from funerals. The subsequent Five Antis Campaign also included anti-superstition propaganda. Finally, if people could not be persuaded to cremate bodies, the prices of coffins and graves would be increased.
[87] "Youxie gongshe chuxian gezhong mixin huodong" (Superstitious activities appear in some communes), *Neibu cankao*, January 24, 1962. It was reported that there were 66 instances of "worshiping and rituals," 168 examples of Daoists blessing houses in communes, and the building of 213 altars.
[88] "Nongcun mixin huodong de fazhan yinxiang shengchan he shehui zhi'an" (The development of superstitious activities in the countryside influences production and social order), *Neibu cankao*, December 25, 1962.
[89] Interview in Shanghai, July 21, 2013.

situation."[90] Perhaps it was such defiance that prompted the Socialist Education Movement to attack superstition, constricting temple life and intensifying propaganda.

In the end, the text of the Love Science and Eliminate Superstition Exhibition may also provide clues into why the anti-superstition rhetoric failed. The exhibition, reflecting anti-superstition propaganda as a whole, created a *category* of superstition that was in opposition to science. Its narrative taught a new history and a new vocabulary, but "superstitious thinking" was merely replaced with an ideology of and faith in science, one that resulted in the use of science as a set of facts or principles, not as a form of questioning. Furthermore, though curators proposed the use of material evidence, the vast majority of the exhibition ended up being texts written on display boards; unlike a health exhibit that could show bacteria under a microscope, it was much harder to show the absence of the supernatural. It is little wonder that the administrators, teachers, and teaching assistants whom the Science and Technology Education Station surveyed remained at a loss. "Some teachers," its report explained, "feel that education about atheism is very hard to carry out, that there are some questions that even they as science educators cannot explain, and that their persuasive powers are weak. Therefore, they dare not take initiative in this work."[91] While the text of the exhibition was in the form of questions and answers, there is little indication that students themselves posed questions on site. But surely they did so back at school, and their teachers did not always know how to reply.

By making science and superstition opposites, the exhibition made them mutually exclusive: because there is an atmosphere, there is no heaven. And yet, just as religion in China was traditionally syncretic, so too was it possible to hold on to more than one idea without their being in conflict. Reports from this period about Youth League members who were also Christians show how some people could assimilate their religious views with the new political ideologies of the state. In a 1963 *Neibu cankao* article on Catholic counties in Sichuan, one Catholic Youth League member, Zhou Yuanying, explained: "Joining the Youth League is to struggle for communism, and embracing religion is to save one's soul after death; so I heed the words of the Party and the words of the Church." Another leader in the Youth League, Li Yuying, concurred: "Believing in Catholicism can keep you from doing bad things. Belief isn't

---

[90] "Zhizhi fengjian mixin huodong buneng caiqu jiandan jizao fangfa" (Stopping feudal superstitious activities cannot depend on simple or hurried methods), *Neibu cankao*, August 15, 1963.

[91] SMA C27-1-51, p. 155.

superstition."[92] Young Pioneers in the city of Tianjin, where church attendance by youth increased, saw no conflict between their religion and Chairman Mao. "Chairman Mao teaches people to study hard, God also makes people study hard," "Chairman Mao cares about our progress, and God also cares about our progress," and "God and Chairman Mao care about me in the same way."[93] For those children less inclined to see the world—known and unknown—in the black-and-white terms of the exhibition, science might have been simply an additional way of believing.

Finally, the kind of propaganda presented in "Love Science, Eliminate Superstition" was not wholly effective because it failed to recognize that one of the reasons for maintaining belief was to appeal to a power higher than the Communist Party, which had failed the people in so many ways. Beginning with the 1953 Xinjing holy water case in the Shanghai countryside, the appearance of superstitious behavior was coterminous with a critique of the state. As Stephen Smith has described, cadres reported peasants stating that they could not afford medical care and therefore they relied upon the sacred water.[94] What Smith does not mention is that the comments also included biting criticism of local cadres and the People's Government, so much so that when the comments passed through the bureaucracy, they were blackened out and eliminated from the record.[95] People continued their religious practices throughout the Mao period because belief was a way to understand the world around them—by offering thanks in 1956 at Shanghai's City God Temple when salaries increased and by burning incense in the countryside when there was a good harvest. In the wake of the devastation that followed the Great Leap Forward, both local officials and local people made offerings. Ironically, the Great Leap Forward was based on a "science" of political

---

[92] "Youxie diqu zongjiao dui qingshaonian de duhai hen shen" (Religion exerts a profound poisonous influence on youth in certain areas), *Neibu cankao*, March 8, 1963. This is a study of Guangyuan, Meishan, Xinfan, and other counties in Sichuan, where there was a high percentage of Catholics. At Rongshan Commune in Guangyuan County, over 83 percent of those under the age of twenty-five regularly participated in Catholic activities, including reading the Bible twice daily with their parents, reciting verses, and singing songs. Among the Youth League members in Hebao Commune, Rongchang County, twenty of the twenty-three members participated in Catholic activities.

[93] "Tianzhujiao yong gezhong yinmou guiji women zhengduo shaonian ertong" (Catholicism uses various schemes to win over our youth), *Neibu cankao*, May 28, 1963.

[94] Smith, "Local Cadres Confront the Supernatural," pp. 148–149.

[95] SMA A22-2-137, p. 60. Before digitization, these comments could be read by holding the documents up to the light. They include accusations of cadres protecting the financial interests of the People's Hospital and of cadres doing nothing but bullying and humiliating the working people. In the end, the pilgrims accused the People's Government of bureaucratism, threatened to withhold their grain taxes, and burned incense as they cursed the cadres.

ideology, on the idea that human revolutionary will would translate into agricultural bounty. People were taught, in this campaign as in others, to have faith in the Communist Party and its policies. In the catastrophic failure of the Great Leap Forward, both its "scientific" and political ideologies were discredited and—exactly as "Love Science and Eliminate Superstition" explained—people reached for religion to make sense of what the state had deemed to be a "natural" disaster.[96] Even though little Luo Genmei was probably too young and too urban to understand her grandmother's visions, it is quite possible that Grandma Luo dreamed of her village temple god because she was reluctant to return to a place where she had seen too many hungry ghosts.

Conclusion: The legacy of superstition versus science

After Mao's death and the end of the Cultural Revolution, to the consternation of officials in Nanshi District, believers began to reappear outside of the locked City God Temple gates. They had been coming for Spring Festival since the early 1980s, and since the temple gates would not admit them they burned their incense outside. Numbers rose yearly, and by 1993 Nanshi District reported that some 3,000–4,000 people gathered to make offerings.[97] Though this reportage did not differentiate between the old and the young, other internal documents from the mid-1980s show an increase in religiosity among youth. In 1986 there purportedly was a growing number of young Buddhists in Shanghai, about 20,000–25,000, with an additional 30,000 youths demonstrating some kind of "religious consciousness." Of the over 40,000 people who went to the Jade Buddha Temple on the first of the first month of the lunar year, young people made up some 54 percent. "Not since Liberation," wrote Xinhua News Agency, "has there been this phenomenon." In the early reform years, these youth—born only slightly after the Young Pioneers from 1963—sought out religion in an era of bewildering change: they felt that the work unit only functioned to administer their lives and that the

---

[96] On recent reflections of scientists on the Great Leap, see Shapiro, *Mao's War Against Nature*. On other reasons for the failure of the state during the Mao era to control religion, see Xiaoxuan Wang, "The Dilemma of Implementation: The State and Religion in the People's Republic of China, 1949–1990," in *Maoism at the Grassroots: Everyday Life in China's Era of High Socialism*, edited by Jeremy Brown and Matthew D. Johnson (Cambridge, MA: Harvard University Press, 2015), pp. 259–278. In studying Rui'an in Zhejiang Province, Xiaoxuan Wang argues that the lack of control was the result of "inconsistent commands" and "the instability and indeterminacy of discourses and categories pertaining to religious policies," pp. 260–261.
[97] HPDA N92-1-637, p. 14.

Party only cared about them in terms of collecting taxes, and said they followed Buddhism to be honest and good people.[98]

Yet despite the reappearance and resurgence of religious faith and practice, it took several more years and both external and internal pressures to restore religious sites to Shanghai's landscape. In 1986 Queen Elizabeth II visited Shanghai and toured the still-closed City God Temple. Her remark about "a temple without gods" was appropriated by both the Shanghai Daoist Association and the Shanghai Bureau of Religious Affairs to argue for the temple's reopening.[99] However, it was not until 1991 that a battle between *Jiefang ribao*, Shanghai's Party newspaper, and local Daoists precipitated the return of the City God Temple. On April 19, 1991 a *Jiefang ribao* editorial used the language of superstition to argue that the City God Temple needed no renewal. "As for other temples," it wrote, "there are some that have cultural value and there are some that are historic sites of religion, but the City God Temple is neither Buddhist nor Daoist. It is only a symbol of the power of the netherworld."[100] The editorial caused a furor in Daoist circles, with the Daoist Association receiving phone calls and letters, a letter-writing campaign to other Daoist associations in China, and finally support from the National Daoist Association that included a protest letter to *Jiefang ribao*. Abbot Chen Liansheng, head of Shanghai's Daoist Association and a member of the Shanghai People's Political Consultative Conference, issued a report declaring the editorial an affront to all religion.[101] On May 3, *Jiefang ribao* finally retracted, apologizing for maligning a "religious and cultural site."[102] In 1992 the Nanshi People's Government recommended its return and in 1994 the site was officially restored as a temple.[103]

But despite a restoration of the legitimacy of religion, an official discourse on superstition remains. Since the Mao era, anti-superstition handbooks have persisted. Insofar as the Love Science and Eliminate Superstition Exhibition reflected contemporary anti-superstition handbooks and indeed—following museological practice—was meant to be a "book," other anti-superstition handbooks reveal how over time, each

---

[98] *Neican xuanbian* (Selections from internal reference), no. 32 (1986), pp. 10–11. The article does not strictly define youth but states that young Buddhists were primarily between the ages of 25 and 30.

[99] HPDA N92-1-637, p. 14.

[100] "Fu si?" (Restore the temple?), *Jiefang ribao* (Liberation daily), April 19, 1991, p. 1.

[101] "Shanghaishi daojiao xiehui di'erjie di'erci lishihui jueyi" (Resolution of the board of directors of the Shanghai Municipality Daoist Association at the second meeting of the second session), *Shanghai daojiao* (Daoism in Shanghai), no. 2 (1991), pp. 1–2.

[102] "Fusi weichang buke" (It is possible to restore the temple), *Jiefang ribao*, May 3, 1991, p. 3.

[103] *SHWWBWGZ*, p. 177; HPDA N92-1-637, pp. 16–20.

text served as an argument against superstition vis-à-vis the state's contemporary project. Thus a 1950 anti-superstition handbook published by the Health Department of the Northeast People's Government presented an argument against superstition and in support of modern public health.[104] The anti-superstition handbooks from the 1960s, as this chapter has shown, were against superstition and for science, against class oppression and for revolution. Then, in the wake of the Cultural Revolution, it was the Gang of Four who stood accused of "modern superstition," a departure from Marxism-Leninism-Mao Zedong Thought, which was regarded as the true science.[105] Today, anti-superstition handbooks continue to teach the same lessons about whether there are gods and what causes eclipses. There are, however, new superstitions: the computer—once the antidote to fortune-telling in the exhibition—is now a source of "scientific" fortune-telling, and the most dangerous superstition lies in the *qigong* practice of Falungong. The state's response to Falungong, not unlike its Mao-era treatment of redemptive societies like Yiguandao, has been to label it a heretical cult. There are still anti-superstition exhibitions in China, and the heavy presence of police in the photographs of the anti-Falungong exhibits suggests that an anti-superstition display continues to be as much for the state's agents as it is for its people.[106] The anti-superstition exhibition remains a way for a state in power to define orthodoxy and heterodoxy, in politics as in science.

"Love Science and Eliminate Superstition," an exhibition's narrative text, provides a snapshot of what people continued to believe during the Mao period. China never went as far as the Soviet Union, whose League of the Militant Godless created more than forty anti-religious museums from former churches by 1930.[107] Rather, the Communist Party officially

[104] Dongbei renmin zhengfu weishengbu (Health Department of the Northeast People's Government), ed., *Dapo mixin* (Smash superstition), September 1950.
[105] *Pochu Lin Biao "Sirenbang" de xiandai mixin* (Eliminate the modern superstition of Lin Biao and the "Gang of Four") (Beijing: Renmin chubanshe, 1978).
[106] Jian Ping, Shao Zhen, and Dong Hui, "Rang kexue de guanghui qusan 'yinmai'" (Let science's glory dispel the "haze"), *Dangjian zazhi*, no. 5 (2000), pp. 37–38. Here, Falungong is a modern superstition (*xiandai mixin*). Falungong also features in a contemporary scholarly analysis: Huang Longbao and Yan Xiaofeng, eds., *Zhongguo lidai fandui mixin zongheng tan* (A survey of opposition to superstition in Chinese history) (Beijing: Xuexi chubanshe, 1999), p. 9.
[107] Adam Jolles, "Stalin's Talking Museums," *Oxford Art Journal*, vol. 28, no. 3 (October 2005), p. 432. Smith also makes the point that although the Nationalist government closed temples (except the officially approved Confucian temples) and major temples were turned into museums during the PRC period, "none of these museums were anti-religious museums of the Soviet type." S. A. Smith, "Contentious Heritage: The Preservation of Churches and Temples in Communist and Post-Communist Russia and China," *Past and Present*, vol. 226, supplement 10 (2015), pp. 194, 196.

permitted religion, attacking instead superstitions as the antithesis of science, a weapon of the class enemy, and a threat to the revolution. However, the tenuous line between religion and superstition—as evinced both by the exhibition and by the organizers' analyses of student beliefs— did not bode well for the political campaigns to come. Only a few years later, the same generation of children who were subject to the anti-superstition campaign would be the Red Guards who conflated all old things as excrescences on the revolution. Then their new faith, and the lessons they had come to repeat so well, were turned upon class enemies whom they submitted to struggle. The identification of such class enemies was also articulated in a new genre of exhibition that preceded the Cultural Revolution: the class education exhibition, or *jiezhan*. In such exhibits, examined in the following chapter, the likes of Grandma Luo's landlord, Shanghai's Bishop Gong, and Yao Jin—the counterrevolution-ary saboteur—were all made to join hands. Through display—rather than dreams—the ghosts of class enemies came to live in China's midst.

4　Cultivating consciousness: The class education exhibition

Li Hongyan was skeptical. Returning home from an *yiku sitian* exhibition with his classmates from Shanghai East Middle School, he asked his father, Li Jinhong, "Were the workers' lives *really* so bitter before Liberation?" Stunned into silence, Li Jinhong reached into the cupboard and produced several objects: an old employment contract, his worker's identity card, and a uniform covered with oil. Using these props, he told of a life like that of "cattle and horses," explaining how he worked from five in the morning until nine at night, how his daily rice was filled with gravel, and how he always feared losing his job. Then it was the son's turn to be wordless, as tears sprang to his eyes. Thus Li Hongyan's 1964 class trip for "recalling bitterness and reflecting on sweetness," like a visit to Fangua Lane, had its desired effect. Though born "under the red flag," Li Hongyan nonetheless came to understand the importance of his family's working-class origins. His prize-winning essay, entitled "I Must Remember the Employment Contract," was retold on two occasions; it first appeared as a story in Shanghai's *Wenhui bao*, and then it was part of his own school's exhibition, on display with three gifts from his father: the identity card, the uniform, and a set of the *Selected Works of Mao Zedong*.[1]

Representing the ideal reception of a propaganda message, the transformation of Li Hongyan's consciousness was echoed in the model opera *On the Docks*, which premiered in the following year under the direction of composer Yu Huiyong.[2] In Act Six, the young Shanghai dockworker Han Xiaoqiang stands in an exhibition hall, holds a worker's identity card in his hands, and sings of revolutionary awakening.[3] This exhibition is

---

[1] "Xianshen shuofa, jiaoyu ernü jizhu guoqu nanku, yishen zuoze, peiyang haizi jianku pusu zuofeng" (Use your experience as an example and educate sons and daughters to remember past bitterness, set an example and cultivate hard work and plain living), *Wenhui bao* (Wenhui daily), January 4, 1964, p. 2.

[2] Yawen Ludden, "Making Politics Serve Music: Yu Huiyong, Composer and Minister of Culture," *TDR: The Drama Review*, vol. 56, no. 2 (Summer 2012) (T214), p. 157.

[3] Shanghai jingjutuan "Haigang" juzu ("On the Docks" crew of the Shanghai Opera Troupe), ed., *Haigang* (On the docks) (Beijing: Renmin wenxue chubanshe, 1974), pp. 48–58, 167–209.

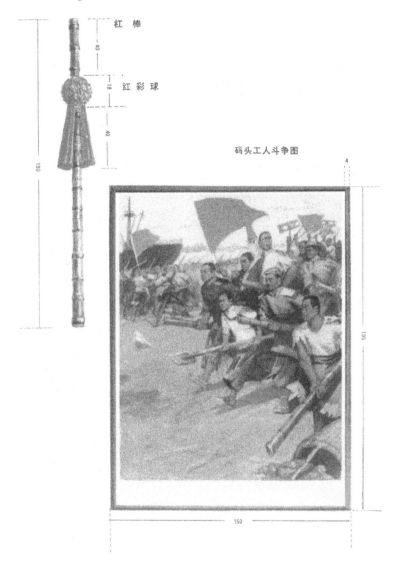

杠 棒

红 彩 球

码头工人斗争图

Ill.4.1. Prop design for the class education exhibition, *Haigang* (On the docks), 1974 (p. 324)

a class education exhibition, a genre of display that originated during the Socialist Education Movement (1962–1966) and that was mounted by all units, from the village to the city, from the school to the factory. With art imitating life, the staging directions for *On the Docks* include an

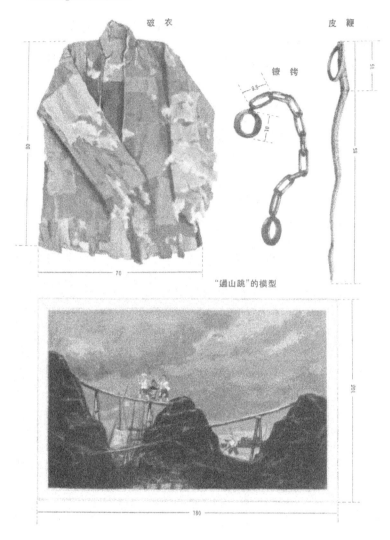

破 衣   皮 鞭

镣 铐

"遍山跳"的模型

Ill.4.2. Prop design for the class education exhibition, *Haigang* (On the docks), 1974 (p. 325)

illustration of the set which shows the items to be displayed: a diorama of workers' lives in the old society; a bamboo pole used in an uprising; a tattered jacket, chains and leather whip; a Mao quotation, "Carry out the revolution to the end!"; and an oil painting of the dockworkers' struggle. For the fictional Han Xiaoqiang and the real Li Hongyan, the

Ill.4.3. Scene from *Shouzuyuan* (Rent Collection Courtyard), 2016. Photo by the author

exhibition was a site where a young man doubts, is shown real artifacts and told a bitter tale, is moved to tears, and ultimately pledges his resolve to follow Chairman Mao. It is objects—the worker's identity card, the employment contract—and the stories they represent that create class consciousness.

The class education exhibition as a genre drew on the techniques used in preceding displays. Intended for the masses, such exhibitions were didactic and visits were ritualistic; the *jiezhan* was deemed a classroom for class education. Involving the masses in curation, incorporating the familiar routine of *yiku sitian*, and using objects as lessons, the class education exhibition fulfilled the requirement that propaganda be "living." Like the omnipresent history displays that sprang up during the Great Leap Forward, the genre was intensely local. The most famous class education exhibition was Sichuan's *Rent Collection Courtyard* (Shouzuyuan), which turned the Anren Township home of the landlord Liu Wencai into a showcase of the horrors of the old society, complete with a life-size series of sculptures depicting the extraction of rent from peasants.[4] But though the *jiezhan* had roots in earlier exhibitionary culture and shared many of its themes, it was specifically developed to accompany the Socialist Education Movement and with it, a heightened emphasis on class struggle. A study of the class education exhibition is thus a way to understand how the ideology of class was presented at the grassroots and on the eve of the Cultural Revolution.

This chapter first describes the Socialist Education Movement and what scholars have described as the late Mao revival of class, providing the background for the class education exhibitions. Then, it turns to class education and the ways in which teachers incorporated the ideology of class into all aspects of pedagogy, from inviting old workers to tell their stories to participatory propaganda in which students conducted interviews from which they mounted and narrated exhibitions of their own. Under the Socialist Education Movement, *jiezhan* were organized and used to propagate Mao's interpretation of class and class struggle. Taking as an example the Shanghai Class Education Exhibition (1965–1966), this chapter traces its curation and presentation, its focus on capitalism and its arguments against the idea of "peaceful evolution," or the specter of revisionism over the socialist road. In these ways, the display accompanied the nationwide Socialist Education Movement, interpreting it with local examples and giving visitors a template for understanding its development. Finally, the chapter considers the response to the exhibition, which included attacks by Red Guards who combed through its records and wrote their own critiques. To those involved in the Shanghai *jiezhan*—from leaders like Shanghai Party Secretary Chen Pixian and Gang of Four member Zhang Chunqiao to capitalist visitors to Red Guards—the exhibit articulated an ideology of class in a preface to the Cultural Revolution's class struggle.

The Socialist Education Movement, class education, and the class education exhibition

The Socialist Education Movement is often seen as a precursor to the Cultural Revolution. Richard Kraus dates Mao's revival of class rhetoric to 1962, when Mao "placed the class issue squarely on the agenda of the Party."[5] At the 1962 Tenth Plenum of the Eighth Central Committee, Mao stated,

---

[4] Denise Y. Ho and Jie Li, "From Landlord Manor to Red Memorabilia: Reincarnations of a Chinese Museum Town," *Modern China*, vol. 42, no. 1 (2016), pp. 3–37.
[5] Richard Curt Kraus, *Class Conflict in Chinese Socialism* (New York: Columbia University Press, 1981), p. 78.

Now then, do classes exist in socialist countries? Does class struggle exist? We can now affirm that classes do exist in socialist countries and that class struggle undoubtedly exists ... In our country we must come to grasp, understand, and study this problem really thoroughly. We must acknowledge that classes will continue to exist for a long time. We must also acknowledge the existence of a struggle of class against class, and admit the possibility of the restoration of reactionary classes. We must raise our vigilance and properly educate our youth as well as the cadres, the masses, and the middle and basic level cadres.[6]

In this speech Mao articulated two aspects of a class ideology that would form the core of class education and its exhibitions. First, class continued to exist in socialism. Before 1949, class was defined by one's relationship to property, and even though the 1950s saw the collectivization of agriculture and the socialist transformation of industry, class labels remained and continued to be used to determine one's status. Second, class struggle persisted in New China and class enemies threatened to make a comeback, restoring capitalism and returning to their former positions. The ideology of class also had a third component, defining class enemies not only as those bearing negative class labels, like landlord or capitalist, but also those among the new elite of Communist China's bureaucracy whose status came from their power. Yiching Wu points out that the old and the new criteria for class "coalesced within a common political framework," and in the imagined alliance between old and new class enemies lay many of the "fateful consequences for the mass politics of the Cultural Revolution."[7]

It was the Socialist Education Movement, whose origins Richard Baum traces to the Tenth Plenum, that articulated the threat of revisionism from those holding power.[8] The movement, called the "Four Cleanups" (*siqing*) in the countryside and sometimes the "Five Antis" (*wufan*) in the cities, was at base a rectification movement targeting local and grassroots cadres.[9] The scope of the Socialist Education Movement was at once

---

[6] Ibid., p. 79; Stuart R. Schram, ed., *Chairman Mao Talks to the People: Talks and Letters, 1956–1971* (New York: Pantheon, 1974), p. 189.

[7] Yiching Wu, *The Cultural Revolution at the Margins: Chinese Socialism in Crisis* (Cambridge, MA: Harvard University Press, 2014), pp. 46–50.

[8] Richard Baum places the origins of the Socialist Education Movement at the Tenth Plenum in September 1962, whereas Roderick MacFarquhar notes that there was no mention of the movement during the plenum, though before the end of 1962 Fujian, Heilongjiang, Shandong, and Sichuan had already seen "measures ... to remedy such misbehavior [as corruption] and to re-indoctrinate the peasants with socialist ideals in line with the decisions of the 10th plenum." Richard Baum, *Prelude to Revolution: Mao, the Party, and the Peasant Question, 1962–66* (New York: Columbia University Press, 1975), p. 1; Roderick MacFarquhar, *The Origins of the Cultural Revolution Vol. 3: The Coming of the Cataclysm, 1961–1966* (Oxford: Oxford University Press, 1997), pp. 334–335.

[9] See, for example, Anita Chan, Richard Madsen, and Jonathan Unger, *Chen Village: The Recent History of a Peasant Community in Mao's China* (Berkeley: University of

specific and broadly ideological: it targeted particular kinds of cadre corruption—unclean work styles—while also attributing the reemergence of individual farming in the wake of the Great Leap to the erosion of socialism. Roderick MacFarquhar suggests that it was "as harsh as previous rural campaigns," and that attempts to revise its directives only succeeded in producing more violence.[10] In its later stages, Baum estimates that between 1.25 and 2.5 million basic-level cadres were purged, making it possibly the "most intensive purge of rural Party members and cadres in the history of the Chinese People's Republic."[11] With the issuance of the Twenty-three Articles in 1965, the final major directive of the Socialist Education Movement, its goals were redefined to be the resolution of the contradiction between the proletariat and the bourgeoisie and the struggle between socialism and capitalism.[12]

Although the Socialist Education Movement ostensibly focused on official corruption, it resulted in attacks on both old and new class enemies. Jeremy Brown points out that one of the most important parts of the movement in the countryside was the examination and reassignment of class labels. Referred to as the "cleansing of class status," the policy beginning in 1964 was to investigate every rural Chinese family and reclassify it accordingly. Though class status could be improved, it could also become less favorable, resulting in deep social instability as well as outright attacks on former landlords and rich peasants.[13] Everywhere the Socialist Education Movement manifested itself as a heightened and intensified propaganda of class. For example, as Shanghai's Five Antis Campaign unfolded in 1963, the Shanghai Party Committee explained that its primary objectives were to "carry out class education, engage in comparing the past and the present, arouse class feeling (*jieji ganqing*), and stimulate consciousness." In reference to the Five Antis Campaign in the factories, the Shanghai Party Committee suggested meetings for speaking bitterness and singled out class education exhibitions or *yiku sitian* exhibitions as "battlefields for propaganda."[14] In this atmosphere, it

California Press, 1984); Ezra F. Vogel, *Canton Under Communism: Programs and Policies in a Provincial Capital, 1949–1968* (Cambridge, MA: Harvard University Press, 1969). Note that this is different from the earlier Five Antis.

[10] MacFarquhar, *Origins*, pp. 343–346.   [11] Baum, *Prelude*, pp. 104–105.

[12] Richard Baum and Frederick C. Teiwes, *Ssu-Ch'ing: The Socialist Education Movement of 1962–1966* (Berkeley: Center for Chinese Studies, University of California, 1968), pp. 35, 118–126.

[13] See Jeremy Brown, "Moving Targets: Changing Class Labels in Rural Hebei and Henan, 1960–1979," in *Maoism at the Grassroots: Everyday Life in China's Era of High Socialism*, edited by Jeremy Brown and Matthew D. Johnson (Cambridge, MA: Harvard University Press, 2015), pp. 51–76. See also Wu, *The Cultural Revolution at the Margins*, p. 49.

[14] "Shanghaishi gongchang qiye da jiang jieji douzheng xingshi, renren canjia huiyi duibi" (Shanghai Municipality's factories and industries speak of class struggle, everyone

is likely that worker Li Jinhong—the father who used his employment contract to *yiku sitian* with his son—had already experienced the campaign in his factory.

What kind of class education was the son, Li Hongyan, experiencing at school? The pages of the periodical *Shanghai jiaoyu* (Shanghai education) from 1963 show how class education was emphasized concurrent with the Socialist Education Movement.[15] Some of these articles were reproduced in a book entitled *Jiaqiang dui qingshaonian de jieji jiaoyu* (Strengthen class education for youth), published in the same year. Written by representatives of the Communist Youth League and various middle schools—from the elite (Fuxing Middle School) to county schools for peasants' children (Number Two School of Songjiang County)—the book's essays highlight the necessity to train revolutionary successors.[16] Pan Wenzheng of Shanghai's Communist Youth League, for example, stressed that knowledge of communism must be taught, that students "must be made to understand what class is, what exploitation is, what class struggle is, and what capitalism is."[17] Shanghai teachers sounded the alarm that even children of workers did not know about their parents' past suffering, that their lives were so rich with consumer goods that they only focused on enjoyment, and that students lacked a "proletarian standpoint." Two teachers, Xi Eryin and Pan Shunlin of Kongjiang Middle School, suggested that students be directed to examine the physical changes around them: Which of the factories and schools were newly built? Which roads were freshly paved? How many students' families had moved into workers' new villages? By asking and answering such questions about material improvements, Xi and Pan wrote, students could be "taught to trust the Party's correct leadership and the superiority of the socialist system."[18]

In order to cultivate a proletarian standpoint, Pan Wenzheng of the Communist Youth League argued that class education should not come only from Youth League activities. Rather, it should infuse everything—from classes on politics to participation in labor, from singing revolutionary songs to celebrating revolutionary holidays—"these activities should all come together to form a system."[19] In this totalizing system of "living

participates in comparing past and present), *Neibu cankao* (Internal reference), August 20, 1963.

[15] See *Shanghai jiaoyu* (Shanghai education), no. 4 (1963), pp. 3–6; no. 5 (1963), p. 20; no. 6 (1963) pp. 9–12. Similar articles on thought education, living thought education, class education, Mao Zedong Thought, proletarian class thinking, and class consciousness fill subsequent issues through 1965. Publication ceased during the Cultural Revolution.

[16] *Jiaqiang dui qingshaonian de jieji jiaoyu* (Strengthen class education among the youth) (Shanghai: Shanghai jiaoyu chubanshe, 1963).

[17] Ibid., pp. 6–10.   [18] Ibid., pp. 15–16.   [19] Ibid., pp. 6–10.

class education," students were taught to see class all around them and class embodied in people. Of many examples, two from Fuxing Middle School stand out. On a trip to engage in labor in Hongkou Park, Fuxing Middle School students unearthed golf balls. Workers at the park explained that they were left over from a game once played by foreigners: "When the foreigners played with such balls, they hired Chinese children to pick them up. If the children lost the balls, the foreigners beat them." In a second example, Teacher Xu Yun told her own bitterness tale, describing her life in the old society, first as a servant girl in a landlord's house and then as a worker in an orphanage. When she displayed her scars from being stabbed with an opium pipe, the students exclaimed, "I would never have imagined that her life was just like that of [the model opera character] the White-Haired Girl!" The lesson of the golf balls was to make Shanghai itself a classroom, where once "had been the fortress of the three great enemies and their counterrevolutionary rule," where Yong'an Department Store was a warehouse of imported luxuries, and where Sheshan Cathedral stood as a monument of imperialist invasion.[20] In the case of Teacher Xu, class education made individuals and their scars evidence for the old society and its cruelties. People could thus also be material.

Living class education required active student participation. Interviews with Shanghai informants who were children during this era suggest that *yiku sitian* left a strong imprint. A child (b. 1959) of two worker parents remembers going to a site to listen to poor or middle peasants. "They'd show us clothing covered with patches and tell us how we should be thankful for the new society. What did we think? We thought it was really honorable—tattered clothes meant that you were poor, and poor was good."[21] Most interviewees stressed that they never thought to challenge such stories, explaining that "everyone was innocent at that time, not like today," and that this was "just part of education." Only those with less ideal family histories might feel a flicker of doubt. Describing *yiku sitian* at a middle school, a historian (b. 1949) remembers shouting slogans, "Don't forget class bitterness! Remember blood-and-tears hatred! Never forget class struggle! ... But those of us who came from bad class backgrounds felt really nervous, very pressured, and we didn't dare say very much."[22] In interviews, the strongest memories were the descriptions of eating a bitterness meal, when the students as a group ate coarse buns or leaves mixed with flour. Though a few actually found their variation delicious—and described methods for improving the food by secretly

[20] Ibid., pp. 25–29, 42.   [21] Interview in Shanghai, July 3, 2013.
[22] Interview in Shanghai, July 2, 2013.

adding oil—many found it difficult to bear. A retired factory technician (b. 1944) explained that "You'd put it in your mouth and try to chew it, and then shift the wad from one side of your mouth to the other, really wanting to spit it out ... it was stuff only fit for pigs!"[23]

The highest level of living class education was to have students be active participants in propaganda. Hence a student could write an essay as Li Hongyan had, or even a play to be performed. Students, as Teachers Xi and Pan at Kongjiang Middle School suggested, could mount an exhibition and then become its docents. Teachers Xi and Pan argued that the advantage of an exhibition was that students would determine from interviews which materials were the most exemplary. They wrote that having to integrate individual stories required that the students see things in class terms.[24] One informant (b. 1949) from a workers' family recalled writing an essay,

In our thinking, only under the Communist Party did poor people stand up and become their own masters. There was even a song called "Listen to mother talk about the past," and this song was really, really beautiful. When we were little, if we imagined the old society, of course it was evil. Because of the lessons at school, I would ask my father what the old society was like when he was an apprentice during the Japanese Occupation. And then (starting to laugh), I had to write an essay for school, an *yiku sitian* essay, right? The teacher said we had to take our family histories and our lessons and tie them together. Anyway, when my father was doing his apprenticeship, he lost part of a finger ... so I asked him how it hurt and how he had to go to the hospital ... and then I had the material for an essay! So I went back to school to tell the story of the evil old society ... with my father's hand! (Laughing) Now for many things, there was some truth to them. The teacher came up with a topic and you had to think about it, right? And you'd think, well of course it was like that because the boss was so evil ... you'd add a little more evil to it, because they didn't fix the machines properly. Then I'd embroider it a little more, and say the boss didn't fix them because he wanted to exploit the working classes, to make more money, to use the workers' blood and sweat. I'd add in all of these things. This is what we all did ... and as long as we followed these lines, we could never go wrong.[25]

From one father's employment contract to another's lost fingertip, from the dockyards to the department store toured by Fuxing Middle School students, living class education taught that objects, bodies, and landscapes were embodiments of class.

Class education in schools was part of the heightened class rhetoric at large, and it also responded to the perceptions of discontent among youth. In *Jiaqiang dui qingshaonian de jieji jiaoyu*, the essays broadly refer to

[23] Interview in Shanghai, July 20, 2013.
[24] *Jiaqiang dui qingshaonian de jieji jiaoyu*, p. 14.   [25] Interview in Shanghai, July 9, 2013.

Shanghai students' ignorance of the past and discontent in the present. In a few instances, the teachers revealed that their students had been influenced by the aftermath of the Great Leap Forward, which had resulted in famine in the countryside and privation in the cities. Yang Shichang of Fuxing Middle School explained that his students had no experience of "serious natural disasters" and had to understand that their current hardships were not comparable to those of "working-class families torn asunder in the past." Teachers Xi and Pan also referred to the Great Leap Forward famine as "successive years of natural disasters," describing their students' "confused understanding," selfishly thinking first of their own or their families' interests, without realizing that the Party's policies "represented the most basic interests of the working people."[26] Classified reports from 1963–1964 registered the discontent among Shanghai youth, the "capitalist elements" that had influenced them, and their unwillingness to make personal sacrifices for socialist construction.[27] But with class education, declared Teachers Xi and Pan, students would become selfless, and even happy to be sent to far-away Xinjiang Province.[28]

Similar accounts of "confused understanding" had appeared early in 1961 in internal newsletters circulated by the Political Department of the PLA, where the practice of *yiku sitian* had begun. In the movement called "two remembrances and three investigations," soldiers engaged in what became the standard *yiku sitian* repertoire: telling bitterness at large meetings, comparing past and present by "settling accounts," eating bitterness meals, and receiving propaganda through books, films, and exhibitions. Notably, it was ordered that the "two remembrances and three investigations" *not* be carried out among soldiers whose families lived in areas with "serious natural disasters" or among those with a "relatively high percentage" of "unnatural deaths."[29] Among the various propaganda techniques, one Yi Qiuting suggested that letters from home should become object lessons. Acknowledging that it was through such letters that soldiers learned about conditions in the countryside, he

---

[26] *Jiaqiang dui qingshaonian de jieji jiaoyu*, pp. 15–16, 26.

[27] See *Neibu cankao*, March 22, 1963, May 12, 1964, and July 22, 1964. Note that Shanghai still suffered food shortages, with one informant (b. 1957) reporting that his three sisters gave him their food, whereas they only ate carrot peels; another informant, a physical education teacher (b. 1942), explained that students often did not exercise so as to conserve energy. Interviews in Shanghai, July 20, 2013 and July 24, 2013.

[28] *Jiaqiang dui qingshaonian de jieji jiaoyu*, pp. 21–22.

[29] *Gongzuo tongxun* ([PLA] work bulletin), no. 4 (January 11, 1961), pp. 9–11. The PLA reported that there were still people with "opinions" who needed to be persuaded and who were not allowed to debate or to air their opinions. This bulletin was circulated within the armed forces, not unlike *Neibu cankao*.

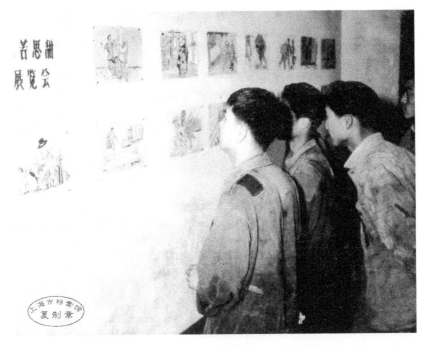

Ill.4.4. Workers at an *yiku sitian* exhibition, undated. SMA H1-23-24-8

praised the example of Unit 7352, which mounted an exhibit of twenty-four letters containing positive news in the company clubhouse. Other soldiers, whose letters included family difficulties or economic dissatisfaction, were encouraged to hand them over and to receive instructions on how to reply. Both personal family letters and the "letters from home exhibition," Yi declared, became "living teaching material."[30] Thus class education was a direct response to the famine. But soldiers were not the only ones with ties to the countryside: class education exhibitions for Shanghai factory workers also began in 1961, a similar response to the "temporary difficulties and inconveniences" and the "many new ideas" brought about by the "successive and serious natural disasters."[31]

By the time the Socialist Education Movement was underway, displays on the topic of class were in place everywhere. On International Workers' Day on May 1, 1963, the Shanghai Workers' Palace was bedecked with at least four exhibits: on class education, the model soldier

[30] *Gongzuo tongxun*, no. 17 (April 26, 1961), pp. 16–18.
[31] SMA C1-2-3596, pp. 46–53.

Lei Feng, the five-good industries, and the five-good workers.[32] The Shanghai Museum celebrated Spring Festival of 1964 by mounting an exhibition called "Comparing Shanghai Society Past and Present," which included a display of shantytown housing.[33] Senior Two students at Xikang Middle School interviewed residents in the former shantytown of Yaoshui Lane, and created a class education exhibition that used the interview material to accuse, with their own voices, the evil old society.[34] All over Shanghai, objects of the past were compared with the material improvements of the present, in propaganda and exhibitions both grass-roots and local.

The situation in Shanghai reflected class education throughout China. From 1963 to the outbreak of the Cultural Revolution in 1966, Party Committees created exhibitions in support of the Socialist Education Movement. The smallest localities mounted their own exhibits—perhaps immediately following a Socialist Education Movement struggle session—and higher levels culled and assembled artifacts from these displays to create large-scale municipal and provincial exhibitions.[35] The *Rent Collection Courtyard* exhibition in Sichuan's Anren Township is perhaps the most famous, but other localities were also elevated as examples. Tianjin's Santiaoshi History Museum, established during the Great Leap in 1958 and anointed with Zhou Enlai's calligraphy and a visit from Chen Boda in 1964, displayed Tianjin's working-class history.[36] In Gejiu, in Yunnan Province, the tin mines provided on-site class education and its example was reproduced in Yunnan's Provincial Class Education Exhibition Hall.[37]

The provincial exhibits were vast and sophisticated. The Shandong multi-media exhibit, which became a model, included movies and lantern

---

[32] "Qingzhu wuyi guoji laodongjie" (Celebrate May 1, International Workers' Day), *Wenhui bao*, April 29, 1963, p. 2.

[33] "Jinxi duibi qifa jieji ganqing" (Comparing past and present stimulates class feelings), *Wenhui bao*, February 16, 1964, p. 2.

[34] "Yi lilongshi dui shisheng jinxing jieji jiaoyu" (Use lane history to carry out class education for teachers and students), *Wenhui bao*, October 27, 1964, p. 1.

[35] Zhensheng Li's photography documents a May 1965 case in Ashihe Commune, Acheng County, Heilongjiang Province, in which a struggle session is followed by a denunciation, and then the personal property is turned into a class education exhibition. See Zhensheng Li, *Red-Color News Soldier* (New York: Phaedon Press, 2003), pp. 44–53.

[36] *Qianwan buyao wangji jieji douzheng: Tianjinshi Hongqiaoqu Santiaoshi lishi bowuguan/jieji jiaoyu zhanlan: Xueleishi bufen jianjie* (Never forget class struggle: History museum and class education exhibition of Santiaoshi, Hongqiao District of Tianjin Municipality: Introduction to a blood-and-tears history), n.d.

[37] *Qianwan buyao wangji jieji he jieji douzheng: Yunnansheng jieji jiaoyu zhanlanguan neirong jianjie* (Never forget class and class struggle: An introduction to Yunnan Province's Class Education Exhibition Hall), January 1966, p. 22.

slides.[38] Hunan's exhibition, covering 4,000 square meters, included 6,200 artifacts, 1,800 photographs, and 150 charts and sculptures. When it opened in the spring of 1964 in Changsha's Provincial Exhibition Hall to one thousand celebrants, as red flags surrounding the newly renovated building blew in the wind, Hunan Party Secretary Wang Yanchun declared the exhibit to be a "living textbook" that would provide "socialist education for cadres and the masses ... In China, there is currently serious, severe, and complicated class struggle. The exhibition's artifacts prove this truth: members of the counterrevolutionary ruling class, though toppled, are unwilling to be destroyed. They are always plotting their restoration." In exhibition halls, provincial museums, and Sino-Soviet Friendship Palaces, Party officials hung welcome banners and cut ribbons on displays that were, as Wang Yanchun argued, richer and of greater meaning than displays that had come before.[39]

The display of current class struggle did not preclude the exhibition of the past; indeed, portrayals of the old society's calumny made the threat of class restoration all the more visceral. Though class education exhibitions were particular to the location and varied accordingly, pamphlets and ephemera reveal that they all began with objects representing imperialists, capitalists, and landlords during the pre-Liberation class struggle. On imperialism, Wuhan provided object lessons using banknotes and stocks, while Yunnan curators included stories about the American Flying Tigers and foreign missionaries.[40] Capitalist exploitation was most often depicted in terms of documents of control: labor contracts, identification cards, and workers' passes. Several exhibitions used clocks as symbols of oppression, explaining how three minutes of tardiness on the "soul-stealing clock" would cost a worker his job.[41] Museum workers in Tianjin created a miniature "cannon-cabinet," or a central surveillance room in a factory which—like Bentham's panopticon—allowed managers

---

[38] *Shandongsheng jieji jiaoyu zhanlanhui huikan* (Proceedings of the Shandong provincial class education exhibition), October 1964, p. 5. For a description of the 1965 film on the exhibit, see Guo Wu, "Recalling Bitterness: Historiography, Memory, and Myth in Maoist China," *Twentieth-Century China*, vol. 39, no. 3 (October 2014), p. 259.

[39] *Hunansheng shehuizhuyi jieji jiaoyu zhanlanhui jianjie* (Introduction to Hunan Province's socialist class education exhibition), March 1964, pp. 1–2. Note Wang Yanchun's comparison is a 1952 exhibition on land reform. The largest exhibition in terms of area was thought to be in Henan, covering over 10,000 square meters. Among the provincial exhibitions, some thought that those in Shanxi and Hunan were the most successful because of the well-selected models and the best form; SMA C4-2-1, p. 76.

[40] *Wuhan shehuizhuyi jieji jiaoyu zhanlanhui huikan* (Proceedings of the Wuhan socialist class education exhibition), June 1, 1964, p. 1; *Qianwan buyao wangji jieji he jieji douzheng: Yunnansheng*, p. 2.

[41] *Qianwan buyao wangji jieji he jieji douzheng: Yunnansheng*, p. 21. Clocks also appeared in the Shandong exhibit; see *Shandongsheng jieji jiaoyu zhanlanhui huikan*, p. 17.

a four-sided view of the entrance, the shop floor, the storeroom, and even the toilet.[42] To illustrate the landlords, class education exhibitions included tools of oppression—from the physical (knives and guns) to the economic (threshing machines and pecks designed to extract extra grain).

In addition to displaying similar artifacts, these portrayals of the past shared at least three common curatorial techniques. The first was juxtaposition. Whereas Fangua Lane's display relied on comparing working-class lives in the past with those in the present, the class education exhibition juxtaposed the possessions of the rich and the poor *before* Liberation, drawing on the land reform definition of class as related to property and exploitation, and benefiting from the visual spectacle that such material comparison allowed. The second curatorial focus was an emphasis on the injured body. As Shanghai instructions on exhibitions in factories suggested, "the best material comes from old workers, old industrial workers with a real blood lineage, because on their bodies is concentrated the excellent character of our working classes."[43] Whether through photographs or actual specimens, a repeated technique in the class education exhibition was to use scars and crippled hands, organs and body parts preserved in jars, or skulls and skeletons, as witnesses to the old society's cruelty. Finally, the exhibition served as a site for the visitors' *yiku sitian*. The best measure of an exhibition's success, as reported in *Neibu cankao* (Internal reference), was for viewers to see themselves— sometimes literally—in the display, and for curation to prompt the telling of bitterness.[44]

But compared to curating past class struggle, with its standard narrative and familiar tropes, exhibiting contemporary class struggle proved less obvious. Apart from citing texts that affirmed its existence and linking old class enemies with new class enemies, how could a class education exhibition portray *hidden* enemies, and what artifacts might convey their desire to be restored? Some displays took the idea of class enemies quite literally. Jiangsu Province's exhibit, for example, portrayed Nationalist spies and Shandong's curators displayed piles of American weapons and military equipment.[45] Positive examples featured individuals ready for class

[42] *Qianwan buyao wangji jieji douzheng: Tianjinshi Hongqiaoqu Santiaoshi lishi bowuguan jieji jiaoyu zhanlan*, pp. 7–8. See Michel Foucault, *Discipline and Punish: The Birth of the Prison*, trans. by Alan Sheridan (New York: Vintage Books, 2nd ed., 1995), pp. 195–228.
[43] SMA C1-2-3596, p. 47.
[44] "Shandongsheng jieji jiaoyu zhanlanhui de tedian" (The special characteristics of the Shandong provincial class education exhibition), *Neibu cankao*, November 27, 1964. See also *Shandongsheng jieji jiaoyu zhanlanhui huikan*, pp. 30–31.
[45] *Jiangsusheng jieji jiaoyu zhanlanhui shuomingshu* (Guide to Jiangsu Province's class education exhibition), 1965, p. 6; *Shandongsheng jieji jiaoyu zhanlanhui huikan*, p. 8.

struggle; on display in Shandong were the three hand grenades and the broadsword of a sixty-seven-year-old in charge of security in his production brigade. Overlooking the problem of their utility in a glass case, the catalogue described how he pointed to the artifacts as his own, declaring, "When we take up [these weapons], it will fill the landlords, rich peasants, and bad eggs with fear!"[46] Some class education exhibitions illustrated contemporary class struggle by focusing on the types of activities that were first investigated during the Socialist Education Movement. Yunnan's display borrowed from the anti-superstition exhibitions, choosing to portray charlatans who spread counterrevolutionary rumors and made "celestial medicines," equating superstition with counterrevolution.[47] In Hunan and Jiangsu, the section on class struggle described private underground workshops and included dioramas with miniature scenes of cadre corruption.[48]

But the most emblematic objects of a hidden class enemy were those known as "*biantiantu*" or "*biantianzhang*," the maps and ledgers secretly saved for a "change in the sky." In the narratives of the class education exhibitions, past class enemies who had not reformed—landlords, rich peasants, counterrevolutionaries, and bad elements—preserved land deeds, loan receipts, rent registers, and property maps in anticipation of a restoration when they could reclaim their property and power. In the absence of the original documents, the display demonstrated, *biantianzhang* were etched into tiles and scrawled on rags, buried together with weapons and ammunition.[49] In the *biantianzhang*, the Maoist revival of class rhetoric resurrected material evidence of the property that had once determined class. After viewing Shandong's class education exhibition, PLA soldier Xing Shudi wrote of this numinous danger,

> Have a look at the exhibition,
> The class enemies are not asleep.
> A black hand writes "*bian-tian-zhang*,"
> Sharpening his knives with his own teeth.
> Old scars still feel pain,
> New hatred is even harder to eliminate.

---

[46] *Buke wangji jieji douzheng: Jieshao Shandongsheng jieji jiaoyu zhanlanhui* (Never forget class struggle: Introducing Shandong Province's class education exhibition), p. 538.

[47] *Qianwan buyao wangji jieji he jieji douzheng: Yunnansheng*, p. 35.

[48] *Hunansheng shehuizhuyi jieji jiaoyu zhanlanhui jianjie*, p. 6; *Jiangsusheng jieji jiaoyu zhanlanhui shuomingshu*, pp. 7–8.

[49] For examples, see *Hunansheng shehuizhuyi jieji jiaoyu zhanlanhui jianjie*, pp. 6, 11, 15; *Shandongsheng jieji jiaoyu zhanlanhui huikan*, pp. 8, 21; *Jiangsusheng jieji jiaoyu zhanlanhui shuomingshu*, pp. 6–7.

154   Curating Revolution

Old anger and new hatred collect in heart-and-mind,
Furious fire in the breast rushes toward the sky.[50]

In this soldier's doggerel, by one for whom remembering class bitterness first began, was the Socialist Education Movement's ideal reception. *Biantianzhang* and a knife signified restoration's desire, past wounds freshened into new hate, and class enemies paced, awake.

Making Shanghai's class education exhibition

Work on the Shanghai Class Education Exhibition began in December 1964. In the words of the Party Committee's Propaganda Department, the purpose of the display was to accord with the Socialist Education Movement and to provide a "fixed battlefield" for class education. To that end, the Propaganda Department established a special Class Education Preparatory Committee and placed it under the direction of Zhang Chunqiao, an alternate secretary on the Secretariat of the Shanghai Municipal Party Committee, who later would become a member of the Gang of Four.[51] Four teams were responsible for collecting materials, creating the exhibition, administration and publicity, and secretarial work. Team cadres were drawn from the Shanghai Bureau of Culture, the writers' and artists' associations, and publishing houses.[52] Beginning later than other displays and their respective local Socialist Education Movements, Shanghai had the benefit of being able to learn from others. For example, during the following February a delegation from Shanghai visited Shandong to study its class education exhibition. The assessment of the Shanghai representatives was that the Shandong exhibition was too overwhelming. Featuring eighty to ninety individuals and thousands of artifacts, it would take a full day to read it carefully. At the same time, they praised Shandong's display for its ability to move peasant visitors, saying that the organizers "deeply understood that if the workers and peasants do not have strong class feelings, then the exhibition is a failure." Well-chosen examples, the representatives concluded, were those that "matched [the viewers'] own experiences," and the more they

---

[50] *Buke wangji jieji douzheng: Jieshao Shandongsheng jieji jiaoyu zhanlanhui*, pp. 550–551.
[51] Jiang Yi and Shao Youmin, eds., *Zhonggong Shanghai dangzhi* (Gazetteer of the Shanghai Chinese Communist Party) (Shanghai: Shanghai shehui kexueyuan chubanshe, 2001), p. 61. In this capacity, Zhang Chunqiao was in charge of propaganda and culture.
[52] SMA A22-2-1241, pp. 1–10. Other units later became involved, including an economics research institute and the Shanghai Museum. The Propaganda Department transferred painters, designers, photographers, and makers of models from other work units, which included studios for oil painting, sculpture, and film, the opera house, and the Shanghai Bureau of Handicrafts. See SMA C4-2-1, pp. 49–51; SMA C4-2-30, p. 35b.

Ill.4.5. Photograph from the Shanghai Class Education Exhibition showing a worker's scar (labeled) in the center of his back, undated. Note the low-rise housing in the background, possibly a shantytown. SMA H1-23-29-18

matched the viewers' experiences, the more likely the exhibition would "spark class feeling."[53]

In the same month that the Shanghai curators visited Shandong, they also studied the example of Pinghu County, located in the countryside just outside of Shanghai. Pinghu officials had made a former landlord's house into an exhibition hall and shared their experience of gathering materials—from locating documents on land reform in the archives, to using the local library and the museums for background history, to borrowing artifacts and photographs from the PSB or the courts.[54] Not unlike the work teams sent by the Party to assess political conditions, or artists and writers experiencing peasant life, exhibition workers went to

[53] SMA C4-2-1, pp. 117–118.   [54] Ibid.

the grassroots to study the historical past. Such interviewers even had a checklist:

ASK: Before and after Liberation, what was the family's life like? What were the conditions of production?

LISTEN FOR: The rent collection and the forcible collection of rent.

LOOK AROUND: How has the victim stood up? Has he preserved any artifacts?

HELP HIM (REMEMBER): Inspire his class consciousness; raise his ideological understanding.

WRITE IT DOWN: Record the victim's accusations of the landlord and his deep experience of *fanshen*.[55]

In a similar way, Shanghai exhibition workers conducted research, asking the PSB for examples of counterrevolutionaries and searching for workers who had been injured in accidents, with instructions to gather artifacts and to take photographs of the victims' bodies.[56]

As the worker's body makes clear, however, the purpose of Shanghai's Class Education Exhibition was not to tell the rural tale of landlords and peasants, but rather to tell the urban story of capitalists and workers. When the first draft of the exhibit was reviewed in May 1965, the Propaganda Department declared that the exhibition should "take 'anti-capitalism' as its core, stress the struggle between the proletariat and the bourgeoisie, and focus on the two-line struggle between socialism and capitalism." A focus on the city's capitalist past would thus "reflect Shanghai's characteristics."[57] The revised, anti-capitalist version of the exhibition went up at the Shanghai Party School, borrowing the auditorium of nearby Xiangming Middle School for additional space. It occupied 1,240 square meters, including 237 bulletin boards, 228 illustrations, 164 photographs, 926 artifacts, and 21 scale models, and it was staffed by a team of 25 cadres.[58] The docents or the narrators, the public faces of the exhibition, came from good class backgrounds and had politically correct behavior and ideology. Standing in front of assigned bulletin boards, measuring 150 cm by 100 cm, the best docents spoke "as if they [were] speaking their own hatred and bitterness, so much so that they themselves would shed tears. One docent said that when he got to the bulletin board about workers being exploited and oppressed, his voice would go as low as possible and his heart could not remain still."[59]

---

[55] SMA C4-2-1, p. 121.　　[56] SMA C4-2-11, p. 4b; SMA C4-2-8, pp. 7–8.

[57] SMA A22-2-1241, pp. 28–29.

[58] SMA C4-2-1, pp. 5, 41. The Shanghai Party Committee planned to eventually relocate it to the Sino-Soviet Friendship Hall as a permanent exhibition administered by the Shanghai Bureau of Culture, but I have seen no evidence that it was ever moved.

[59] SMA C4-2-1, pp. 93, 111. There were about one hundred docents and twenty guards.

Visitors were expected to spend a total of two hours at the exhibition, much less time than the six or seven hours required to visit the displays in Shandong and Jiangsu. An early report suggested that during the seven hours an audience could not retain more than seven examples; the authors of the report argued to Zhang Chunqiao and other leaders that the Shanghai exhibition should aim for the "few but essential."[60] The exhibition was originally intended for work units undergoing the Four Cleanups Campaign. But in addition to those cadres, workers, and members of the masses, the audience eventually expanded to other cadres and factory workers, PLA officers and soldiers, teachers and students, and people representing the democratic parties.[61] It was classified as an internal exhibition, not to be publicized nor shown to foreigners, so there is no record of the exhibition in official newspapers. All the same, many people from outside of Shanghai visited, including propaganda officials, journalists, and workers from other class education exhibitions. Shanghai's Class Education Exhibition Committee maintained detailed, bi-weekly reports on the attendees—including any notable personages—what they said during their visits, and their participation in subsequent discussions. Thousands of people visited each day, and by August 1966 it was estimated that over 700,000 people had seen the exhibition.[62]

Before the Cultural Revolution brought out-of-town Red Guards to the exhibit, the typical visitor was part of an organized group. But even if an individual was compelled to participate, he or she was highly motivated to pay attention and to remember its contents. In many ways, an exhibition functioned as an up-to-the-minute ideological text. Like the First Party Congress Site with its revisions of revolutionary history, a class education exhibition was a broadside of the latest and most relevant Mao quotes and a snapshot of the Socialist Education Movement as it unfolded. For Shanghai's Class Education Exhibition, focusing on the problem of capitalism and its vestiges, the display explained and refuted the concept of "peaceful evolution." Referring to a strategy proposed by American Secretary of State John Foster Dulles in 1953 and thereafter adopted

---

[60] SMA C4-2-1, pp. 2, 76. The first draft planned for three hours, but then it was cut to two. Officials calculated that it would take one to one-and-a-half minutes to reach each bulletin board, so a visitor could read 180 boards within three hours. Visitors who had been to numerous class education exhibitions concluded that less was indeed better. See also SMA A22-2-1241, p. 29.

[61] SMA A22-2-1401, p. 10; SMA C4-2-1, p. 25.

[62] SMA C4-2-1, p. 94. This estimate of 711,675 people is from August 4, 1966. By the end of 1966 it had been seen by a total of almost one million people. In October 1966, crowds could total 6,000 people each day, with long lines starting to form at four o'clock in the morning. A group from Pinghu County made the ten-hour trip by boat. SMA C4-2-16, p. 1.

by the Eisenhower administration, it claimed that the socialist countries would be peacefully subverted from within and that communism would change of its own accord. After reading Dulles's speeches on "peaceful evolution," Mao's commentaries were circulated among the leadership in 1959. As Vice Premier Bo Yibo's memoirs suggest, Mao regarded revisionism and "peaceful evolution" as two sides of the same coin. With the 1962 Tenth Plenum and the beginning of the Socialist Education Movement, historian Qiang Zhai explains, "the struggle to oppose 'revisionism' and to prevent a 'peaceful evolution' was accelerated at home."[63]

With the attack on "peaceful evolution" on many a 150 cm by 100 cm display board, the Shanghai Class Education Exhibition became a way for hundreds of thousands of people to see it made manifest in stories and artifacts. As the preface to the exhibit read, its purpose was "to accord with the Socialist Education Movement, to expose the exploitive nature of the bourgeoisie and the hidden plot of contemporary class enemies to use 'peaceful evolution' to restore capitalism, to raise our consciousness, and to actively engage in the revolutionary struggle of fostering proletarian ideology and eliminating bourgeois ideology."[64]

In choosing both positive and negative examples and in searching for artifacts, curators of class education began with an ideological argument and then looked for evidence. From February 1965 when the committee first began its work, it was said that examples should first be chosen and then be "refined."[65] In November 1965 when representatives of the All-China Federation of Labor suggested how to choose positive examples that had resisted class enemies, they explained that if one person did not exemplify everything that was desired, the curators should make a composite.[66] With this strategy, curators were following an early injunction by the writer Lu Xun on defining people as models: "observe many and combine."[67] In February 1966 Party Secretary Chen Pixian declared, "First have your outline, and after it has been determined, then go and look for materials." In the exhibition, class education began with a lesson in search of objects.[68]

---

[63] Qiang Zhai, "Mao Zedong and Dulles's 'Peaceful Evolution' Strategy: Revelations from Bo Yibo's Memoirs," *Cold War International History Bulletin*, nos. 6–7 (Winter 1995/1996), pp. 228–331.

[64] SMA C4-2-8, p. 151.   [65] SMA C4-2-1, p. 118.

[66] SMA C4-2-1, pp. 64b–69. At an undated meeting, Zhang Chunqiao explicitly instructed not to use names: "We can discuss A Factory with John Doe, but we don't have to give his real name, nor do we have to give the factory's name. However, the facts will be real and can be used to carry out education among the masses." SMA C4-2-11, p. 8b.

[67] See Boyd Compton, trans., *Mao's China: Party Reform Documents, 1942–1944* (Seattle: University of Washington Press, 1952), pp. 252–253.

[68] For collecting instructions, see SMA C4-2-16, pp. 1–2.

The first of the display's three parts, "Understand the Inherent Exploitation of the Bourgeoisie," would have been familiar. Mirroring the history of Fangua Lane, the beginning section offered the textbook account of Shanghai as a "heaven for the exploiting class and a hell for the working people. It was a microcosm of semi-feudal and semi-colonial old China."[69] Docents first explained imperialism and the impact of foreign capital on the Chinese economy, with bureaucratic and comprador capital blamed for the wartime inflation. The suffering of Shanghai's working people was contrasted with the extravagance of the capitalists. Like class education exhibitions elsewhere, curators used stocks and tax stamps, employment contracts and workers' clothing, and even models of the shantytowns to tell the story of life in the "old society." The first part focused on Shenxin Cotton Mills, the largest in Shanghai. The display included labor and indenture contracts, the clothing of a contract worker named Zhou A'da, and perhaps this following photograph of a woman textile worker. As in a *yiku sitian* narrative, she points to the site of a past injury. Juxtaposed with the tattered worker's clothing was a gleaming pair of golden horses from the inventory of gifts on the occasion of the sixtieth birthday party of Rong Zongjing, one of the two brothers who controlled Shenxin's cotton and flour mills.[70]

Though the contours of this exhibit's history would have been familiar, there were two differences—the first was one of emphasis and the second was one of degree. On the former, while displays of Fangua Lane juxtaposed the workers' past and present conditions, this exhibit compared workers' past lives with capitalists' past lives. Through this pairing, the class education exhibition drew attention to the gulf between them and made material the threat of "peaceful evolution." On the latter difference, capitalism was presented not simply as the story of a big fish like Rong Zongjing but also as any kind of self-interested behavior or profit. The argument was presented almost as if it were a proof: "All capitalists build their fortunes on exploitation." Refuting claims that capitalists are successful because of their own labor, or because of a combination of work and thrift, the display included a number of case studies and reiterated that—big or small, born a capitalist or a worker-turned-capitalist—no one could be successful without exploitation.[71] The purpose of this

---

[69] SMA C4-2-8, p. 152.

[70] SMA C4-2-8, p. 162. Note that Rong Zongjing's name was not used, but the date of the birthday matches what would have been his sixtieth birthday. Also note that though the docent does not mention it in the script, the horses are actually replicas. For the major strike at Shenxin Number Nine Mill, see Elizabeth J. Perry, *Shanghai on Strike: The Politics of Chinese Labor* (Stanford, CA: Stanford University Press, 1993), pp. 213–214.

[71] SMA C4-2-8, pp. 157–158. See also the docents' script in SMA C4-2-8, pp. 88–89.

Ill.4.6. Photograph from the Shanghai Class Education Exhibition of
a worker from Shenxin Number Nine Mill (on the apron), indicating
a former injury from the "old society," undated. Note that this was the
mill where a great strike was held in 1948, for which the women were
celebrated after 1949. SMA H1-23-29-13

argument, clearly keyed toward the targets of the Socialist Education
Movement, was to eliminate the possibility of capitalism being defined as
a matter of degree.

Parts Two and Three, "Defend Against the Furious Attacks of the
Bourgeoisie" and "Smash the Hidden Plot by Class Enemies to Use

'Peaceful Evolution' to Restore Capitalism" both took "peaceful evolution" as the main theme. The shorter second part used examples from the original Five Antis Campaign in the 1950s to suggest that although some capitalists had turned their businesses over to the state, they secretly saved deeds and stockholder lists—the *biantianzhang*—in anticipation of Chiang Kai-shek's return.[72] Part Three presented, one after another, cases reflecting "peaceful evolution" in contemporary Shanghai. Some of the examples admonished the corrupting influence of bourgeois lifestyles. One woman named Weng Huayu, for example, was noted for keeping candies and makeup in her factory workbench. Pointing to the offending objects, the docent declared that "some workers, without knowing it, were corrupted by her and mimicked her concern about what to eat and what to wear."[73] Other case studies documented the corruption and speculation that was attacked during the Four Cleanups. One worker at the Shanghai Watch Factory, Zhang Rurong, was accused of stealing watches and supplies to open his own private shop. As an example of private moneylending, receipts in the display illustrated the tale of a Ms. Cheng, whose demands for usurious interest robbed a sick boy of his medicine, eventually leading to his loss of sight. For a case of speculation, the exhibition told the story of one Jin Zuyin, who used his Yong'an Department Store connections to buy up cameras and then to resell them at a profit. The most dramatic of the speculation stories was that of a capitalist element named Chen Huixiu, whose 70,000 yuan of diamonds no doubt dazzled the imagination.[74] In these examples big and small, Shanghai's Class Education Exhibition revealed the targets of the Socialist Education Movement.

Still, capitalist longing and restoration's intent were harder to depict than candies in a drawer or a collection of pilfered watch mechanisms. To portray these, the Shanghai Class Education Exhibition turned to the capitalists' own words, in the form of diaries and confessions. On display was the diary of capitalist Chen Rongxuan, the former boss of his family's construction company. The eight-volume diary, seized during the Four Cleanups, was opened to entries from 1962 to 1964, in which Chen expressed his sadness over his empty garden, his shame in losing his family's company, his sorrow at his father's grave, and his regret over the loss of his two automobiles. If visitors had any trouble reading the classical language of the diary, the docent provided the correct conclusion: "In this way, he reveals that he is not happy with socialist

---

[72] See, for example, SMA C4-2-8, p. 185.   [73] SMA C4-2-8, p. 128.
[74] SMA C4-2-8, pp. 205–219.

transformation."[75] The other kind of incriminating words-on-display was confessions, the lengthiest being the case of Tang Yuman, who had once owned a candy store on Fuyou Road in Shanghai's Nanshi District. During the Four Cleanups, Tang composed the following confession:

From Liberation until today, our family has preserved a set of *biantianzhang*. Because of our class nature, we nurtured strong hopes for the life we lived in the old society, when we lived without having to labor. We always wished that one day history would return us to those old days ... then [we could] use these *biantianzhang* ... to reestablish our old business.

Tang went on to explain his discontent with working for the public manager of the candy store and how he had decided to undermine him by pretending to be an activist and gaining his trust, sharing advice on the candy business as they walked home every day after work. The exhibition did not explain exactly how Tang Yuman "seized power," except that his friendship with the public manager resulted in some of his friends being promoted.[76] In any case, visitors to the class education exhibition frequently cited the confession as the most striking item on display, and the confession was taken as evidence of the first order, no different from other quotations or hearsay.[77] The confession—as in imperial times written to accord with the crime—was made public with its exhibition.[78]

To the capitalists' self-incriminating words were added the accusations of their alleged victims. Thus the Shanghai Class Education Exhibition also included *yiku sitian*. One young leader, Chen Minsheng, in a production team at Shanghai's Number Six Wireless Factory, allegedly had been corrupted by a capitalist named Ye Xiulan until his mother took it upon herself to carry out "family history education." Hearing the stories of his father's forced labor as a coolie for the Japanese and then as a dockworker, Chen Minsheng "drew a line" to separate himself from Ye Xiulan, turning in the various gifts he had received.[79] During political

---

[75] SMA C4-2-8, pp. 127, 203–204. Unfortunately, no further information about exhibited diaries exists in these files. For a discussion on the authenticity of the most famous Mao-era diary, that of model soldier Lei Feng, see Xiaofei Tian, "The Making of a Hero: Lei Feng and Some Issues of Historiography," in *The People's Republic of China at 60: An International Assessment*, edited by William C. Kirby (Cambridge, MA: Asia Center, Harvard University, 2011), pp. 293–305.

[76] SMA C4-2-8, pp. 196–198. Though other examples included excerpts of confessions, this seems to be the only one that includes the confession as an exhibition object.

[77] SMA C4-2-1, p. 64. Weng Huayu's confession about her candies was also used against her. See SMA C4-2-8, p. 128.

[78] Susan Naquin, "True Confessions: Criminal Interrogations as Sources for Ch'ing History," *National Palace Museum Bulletin* [Taibei], vol. 11, no. 1 (March–April 1976), pp. 1–17.

[79] SMA C4-2-8, p. 208.

campaigns, presents given by the accused were often submitted as proof of bribery or corruption, and here in the exhibition's glass case workers piled up Ye Xiulan's gifts as evidence.[80] The examples of Chen Rongxuan, Tang Yuman, Ye Xiulan, and others show how an exhibition reflected each step in a political campaign: the pressure to hand in diaries or to write confessions, the use of material proof in objects and words, and finally the curation of evidence so that hundreds of thousands could see for themselves.

Behind the scenes, however, curators continued to struggle with how to represent Mao's interpretation of "peaceful evolution" and how to definitively depict a movement as it was unfolding. The central tension was how to portray hidden class enemies that were simultaneously dangerous and doomed to failure. At the same time, how was one to portray class victims as at once menaced and triumphant? The lines between past and present, which were meant to be so clear in propaganda, were actually blurred and easily misunderstood. In a set of meeting minutes from October 1965, Yang Xiguang—like Zhang Chunqiao, alternate secretary on the Secretariat of the Shanghai Municipal Party Committee—suggested that one should shy away from terms like "short-term worker" that might prompt comparisons to labor practices in New China. Yang's concern was prescient; as Elizabeth Perry and Li Xun show, hundreds of thousands of Shanghai workers had been laid off between 1960 and 1962, returning only as discontented temporary workers and later as activists in Cultural Revolution rebel groups.[81] On the question of how the evils of capitalism past compared with the present, Party Secretary Chen Pixian admonished the curators for making the post-1949 capitalists appear to be worse than the pre-1949 capitalists, when "in actuality the biggest crimes occurred *before* Liberation, with the earliest period the darkest."[82] Finally, the premise of "peaceful evolution" was that capitalist elements would secretly infiltrate socialist society, so how should they be drawn? In meetings with illustrators, Zhang Chunqiao's reply was that there should be as much realism as possible,

Making the negative characters and capitalists so ugly makes them obvious ... If they are all drawn like this, then "peaceful evolution" would not be possible; the

---

[80] For an example of gifts as evidence during the Socialist Education Movement, see Denise Y. Ho, "Reforming Connoisseurship: State and Collectors in Shanghai in the 1950s and 1960s," *Frontiers of History in China*, vol. 7, no. 4 (2012), p. 627.

[81] Elizabeth J. Perry and Li Xun, *Proletarian Power: Shanghai in the Cultural Revolution* (Boulder, CO: Westview Press, 1997), pp. 100–107. See also Wu, "Revolutionary Alchemy: Economism and the Making of Shanghai's January Revolution," ch. 4, in *The Cultural Revolution at the Margins*, pp. 95–141.

[82] SMA C4-2-11, p. 13b.

masses would see through them right away ... They should be drawn as they are. Do you think [the capitalist] Rong Yiren is ugly? He's a good-looking guy. How is he ugly? You insist that he's ugly, but we want to reflect his original nature.[83]

The difficulty of curating hidden threats and vain desires, against a landscape of class and history far more complicated than class education's slogans, was never fully resolved. As the Socialist Education Movement became the Cultural Revolution, the class education exhibition wrote and rewrote the pages of its textbook.

Reception

A visit to the Shanghai Class Education Exhibition was a serious affair. Attendees had to apply, and once there many made it a careful study. Officials noted that "some comrades hand-copied all of the materials on the site, primarily to prepare reports for their work units or to use them as teaching materials."[84] From slogans to Mao quotations, from *yiku sitian* to confiscated diaries, work units could use the displays to understand how others across the municipality were conducting the Socialist Education Movement. Even out-of-town cadres visited the exhibition as a way to be briefed on the progress of the campaign in Shanghai.[85] Exhibition officials took visitor feedback equally seriously. During the trial exhibition that went up at the end of 1965, up to 4,000 people viewed it each day, and within a little more than one month, officials gathered over 3,000 comments and held almost twenty focus-group meetings.[86] In these materials—later collected by Red Guards who used them for denunciations—there is a far more variegated response than in those selected for reprinting in the pamphlets prepared for other class education exhibitions. While official reports about ordinary visitors affirmed a lesson learned—much like students after visiting an anti-superstition display—others were less than models: capitalists who were compelled to view the exhibition expressed deep unease, and the Red Guards who arrived at the end of 1966 chose to attack it as a "black exhibition."

The measure of success of the Shanghai Class Education Exhibition was both emotional and didactic. As Party Secretary Chen Pixian said during a February 1966 meeting, "Right now, only those who suffered cry when they see it. This will never do ... you want everyone to walk away

---

[83] SMA C4-2-11, p. 8b. These meeting minutes are undated.   [84] SMA C4-2-1, p. 65.
[85] SMA C4-2-1, p. 70. In March 1966, of the 430,749 people who had attended so far, 30,000 were from Socialist Education Movement work teams, 210,000 were from units undergoing the Four Cleanups, and 30,000 were from Socialist Education Movement work teams in the countryside. SMA C4-2-1, p. 90.
[86] SMA C4-2-1, p. 41.

weeping. Put in some more models, mobilize the artists!"[87] Portrayals of the pre-1949 working class were praised for their verisimilitude, as one old factory worker related: "The display objects (*zhanpin*) in the exhibition are just like those from my life in the old society."[88] As with other class education exhibitions, workers condemned the past with words and tears. When Ma Shichao, a worker for Shanghai Transport, confronted his own pre-Liberation patched clothing in the exhibit, "he cried so much that he could not speak." Some women workers, seeing in the exhibition women whose hands had been crippled by the capitalists, "clutched at where their own hands had been pierced, at once crying and looking [at the display]."[89] These manifestations of perceptual knowledge were combined with rational knowledge, as visitors demonstrated that they had imbibed the class lesson.

Visitors felt the exhibition's "anti-capitalist" focus was appropriate for Shanghai. Soldiers from the countryside who had not known capitalists declared them equal to landlords or rich peasants, and one worker from Minhang's Electric Tools Factory, Chen Yuhui, declared that the exhibition taught him "how to recognize enemies."[90] Comments suggested that visitors could repeat back the lessons of the exhibition, including that all capitalists built their fortunes from exploitation, that big and small capitalists were all alike, and that every capitalist dreamed of restoration.[91] According to the feedback, the exhibition motivated visitors to return to their work units and carry out the Socialist Education Movement. One worker from Shanghai Barge Company exclaimed that he had been made to examine his personal behavior—in his case going to others' homes and listening to "yellow" (obscene) music. A member of a Socialist Education Movement work team explained that when he saw the negative examples on display, he compared them "to the situation in [his] own work unit," Shanghai's First Bureau of Machine Building. Some echoed the rightness and timeliness of the political movement, without which, they affirmed, "we would truly be in danger of changing color."[92]

The exhibition's records also reveal that there were critics. There were logistical problems, like overcrowding. Some found the second and third parts imbalanced, not everyone liked the urban focus, and many complained that there were too many words and too few objects.[93] Others criticized the capitalists on display for not being sufficiently cunning or concealed, and some were bored by the succession of case studies, saying

---

[87] Ibid., p. 14.   [88] Ibid., p. 90.   [89] Ibid., p. 44.
[90] SMA A22-2-1401, pp. 10–13; SMA C4-2-1, pp. 41–42.
[91] SMA A22-2-1401, pp. 11–12.   [92] SMA C4-2-1, pp. 46–47.
[93] SMA A22-2-1401, p. 13; SMA C4-2-1, p. 48.

that the exhibition lacked a plot.[94] There were also tough questions that the exhibition officials noted but did not answer. Was "peaceful evolution" meant always to be peaceful? If the capitalists were really so bad and unable to reform, then why should they be employed in the new society? Also, during the trial exhibition visitors pointed out that some of the stories "did not name names."[95] But despite the criticisms and questions, the overwhelming majority of the comments were enthusiastic. An editor from *Xinmin wanbao* (New people's evening news) described it as "fresh, outstanding, distinctive, and succinct," workers thought it better than a film, and Jiaotong University students declared that it surpassed ten politics classes.[96] In the totalizing system of class education, visitors suggested that it be replicated: as duplicates in workers' palaces, in photographs and lantern slides for traveling exhibitions, and even as textbooks or comic books for children, workers, and peasants.[97]

Of all the visitors to the class education exhibition, those who were most carefully observed for their reactions were the capitalists. On December 23, 1965, a group of about eighty people from the Shanghai People's Congress and the Shanghai People's Political Consultative Conference toured the exhibit. The exhibition staff watched them closely. They reported that some visitors only briefly glanced at the displays and seemed not to listen to the docents. One Zhu Hongyi, a vice director of the Association for Industry and Commerce, "entered the hall and looked right and left. At each example, he'd look at the title and walk right past ... You could tell he was probably worried about finding his name." Though this did not come to pass for Zhu, Rong Shuren—vice director of Putuo District Business Association—actually did see her own Rong family in the exhibition. The staff reported that she first hung back behind the other visitors, and then, seeing the description of worker exploitation at Shenxin Number Nine Mill, muttered with annoyance that she had already seen this in a movie. Before the display of her father's extravagant sixtieth birthday party, she shrugged it off, saying, "This was in 1932. Two years later the family's economic circumstances worsened. I was really young then and I didn't understand anything." After the visit, the group participated in a discussion meeting at which individuals allegedly tried to deflect attention away from themselves: some declared that they were only low-level bosses; others did not talk about themselves at all; and Rong Shuren said she had nothing to do with the cotton mills,

---

[94] SMA C4-2-1, p. 74.   [95] SMA A22-2-1401, p. 13; SMA C4-2-1, p. 69.
[96] SMA C4-2-1, p. 25.
[97] SMA C4-2-1, pp. 47, 69. Among other exhibitions, Shandong's exhibition was made into a film, SMA C4-2-11, p. 5b. The *Rent Collection Courtyard* sculptures also became the subject of a film in 1966.

only the flour mills. Somehow exhibition officials found out what she said after she went home: she summarized to her husband the parts of the exhibit that included the Rong family, and both husband and wife downplayed their family connection. Rong's husband demurred, "I'm only a son-in-law; I have no connection to the Rong family affairs." Rong Shuren distanced herself as well, saying, "I am a Rong family daughter and daughters marry out—like spilled out water. The exploitation at Shenxin had nothing to do with me."[98]

But some at the discussions were more amenable to the exhibition's lessons, and for them the meetings became a stage for self-criticism. If workers who saw themselves in the display would *yiku sitian*, the ideal capitalist visitor would reflect on his past life accordingly. Several individuals from the People's Congress and the People's Political Consultative Conference took the opportunity to enumerate their own errors of the past: exploiting and cheating workers, buying up foreign currency and raising interest rates, and benefiting from wartime inflation. Some referred to the exhibition as an inspiration. Xu Yifang, director of the Shanghai Bureau of Construction, described it as a mirror. "I could clearly see my own hideous nature." Viewing the newspaper clipping about Rong Zongjing's birthday, Xu Zhucheng from the Shanghai Bureau of Publications concluded that journalists had served the exploiting classes. "When I saw it, it shook me to the core." As in the case of Rong Shuren, exhibition officials noted reports of behavior after viewing the exhibition: one daughter-in-law of a capitalist, chastised by the story of Weng Huayu and her candies, became quiet, and no longer challenged others' accusations of her corruption.[99]

Apart from such special tours, visits by individuals with capitalist class backgrounds were recorded as demonstrations of the exhibition's influence. Zhi Yangtai, a son of the director of Dalu Machine Factory, told exhibition workers of his sorrow. "In the past I thought my father rose from apprentice to director because of his technical skills and obedience; now I know that he was oppressing workers." Ding Xunxiang, a worker at Hongkou Youth Palace and the son of a capitalist, wrote a confession letter after his visit. "All crows are equally black; my father was like all

---

[98] SMA C4-2-1, pp. 45, 78. Rong Shuren's comment about Shenxin's fortunes was true. As Parks Coble has shown, by 1934 Shenxin faced the worldwide economic depression and competition from the Japanese. Despite Rong Zongjing's political connections and, as Coble argues, his payment of 10 million yuan in taxes during the preceding years, he was unable to finance loans to keep Shenxin afloat. See Parks M. Coble, *The Shanghai Capitalists and the Nationalist Government, 1927–1937* (Cambridge, MA: Council on East Asian Studies, Harvard University, 1980), pp. 154–155.
[99] SMA C4-2-1, p. 80.

other capitalists. Was I not brought up on the blood and sweat of workers? I must reform my thinking and become a proletarian successor."[100] The class education exhibition, the reports explained, prompted Zhi Yangtai and Ding Xunxiang to "draw a line" between themselves and their parents.

When the Cultural Revolution broke out, the proletarian successors— in the form of the Red Guards—came to the exhibition en masse. In September 1966, about 2,000 Red Guards attended, or about 100–200 per day, carrying their student ID cards or university letters of introduction.[101] At first, the curators treated the Cultural Revolution as simply the next stage of class struggle to be put on display; since May 1966 they had been racing to update the exhibition with the latest news: Yao Wenyuan's critique of *Hai Rui Dismissed from Office*, his attack on the *Three Family Village*, and the Central Committee's "Decision Concerning the Great Proletarian Cultural Revolution."[102] As the Red Guard movement began in late summer, curators quickly put up photographs of the "Attack on the Four Olds" (*po sijiu*) and of people being struggled by Red Guards.[103] Exhibition workers formed their own groups, calling themselves "Red Propagandists" and "Red Defenders." It was the exhibition's own Red Guards who added new examples, using their contacts in factories and among Socialist Education Movement work teams to select cases, collect artifacts, and take photographs of confiscated possessions.[104] One exemplary addition was the case of Gong Xuren of Fufeng Flour Factory. Born into a landlord family and making his own fortune in flour mills, Gong's life was exhibited via objects that Red Guards had seized: weapons in the form of guns, bullets, and gunpowder; *biantianzhang* such as property deeds; and treasures including not only gold and jewels but also art and antiques.[105] Throughout most of November, visiting Red Guards treated the display as others had in the past—as a contemporary broadside of an unfolding political movement.[106]

But when the political situation began to unravel in late November, the Shanghai Class Education Exhibition—a proxy for one narrative of class and for the Shanghai Party Committee that shepherded its curation—

[100] SMA C4-2-1, p. 77. For other examples, see SMA A22-2-1401, pp. 11–12.
[101] SMA C4-2-1, p. 105.
[102] SMA C4-2-1, p. 54; SMA C4-2-8, pp. 146–147; SMA C4-2-8, pp. 4–5, 148.
[103] SMA C4-2-8, pp. 5, 149.
[104] SMA C4-2-1, pp. 102–103. For plans to update the Cultural Revolution section, see SMA A22-2-1401, pp. 3–5.
[105] SMA C4-2-8, pp. 11–12, 65.   [106] SMA C4-2-1, pp. 109–110.

came under attack as a "black exhibition," a "great poisonous weed of anti-Mao Zedong Thought," and the work of "reactionary academic 'authorities'" who had enshrined "the bourgeoisie on the exhibition's throne."[107] Making such accusations were no fewer than seven organizations, from universities and museums in Shanghai and elsewhere. These organizations included Beijing Agricultural University's Red Guards (the August 1 Combat Brigade), Beijing Steel Institute's East is Red Commune, Beijing Light Industry Institute's Little Red Army (Long March Team), Shandong University's Red Guards (Face the Sun Combat Team), Jiaxing [Zhejiang] Museum's Small Spark Combat Force, the Shanghai Class Education Exhibition's Lu Xun Spirit Combat Force, and the Shanghai Universities' Red Guard Headquarters (Right to Rebel Combat Force).[108] The attacks demonstrate that the Red Guards did detailed research: they visited the display on numerous occasions, they dug through the exhibition's documentary paper trail, and they even interrogated propaganda officials. The Shanghai Universities' Red Guard Headquarters used their attack to accuse members of the Shanghai Party Committee of relying on bourgeois scholars to carry out curatorial work, asking, "Why didn't you invite the old workers and the old poor and middle peasants?"[109] The Long March Team from Beijing's Light Industry Institute planted itself outside the Shanghai Propaganda Department, demanding that Vice Director Jiang Wenhuan declare the exhibition a "big poisonous weed."[110]

It is likely that none of the exhibition's content, given the determination of the Red Guards to find "weeds," would have been suitable. After all, the purpose of class education had been to guard against class enemies, whereas the prerogative of the Cultural Revolution was open struggle. In the vituperative language of the attacks, items included were vilified and anything omitted was imputed with maliciousness. The focus on capitalism, once praised for its concision, was interpreted as disregarding imperialism and feudalism and therefore being the antithesis of Mao Zedong Thought. Red Guards from Beijing Agricultural University accused the curators of "whitewashing imperialism and exonerating it for its crimes."[111] The Shanghai Class Education Exhibition was called to

[107] SMA C4-2-30, pp. 21a–b, 23, 33, 38b. For the names of the "scholars and authorities," see SMA C4-2-30, p. 34b. These included individuals from the Shanghai Academy of Social Sciences (Institute of History and Institute of Economics), Fudan University, the Union of Philosophy and Social Science, and the Shanghai Party School (Political Economy and Party History). On links to the Shanghai Party Committee, see SMA C4-2-30, p. 38b.
[108] SMA C4-2-30.   [109] Ibid., pp. 27b, 34b.   [110] Ibid., p. 27b.   [111] Ibid., p. 1b.

task for everything it allegedly left out or underemphasized: there were not enough Mao quotations, there was little history of the Party, and there was no portrayal of the pre-1949 class struggle. Though the purpose of the Socialist Education Movement had been to highlight contemporary class struggle, Red Guards attacked the exhibition for not celebrating the socialist present.[112] In a head-spinning brew of accusations, special fury was reserved for the part on "peaceful evolution." By portraying the capitalist threat, the Red Guards argued, the exhibition disregarded resistance; its telling, they alleged, implied that "Shanghai is not socialist Shanghai under the leadership of the CCP. Rather, it is cloaked with American White Terror! Shanghai is not the prosperous metropolis of New China. Rather, it is the Moscow of the revisionist Soviet Union. This clearly slanders our proletarian dictatorship!"[113] Several Red Guard groups called the exhibition to account for not including the First Party Congress, a slight to revolution both past and present.[114]

The Red Guards' accusations also extended to the visuality of the display. The Shandong Red Guards picked up on Zhang Chunqiao's comment on how to draw Rong Yiren; they and their Beijing comrades read Zhang's directions as making the working class ugly and the capitalists beautiful.[115] Photographs also came under attack. Regarding a photograph displaying workers and capitalists sitting together, captioned "labor and capital cooperating," the Shanghai Red Guards spat, "Pah! Sheer nonsense!"[116] An image of a capitalist being arrested was found offensive because he was both well dressed and calm. "In what way does he look like a criminal? He looks just like one of our martyrs, facing danger without fear. And in the photograph the PSB and the masses do not hate the enemy; they are even smiling! This is counterrevolutionary propaganda to the core!"[117] Even a photograph that happened to capture a cat (*mao*) in the frame was interpreted as anti-Mao. Red Guards from Beijing Light Industry Institute declared, "Whoever opposes Chairman Mao, we will smash his dog's head to a pulp!"[118] A historical photograph, an image of a capitalist in glasses and pomaded hair, a cat caught at a picture's edge: Red Guard critiques of the class education exhibition replaced its original narrative script—once carefully approved as an ideological lesson—with the language and vitriol of the Cultural Revolution. The Red Guards attacked the display with words they had lifted from visitor comments to defend mass opinion, and even interpreted taboo remarks as evidence of a curatorial conspiracy. To make their point,

[112] Ibid., p. 34.   [113] Ibid., p. 33.   [114] Ibid., pp. 26b, 32, 37.
[115] Ibid., pp. 1b, 37b. Here the Red Guards quote "Shanghai Party Secretary Zhang XX"; the quotation matches an earlier transcript.
[116] Ibid., p. 32b.   [117] Ibid., p. 26.   [118] Ibid., p. 26b.

Shandong Red Guards cited a student's reaction to Rong Zongjing's golden birthday horses, "Oh my! How very beautiful! How very beautiful!"[119] Such words, the Red Guards contended, showed clearly that the objects on display had a corrupting effect, making the curators who chose them into bedfellows with the very capitalist elements whom they were meant to expose. The Shanghai Red Guards pledged to "rebel until the end, until we create a bright-red class education exhibition that propagandizes Mao Zedong Thought!"[120] But their accusations, awash with slogans, never defined what such an exhibition would be.

Conclusion: Class displays and big-character posters

Presented on the eve of the Cultural Revolution, Shanghai's Class Education Exhibition reflected one propaganda genre of the Socialist Education Movement. Like the First Party Congress Site and Fangua Lane, the Shanghai Class Education Exhibition curated a story of Shanghai history in the lexicon of class, of a working class triumphant under the leadership of the Party. But unlike Fangua Lane's celebration of life in New China, class education warned of its perils. Not only were past beliefs obstacles to scientific understanding, as anti-superstition exhibits cautioned, but class enemies lurked in the midst of New China, threatening nothing less than restoration. With stories, artifacts, and individual examples, the Shanghai Class Education Exhibition taught visitors to see class in people and in things, to hold a mirror to themselves and to those around them. Curators relied on visual and material culture in order to, as Party Secretary Chen Pixian explained, relate perception to reason.[121] But perhaps in the crucible of class struggle, as the Red Guard attacks suggest, emotion became its own kind of reason.

More than the exhibitions in the previous chapters, Shanghai's Class Education Exhibition was part of a political campaign. The purpose of its examples was at once to teach the work teams how to conduct the Socialist Education Movement and to explain to ordinary people the campaign's import and ideological underpinnings. The exhibition was always approved by the Shanghai Party Committee, and in this way it was the most up-to-date interpretation of the Socialist Education Movement as it was occurring. Whether or not visitors were required to attend, and

---

[119] Ibid., p. 38b. For other examples of Red Guard citations of comments by previous visitors, see Ibid., p. 24b.

[120] Ibid., pp. 22b, 35b.

[121] SMA C4-2-1, p. 88. For more on the relationships among image, emotion, and reason, see, for example, *Hunansheng jieji jiaoyu zhanlanhui jianjie*, p. 4; SMA A22-2-1241, p. 9; SMA C4-2-1, pp. 5, 93; SMA C4-2-11, p. 15b.

whether or not the display was actually interesting, it was in one's best interest to learn the latest political line. Hence, some copied the exhibition boards word-for-word, some requested repeat visits, and over the course of the summer of 1966 increasing numbers clamored to see the revised Cultural Revolution version. The swiftness with which these new displays went up underscores the role of the exhibition as revolution's textbook. Curators added pages as events happened, very soon after the fact. The updated display explained the Red Guards' "Attack on the Four Olds," it showed a photograph of Yong'an Department Store's signboard torn from the landscape of Nanjing Road, and it included an image of the Shanghai Customs House, whose bell now tolled "The East is Red."[122]

But the Shanghai Class Education Exhibition did more than explain the origins and outcomes of the Socialist Education Movement as it became the Cultural Revolution. Curated in parallel with the political campaign, it taught viewers how to act and how to make class struggle on their own. Class education exhibitions therefore represent the revolutionary mode of exhibitionary culture. The exhibition boards so assiduously copied became templates for attacking class enemies. In August 1966, visitors from industrial, trade, and transportation work units reported to the exhibition staff that,

the content of their units' big-character posters is nearly the same as that in the third section of the exhibition. So the exhibition inspires and motivates the masses to write big-character posters and to participate in the Cultural Revolution. The exhibition has a definite effect.[123]

Though the propaganda system of Mao's China surely provided many other sources of inspiration, this comment as related by the work units themselves is telling: in form and in content, exhibition boards became big-character posters.[124] A class education exhibition was also a revolutionary handbook.

Even before the display boards sparked the Cultural Revolution's big-character posters, visitors recognized the exhibition's power to denounce. In the summer of 1966, a member of a group of factory managers said, "When the exhibition docents accused the bourgeoisie of evil crimes, it was as if they were accusing me. Several of the maquettes seemed to be pointing at me. When I saw them, my whole body trembled."[125] One visitor's class lesson was thus another's premonition, as a political

---

[122] SMA C4-2-8, pp. 4–5, 148.   [123] SMA C4-2-1, p. 94.
[124] Guo Wu suggests that *yiku sitian* contributed to the Red Guard violence, citing a Red Guard memoir of doing *yiku sitian* to encourage the beating of class enemies. See Wu, "Recalling Bitterness," p. 264.
[125] SMA C4-2-1, p. 92.

repertoire was cultivated and subsequently applied. When Red Guards began their movement by invading private homes to search for counter-revolutionary evidence, they may have been thinking of the artifacts in the class education exhibitions: the gold horses, the *biantianzhang*, and the diaries. One form of revolutionary action, as the next chapter will show, was to make a display of the items they discovered. In the exhibition of confiscated possessions, the Red Guards found a stage for Cultural Revolution's class struggle.

5 The Cultural Revolution's object lessons: The Exhibition of Red Guard Achievements

As the narrative litany of Guo Linshuang's crimes reached a climax, a shout arose from among the masses. "In the name of the Red Guards, I sentence him to death!"[1] In the preceding moments, a worker from Yong'an Department Store—once Guo Linshuang's family business—outlined a life of ignominy. Before Liberation, the worker explained, the reactionary capitalist colluded with imperialists and Guomindang bandits, profiting from his exploitation of labor. After 1949, the accusation continued, Guo Linshuang never reformed, maintaining his capitalist lifestyle and hiding both assets and documents in anticipation of a restoration. Gesturing at photographs of Yong'an Company's former foreign licenses and pointing to a lavish display of luxury clothing and imported foodstuffs, the worker drew the audience's attention to a hefty set of keys.[2] In a practiced voice he cried, "These keys were *often* used in Guo Linshuang's home; they weigh 12.5 *jin*. Comrades! Each and every key is completely soaked with the blood and sweat of us working people!" The crowd, full of class feeling, roared.[3]

This scene evokes Cultural Revolution struggle sessions, in which Red Guards accused alleged class enemies before the masses, but with one conspicuous absence: Guo Linshuang himself was not there. Instead, Guo was denounced in an exhibition, through the display of objects confiscated when waves of Red Guards made revolution by ransacking his stately home at 1375 Middle Huaihai Road.[4] These objects were

---

[1] SMA B123-6-1536, p. 15.
[2] SMA B123-6-1540, pp. 20–21b, 32–40. Three photographs of a struggle session of someone who looks like Guo, under a banner labeled "capitalist," appears on an unnumbered page, probably p. 31.
[3] SMA B123-6-1534, p. 2; SMA B123-6-1536, p. 15; 12.5 *jin* is equal to about 13.78 pounds. Note that preparations for this exhibition mounted by the Shanghai Bureau of Commerce began at the end of September and lasted for two weeks, with the official opening on October 17.
[4] SMA C48-1-146-49; SMA C48-1-176-142. The registration documents, which include Guo's address, valued his residence at 228,672 yuan.

presented as part of the Red Guards' "achievements" (*gongxun*), and they were mounted as an exhibition by the Shanghai Bureau of Commerce that ran from October to November 1966. Workers from Yong'an Department Store—renamed The East is Red Department Store— curated displays depicting various aspects of Guo's life, which was the primary negative example among many in the Exhibition of Red Guard Achievements. Together with docents assembled by the Shanghai Bureau of Commerce, the workers wrote and honed a narrative script. The line about Guo Linshuang's keys was revised as the docents assessed the listeners' reactions. Stressing the word "often," they concluded, "stimulated even more class feeling" and the addition of the final line spurred the crowd to shout expletives and hurl insults. Their narration, together with the exhibition's material artifacts (*shiwu*) as criminal evidence, unmasked the class enemy.[5]

Visitors to the Exhibition of Red Guard Achievements numbered between one and two thousand daily; in the first two weeks after its opening it attracted 19,900 people, of which 15,300 were from various work units of the Shanghai Bureau of Commerce, and the remainder representing over 200 other units. In addition to workers and staff from the city, the audience included soldiers from the PLA, peasants from the people's communes, and other Red Guards from as far away as Guangzhou, Harbin, and Tibet.[6] Local visitors would have been familiar with some of the content of the exhibit, and all visitors would have recognized its form. The history of Shanghai and its capitalist past was told at the First Party Congress Site, with displays of the shantytown, and in the recent and ubiquitous class education exhibitions. The practice of remembering past suffering, illustrated at Fangua Lane with *gundilong* and begging bowls, was replicated in the Exhibition of the Red Guard Achievements through the inclusion of artifacts, such as a rickshaw puller's patched thousand-layer pants or a photograph of a coal worker's machine-mangled arm.[7] If the portrayal of individual class enemies called to mind the genre of class education exhibition, it was at least partly because Red Guard docents trained themselves through repeat visits to the *jiezhan*.[8] But while the genre of the Red Guard exhibition mirrored class education exhibition in form and replicated some of its content, it made a new argument: it was the Red Guards who had exposed the

---

[5] SMA B123-6-1536, p. 15.
[6] SMA B123-6-1534, pp. 11–14. The exhibition was reported to be so popular that each day several hundred people were turned away, and by October 29, there was a waiting list of 70 units consisting of 8,800 people.
[7] SMA B123-6-1540, p. 14b.   [8] SMA B123-6-1534, p. 5.

hidden class enemies. With its sheaves of "counterrevolutionary documents" and heaps of silk stockings, the Red Guard exhibition was justification for the Cultural Revolution.

The Red Guard movement that began the Cultural Revolution has been described as a "Red Terror," hot summer weeks of chaos and confusion. Describing this season of violence, Roderick MacFarquhar and Michael Schoenhals explain, "whereas party violence had normally been carefully controlled and calibrated, now the rules had been suspended."[9] Writing on the cult of Mao, Daniel Leese observes that Mao's reception of Red Guards at Tiananmen mass rallies was anarchic and that forms of making revolution were so many and diverse that one Beijing middle school made a list of one hundred ways to "destroy the old culture and establish the new."[10] At the same time, the Red Guards shared a repertoire of class struggle, from tearing down street signs with feudal names to parading perceived enemies with dunce caps on their heads and heavy placards around their necks. In the same way that these forms of condemnation, referred to as "struggling," replicated themselves throughout China, Red Guard showcases were mounted from the Beijing Exhibition Hall to the smallest county schoolhouse. This chapter studies Shanghai's Exhibition of Red Guard Achievements, which claimed to be a revolution in exhibition work but actually drew from a longer political culture.[11] Its display was an argument for the Cultural Revolution, and its curators and docents understood their work as a form of revolutionary action. As they explained, "to do narration in the exhibition is also to make revolution."[12]

The Cultural Revolution house search and its "fruits of battle"

The Exhibition of Red Guard Achievements was not the first glimpse a Shanghai visitor or a Yong'an worker had into Guo Linshuang's life or home. The manager of Yong'an Company—originally a subsidiary of Hong Kong's Wing On (Yong'an) Company that opened in Shanghai in 1918—had long been a public figure. Historian Wen-hsin Yeh describes Guo, also known as Leon Kwok, as one of Republican Shanghai's self-styled patriarchs, offering relief when the department

---

[9] Roderick MacFarquhar and Michael Schoenhals, *Mao's Last Revolution* (Cambridge, MA: Belknap Press of Harvard University Press, 2006), p. 131.

[10] Daniel Leese, *Mao Cult: Rhetoric and Ritual in China's Cultural Revolution* (Cambridge: Cambridge University Press, 2011), pp. 133–135.

[11] SMA B123-6-1534, p. 6.   [12] SMA B123-6-1536, p. 11.

store on Nanjing Road was bombed in 1937 and encouraging patriotic donations during wartime.[13] On the eve of Liberation, Guo did not board the family's flight to Hong Kong; instead he threw his lot in with New China, presiding over Yong'an Company's transition to joint state-private management in 1956.[14] As Yong'an Company's manager and as a delegate to the Shanghai's People's Congress beginning in 1954, Guo Linshuang was frequently in the news. He was present at the establishment of Yong'an's first union in 1949, he laid a wreath to remember Yong'an workers in the Republican-era National Goods Movement, and when Yong'an Company underwent socialist transformation, as state-private management was called, his congratulatory speeches filled the local papers.[15] In addition to his continued public pronouncements on the effectiveness of socialist transformation and its benefits for Chinese consumers, depictions of Guo Linshuang's home life also appeared in the press.[16] In 1957 *Xinwen ribao* (News daily) led its readers to his Western-style garden home, describing how from a distance one could hear "the sound of a violin rippling through the still of the night." The article in *Xinwen ribao* was accompanied by a portrait of Guo and his wife sitting in an elegant room under a chandelier, listening to their two daughters play the piano and the violin.[17] During Spring Festival, Guo was depicted receiving past and present Yong'an Company workers in rooms spacious and refined, his tables laden with hometown Cantonese delicacies and adorned with flowers he had cultivated himself.[18]

[13] Wen-hsin Yeh, *Shanghai Splendor: Economic Sentiments and the Making of Modern China, 1843–1949* (Berkeley: University of California Press, 2007), pp. 57–63, 162–163, 170, 176. Yeh also notes the occasional criticism that such philanthropy was self-serving.

[14] See Xiaocai Feng, "Rushing Toward Socialism: The Transformation and Death of Private Business Enterprises in Shanghai, 1949–1956," in *The People's Republic of China at 60: An International Assessment*, edited by William C. Kirby (Cambridge, MA: Asia Center, Harvard University, 2011), pp. 240–258.

[15] "Yong'an gongsi fenhui zuowan zhenshi chengli" (The union of Yong'an Company was formally established yesterday evening), *Wenhui bao* (Wenhui daily), November 24, 1949, p. 2; "Shanghai jihui jinian Liang Renda" (Shanghai gathers to remember Liang Renda), *Wenhui bao*, February 10, 1957, p. 1. On Guo's congratulatory speeches, see, for example, *Jiefang ribao* (Liberation daily), August 16, 1956; *Xinmin wanbao* (New people's evening news), November 22, 1955, November 23, 1955, January 14, 1956, January 20, 1956, January 21, 1956.

[16] SMA C48-2-2676, pp. 11–12; *Xinwen ribao* (News daily), January 13, 1957; *Xinmin wanbao*, June 19, 1957, August 31, 1957, January 20, 1958; *Renmin ribao* (People's daily), April 9, 1960.

[17] "Guo Linshuang zhe yinian lai" (Guo Linshuang during the past year), *Xinwen ribao*, January 13, 1957, p. 1.

[18] "Yijian zhide gaowei de xishi: Guo Linshuang daibiao de fayan" (A happy matter worth telling: Speech by Delegate Guo Linshuang), *Jiefang ribao*, August 16, 1956, p. 6; SMA C48-2-2368, pp. 158–162.

Like Wang Lanhua of Fangua Lane, Guo Linshuang became a spokesperson for life in New China. Foreign journalists and leaders were invited to dinner at his home, where they would admire his chickens and flowers. At the end of such dinners, they were asked to leave comments in a booklet, as if they were visiting an exhibition. Florid and smiling in a Western suit, Guo Linshuang brought foreign friends on tours of Yong'an Department Store, where a Mao portrait overlooked the glass counters. His interview with the Soviet magazine *Iskra* was even republished in a Shanghai newspaper.[19] In his speeches, Guo presented a standard narrative, which went something like this: he and his family were overseas compatriots who had incorrectly believed that industry would save the nation. At the same time that Yong'an was facing oppression by foreign businesses, it was also colluding with the imperialists by registering for their licenses. With its luxury products, the department store served the rich while exploiting its workers. At Liberation, Guo explained, he stayed, seeing Shanghai as his motherland. Although he took the socialist road, he realized that he still needed to reform his capitalist thinking.[20] In the aftermath of Yong'an Company's socialist transformation, Guo's speeches attributed its success to the superiority of the socialist system: he noted its stocks of Chinese products for sale at modest prices, its high rate of business turnover, and the flood of customers served by a new motto—"everything starts with the interests of the consumer."[21]

Constantly telling a tale of material improvement through consumer goods—not only in Shanghai but also in the surrounding countryside and even during the Great Leap Forward—Guo's public face never betrayed the doubts that appear in his political evaluations.[22] Writing confessions, Guo Linshuang revealed his anxieties in the face of political campaigns, his sufferings *after* Liberation that had made his hair turn

---

[19] "Guo Linshuang zhe yi nianlai" (Guo Linshuang during the past year), *Xinwen ribao*, January 13, 1957, p. 1.

[20] SMA C48-2-1013, pp. 201–202. For a discussion of class during the Mao era, see Yiching Wu, *The Cultural Revolution at the Margins: Chinese Socialism in Crisis* (Cambridge, MA: Harvard University Press, 2014), pp. 38–46. Guo Linshuang's class status was industrial capitalist, a subcategory of capitalist. See SMA B52-2-81, p. 133.

[21] SMA C48-2-2676, pp. 11–12. See also *Xinwen ribao*, January 13, 1957; *Xinmin wanbao*, June 19, 1957, August 31, 1957, January 20, 1958; *Renmin ribao*, April 9, 1960.

[22] In 1960 Guo was asked to report on Shanghai's neighboring communes, and in doing so he made an inventory of the types of goods in the people's communes since the beginning of the Great Leap Forward in 1958, enumerating the increase in wool coats, shoes, fountain pens, sweaters, and so forth. "Nuli xuexi, wei shehuizhuyi duochu yifen liliang: Guo Linshuang weiyuan de fayan" (Study hard and socialism will gain more strength: Speech by Member Guo Linshuang), *Renmin ribao*, April 9, 1960, p. 17.

white and exacerbated his pancreatic illness, and that on his salary—cut by three-fourths—it was difficult to make ends meet. He admitted that he was backward compared to the younger generation and that "when I see my own name I become nervous."[23] But to the outside world Guo Linshuang asserted that he was living in his own "golden age," scoffing at his previous superstitious belief in fortune-telling: "After a few years of study, I think these attitudes are really laughable. Only by understanding the laws of social development and taking the socialist path can one seize one's own fate."[24] Expressing such a spirit, Guo became a model spokesman for Shanghai's former capitalists.[25] Initiated by Guo Linshuang, Yong'an Company was the first department store to undergo socialist transformation. At the celebration, he stepped onto a Cantonese opera stage to commemorate Yong'an's new life.[26] Into the 1960s, Guo continued to receive foreigners and tout the advantages of the socialist system. On a family visit to Hong Kong, he reassured his father of his social position by showing him a pictorial magazine spread featuring his life, including photos of Guo sitting at his desk, making speeches, feeding his chickens, and working in the garden.[27] Internal documents about Guo Linshuang's political performance notwithstanding, he played his part well. He did not appear in Shanghai's class education exhibition.

But when the Cultural Revolution began in 1966, Yong'an Department Store was one of the first and most visible targets of the Red Guards. Beginning at dawn on August 23, *Renmin ribao* reported, Shanghai Red Guards announced their critique of the old world, attacking the "Four Olds" of thinking, culture, customs, and habits.

---

[23] SMA C48-1-153-69, pp. 69–70. For the effects of the various campaigns on individuals like Guo, see Karl Gerth, "Wu Yunchu and the Fate of the Bourgeoisie and Bourgeois Lifestyles under Communism," in *The Capitalist Dilemma in China's Communist Revolution*, edited by Sherman Cochran (Ithaca, NY: East Asia Program, Cornell University, 2014), pp. 175–201.

[24] "Jianchi buyu de tuanjie zai dang de qizhixia wei fazhan kexue wenjiao shiye gongxian liliang" (Persistently rally around the flag of the Party and contribute to the development of science, culture, and education), *Wenhui bao*, July 25, 1961, p. 1.

[25] For other examples of model capitalists, see Christopher R. Leighton, *The Revolutionary Rich: Political Fortune and Red Capitalism in China, 1949–1979*, forthcoming.

[26] "Yong'an gongsi zhenshi shenqing gongsi heying" (Yong'an Company formally applies for joint public-private management), *Xinmin wanbao*, November 22, 1955; on the opera, *Xinmin wanbao*, January 14, 1956, January 20, 1956, January 21, 1956. Note that all contemporary accounts report that the opera was "Jin ma'an" (The golden saddle).

[27] Hong Hong, "Guo Linshuang he Shanghai Yong'an gongsi (Guo Linshuang and Shanghai's Yong'an Company), in *Zhongguo bainian shangye juzi* (One hundred years of China's business magnates), edited by Liu Yu (Changchun: Dongbei shifan daxue chubanshe, 1997), pp. 272–274.

Red Guards gathered on the famed shopping street of Nanjing Road, a symbol of Shanghai's capitalist past. They plastered the windows of Yong'an Department Store's windows with big-character posters, demanding that its name be changed to "Forever Red," "Struggle Forever," or "Red Guard." "Yong'an," the Red Guards maintained, "was the name given by the old society's big boss, who had planned to forever (yong) and secretly (an) exploit the working people ... today the stinking placard of 'Yong'an' will hang no longer!"[28] Thus, the Yong'an Department Store sign came down and it was replaced by a sign that read "The East is Red Department Store." As the "Attack on the Four Olds" spread, Red Guards made revolution in public and in private. On the streets, they assailed feudal shop names and accosted individuals with permed hair, and in individual homes they scoured every corner for evidence of counterrevolution. Such ransacking, known as a house search, affected Shanghai more than any other city in China and yielded the largest quantity of confiscations. Between August 23 and September 8, 1966, 84,222 Shanghai homes were searched.[29] A report prepared in April of 1967 for the Shanghai Revolutionary Committee suggests that by that time the house searches had produced—among other things—30 tons of gold, 2.4 million silver dollars, 400 counterrevolutionary documents, and 598 guns with 117,000 bullets.[30]

The "old society's big boss" was undoubtedly Guo Linshuang, whose home was searched numerous times, first by Red Guards from The East is Red Department Store, then by Red Guards from the

[28] "Shanghai Tianjin geming xiaojiang he shangye zhigong xiang boxue jieji 'sijiu' fadong zonggong: Huiqi geming tie saozhou, hengsao yiqie jiuxisu" (Revolutionary little generals and commercial workers in Shanghai and Tianjin make a general offensive against the "Four Olds" of the exploiting classes: Raising the revolutionary iron broom, they sweep away all old customs), Renmin ribao, August 25, 1966, p. 2.

[29] Wang Nianyi, Da dongluan de niandai (The age of great turmoil) (Zhengzhou: Henan renmin chubanshe, 1988), p. 54. This is in comparison to 33,695 house searches in Beijing. According to archival documents, by the end of the Cultural Revolution over 250,000 homes had been searched in Shanghai. See SMA B1-9-228-74, p. 74.

[30] Perry and Li use a 1986 Bank of China report, in which some of the numbers match contemporary records and some do not. Matching numbers include the amount of U.S. dollars, foreign currency, silver dollars, cash, and bonds. The amount of gold is off—contemporary reports cite 30 tons and Perry and Li cite 65 ounces. As Beijing Red Guards reported 5.7 tons of gold, it is possible that gold was sent through a different channel. Elizabeth J. Perry and Li Xun, Proletarian Power: Shanghai in the Cultural Revolution (Boulder, CO: Westview Press, 1997), p. 12; Wang Nianyi, Da dongluan de niandai, p. 55. I rely on a report to the Shanghai Revolutionary Committee dated April 15, 1967, held in the Jianchuan Museum Cluster, Anren Township, Sichuan Province. For the amounts reported by the Shanghai's Bureau of Commerce, see SMA B123-6-1535, p. 16.

Institute of Finance and Economics, and even by Red Guards from a local middle school. As one group after another conducted their "revolutionary action" and made his home into their headquarters, Guo was imprisoned in the "ox-pen" of his windowless garage. He was only allowed out when he was the object of struggle sessions, such as those of Shanghai Party Secretary Chen Pixian and Mayor Cao Diqiu. When one group of Beijing Red Guards burst into the garage and began beating Guo almost to death, The East is Red Department Store Red Guards surrounded them and said: "You can't beat him like this. We have to keep him as a negative example!"[31] In the Exhibition of Red Guard Achievements, Guo Linshuang became the central "negative example," his possessions proxy for him and his class, and all objects of the house search proof that it was right to rebel.

Where did the idea for the Red Guard exhibitions come from? As Elizabeth Perry and Li Xun explain, "early Red Guard activities in Shanghai were patterned on the Beijing model," whether through imitation from afar or through direct instructions from the thousands of Beijing Red Guards who descended on Shanghai from August to October 1966.[32] According to an estimate by historian Jin Dalu, more than 4,000,000 out-of-town Red Guards visited Shanghai in the second half of 1966, with Beijing students playing a prominent role.[33] Less than one week after the "Attack on the Four Olds" erupted in Shanghai, *Renmin ribao* saluted the Red Guards for their actions, directly linking the exposure of class enemies to the subsequent display of their allegedly counterrevolutionary documents and weapons. The editorial board wrote on August 29, 1966,

---

[31] This paragraph is indebted to Hong Hong, "Guo Linshuang he Shanghai Yong'an gongsi," pp. 274–275. Hong explains that subsequently Guo Linshuang was allocated two rooms in a hotel near Yong'an Company and he lived there under guard; he and his wife were assigned to wash dishes and wipe tables in the cafeteria.

[32] Perry and Li, *Proletarian Power*, pp. 9–12.

[33] Jin Dalu, *Feichang yu zhengchang: Shanghai "wenge" shiqi de shehui shenghuo* (Extraordinary and ordinary: Social life during Shanghai's "Cultural Revolution" period) (Shanghai: Shanghai cishu chubanshe, 2011), 2 vols., pp. 64–88. Li Xun also details the role of Beijing Red Guards in Shanghai, explaining how their criticisms of Shanghai's movement were made in reference to Beijing. See Li Xun, *Wenge zaofan niandai: Shanghai wenge yundong shigao* (The age of revolutionary rebellion: A history of Shanghai's Cultural Revolution movement) (Hong Kong: Oxford University Press, 2015), 2 vols., pp. 121–162. The memoirs of then–Party Secretary Chen Pixian also describe Shanghai Red Guards imitating Beijing Red Guards, and the influence of the Beijing Red Guards on the Shanghai Red Guards. See Chen Pixian, *Chen Pixian huiyilu: Zai "yiyue fengbao" de zhongxin* (The memoirs of Chen Pixian: At the center of the "January Storm") (Hong Kong: Sanlian shudian, 2005), pp. 58–61.

As for these blood-sucking worms, as for these enemies of the people, the Red Guards are currently dragging them out one by one. Red Guards take out their hidden gold, silver, and jewels to be exhibited. Their manifold *biantianzhang* and their murderous hidden weapons of all kinds are also taken out to be exposed to the masses. This is the achievement of our Red Guards; the actions of the Red Guards are truly great![34]

That the Red Guards in Shanghai and elsewhere responded directly to *Renmin ribao* is evident in the reappearance of the article's language. On October 14, 1966, Red Guards at Shanghai's Tongji University, for example, declared that they were following the Beijing Red Guards, using the language in the *Renmin ribao* article word for word.[35] At about this time, Sophia Knight, a British foreign teacher in Shanghai, wrote home to her mother that "more incriminating evidence has been discovered in the houses of capitalists etc., gold bars and such like; and spy rings apparently have been uncovered. In Peking an exhibition has been opened. I'm pretty sure there'll be one in Shanghai too, and I hope foreigners will be allowed to visit it." Knight, who had been documenting rumors of Shanghai house searches since September 14, finally got her wish on November 30. The exhibition she visited at the former Polish Consulate had everything she imagined and more: diaries and letters, Japanese knives and whips once used on workers, and radio transmitters and a fountain pen that shot poison gas.[36]

Organizing an exhibition became part of Red Guard repertoire everywhere.[37] In Beijing, as Daiyun Yue later wrote, the Peking University Cultural Revolution Preparatory Committee set up a display of confiscated materials in a classroom. She describes filing through the exhibit with her department staff and watching a primary school student whom she knew serve as a docent for the items on display: books and paintings, photographs and Nationalist Party documents, and even a string of high heels collected from all around campus.

---

[34] "Xiang women de hongweibing zhijing!" (Salutations to our Red Guards!), *Renmin ribao*, August 29, 1966, p. 1, in *Zhongguo wenhua da geming wenku* (Chinese Cultural Revolution database), edited by Song Yongyi (Hong Kong: Xianggang Zhongwen daxue, Zhongguo yanjiu fuwu zhongxin, 2002), CD-ROM (cited hereafter as *WDGW*).
[35] "Tongji daxue wuchanjieji wenhua da geming dashiji" (Chronicle of Tongji University's Great Proletarian Cultural Revolution), October 14, 1966, in *WDGW*.
[36] Sophia Knight, *Window on Shanghai: Letters from China, 1965–67* (London: Deutsch, 1967), pp. 219–227.
[37] Informal "exhibitions" at struggle sessions may have preceded the organized exhibitions described below. For the objects on display at the struggle session of Li Fanwu, governor of Heilongjiang Province, in Harbin, September 12, 1966, see Zhensheng Li, *Red-Color News Soldier* (New York: Phaedon Press, 2003), pp. 114–115.

Yue explains in her memoir that the purpose of the exhibit was "to reveal the seriousness of the class struggle at Beida [Peking University]; to make clear the sufferings of the workers, peasants, and soldiers; and to unmask the bourgeois lifestyle of the faculty and cadres." She also suggested that the exhibition was a way for Nie Yuanzi, a Red Guard leader at Peking University, to define the crimes of those under attack.[38] Elsewhere in Beijing, Red Guards put on class education exhibitions and "Attack on the Four Olds" displays; at Beijing Normal University fur coats and leather bags were laid out in the teachers' cafeteria.[39] In a field where intellectuals, labeled ox-demons and snake-spirits (*niugui sheshen*), were made to weed the grass, a Red Guard raised his camera to photograph them for an exhibition. All turned their backs to the lens save one Li Helin, a scholar of Lu Xun. Li raised his "yin-yang" shaved head to face the camera, waited for the click, and requested a copy as a souvenir.[40]

Away from Shanghai and Beijing, other Red Guards followed suit. Guangzhou organized an exhibition which was part history of the Red Guard movement, part denunciation of individuals, and part accounting of the house searches. In addition to enumerating confiscated possessions, Guangzhou also counted the changing of street and shop names, churches "mopped up," and individuals deported from the city.[41] In Chongqing, the Mao Zedong Thought Red Guards put on a Chongqing Red Guards Revolutionary Rebel Exhibition in the municipal museum, which gained a reputation beyond the city, attracting crowds who came to witness the spectacle. As Yang Yaojian, a "Red Little Guard" working on the exhibit remembers, "They wanted to see with their own eyes what kind of life the landlords and the capitalists had led. The visitors would discuss all the while, wondering whether eating exotic delicacies would be bad for the health, or what it would feel like to sleep in such a big, elegantly carved bed." Beyond the fascination with unknown decadence, Yang confirms that visitors "would be even more convinced that the 'five black elements' [landlords, rich peasants, counterrevolutionaries, bad elements, and rightists] were still dreaming of a restoration and were

[38] Daiyun Yue and Carolyn Wakeman, *To the Storm: The Odyssey of a Revolutionary Chinese Woman* (Berkeley: University of California Press, 1985), p. 171.

[39] Beijing Municipal Archive (hereafter cited as BMA), 2-18-123, p. 40; BMA 147-2-128, p. 1.

[40] Guang Qin, "Xihou wangzeng wo yi zhang" (After you develop it, I hope you will give me a copy), *Lu Xun yanjiu dongtai* (Lu Xun research trends), no. 1 (1989), p. 24.

[41] *Guangzhou diqu hongweibing geming zaofan zhanguo zhanlanhui* (Guangzhou area Red Guards' fruits of rebellion exhibition), December 1966.

unanimous in their praise of the Mao Zedong Thought Red Guards digging up these 'time bombs.'"[42]

As part of the Red Guard repertoire, such exhibitions spread to the countryside. In Hebei, as Gao Yuan describes in his memoir, his middle school displayed "The Startling Realities of Class Struggle," with the most vivid artifacts being piles of grain coupons.[43] Exhibition became a way for one faction to demonstrate its victory over another; in Guangxi one faction became known for parading its enemies in metal cages as "displays of beasts" (*qinshou zhanlan*).[44] Some exhibition halls, such as those in Chongqing, came under attack by members of opposing factions, becoming not only a way to struggle class enemies but also sites of internecine warfare.

While part of the impetus to exhibit came from signals emanating from Beijing, Red Guard exhibitions at all levels bore the stamp of direct Party organization. In the case of the Hebei middle school, it was the work team that helped the rebel students arrange a display of the teachers' confiscated property.[45] In Chongqing, the Party Committees at the municipal and district levels coordinated visits from each work unit.[46] Beijing organized the largest and most centralized display, the Capital Red Guards Revolutionary Rebel Exhibition (Shoudu Hongweibing Geming Zaofan Zhanlanhui).[47] Directed by Lin Biao's office, this showcase began mobilizing members of the military in October 1966, eventually assembling over two hundred workers from units as disparate as the rebel groups, the military, the museums, and the branches of the public security apparatus. Arrayed across four wings of the Beijing Exhibition Hall and even publishing its own booklet, the Capital Red Guards Revolutionary Rebel Exhibition had access to powerful resources. Its workers flashed military badges and moved unimpeded through warehouses. Every day a private ministry-level car would drop off and pick up four Song dynasty (960–1279) basins ranked first-grade national treasures; the display was personally approved by Jiang Qing and members of the Central Cultural Revolution Group (CCRG) as well as the Beijing

---

[42] Yang Yaojian, "Shouwei zaofan zhanlan" (Guarding the rebels' exhibition), *Hongyan chunqiu*, no. 1 (1998), p. 41.

[43] Gao Yuan, *Born Red: A Chronicle of the Cultural Revolution* (Stanford, CA: Stanford University Press, 1987), p. 73.

[44] Li Guohe, "Wo chengle 'huoren zhanlan' de zhanpin" (I became an artifact in a "living exhibition"), *Yanhuang chunqiu*, no. 1 (2012), pp. 58–60.

[45] Gao Yuan, *Born Red*, p. 72.   [46] Yang Yaojian, "Shouwei zaofan zhanlan," p. 41.

[47] *Shoudu hongweibing geming zaofan zhanlanhui* (Capital Red Guards revolutionary rebel exhibition) (Beijing: Shoudu dazhuan yuanxiao hongdaihui, 1967). Some memoirs use a slightly different title, but this is the name printed on the official booklet.

Red Guard leaders.[48] In addition to Lin Biao, who stressed that each locality should have an exhibition of Red Guard successes, other top leaders made similar suggestions, from Foreign Minister Chen Yi to CCRG Director Chen Boda. It was Lin Biao who coined the term "Red Guard Achievements" and Chen Boda who repeatedly spoke of the necessity to exhibit the "fruits of battle" (*zhanguo*).[49] Shanghai's Exhibition of Red Guard Achievements was a response to these suggestions.[50]

The genre of Red Guard exhibition was manifested in different forms, from a classroom display with a few specific teachers as targets to Beijing's Capital Red Guards Exhibition, which was tasked with the goal of "letting the exhibition shake the whole world."[51] The latter was probably the most elaborate, with four halls, elaborate kiosks, and sculptures: of Mao wearing a Red Guard armband, of Mao surrounded by Red Guards, and even of a struggle session.[52] Its four halls were entitled: "Long Live the Victory of Chairman Mao's Revolutionary Line," "Strike Down China's Khrushchev," "Sweep out the Ox-Demons and Snake-Spirits," and "The Great Red Guard Movement

---

[48] Ding Dahua, "Shisuo hanjian de hongweibing chaojia zhanguo zhanlanhui" (A sight seldom seen: The Red Guards' house search fruits of battle exhibition), *Wenshi jinghua*, no. 1 (January 2008), pp. 25–31. Units involved in its planning and execution included the Capital Universities' Red Guard Revolutionary Rebel Alliance, the Beijing Military Region, the Ministry of Public Security, the Beijing PSB, the Museum of the Chinese Revolution, and the Museum of History. In attendance at the final approval were Chen Boda, Jiang Qing, Zhang Chunqiao, Kang Sheng, Yao Wenyuan, Wang Li, Guan Feng, Qi Benyu, and other CCRG members, as well as Nie Yuanzi, Kuai Dafu, Tan Houlan, and other Red Guard leaders. Ding's memory is confirmed by the official booklet, which lists Lin Biao, the CCRG, and the PLA as supporters. See *Shoudu hongweibing geming zaofan zhanlanhui*, introduction. The BMA shows similar precedents in organizing class education exhibitions, with the PSB, the Five Antis Office, and the BMA involved in procuring historical materials. See BMA 101–189, p. 10.

[49] Lin Biao, "Zai zhongyang gongzuo huiyi xiaozu huishang de jianghua" (Speech at a meeting of the Central Committee's small work group), October 12, 1966; "Chen Yi zai waiwen chubanju quanti zhigong dahuishang de jianghua" (Chen Yi's speech at an all-staff meeting of the foreign languages publication house), September 14, 1966; Chen Boda, "Chen Boda zai zhongyang gongzuo huiyishang de jianghua" (Chen Boda's speech at the Central Committee's work meeting), October 16, 1966; Chen Boda, "Chen Boda dui liangge yue yundong de zongjie" (Chen Boda's summary of two months of the movement), October 24, 1966; Chen Boda and Wang Li, "Chen Boda Wang Li tong Fujian Hui'an yizhong ershiwu ming zhanshi zuotan jiyao" (Summary of a meeting of Chen Boda and Wang Li with twenty-five soldiers of Hui'an's Number One Middle School in Fujian), October 29, 1966, all in *WDGW*.

[50] Even in the following year, the Shanghai Revolutionary Committee invoked one of Chen Boda's speeches to justify the continued display of the Red Guard movement. SMA B244-2-36, pp. 11–12.

[51] Ding Dahua, "Shisuo hanjian de hongweibing chaojia zhanguo zhanlanhui," p. 26.

[52] *Shoudu hongweibing geming zaofan zhanlanhui*, pages unnumbered.

Reverberates Around the World." More formal and comprehensive than the ad hoc classroom exhibits, the first two halls outlined the development of the Beijing Red Guard movement, including prominent big-character posters penned by Red Guard leaders such as Nie Yuanzi and even one big-character poster attributed to Chairman Mao.[53] The section that attracted most visitor attention was the third hall, the display of the house search.[54] Following *Renmin ribao*'s prescription to exhibit riches, documents, and weapons, each Red Guard Exhibition—no matter how modest—included a variation on these themes.

By exhibiting the confiscated possessions of the house search, the Red Guard Exhibition engaged in different kinds of work. At the most basic level, curating worked as a kind of inventory, with objects recorded as they arrived at the exhibition site. In Shanghai, for example, charts enumerating the spoils served as a backdrop for the display. On another level, the exhibition made private house searches public, with thousands of people able to continuously view the process and review its results. As Ding Dahua, then a twenty-seven-year-old political cadre in the military assigned to the Capital Red Guards Exhibition, later remembered, "a number of important house search incidents were made known through the exhibition." Ding's fellow workers relived the house searches in film, as they watched original documentary footage of house searches and struggle sessions. He writes, "I remember that from beginning to end we watched them for about a week, each day from morning to afternoon we'd watch for many hours ... afterwards we became inured to it, watching until our heads were dizzy."[55] Above all, the Red Guard exhibition was a form of rendering judgment, defining a particular enemy through his crimes, and making the struggle of individuals part of the larger movement. But in an atmosphere where political fortunes would

---

[53] As MacFarquhar and Schoenhals explain, Mao wrote the text on an old copy of *Beijing Daily* and his secretary copied it onto a blank sheet of paper. See *Mao's Last Revolution*, p. 90.

[54] Ding Dahua, "Shisuo hanjian de hongweibing chaojia zhanguo zhanlanhui," pp. 29–30; Du Xing, "'Posijiu' zhanlan ji" (A record of an "Attack on the Four Olds" exhibition), *Shidai jiaoyu* (January 2010), http://news.ifeng.com/history/zhiqing/xiaohua/detai l_2012_07/04/15759320_0.shtml (accessed September 30, 2016). Some footage of house searches is included in a video held in the Fairbank Collection of the Fung Library, Harvard University. See *Cultural Revolution Video Collection*, DVD (VHS Tape Transfer) (Decade in the Great Cultural Revolution, ca. 1978). Special thanks to Nancy Hearst for locating the original VHS.

[55] Ding Dahua, "Shisuo hanjian de hongweibing chaojia zhanguo zhanlanhui," pp. 28–29.

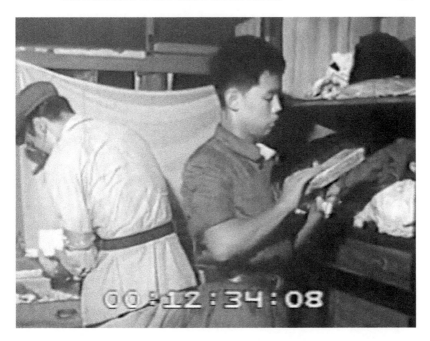

Ill.5.1. Film still of a house search, undated. Cultural Revolution Video Collection: Decade in the Great Cultural Revolution, Fairbank Collection, Fung Library, Harvard University

rise and fall, curating an exhibition was dangerous. Ding recalls the fear that hung over all the workers. Never knowing what political change might next occur, he writes that everyone "trembled with fear, everyone felt insecure, like a clay Buddha crossing the river, unable even to fend for himself."[56] Like the docents at the First Party Congress Site, Red Guard exhibition workers stood in the midst of political tumult.

As political action, the Red Guard exhibitions harkened back to the repertoire of land reform in the 1940s, particularly the "Settling Accounts Movement" or the redistribution of landlord property to the peasants. As William Hinton describes in the case of Shanxi's Long Bow Village, the property of the wealthy was laid out in a temple yard, from farm implements to furniture and from fine clothing to brightly-colored quilts, all as the "fruits of struggle" (*douzheng guoshi*).[57]

---

[56] Ibid., p. 26.
[57] William Hinton, *Fanshen: A Documentary of Revolution in a Chinese Village* (New York: Vintage Books, 1966), pp. 147–151.

Ill.5.2. Film still of a house search, undated. Cultural Revolution Video Collection: Decade in the Great Cultural Revolution, Fairbank Collection, Fung Library, Harvard University

Elsewhere, contemporary reports show that such spoils were not so quickly dispersed. Instead, the "fruits of victory" (*shengli guoshi*) were exhibited for days on end with the express purpose of cultivating class hatred. In 1947, one Zhen Linfeng wrote an article in *Dongbei ribao* (Northeast daily news) that explained step by step how to "exhibit the wealth of victory and inspire class consciousness," enumerating the items to be put on display and explaining how to employ a narrator and what questions to ask of the crowd. Showing an object as a lesson, Zhen stressed, would lead an audience to vent its grievances. In Changxin Village, "once they put the landlord's gun on the table and let everyone see it, the peasants' anger quickly became a speaking bitterness meeting." As one after another spoke their bitterness, Zhen explained, "even more [political] activists emerged." In the same year, Jilin Province reported the creation of a "new kind of exhibition" that included the class enemies themselves: concubines clutching their parasols, Guomindang "spies" in military uniforms wearing "American" hats, and landlords in long gowns holding the pecks they had used to measure tax grain. So attired, the landlord was made to narrate a pictorial exhibition drawn about him, reflexively describing how he had oppressed and beaten the poor.[58] Land reform's new exhibitions thus inaugurated the second mode of socialist China's exhibitionary culture—that of a revolutionary movement. Displaying its own "fruits of battle," with a Red Guard docent in place of the landlord narrator and with objects in place of their owners, the Exhibition of Red Guard Achievements curated in the revolutionary tradition.

Curating the Cultural Revolution in Shanghai

The most emblematic object in Shanghai's Exhibition of Red Guard Achievements was not to be found among the glinting weapons, the glittering jewels, or the photographs of Guo Linshuang's bathroom, labeled to indicate that the gleaming fixtures were all American imports. Instead, it was a plain metal teakettle, cocked open to show a false bottom. It was found in the home of Yao Shifeng of the Petroleum and Coal Company, and docents related how Red Guards had staged a dramatic invasion of the house, climbing through the second-story windows and threatening the daughter who attempted to block their way. They discovered the teakettle in the garbage and were surprised by its unusual weight. The Red Guards measured the kettle and found the interior shallow, so they pried it open to discover gold bars wrapped in thick cotton wadding. With similar perspicacity, they observed the way that Yao's wife and four children stood soaking in two layers of clothing in the summertime, curiously bent at the middle; some forty gold rings were hidden on their bodies and even in the heels of the children's shoes. "But," the docent declared, "none can escape the penetrating eyes of the Red Guards!"[59]

With the teakettle as object lesson, three things were simultaneously on display. The gold was evidence of exploitation, a stand-in for Yao Shifeng as a landlord who had supposedly evaded political reform. This allegation meant that he and the other people on display had refused to accept their place in New China, and the gold served as evidence of crimes past and plots present. Gold took

---

[58] Zhongguo geming bowuguan (Museum of the Chinese Revolution), ed., *Jiefangqu zhanlanhui ziliao* (Materials on exhibitions in the liberated areas) (Beijing: Wenwu chubanshe, 1988), pp. 254, 363–366. For an example of a land reform exhibition in Shanghai's suburbs, see SMA B14-1-172-66.

[59] SMA B123-6-1540, p. 18; SMA B123-6-1535, p. 33.

on a numinous power that informants feel even today. A retired worker (b. 1947) who participated in a house search recalls the heft of a bag from the manager of her former factory, the gold bars proof of a crime.[60] A former Red Guard (b. 1952) relates a "Four Olds" exhibition in a temple in Shanghai's neighboring Zhenru County and how "the old-hundred-names, the ordinary people, had never seen anything like gold bars ... where did they come from? And you would think, well, it came from exploitation."[61] Ye Zhaoyan, age 9 at the beginning of the Cultural Revolution, writes that among the objects at the Red Guard exhibition, the children only had eyes for the gold. So powerful was the notion that "bad people's houses surely had gold" and that "where there was hidden gold, there were bad people," that when Ye watched his own parents being searched, he was certain that gold would come tumbling out of the family's bookcases.[62]

The second thing the false-bottomed kettle displayed was that the gold was *hidden*, and indeed fifty years later Ye describes how an entire room in a Red Guard exhibition that he visited was devoted to the way gold was tucked away: placed in the toilet, sewn into shoes, secreted under stoves, and bricked into walls. That gold was concealed was taken to represent one skein with two threads: its owners harbored secret capitalist desires and counterrevolutionary intentions and they were saving the gold to make a comeback. Accordingly, the kettle taught a third lesson, that the Red Guards were responsible for its discovery, making it—with the gold bars—one of the "fruits" of the Red Guards' battle. But as Ye Zhaoyan writes, in an era when "gold was not gold," the treasures on display as the revolution's triumphs masked the owners' tragedies. During one Shanghai house search, the son of a capitalist tried to draw a line between himself and his parents by showing the Red Guards where the family gold was hidden. His mother, unable to bear the Red Guards' accusations and her son's betrayal, jumped off a building.[63] Another boy (b. 1957) remembers seeing the body of a woman who had hung herself, with all of her gold and jewelry on her person.[64] The object of one child's fascination and another child's conscience was the subject of many families' terror and some individuals' undoing.

The kettle with its hidden gold was one of the many artifacts on display at the Exhibition of Red Guard Achievements, appearing in

---

[60] Interview in Shanghai, July 21, 2013.   [61] Interview in Shanghai, July 15, 2013.
[62] Ye Zhaoyan, "Huangjin bushi huangjin" (Gold is not gold), *Xinmin wanbao*, July 7, 2013.
[63] Interview in Shanghai, July 9, 2013.   [64] Interview in Shanghai, July 24, 2013.

the middle of a showcase divided into two parts. The first half was devoted to objects and the second focused on individuals such as Guo Linshuang and Yao Shifeng. At the start of a tour, visitors stood in a prefatory room and gazed upon a white bust of Chairman Mao. They raised their Little Red Books and were led in the reading of a selection of Mao quotations.[65] The first part of the exhibit began with a table that enumerated the objects the exhibition displayed, the triumvirate of things first listed in *Renmin ribao*: weapons, *biantianzhang*, and treasures (gold, silver, and jewels). On the left-hand column of the chart, the weapons and *biantianzhang* included 14 guns and 11 transmitter-receivers, 329 counterrevolutionary flags or badges, and 1,020 land deeds. On the right-hand column of the chart, Red Guards documented 28,330 *liang* (or 1,416,500 grams) of gold, 2,102 diamond rings, 2,180 watches, and 87,525 meters of fine fabrics.[66]

After reviewing the chart, visitors walked the length of long tables covered in cloth and densely laid with a sampling of each object. Behind the tables, the walls were decorated from top to bottom with Cultural Revolution slogans, Mao quotations, large labels (i.e., "instruments of restoration"), and explanatory texts. Additional confiscated possessions were secured to the backdrop, like butterflies in a case or as in a cabinet of curiosities. Among the weapons were sabers arrayed along the wall and bullets spread out in careful lines: "These are the guns and butchers' knives used by class enemies to murder Communist Party members and the revolutionary people." Draped Nationalist and American flags made for "reactionary evidence," and even more startling, the visitor was presented with desecrated PRC flags and a hidden portrait of Chiang Kai-shek on a pillow. Piled up against the backdrop were heaps of land deeds, so that they appeared

---

[65] SMA B123-6-1540, p. 3.

[66] SMA B123-6-1535, p. 16; SMA B123-6-1540, p. 4. As a point of comparison, Beijing's Capital Red Guards Exhibition enumerated 268 guns, 19,676 other weapons, 14,398 counterrevolutionary badges and documents, 41,294 land deeds, and 103,131 *liang* of gold. Additional categories included 6,820 counterrevolutionary diaries and poems and 613,618 *wenwu* and jade objects. See *Shoudu hongweibing geming zaofan zhanlanhui*; these numbers match Wang Nianyi's estimates; see his *Da dongluan de niandai*, p. 55. Of course, the Beijing numbers are meant to represent the city, whereas the Shanghai numbers represent a unit. For a more equal comparison, Li Xun finds the amount Shanghai confiscated a total of 480,000 *liang* of gold; she calculates this to be more than ten times that confiscated in Beijing. See Li Xun, *Wenge zaofan niandai*, p. 113. For a comparison with Guangzhou: 31 handguns, 15 rifles, over 500 sabers, 5 transmitter-receivers, 850 counterrevolutionary IDs and 76 counterrevolutionary flags, 35,000 *biantianzhang*, and over 930 *jin* of gold—see *Guangzhou diqu hongweibing geming zaofan zhanguo zhanlanhui*, p. 4.

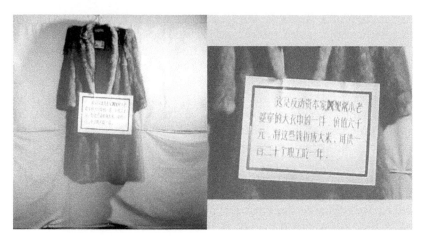

Ill.5.3. Yan Jichang's fur coat from the Exhibition of Red Guard Achievements

to spill out as from a *trompe-l'oeil* painting. Finally, shining against dark cloth were delicate pieces of jewelry identified by their value: a piece of platinum worth 2,800 yuan, a diamond ring costing 4,800 yuan, a diamond bracelet priced at more than 10,000 yuan, and a piece of jade valued at 150,000 yuan. Throughout, the presentation of the weapons, land deeds, and treasures was supplemented by stories of individuals and their possessions, though it should be noted that for some of the most nefarious crimes, names were omitted and replaced with "a class enemy."[67] The three categories of objects each had auxiliary displays to highlight their villainy; a section on feudalism made sectarian religion bedfellow with counterrevolution, and beyond the treasures there were other luxury items, from exotic *materia medica* to fur coats.[68]

The inclusion of the fur coat provided an opportunity to introduce the curatorial method of juxtaposition. Akin to Fangua Lane's comparison of past to present, the Red Guard exhibition—like the class education exhibition—compared capitalists to workers and landlords

---

[67] Names are mentioned in B123-6-1535, p. 7, for the violated flags and the pillow hiding the portrait of Chiang Kai-shek. However, in B123-6-1540, p. 6, the individuals are referred to as "class enemies" or "a bureaucratic landlord class element."

[68] SMA B123-6-1540, pp. 4–16.

to peasants. The fur coat, identified as belonging to bank manager Yan Jichang's concubine, was said to be valued at 6,000 yuan, a sum that would purportedly feed 120 workers for a year. Regardless of whether this was true, the fur coat established a pattern for presenting other luxury goods throughout the Exhibition of Red Guard Achievements: objects were described by listing their value, that sum's conversion to rice, and the number of workers who could fill their bellies from it. To underscore these juxtapositions, the curators appended an obligatory section displaying the patched thousand-layer pants of a rickshaw puller and a photograph of one Lu Xiaogen, a worker in a coal briquette factory whose arm had been caught in a swiftly spinning machine whose repairs had been neglected by the tight-fisted capitalist.[69]

With the vivid image of Lu Xiaogen's crippled body closing the first part of the exhibition, the second part introduced class enemies one by one as topics (*zhuanti*) and as targets (*duixiang*), as the docents referred to them behind the scenes. In addition to Guo Linshuang and Yao Shifeng, there were six other targets. The first was Wang Chengde, portrayed by way of heaps of foodstuffs: baskets of rice, new year's cakes, noodles, and beans; tinned products from fish and meat to infant milk powder; containers of alcohol and every kind of cooking oil; and jars of vegetables and four kinds of sugar. Wang Chengde's pantry was displayed with a message, indicating not simply abundance and waste (as the narrator described how the food had rotted) but also the hoarding of household goods and manipulating the market at precisely the time of the "three years of natural disaster." Guo Linshuang and Yao Shifeng were followed by Yao's colleague at the Petroleum and Coal Company, Luo Huailian, who was also accused of hoarding and preserving photographs of his *biantianzhang*. In Luo's section appeared the trope of medicine, one stalk of ginseng he consumed equated to twenty years of a worker's salary. With medicine derived from "workers' bodies" and "workers' blood and sweat," Luo Huailian was literally called an eater of human flesh and a drinker of human blood. The following two targets were displayed as examples of feudalism

[69] SMA B123-6-1540, pp. 14b–17. It is unclear how the Red Guards calculated the value of such property. If a piece of ephemera showing the prices at which confiscated possessions were liquidated during the Cultural Revolution is any indication, then a long fox fur coat of top quality went for 163 yuan (an average of 94 yuan for all levels of quality) and a long mink coat sold for an average of 48 yuan. "Chuli chachao wuzi jiage cankao biao" (Reference price list for processing confiscated property), Jianchuan Museum Cluster, Anren Township, Sichuan Province.

and a desire for restoration. Xie Dingfan was illustrated via portraits of his grandfather in the robes of officialdom and couplets written with Kang Youwei's brush, and Qu Liekun was represented by pharmaceutical agents found in the home of his daughter, stockpiled from state property in anticipation of the return of capitalism. Finally, Wen Hongchang and Chen Qinghua were presented as vignettes of counterrevolutionaries and spies—their radios, cameras, and telescopes part of the inventory on display.[70]

If these targets each represented only a few facets of the class enemy and his threat to the revolution, Guo Linshuang was the central and most comprehensive target. The East is Red Department Store Red Guards who had saved him from being beaten by the Beijing Red Guards spared no effort in dragging out every scrap of evidence for the exhibition, from Yong'an Company records to the prize flowers from his garden. The display on Guo Linshuang started with his pre-1949 history, establishing his relationship with Guomindang leaders via a family history bearing an inscription by Chiang Kai-shek, a copy of the constitution with the signature of his father Guo Quan, and even a Cantonese opera banner showing his affiliation with Minister of Finance Kong Xiangxi. A spread of Yong'an's licenses showed that indeed the company was registered first with the British, next as an American company, and then as a Chinese company under the Wang Jingwei puppet government.[71] To add the charge of exploitation to counterrevolutionary and imperialist collusion, curators included the tattered clothing of a worker, complete with his dismissal slips; the latter supported the docent's enumeration of Yong'an's rules of discipline and the alleged quotes by Guo Linshuang about the dispensability of workers.[72] The remainder of the Guo Linshuang display depicted the contents of his house. Heaps of food were presented with their country of origin; clothing was piled helter-skelter in a corner, with hand-lettered characters arching across the jumble reading, "This is one part of the old blood-sucker's clothing. There were over 80 boxes." Finally, to give the visitor a glimpse into Guo's rooms as a Red Guard might have seen them, photographs illustrated the Western or foreign parts of his

---

[70] SMA B123-6-1535, pp. 20–46. Here I rely on the docents' scripts from November 19, 1966, supplemented by the photographic account. Note that the two narratives are not entirely the same, but the differences do not alter the trajectory.

[71] Parks M. Coble, Jr., *Chinese Capitalists in Japan's New Order: The Occupied Lower Yangzi, 1937–1945* (Berkeley: University of California Press, 2003), pp. 147–149.

[72] Yeh, *Shanghai Splendor*, pp. 170, 180. Yeh shows that employees were unhappy about the disciplinary regulations and that the wartime excess labor supply allowed Yong'an managers to fire workers at will.

house: the bathroom with its flush toilet, the separate Western kitchen, and the garden, its flowers labeled front to back as coming from Germany, Japan, America, and England. To emphasize both the vastness of the household's wealth and its rightful seizure, the exhibition included its keys, weighing 12.5 *jin*.[73]

What did it mean to have the objects of a house search on display? First and foremost, it made material objects evidence by equating *objects* with *people* with their alleged *class crimes*. Luxury possessions were both symbols of capitalist desires and literal measures of exploitation; a piece of jewelry was identified by its value, then converted into an amount of grain or hours of labor. Objects associated with what the propaganda of New China had deemed counterrevolution were by necessity proof of intention; one could not save an old document for family nostalgia or retain a piece of fabric with Chiang Kai-shek's image simply because materials were scarce. In an era of Red Terror, the only valid lesson for the object was the one the exhibition wished to tell. Though cartoons pinned on the backdrop might depict individuals, the display relied on objects, which in turn were metonyms for the owners, their class, and their crimes.

The powerful link between objects and class status—already established by the class education exhibitions—primed Red Guards in what to look for. In addition to the little boy Ye Zhaoyan who imagined that his parents *must* have gold, other informants report going on house searches with specific objects in mind. One man (b. 1956)—then ten years old in the Zhejiang countryside—admits, "At that time we were mostly looking for *biantianzhang*. At that age, we'd think that, well, landlords were always thinking of restoration. Also weapons. And then there were radio transmitters, because we also thought that they were spies."[74] Another interviewee (b. 1952) who participated in house searches remembers one particular house and how the Red Guards pried open a rosewood chair, slashed a leather sofa, "and, because we thought maybe there might be guns or swords hidden in the floorboards, we broke them up."[75]

On the other side, it is little wonder that individuals during the Cultural Revolution were so fearful to be found with such markers of class in their possession that they destroyed them preemptively. Many

---

[73] SMA B123-6-1535, pp. 24–32; SMA B123-6-1540, pp. 20–21, 32–35, 38–40; 12.5 *jin* is equal to about 13.78 pounds. Note that I follow the chronological narrative in the former file; in the latter file the photographs (some on unnumbered pages) are not in order. It is unclear whether this was intentional.

[74] Interview in Shanghai, July 1, 2013.   [75] Interview in Shanghai, July 15, 2013.

informants specifically remembered what they hastily burned or otherwise got rid of: books, photographs, swords and other antiques, Western clothing, and even their own diaries.[76] A retired cadre (b. 1950) from a capitalist family remembers, "We were all afraid, because even if our family wasn't rich, everybody had some of these old things ... at that time, we didn't even dare *look* at such things. If people said they should be burned, we burned them. What if these things were found and you were already [labeled] a capitalist?"[77] In a time when class origin was conflated with class status, possessions of the past could be ventriloquized to accuse, their danger enough for people to consign them to flames.

In the Red Guard exhibition, material objects were proof of class crimes and evidence of the rightness of Mao Zedong Thought. Throughout, the language of the docents' narrative was peppered with terms that equated artifacts with evidence. Things on display were referred to, for example, as "*zuizheng*," or proof of crime, and alternatively as "ironclad evidence." When luxury items were listed, from pieces of gold and silver to boxes of silk and nylon stockings, they were called "living facts." In turn, the "proofs of crime spoke" and the *biantianzhang* "testified." Taken together, exhibition objects were referred to as a "veritable record."[78] Even the language of the house search had embedded within it the idea of illegitimate possession, the confiscation of property in the hands of a criminal. Like Ye Zhaoyan waiting for his parents' gold to be discovered, guilt was already assumed and the object only served to confirm. With these words attached to objects, even the format of the docents' script followed that of a crude proof of Mao Zedong Thought. The narrative on Guo Linshuang began with a quote by Mao, saying,

Comrades! Chairman Mao says, "The enemy will not perish of himself. Neither the Chinese reactionaries nor the aggressive forces of U.S. imperialism in China will step down from the stage of history of their own accord." Comrades, here we have exhibited part of the criminal evidence that reactionary capitalists plot restoration ...[79]

The Guo Linshuang display, like the other sections, was bookended with another of Mao's teachings. The Exhibition of Red Guard Achievements

---

[76] Interviews in Shanghai, July 2, 2013, July 7, 2013, July 8, 2013, July 15, 2013, and July 18, 2013.

[77] Interview in Shanghai, July 2, 2013.

[78] SMA B123-6-1535, p. 7; SMA B123-6-1536, p. 20.

[79] SMA B123-6-1535, p. 24. Translation from Mao Zedong, *Quotations from Chairman Mao Tsetung* (Peking: Foreign Languages Press, 1972), p. 11.

was therefore described as a tool to propagandize Mao Zedong Thought, both the process of curating and the experience of visiting a veritable classroom.[80]

That material things were proof of the correctness of Mao Zedong Thought was of course an echo of the Socialist Education Movement's class education exhibitions, which had also served to expose and to denounce. What was new in the genre of the Red Guard exhibitions was that the objects on display were arguments for the Cultural Revolution and for the Red Guards as the correct interpreters of Mao Zedong Thought. Hence the display showed how evidence was discovered— as in the story of Yao Shifeng's teakettle—and in using the phrase "we Red Guards" the docents stressed how things were hidden and how they were found. Although other workers in The East is Red Department Store could not but have approved of the Exhibition of Red Guard Achievements, nonetheless their feedback demonstrates that the display prompted the desired verbal response. One Chen Kuan declared that "after seeing the exhibition [he] felt that the Cultural Revolution was timely," several workers stressed that they must continue to struggle Guo, and one unnamed worker highlighted the impact of seeing the actual objects, as he had as a participant in a house search. "If I had not seen the capitalists' houses with my own eyes, I would not have understood."[81] Another visitor, Zhu Longmei, explained that young people had no personal experience with class enemies—"we only read about them in books, and therefore we didn't have a very deep understanding."[82] A docent surnamed Wang equated seeing Guo's possessions with "seeing Guo Linshuang," and seeing the exhibition's evidence was also believing.[83]

But curating the Cultural Revolution was not simply an expression of victory. While the objects on display were used to justify the Red Guard movement, the exhibition's curation was meant to further political action. It revealed to all comers the events and the objects of the house search and gave them a common narrative with which to understand them. In an era of continuous revolution, the display made people increase their hatred, polish their eyes, and realize that Guo Linshuang was still riding in his own private car, "exploited from the blood and sweat of the working people."[84] In the same way that Michael Schoenhals writes of "doing things with words in Chinese politics," exhibitions can be seen as doing things with objects in

---

[80] SMA B123-6-1534.   [81] SMA B123-6-1534, pp. 47–49.
[82] SMA B123-6-1536, p. 20.   [83] Ibid., p. 29.   [84] SMA B123-6-1534, pp. 47–48, 52.

Chinese politics.[85] The formal and formulaic language of classes, of enemies, and of revolution was here applied to material things, so much so that a display of the house search became an extension of an individual struggle.

Narration as class struggle

The young docents of the Exhibition of Red Guard Achievements had no experience with museum work. There were about fifty of them in total, sent from various units that reported to the Shanghai Bureau of Commerce, and they were divided into teams based on a theme or on individual targets. Workers from The East is Red Department Store, for example, were assigned to narrate Guo Linshuang's story. In their post-exhibition work summaries, the docents admitted that some had been reluctant to take part. Initially, some thought that the Cultural Revolution struggle was greatest in their original work units, and others felt that the house searches had already defeated the enemies of the people. But by the end of the process, the docents claimed that they, too, had received a class education. Multiple teams described how they cried bitter tears with their audiences; several reported that they steeled themselves against sore and bleeding throats with Mao Zedong Thought. The docents called themselves Red Propagandists and their own work the battlefront. In their own words, narration was class struggle and exhibition was revolutionary action.[86]

For the docents, even more than for the audiences they received, creating the exhibition was participatory propaganda. In the process of their own conversion, the docents grappled with questions that predated the Cultural Revolution and that were not specific to the exhibition. For example, how did one cultivate one's own class feeling? How should one speak so that listeners would pay attention, so that one's class feeling would touch the wellspring of another's? How could narration create hatred of a class enemy? Though the docents' reports were surely mediated and written to demonstrate final success, the handwritten pages reflect a striving to turn feelings into words and words into emotion, all underpinned by a belief in the truth and power of Mao Zedong Thought.[87] As Elizabeth Perry has argued, the Chinese Communist revolution owes much of its success to "emotion work," and it

---

[85] Michael Schoenhals, *Doing Things with Words in Chinese Politics* (Berkeley: Institute of East Asian Studies, University of California, 1992).

[86] SMA B123-6-1536, p. 11.

[87] See Nicole Eustace et al., "AHR Conversation: The Historical Study of Emotions," *American Historical Review*, vol. 117, no. 5 (December 2012), pp. 1487–1531.

bequeathed this legacy to post-1949 political campaigns like the Cultural Revolution.[88] Echoing the displays of landlord property in struggle sessions during land reform, the Exhibition of Red Guard Achievements provides a case study of exhibition halls as a stage for the performance of emotions.

Preparation began with the study of Shanghai's class education exhibitions, which were still up from the Socialist Education Movement. Thus, at least in Shanghai the two kinds of display were temporally linked in both directions; class education exhibits provided templates for the Red Guards' big-character posters, and in determining how to display the crimes of the Red Guards' targets, the novice curators and narrators turned back to the *jiezhan* to look for models. As a first step, the Red Guards fanned out to study and to ask questions at eleven other exhibitions and they were instructed to make a record of each and every key artifact. They discussed the scope of their own display, including the themes and individuals in each section, and then they divided into groups to collect artifacts, draft the narrative, and put up the display. A preliminary outline was created within three days.[89] This division of labor reflects the memories of painter Li Bin (b. 1949), who recalls being responsible for exhibitions in Heilongjiang as a sent-down youth. "They would give you a script, or a story, or some events, like a comic strip ... we would have to draw it out, one scene at a time. There'd be several teams, those who could draw, those who could write ... We'd be very happy to paint. We just seized our colors and started painting."[90]

To write their own scripts, Red Guard docents started with artifacts and stories. Taking a page from the example of the class education exhibitions, they interviewed the victims of alleged capitalist crimes. For example, Team 8, the group in charge of the display on Chen Qinghua, interviewed Lin Kanglian, identified as his victim. Condemned in the exhibit for being a counterrevolutionary and portrayed via a panoply of spy equipment, Chen Qinghua was also accused of beating and tormenting the servant girls in his household.[91] All of the members of Team 8 listened to Lin Kanglian's bitter tale and cried when they heard her story. Seeing the scars all over her body, the narrators reported, "aroused our brotherly class feeling and sympathy still further, making us incomparably furious with the class enemy. This interview was a deeply impressive

---

[88] Elizabeth J. Perry, "Moving the Masses: Emotion Work in the Chinese Revolution," *Mobilization*, vol. 7, no. 2 (June 2002), pp. 111–128.

[89] SMA B123-6-1534, pp. 2–6.   [90] Interview in Shanghai, July 10, 2013.

[91] SMA B123-6-1535, p. 45.

education and it made us truly hate Chen Qinghua, so much so that when
we were narrating, deep in our hearts we would be stirred to the point of
crying." Team 8 concluded that only by combining class love with hatred
of the enemy could one "stimulate the visitors' feelings and meld them
with our own, so that when [the audience] heard Chen Qinghua's crimes,
they'd cry for his execution." In this way, they wrote, "we educated
ourselves and educated the audience."[92] If Team 8's experience represented a model trajectory, then the narrator's role was to go to the masses,
to transmit their stories, and then to transfer the emotion into shared class
feeling.

While the interviews provided context, the central focus of the exhibition was on the house search itself. By putting out the spoils and describing the process by which they were found, the docents reenacted the
house search. Hearing the narrative, visitors followed the Red Guards
through the windows of Yao Shifeng's house and opened the teakettle
together with them. The audience accosted Qu Liefang when he allegedly
dropped gold into a wastebasket, "carrying out sabotage."[93] The docents
of the section on counterrevolutionary crimes relived the discovery of
the pillow with the hidden portrait of Chiang Kai-shek, explaining how
"the courageous Red Guards took off one pillowcase after another,
and on the fourth layer the portrait appeared. This shows that night
and day, class enemies dream of the bastard Chiang, and dream of his
restoration!"[94] With both objects and words, the display repeated and
ritualized the house search.

The exhibit allowed the docents to continue to struggle against individuals via their confiscated possessions. From the beginning, the teams
were divided up according to the target, with the parallel between the
exhibition and the struggle session so strong that one individual on
Team 6, "because he was familiar with the target, did not dare to take
up the fight."[95] As illustrated above, each part of the text was structured
as an argument for Mao Zedong Thought. The argument's conclusion
reached a climax when the docent called for further class struggle.
The narrators from The East is Red Department Store, for example,
concluded their lengthy condemnation by shouting, "We must raise
high the great red flag of Mao Zedong Thought, and struggle the counterrevolutionary capitalist Guo Linshuang. Struggle until he reeks, struggle
until he collapses, and struggle until the end, such that he will never turn
over his body!"[96] Docents articulated their work as class struggle; one

[92] SMA B123-6-1536, p. 25.   [93] SMA B123-6-1535, p. 40.
[94] SMA B123-6-1540, p. 6.   [95] SMA B123-6-1536, p. 18.
[96] SMA B123-6-1535, p. 32.

explained that narration was his battlefield where "I expose the enemies ... I must expose their counterrevolutionary nature, let them be criticized ... only in this way can I inspire the comrades' feelings, their hatred of the enemy."[97] Like the curators of the First Party Congress Site, the Red Guard docents spoke of the red thread of Mao Zedong Thought. But exhibits at the former were those of a state in power, whereas the Red Guard exhibitions were those of a revolutionary movement. At the First Party Congress Site the "Red Line" was an interpretation of history, at the latter the "Red Line" was a call to arms.

Even as the exhibit became a site of class struggle, the narrators grappled with the problem of calling forth class feelings. This was a two-step process. First, they had to cultivate their own feelings. As one team member stated, "We have to make the visitors feel moved, and in order to do this we ourselves must first be aroused. If we are not moved, then how can we move the audience?"[98] Moving oneself involved remembering the victims whom one may have interviewed, or contemplating the artifact: the servant girl's scars, the tattered clothing. One's own class hatred was key, the docents argued, to doing a good job of narration, which in turn brought out the class hatred of others. One of the team members asked, "When one has called forth one's hate, how does one call on the audience to give a sympathetic response that gives rise to its hate? In addition to the material artifacts and the criminal evidence, it is primarily our narration that carries with it class feeling."[99] To make emotion with things, one needed words.

The second step was therefore to perfect the performance of the script. The docent who spoke of his work as a battlefield wrote, "I must use the lightness and heaviness of my words, my facial expressions and gestures, to express my own class feeling."[100] Others also spoke of narration as if it were a performance:

One should have memorized the script, one should have it mastered, and most of all it should become the words that one's own heart wants to say ... While we are narrating, every act and every movement of the speaker, and every one of his words and phrases, will give rise to a response from the audience. Therefore, when we appear on the stage, we must be somber.[101]

Acutely concerned with audience reception, the docents worked to ensure the uniformity of the narration across each member of the team,

---

[97] SMA B123-6-1534, p. 44.   [98] SMA B123-6-1536, p. 12.

[99] Ibid., p. 15. Other reports explained the verb "*gandong*" (to move, to touch) as the result of linking the feelings of the speaker, or "*gan*" (feelings, emotions), and the listeners' being moved, or "*dong*" (to move, to change). SMA B123-6-1534, p. 8.

[100] SMA B123-6-1534, p. 44.   [101] SMA B123-6-1536, p. 15.

attributing less-than-ideal responses to a lack of consistency. They debated when they should raise or lower their voices "in order to fully give free rein to the intelligence of the masses and their creative power."[102] The post-exhibition reports are replete with notes about speaking until throats were hoarse and bleeding; pain—a badge of loyalty—was to be combatted with Mao Zedong Thought. The performance of narrative was also a performance of class. Team 6, for example, reported that after its members realized that narration was "a question of whether or not one has class feeling," they threw themselves into their work, "determined to overcome all difficulties."[103] As one report asked rhetorically, "In the face of facts that drip with blood, how could we not hate? If . . . you are not able to call forth your own hate, it is because you have forgotten your roots."[104] The material on display, in turn, embodied such facts. Wrote one docent, "as soon as I come into contact with these exhibition objects, fury rises up in my breast."[105]

The final arbiter of the narration's success was the response of the audience. To be sure, the Exhibition of Red Guard Achievements' reports on visitors' class feelings were already subject to two filters. First, most attendees were like the docents in being highly conscious of their moods. They had likely been to similar displays before—in schools, factories, or exhibition halls—and they knew which emotions were appropriate. The second filter lies in the selections made and written down in the reports, with the express purpose of showing that the narration had indeed struck a chord. Hence, The East is Red Department Store team wrote that other Red Guard visitors "were so angry that they gnashed their teeth and said, 'Beat them to death!'; that PLA soldiers clenched their fists and asked if the enemies had been swept away; and that old workers responded with hot tears and comments like 'We will never forget our deep-seated hatred!'"[106] Other reactions in the reports confirm that the Red Guard exhibition provided a lesson in class education, that it proved the rightness of Mao Zedong Thought, and that the Cultural Revolution was timely and the Red Guards were victorious. The feedback suggested that the materiality of the exhibition mattered; to see the possessions of the capitalists was something more than simply reading about them in books, and the tangibility of the knives and guns made for a "living education."[107] The Exhibition of Red Guard Achievements, docents and visitors

---

[102] Ibid., pp. 11, 18, 25.   [103] Ibid., p. 17.   [104] Ibid., pp. 14–16, 18, 24.
[105] SMA B123-6-1534, pp. 43–44. In the same account, the docent describes fusing the exhibition objects with his thoughts and feelings.
[106] SMA B123-6-1536, p. 12.   [107] Ibid., pp. 28–29.

alike reported, had given them new eyes: one Xu Qi from the China Department Store remarked that seeing the pillow with the hidden portrait of Chiang Kai-shek and all the gold made him "reflect that when we searched [people's houses], we did not search carefully enough. We should have been searching with the maximum amount of hatred."[108] Said one docent after seeing the remainder of the exhibition, "I realized that there are even more ferocious class enemies."[109]

If the exhibition's reports are primarily filled with comments that show object lessons learned, its edges admit that there were variations in reception. Among the docents, the team summaries reveal that some did not take their work seriously, and they were criticized for being insufficiently plain in appearance or for chatting and joking when they should have been serious and stern-faced.[110] The reports also relate how some docents were discouraged by the visitors' lack of attention; if the model was the attendee who read for three hours and then requested to return, the negative example was the visitor who stopped listening or even wandered off before the docent had completed his narration.[111] The difficulty of getting visitors to view the objects with class feeling is obliquely hinted at. During the preview, several people called for more comparisons between the rich and the poor, and one stressed that curators should not just "put out everyday items like they are commercial products, or put out feudal superstitious things like Buddhas in a temple."[112] Without saying why, the docents confessed that the hardest section to narrate was the part themed "treasures," and an alert was raised about a suspicious-looking youth circling the table of gold, silver, and jewels.[113] Shandong Red Guards who critiqued the Shanghai Class Education Exhibition recorded that one middle-school student could not control himself, saying, "If you were to give me one of these, I could live off of it for my entire life!"[114] Read between the lines, reports suggest that some visitors saw not the lesson, but instead were dazzled by the treasures, perhaps even tempted to slip one away. As one team commented to underscore the importance of narration, "Deep class feelings are not innate."[115]

Today, memories of visiting a Red Guard exhibition are mixed. Some recollections are faded, with people naming typical objects—gold bars, guns, perhaps a Bible—and others only remembering that such a genre existed. One man (b. 1950), who had been a student at Fuxing Middle

---

[108] SMA B123-6-1534, p. 52.   [109] SMA B123-6-1536, p. 24.
[110] SMA B123-6-1636, p. 19.
[111] SMA B123-6-1534, p. 11; SMA B123-6-1636, pp. 11, 16, 19.
[112] SMA B123-6-1534, p. 9.   [113] Ibid., p. 38.   [114] SMA C4-2-30, p. 38b.
[115] SMA B123-6-1536, p. 12.

School, recalls that exhibitions followed the searches of the principal and others, and that battling factions going after two different principals would collect criminal evidence and exhibit the items, even traveling to the countryside to the former home of one of the principals for materials.[116] A high-school physical education teacher (b. 1942) laughed ruefully when asked about the Red Guard exhibitions, "And they did this with my things too! At the school gate, they hung up a pair of my shoes and said they were capitalist leather shoes. They hung a sign, saying that these were Teacher X's shoes. And what were you going to do about it?"[117] Some remember the anger or fear inspired by a particular object. The memoirist Gao Yuan recounts his feelings on seeing grain coupons confiscated from the Party secretary, "Did he have so much fruit and meat to eat that he could not use up his grain rations? ... The more I thought about the small dining hall, the more indignant I felt."[118] One informant (b. 1954) remembers his childlike terror at seeing a human skull on display, realizing years later that it was perfectly normal for a doctor at Fudan Medical School to have one in his possession.[119] Like the astonished observers of the gold, others retain that which was simply fantastic. The former Fuxing Middle School student reports that "the Qing dynasty robes gave me the deepest impression. Because one really had never seen them before, except maybe in the movies. That was really amazing."[120] To these varied reflections are added recently published remembrances: the fascination of the Chongqing child with confiscated Buddhist pictures, the dread of the Beijing political cadre about the possibility of making a curatorial mistake, and the irony of the Lu Xun scholar who asked for a copy of his own exhibition photo.

But in its own time, the Exhibition of Red Guard Achievements made no allowance for alternative narratives. It presented a template for house searches, providing the most nefarious examples of what a Red Guard was meant to find. It modeled how such material should be used for class struggle and how the "fruits of battle" should be described. The experience of curating and narrating the display was, as the docents understood, a class education—formative in the same way that the land reform "living exhibitions" had created activists. Although recent research on Cultural Revolution factionalism by Dong Guoqiang and Andrew Walder questions our ability to use class

---

[116] Interview in Shanghai, July 3, 2013.   [117] Interview in Shanghai, July 20, 2013.
[118] Gao Yuan, *Born Red*, p. 73.   [119] Interview in Shanghai, July 20, 2013.
[120] Interview in Shanghai, July 3, 2013.

categories to analyze how or why people acted as they did, the persistent language of class still requires us to attend to how it was articulated.[121]

For the language of class could have real and tragic consequences. Exhibiting the Red Guards' achievements appeared to be a verbal struggle over a physical struggle, even as it was centered on material objects. But what if the search of a class enemy did not turn up any gold, or what if only one diary—not a second private diary as the exhibit suggested—was found? Objects—or alternatively their absence—combined with words had the power of terror. By engendering class hatred, by arming the visitors to search for and interpret material as embodying class, and by providing examples of the most "ferocious class enemies," the Red Guard exhibitions may also have exacerbated the violence.[122] At the end of Guangzhou's Red Guard exhibition, entitled a "conclusion without a conclusion," the organizers proclaimed, "Fellow Red Guard fighters, comrades in revolution! Here our exhibition comes to an end. But class struggle is not yet over."[123]

Conclusion: Object lessons

The Red Guard exhibition, like the Red Guard movement, was short-lived. The end of the Red Guard movement dates to July 1968, after which time millions of young people were demobilized to the countryside as "sent-down youth."[124] The exhibit of the Beijing Red Guards, the largest and most official, was disbanded at the beginning of 1969.[125] In Shanghai, although some publications retained the format of an exhibition, including photographs of seized guns and bullets, Guomindang badges and counterrevolutionary documents, the Red

---

[121] Dong Guoqiang and Andrew G. Walder, "Local Politics in the Chinese Cultural Revolution: Nanjing Under Military Control," *Journal of Asian Studies*, vol. 70, no. 2 (May 2011), pp. 425–447; Andrew G. Walder, *Fractured Rebellion: The Beijing Red Guard Movement* (Cambridge, MA: Harvard University Press, 2009).

[122] In Hu Jie's documentary film *Though I am Gone*, an interviewee named Pan Shihong, then a student at Beijing Number Thirty-five Middle School, tells the story of some Red Guards who were absolved of a murder because the elderly female victim had been found with a land deed; it was said that Jiang Qing and Minister of Public Security Xie Fuzhi had agreed that, with such evidence, the Red Guards were not guilty. I have not been able to find the documentary evidence, though Li Xun shows that in Xie Fuzhi's speeches he tacitly approved of the beating of "bad people" and stressed that Red Guards who beat people to death should not be punished as they were not acting under ordinary circumstances. Nevertheless, the existence of such rumors underscores the role of material evidence in justifying violence. See Hu Jie, director, *Though I am Gone* (New York: dGenerateFilms, 2007), and Li Xun, *Wenge zaofan niandai*, p. 107.

[123] *Guangzhou diqu hongweibing geming zaofan zhanguo zhanlanhui*, p. 11.

[124] MacFarquhar and Schoenhals, *Mao's Last Revolution*, pp. 251–252.

[125] Ding Dahua, "Shisuo hanjian de hongweibing chaojia zhanguo zhanlanhui," p. 31.

Guard exhibits were more ephemeral.[126] With Shanghai's January
Revolution of 1967 and the restoration of order under the Shanghai
Revolutionary Committee, a formal exhibit, complete with pamphlets,
commemorated the very same "January revolutionary storm that
shakes the world!" In this exhibit, none of the objects from the
Exhibition of Red Guard Achievements appeared; the Red Guards
themselves were found in only a few photos and were represented via
an anonymous diary written by a little Red Guard.[127]

What happened to the objects of the house searches? At the highest
levels of the leadership, it appears that some objects were tracked from
the very start. In his 2015 memoirs, Qi Benyu, the last surviving member of the Central Cultural Revolution Group at the time, describes
a booklet circulated by Premier Zhou Enlai in August 1966. Entitled
"The Fruits of Battle from the Red Guards' 'Attack on the Four Olds,'"
it included photographs of confiscated possessions. At the time, Zhou
only said that "people would look after them," but Qi later discovered
that everything had been handed over to a "Capital Work Group" that
reported directly to Zhou.[128] It is not clear how the Capital Work
Group intersected with the Capital Red Guard Exhibition, if at all,
and whether thereafter it took responsibility for the objects. As for
other Red Guard exhibitions, some of the artifacts were returned to
the original work units, some were retained while the class statuses of
the owners were determined, and some were liquidated as second-hand
goods.[129] The little Red Guard from Chongqing remembers taking his
mother's ticket to the warehouse where the former exhibition objects

---

[126] For an example, see *Gongren zaofanbao* (Workers' rebel news), December 12, 1967, p. 2.
[127] *Weida de yiyue geming shengli wansui zhanlanhui* (Exhibition wishing long life to the
victory of the great January Revolution) (Shanghai: Shanghai wuchanjieji gemingpai,
August 1968).
[128] Qi Benyu, "Huiyi Jiang Qing tongzhi" (Remembering Comrade Jiang Qing), *Fuxing
wang*, July 30, 2015, www.mzfxw.com/e/action/ShowInfo.php?classid=18&id=44595
(accessed June 2, 2016). Qi explains that this was a secret organization led by Marshal
Ye Jianying, and its activities were unknown even to senior CCRG members like Chen
Boda and Jiang Qing. A longer account—which dates the booklet to the fourth quarter of
1966—is found in Qi Benyu, *Qi Benyu huiyilu* (Recollections by Qi Benyu) (Hong Kong:
Zhongguo wenge lishi chuban youxian gongsi, 2016), pp. 474–476. Qi Benyu died
in April 2016. Memoirs by people who actually carried out house searches also suggest
that those who worked with PSB name-lists were required to register and hand over the
items that they found. See Li Xun, *Wenge zaofan niandai*, p. 110.
[129] See Denise Y. Ho, "The Old Society and the New Society: Towards a Material Culture
of China's Cultural Revolution," in *The Oxford Handbook of History and Material Culture*,
edited by Sarah Carter and Ivan Gaskell (Oxford: Oxford University Press, 2017). Du
Xing claims that at the end of the Beijing exhibition the PSB took the guns, the finance
department received the gold and jewelry, and the antiquities and *wenwu* were sent to the
museums; see Du Xing, "'Posijiu' zhanlan ji," p. 93.

were kept; "there were all kinds of daily-use items strewn everywhere, and using the ticket you could buy one or two items very cheaply." In Jie Li's *Shanghai Homes*, one informant recalls her mother buying a wool sweater and two silk scarves at a second-hand shop, remarking that although one could not wear them outside, it was a pleasure simply to own beautiful things.[130] In Shanghai, confiscated cash, foreign currency, and gold were handed over to the bank and in 1970 converted at prices determined by the state.[131] After the end of the Cultural Revolution, the government ordered that restitution be made, and in Chongqing as elsewhere some of the more valuable items, such as antiquities, books, and furniture, were returned if their rightful owners could be traced.[132] However, most objects left no record and were not to be seen again.

Guo Linshuang did not live to see his possessions returned. On October 27, 1974, he died of a heart attack and Shanghai Number Ten Department Store (the new name for The East is Red Department Store) allowed him only a simple funeral at which the adjective "patriotic" was struck from the eulogy.[133] Like many others accused during the Cultural Revolution, Guo was rehabilitated in November 1978, and in the 1980s his overseas descendants returned to invest in China's economic miracle. His son Guo Zhikai, a Canadian citizen, tore down the garden house at 1375 Huaihai Road and built a twenty-five-story high-rise building in its place.[134] In 2005, the department store was renamed Yong'an, complete with a new signboard and neon lights. Today, its workers are taught a new narrative about the place of the department store in the revolution: when Nanjing Road was liberated, the first red flag to be unfurled was that of Yong'an Company.[135] Asked about Guo Linshuang, a Yong'an cadre (b. 1957) in charge of employee education said, "Guo was a national capitalist, he donated airplanes and other things, and Yong'an was the first department store to be handed over to the state. He was here from 1933 to 1955, when he left. Later on, nothing

---

[130] Jie Li, *Shanghai Homes: Palimpsests of Private Life* (New York: Columbia University Press, 2015), pp. 120–121.

[131] Li Xun, *Wenge zaofan niandai*, p. 64.

[132] Yang Yaojian, "Shouwei zaofan zhanlan," p. 42. For archival documents on the restitution of property to national bourgeoisie, see SMA B112-6-205.

[133] Hong Hong, "Guo Linshuang he Shanghai Yong'an gongsi," pp. 275–276.

[134] Ibid., p. 276; *Wenhui bao*, December 2, 1978, July 7, 1985, May 8, 1996; *Xinmin wanbao*, August 5, 1985.

[135] This account is also included in Shanghai shehui kexueyuan jingji yanjiusuo (Economics Institute of the Shanghai Academy of Social Sciences), ed., *Shanghai Yong'an gongsi de chansheng, fazhan, he gaizao* (The emergence, development, and reform of Shanghai's Yong'an Company) (Shanghai: Shanghai renmin chubanshe, 1981), p. 235.

is known about him. Maybe he went back to Hong Kong." Pressed on whether anything had happened to Guo Linshuang during the Cultural Revolution, the cadre replied, "I don't know ... I wasn't here then. Anyhow, there aren't any records ... We just rely on stories that have been handed down."[136]

In 1986, the writer Ba Jin, who coincidentally sat with Guo Linshuang on the Shanghai People's Congress, called for a Museum of the Cultural Revolution.[137] During the 2016 fiftieth anniversary of the ten years of turmoil, Chinese intellectuals and activists asked why there still was not yet a Cultural Revolution museum. They were, as this chapter has shown, only partially right: from the outbreak of the Red Guard movement there were in fact Cultural Revolution exhibitions. Of course, the Red Guard exhibitions are the precise opposite of what Ba Jin had in mind. Rather than a monument that might serve to recall and to warn, these exhibits served to attack and condemn. Contemporary display was part of political action: it was used to reveal the Red Guards' "achievements," it displayed the objects of the house searches to make arguments about Mao Zedong Thought and the Cultural Revolution, and it was itself a form of class struggle.

Even after the Red Guard movement was over, exhibitions continued to be used to denounce class enemies. Sociologist Yang Su's study of collective killings during the Cultural Revolution documents a series of such exhibitions in Guangxi and Guangdong provinces in 1968. In Guangxi, four exhibitions—taking place in government and military offices as well as at Guangxi University—displayed political enemies bound in cages. Labeled traitors and war criminals and tortured on site, tens of thousands of such victims were shown for days to over two million people. Guangdong held similar exhibitions, sometimes designed to display the atrocities allegedly committed by opposing factions.[138] The Shanghai Exhibition of Red Guard Achievements did not use living people, but elsewhere the phenomenon of "living exhibition" (*huoren zhanlan*) was widespread enough that when it appeared in the media in 1984 it provoked debates about which Cultural Revolution practices

---

[136] Interview in Shanghai, July 24, 2013. The cadre joined Yong'an Company in 1986.

[137] See *Wenhui bao*, November 30, 1965, p. 1; Ba Jin, "A Cultrev Museum," in *Seeds of Fire: Chinese Voices of Conscience*, edited by Geremie Barmé and John Minford (New York: Hill and Wang, 1988), pp. 381–384.

[138] Yang Su, *Collective Killings in Rural China during the Cultural Revolution* (Cambridge: Cambridge University Press, 2011), pp. 204–205. One of the studies that he cites for Guangzhou refers to these exhibits as "mass dictatorship exhibitions." See Haifeng, *Guangzhou diqu wen'ge licheng shulüe* (An account of the Cultural Revolution in the Canton area) (Hong Kong: Youlian yanjiusuo, 1971), pp. 401–404.

should be repudiated.[139] Writing of the controversy about twenty-five years later, some have argued that all forms of public humiliation—from being forced to wear dunce caps to being paraded in the streets—regarded people as exhibition pieces and therefore should be called "living exhibitions."[140]

To call all such Cultural Revolution practices exhibitions may be going too far, as other influences—from religion to theater—also left a mark. Guo Linshuang himself, with his fondness for Cantonese opera, would probably have chosen the stage; he was known to have said to fellow actors, "human life is like an opera, and everything in the world is theater."[141] For Guo Linshuang, the Exhibition of Red Guard Achievements literally changed the narrative script of his life. Before the Cultural Revolution, he could tell his own story, however limited: he gave speeches that described his own personal history, he had a poem published in the local paper, and he wrote reviews of his beloved opera.[142] But the Red Guards at The East is Red Department Store told a different tale, even changing the title of the opera he performed to celebrate Yong'an Company's socialist transformation. The Cantonese opera staged in 1956 was called the *Golden Saddle*, but the exhibition's docents claimed that he sang a part in something called the *Mounted Bandits of Shandong*, decrying Guo for attacking socialist transformation as highway robbery.[143]

Even in this ahistorical sleight of hand the focus was on Guo's property, the centerpiece of the Red Guard display. Such exhibitions were a powerful part of Cultural Revolution political action because they equated material possessions and class. Red Guard showcases suggested to viewers what should be found in a house search. In this way, exhibits contributed both to people's fear of what they possessed and

---

[139] Lu Liang and Ye Hui, "Wengezhong zai Hangzhou daxue gao 'huoren zhanlan' de gebie ren zhijin rengrang jianchi jizuo de cuowu guandian bu gai" (Individuals who made "living exhibitions" at Hangzhou University during the Cultural Revolution still hold incorrect ultra-leftist views), *Guangming ribao* (Guangming daily), April 3, 1984, p. 1.

[140] See, for example, Du Xuefeng, "'Wenge' de 'huoren zhanlan'" ("Living exhibitions" during the "Cultural Revolution"), *Zhongshan fengyu*, no. 2 (2010), p. 49; Wei Dongfeng, "Linglei de zhanshi: Wenge shiqi zhanlan huodong anli fenxi" (Another kind of exhibition: An analysis of Cultural Revolution exhibition activities), *Dazhong wenyi*, no. 9 (2009), pp. 98–100.

[141] Jiu Yi, "Guo Linshuang de yize jiuwen" (An old story about Guo Linshuang), *Xinmin wanbao*, August 5, 1985, p. 6.

[142] Zhong Cheng, "Guo Linshuang shengri yinshi" (Guo Linshuang recites a poem on his birthday), *Xinmin wanbao*, March 22, 1957, p. 6; Guo Linshuang, "Wo kan Yueju 'Sou xueyuan' de yanchu" (I saw a performance of the Cantonese opera "Searching for the Academy"), *Xinmin wanbao*, June 6, 1956, p. 5.

[143] For original reportage, see *Xinmin wanbao*, January 14, 1956, January 20, 1956, January 21, 1956. For the docents' scripts, see B123-6-1535, pp. 27–28.

perhaps even to the ruthlessness of the Red Guard struggle sessions, which took as a given the idea that a class enemy must be hiding evidence and that such a discovery was proof of the Red Guards' revolutionary mettle. At the Exhibition of Red Guard Achievements, the lesson was to see class in things and therefore crimes in things. With tangible objects, it taught continuous revolution. But at least two valuable items from Guo Linshuang's house search did not make it into the exhibition: a gold Buddha statue and a jade *ruyi*, or a decorative sceptre.[144] Though they could have been classified as "treasures" for their materials or displayed as superstitious objects for their Buddhist associations, the two pieces simply disappeared. The fate of cultural relics, as well as the Shanghai Museum that housed them, is the subject of the following chapter. If *wenwu* were not to be destroyed as the "Four Olds" or incorporated into a Red Guard exhibition as examples of the "fruits of struggle," what place had they in the revolution?

[144] Hong Hong, "Guo Linshuang he Shanghai Yong'an gongsi," p. 274.

6 Antiquity in revolution: The Shanghai Museum

The Longhua Pagoda, rising seven levels over the landscape in the southwestern corner of Shanghai, was twice encircled—with ropes and with people. Dating from the Song dynasty and celebrated as one of Shanghai's eight vistas, the pagoda and its adjacent temple had long been a destination for pleasure-seekers from the city and for families on annual Spring Festival outings.[1] But on August 23, 1966, at the outbreak of the Cultural Revolution in Shanghai, a scene of destruction unfolded. That morning, in the name of Mao Zedong's call to attack the "Four Olds," Red Guards laid waste to the Longhua Temple. The temple's Buddhas were smashed, its monks subjected to struggle sessions, and its scriptures fed to the flames.[2] Red Guards, calling themselves the "Burn-the-Pagoda Headquarters," tied the base of the pagoda with ropes. But as rumors flew of imminent destruction and a group of college students came to blows with the Red Guards, a second circle—of people—wrapped around the Longhua Pagoda.[3] Part of the human wall made up of students and locals, Zhong Yinlan of the Shanghai Museum remembers that, "We explained to the Red Guards that the pagoda was a *wenwu*, a cultural relic, not one of the

[1] Huang Bi, "Longhua guta de qingchun" (Spring comes to the Longhua ancient pagoda), *Lüxing jia* (Traveler), no. 3 (1956), pp. 20–21. The contemporary structure dates to the Song dynasty, with renovations completed during the Ming and Qing dynasties. In 1953 Shanghai's Bureau of Construction began a new renovation process, which included research on similar pagodas in Nanjing and Suzhou and employed multi-generational families of builders. It was completed in 1955.

[2] Jin Ding, "Budao de Longhua ta" (The Longhua Pagoda that did not fall), in *Shoucang lishi* (Collecting history), edited by Chen Pengju (Shanghai: Shanghai shudian chubanshe, 1998), pp. 235–237.

[3] In Jin Ding's account, students and teachers from the neighboring school of nursing heard the rumors and six students rushed to the site, where they were first beaten and then paraded by the "Burn-the-Pagoda Headquarters." Public sympathy led to the gathering of the crowd. According to Shanghai Museum lore, the students were history majors from East China Normal University. Interview in Shanghai with Li Junjie, July 20, 2011. See also Chen Zhiqiang, *Wenbo xianqu: Shen Zhiyu zhuan* (Museum pioneer: A biography of Shen Zhiyu) (Shanghai: Shanghai wenhua chubanshe, 2011), p. 203.

Ill.6.1. Postcard of the Longhua Pagoda, René Antoine Nus, ca. 1930s.
Image courtesy of the Virtual Cities Project, Institut d'Asie Orientale

'Four Olds.'"[4] To the shouts of "do not burn!" more of the old-hundred-names, Shanghai's ordinary people, linked hands in multiple rings. The Longhua Pagoda remained standing.[5]

For Zhong Yinlan, then a young member of the Shanghai Museum's Department of Painting, this was one of the many rescue missions in which she took part during the late summer of 1966, when the Red Guard movement engulfed the city with its "Attack on the Four Olds." This campaign to eradicate old thinking, old culture, old customs, and old habits was part of making revolution: the old was to be extirpated to make way for the new. The Red Guards went on a rampage in words and deeds. They accosted individuals sporting bourgeois fashions, they tore down street signs with names deemed to be feudal, and, as in the case of the Longhua Temple and Pagoda, they set out to destroy remnants of the old

[4] Interview in Shanghai with Zhong Yinlan, December 25, 2009. Interviews in Shanghai with Li Junjie and Zhong Yinlan suggest that protection of the Longhua Pagoda was more organized than spontaneous, because the Shanghai Cultural Relics Commission and the Shanghai Museum sent workers and local officials mobilized residents.
[5] The event became known as the 8–23 Longhua Pagoda Incident. Shortly thereafter, the Shanghai Cultural Relics Commission and the Shanghai Museum sent leaders to thank the students. On December 19, 1966, the students were received by Premier Zhou Enlai. See Jin Ding, "Budao de Longhua ta," p. 236.

society. To preempt a Red Guard attack, the Shanghai Museum packed up the objects in its exhibition rooms and sealed its doors. Behind them museum workers remained at the ready, as Shanghai's art collectors were doubly vulnerable to the "Attack on the Four Olds"; they were likely to face house searches because of their capitalist backgrounds, and their homes were filled with *wenwu*. Fearful of irremediable consequences, the Shanghai Museum installed a twenty-four-hour hotline, and Chen Peifen—a young student of bronzes with impeccable class credentials— organized the staffing. Joining her in rotation was Zhong Yinlan, who recalls how during the "Attack on the Four Olds" she slept in the museum on a makeshift bed. "If we heard that a certain household was going to be searched, or that there would be Red Guards going to attack the 'Four Olds' in a house at midnight, then we would send people as quickly as we could. At midnight, or at one or two in the morning, no matter what the time, if it was a collection with paintings I would go there at once. I never got to return home."[6] Shen Zhiyu, the Shanghai Museum director who had discovered the First Party Congress Site, stayed on guard at the museum. A small fleet of trucks borrowed from the Shanghai Bureau of Culture waited outside.[7]

This chapter examines the Mao-era history of the Shanghai Museum, which at its founding in 1952 was one of New China's first museums and remains today one of the most eminent art collections in the People's Republic.[8] The chapter first presents an institutional history of the museum, which, with its sister organization the Shanghai Cultural Relics Commission, collected and curated the city's *wenwu*, from the paintings Zhong Yinlan studied to the preserved shantytown housing in Fangua Lane. To collect was to curate, and from its inception the Shanghai Museum intended to build a collection that would encompass China's antiquity, providing an art historical narrative for the nation. In the preface to its earliest catalogue, written in 1952, the museum declared that its guiding principles were the following: to allow the masses

---

[6] Interview in Shanghai with Zhong Yinlan, December 25, 2009.
[7] Chen Zhiqiang, *Wenbo xianqu*, p. 206.
[8] For a major book in Chinese on the Shanghai Museum, see Zheng Zhong, *Bowuguan yu shoucangjia* (Museum and collectors) (Shanghai: Shanghai wenyi chubanshe, 2000). Zheng Zhong had the "museum beat" for *Wenhui bao* (Wenhui daily), wrote biographies of collectors, and also had access to the archives of the Shanghai Museum. For a recent pathbreaking study of the Shanghai Museum, see Di Yin Lu, "Seizing Civilization: Antiquities in Shanghai's Custody, 1949–1996" (PhD diss., Harvard University, 2012). Lu's work uses extensive oral histories conducted in Shanghainese and rigorous statistical analysis to argue that the Shanghai Museum was built from the systematic appropriation of antiquities of private owners, a seizure that was facilitated by the Cultural Revolution. Lu, "Seizing Civilization," pp. 7, 171–172.

to understand that China was one of the world's earliest civilizations and that this was the great product of labor, to allow workers and students to critically absorb China's ancient cultural quintessence and thereby develop new culture, and to cultivate patriotism and desire to struggle on China's behalf. These prescriptions drew from the writings of Mao Zedong, which were prominently excerpted in the frontispiece of the catalogue. "On New Democracy," a 1942 Mao text that became one of the museum's touchstones, argued that the culture of antiquity had both a democratic and a revolutionary essence and therefore was a necessary condition for the development of a new national culture.[9] The story of building the Shanghai Museum shows how representatives of Old China cultivated New China; it was an elder generation of connoisseurs who gave Chen Peifen and Zhong Yinlan their classical training, and it was China before 1949 that bequeathed its *wenwu* to the new socialist museum.

When Zhong Yinlan and others persuaded the Red Guards at the Longhua Pagoda that it was a *wenwu*, not part of the "Four Olds," she was drawing on a long tradition of defining cultural relics as national patrimony. Though May Fourth iconoclasts had criticized the museum as a mere repository for "old tools, old objects, and old classics,"[10] Nationalists, Communists, and even collaborators with the Japanese defended the preservation of China's material culture. In a 1934 telegram circulated by Chiang Kai-shek and Wang Jingwei, the two Nationalist leaders explained the work of the Central Commission on Antiquities by saying that "only by studying old materials is one able to know the new ... If one wishes to revive the nation through [its] long-held culture, it is necessary to know the nation's history."[11] Seven years later Wang Jingwei's collaborationist government created its own Cultural Relics Commission, thanking the Japanese for stepping in at a time when "our nation was lacking in people to take care of cultural relics" and pledging to preserve Chinese culture for the "propagation of the culture of the Eastern Seas!"[12] During the second

---

[9] *Shanghai bowuguan chenliepin shuomingshu* (Guide to Shanghai Museum exhibits) (Shanghai: Shanghai bowuguan, November 1952), frontispiece, p. 4.

[10] Chen Duanzhi, *Bowuguanxue tonglun* (General survey of museum studies) (Shanghai: Shanghaishi bowuguan, 1936), p. 27.

[11] "Wang yuanzhang Jiang weiyuanzhang tongdian yuanwen" (Director Wang and Committee Chairman Jiang's joint circular), in *Zhongyang guwu baoguan weiyuan huiyi shilu* (Proceedings of the Committee to Promote the Preservation of Antiquities), edited by Zhongyang guwu baoguan weiyuanhui (Committee to Promote the Preservation of Antiquities) (Nanjing: Zhongyang guwu baoguan weiyuanhui, June 1935), p. 39.

[12] Zhu Minyi, *Xingzhengyuan wenwu baoguan weiyuanhui niankan* (Annual of the Cultural Relics Commission of the Administrative Yuan) (Nanjing, 1941), preface, and pp. 6–7.

Sino-Japanese War and the subsequent Chinese Civil War, Chinese intellectuals also spoke on behalf of cultural preservation; librarians wrote that cultural projects in Free China would serve future Chinese museology and engineers cited their responsibility to protect historic sites in the war zones.[13] During the final year of the civil war, the historian Xiang Da issued a plea for *wenwu*, arguing that cultural preservation was practiced by all civilized and modern nations and stressing that even though the Nationalists and Communists were fighting an ideological battle, "they should know to love and protect the cultural remains of their forebears."[14] When the Communist Party came to power in 1949, it also used *wenwu* to project political legitimacy, but it was careful to distinguish itself from previous regimes. The renovation of Shanghai's Longhua Pagoda in the mid-1950s was described as restoring a glorious page of national history and in reference to cultural relics work in the Soviet Union.[15]

But it was not enough to curate *wenwu* for the nation. As the "Attack on the Four Olds" demonstrates, the place of antiquity in New China was far from assured. This chapter focuses on the Shanghai Museum during the Cultural Revolution, a decade seen as one of the most critical threats to traditional Chinese culture in the twentieth century.[16] I argue that during this period the new generation of Shanghai Museum workers collected and curated, inscribing antiquity with contemporary meanings of revolution. With their teachers in ox-pens and leaders like Shen Zhiyu sidelined, they mounted an institutionalized and ideologically legitimated defense of *wenwu*, in which the material culture of China's past was returned to the masses who had made it. In this way, the Shanghai Museum revolutionized antiquity, defending cultural relics not only in the name of revolution, but also claiming that preservation was a mission of the Cultural Revolution all along. While today's Shanghai Museum restores *wenwu* to a narrative of nation, its collection nevertheless owes much to the Cultural Revolution period of *wenwu* for revolution.

[13] Yuan Tongli, "Kangzhan qizhong woguo bowuguan zhi dongtai yu qiantu" (The situation and future of our nation's museums during wartime), *Zhongguo bowuguan xiehui huibao* (Journal of the Chinese Museum Association), no. 1 (1941), pp. 2–4; Shen Yi, "Gongchengshi yu difang guji" (Engineers and local historical sites), *Gongcheng: Zhongguo gongchengshi xuehui huikan* (Chinese Engineering Society Journal), vol. 16, no. 2 (1943), pp. 23–24.
[14] Xiang Da, "Wei wenwu qingming" (A plea on behalf of cultural relics), *Zhongjian* (China constructs), vol. 3, no. 6 (1948), p. 8.
[15] Huang Bi, "Longhua guta de qingchun," p. 21.
[16] A recent exception is Mobo Gao, *The Battle for China's Past: Mao and the Cultural Revolution* (London: Pluto Press, 2008).

A socialist museum for New China

When Zhong Yinlan—bookish and shy, with a long braid down her back—first walked through the doors of the Shanghai Museum in 1952, it was a modest collection of 7,000 objects housed in the former race-course building.[17] Symbolically, almost three thousand of the *wenwu* in the earliest collection arrived in Shanghai in two trucks on May 5, 1949, carried from the battlefields on behalf of General Chen Yi by his deputy Li Yanong.[18] Li became the head of the Shanghai Cultural Relics Commission, established by the Shanghai Military Control Committee on September 17, 1949, four months after the PLA entered the city.[19] In 1950 the Shanghai Municipal Government established the Shanghai Bureau of Culture, and the Shanghai Museum—like the First Party Congress Site—was one of the work units under its jurisdiction.[20] Both the Shanghai Cultural Relics Commission and the Shanghai Bureau of Culture shared the work of cultural preservation, the former a United Front group of experts and the latter a municipal administrative unit.

The work of Shanghai's cultural bureaucracy relied on the patronage of Chen Yi, who became Shanghai's first mayor under the new regime. In 1950, it was Mayor Chen who posted the State Council's national regulations to protect ancient culture, adding his personal postscript specifically to protect the Yu Gardens near the City God Temple.[21] During the early years of Liberation the Shanghai Museum received fully one-third of the municipal budget allotted for culture and education, with Mayor Chen Yi intervening to approve purchases of art.[22] Li Junjie, who joined the Shanghai Museum with Zhong Yinlan's cohort, explains, "We would bring out the good stuff and invite Leader Chen to

[17] Zhang Ling, "Kanhua yibeizi zhiqiushi zhenwei: Ji guojiaji shuhua jiandingjia Zhong Yinlan" (A lifetime of viewing paintings in search of the truth: Zhong Yinlan, nationally-ranked appraiser of paintings), *Xinmin wanbao* (New people's evening news), November 27, 2002, p. 3.
[18] Shen Zhiyu, "Huainian Chen Yi tongzhi dui wenbo shiye de juda guanhuai" (Remembering Comrade Chen Yi's great concern for the work of cultural relics and museums), in *SZYWBLJ*, p. 362.
[19] The Shanghai Cultural Relics Commission had a number of Chinese names. It was first called Shanghaishi gudai wengu guanli weiyuanhui, but it was renamed Shanghaishi wenwu guanli weiyuanhui in January 1950. Over the course of the 1950s it was renamed Shanghaishi renmin zhengfu wenwuguanli weiyuanhui (August 1953), and then Shanghaishi wenwu baoguan weiyuanhui (April 1955). It was made part of the Shanghaishi renwei wenyi bangongshi (June 1956) and then incorporated into the Shanghai Museum (February 1960). See *SHWWBWGZ*, pp. 370–371.
[20] In September 1988, the Shanghai Museum was separated from the Shanghai Bureau of Culture and again fell under the leadership of the Shanghai Cultural Relics Commission. See *SHWWBWGZ*, p. 370.
[21] SMA S172-4-67, p. 1.   [22] Shen Zhiyu, "Huainian Chen Yi," p. 362.

have a look. And we would ask, should we buy it? He would respond, yes, let's buy it. And what if we didn't have enough money? He would say, well, hurry up and write a report, and I'll approve it." In this way, the Shanghai Museum had a guarantor in the Shanghai Bureau of Finance, and during Spring Festival when collectors were eager to sell—so that they could pay off their debts as tradition dictated—but the museum was at the end of its fiscal year, Chen Yi's political patronage could replenish the till.[23]

The Shanghai Museum's leadership remained keenly aware of the importance of political attention. Even after Chen Yi became foreign minister in 1958, he would return to visit the museum. In 1961 he brought with him several central leaders, including Premier Zhou Enlai, who asked to see the treasures in the storehouse. Accompanied by a young bronze expert, Ma Chengyuan, Premier Zhou held in both hands a mirror from the Western Han, flashing its engraved patterns on the wall in the midday sunlight.[24] The Shanghai Museum, attuned to what Elizabeth Perry calls "cultural patronage," never missed an opportunity to propagandize its own efforts and to "work on the leaders."[25]

Though the Shanghai Museum was framed as a new-style socialist museum, it relied upon the expertise of the pre-1949 world of museology and connoisseurship. The vice director of the Shanghai Cultural Relics Commission was Xu Linyu, who had been part of the leadership of the Nationalist-era Central Museum and Palace Museum. The Shanghai Cultural Relics Commission—with invitations from Mayor Chen Yi— was stacked with some of Shanghai's most important men of letters, who brought both their knowledge of art history and their personal network of collectors.[26] The Shanghai Museum employed people who had worked in the Republican-era Shanghai Municipal Museum, from its former director Yang Kuan who wrote the outline for the 1952 exhibition to the staff who created the catalogue. While its junior leaders, represented by people like Shen Zhiyu—artists who had joined the Communist underground— had been trained *in* Old China, the Shanghai Museum's youngest generation was trained *by* Old China. The 1952 cohort, which included Chen Peifen, Li Junjie, and Zhong Yinlan (Ma Chengyuan arrived in 1954),

---

[23] Interview in Shanghai with Li Junjie, July 20, 2011.

[24] Zheng Zhong, *Bowuguan yu shoucangjia*, pp. 186–188.

[25] Elizabeth J. Perry, *Anyuan: Mining China's Revolutionary Tradition* (Berkeley: University of California Press, 2012), pp. 11–13. In later years, the Shanghai Museum even organized classes for cadres, telling stories about how objects were preserved and repaired, how to tell the real from the fake, and relating why the *wenwu* were so precious. Interview in Shanghai with Li Junjie, July 20, 2011.

[26] *SHWWBWGZ*, pp. 474–475; interview in Shanghai with Li Junjie, July 20, 2011.

attended lectures on art history by pre-1949 experts. Likewise, in the nationalized Antiquities Market (*Guwan shichang*) a new generation of buyers learned the skill of appraisal, training in master-apprentice relationships.[27]

Among the Shanghai Museum's 1952 cohort, four members were selected in 1959 for further training, to form the mainstays of their young generation. Chen Peifen, who started out at the age of seventeen by working on the museum floor—keeping it clean, guarding the objects, and answering simple questions—rose quickly through the ranks, joining the catalogue team and working on acquisitions. In 1959 she was assigned to study bronzes with an archaeologist called Jiang Dayi. In her oral history she relates how she was first made to hand-copy Rong Geng's 1925 dictionary of bronze inscriptions before her weekly Sunday lessons could begin.[28] Zhong Yinlan's training in painting was similarly traditional. Having also left middle school to join the Shanghai Museum, she began training as a docent, but her beautiful handwriting earned her a position on the catalogue team.[29] Selected in 1959 to study painting for appraisal, Zhong began her training with painter and collector Shen Jianzhi every Monday morning. Like a student in imperial times, she arrived even before Shen had risen—to clean the desk, prepare the water, and grind ink from tablet and inkstone. To his new pupil, Shen explained, "If you don't understand the use of brush and ink in painting, then don't even think about studying appraisal. Chinese calligraphy is made up of brush and ink, and through them each painter's personality is revealed."[30] For the following seven years, Zhong Yinlan painted every night on the one family table, only after her brothers had completed their

---

[27] Interview in Shanghai with Li Junjie, July 20, 2011; interview in Shanghai with Zhu Li, July 18, 2011. Li Junjie still has his original hand-copied textbooks, with titles such as *Kinds of Jade and Their Uses*. Di Yin Lu's oral histories illustrate the training of this group, which she calls the "red antiquarians." See Lu, "Seizing Civilization," pp. 53–62, 112–121, 131–139.

[28] Duan Lian, Song Shijuan, and Chen Ling, eds., *Wangshi yu jiyi: Shanghai diqu bowuguan, jinianguan koushu fangtanlu* (Past and memory: A record of oral histories and interviews from Shanghai local museums and memorial halls) (Shanghai: Shanghai cishu chubanshe, 2010), pp. 14–18. A reprint of the Rong Geng text, *Jinwen bian* (Beijing: Zhonghua shuju, 1985), is over 1,500 pages in length; Chen Peifen completed her task in just three months.

[29] Zhang Ling, "Kanhua yibeizi zhiqiushi zhenwei." See also Li Hongbing, "Kanhua yi beizi: Fang Shanghai bowuguan guojiaji wenwu jianding zhuanjia Zhong Yinlan" (A lifetime of viewing paintings: An interview with Zhong Yinlan, Shanghai Museum's nationally-ranked expert to appraise cultural relics), *Renmin ribao* (People's daily), August 14, 2000 (special supplement), p. 16.

[30] Zheng Zhong, "Zhong Yinlan de shuhua jianding shengya" (Zhong Yinlan's career in painting appraisal), *Wenwu tiandi* (Cultural relics heaven-and-earth), no. 3 (2006), pp. 48–53.

homework. She was made a full-fledged appraiser in 1966, the year the Cultural Revolution began.[31]

Chen and Zhong were classically trained so that they could work in acquisitions for the Shanghai Museum and thus contribute to the growth of its collection. In the early years of the People's Republic, the Shanghai Museum added to its collection in several ways. As part of the takeover of Shanghai, the state absorbed *wenwu* from pre-1949 museums, including those of the Université l'Aurore and the Royal Asiatic Society.[32] From the metal scrap heaps of industrial Shanghai, the Shanghai Museum also rescued fragments of artifacts, sometimes piecing together shards of ancient bronzes collected years apart.[33] But the museum's collection expanded primarily through purchases and donations. In the former case, Shanghai provided an exceptional art market. Historically, the cosmopolitan metropolis had been a center of wealth as required for connoisseurship, and the tumult of wartime during the Republican era made Shanghai—with its foreign concessions—a refuge for collectors from neighboring provinces, who brought with them their most prized possessions. In the 1930s over two hundred antique shops clustered around what is today Guangdong Road between Jiangxi Road and Henan Road, and the area continued to be a market for antiquities after 1949.[34] Private trade in *wenwu* was allowed up until the socialist transformation of 1956, when Shanghai's antique stores—like other private enterprises that were converted to state-private management—came under the administration of the Shanghai Bureau of Trade.[35] Zhu Li, a middle-school graduate who began as a trainee in the Antiquities Market in 1962, explains that whereas before 1956 a private collector might sell his *wenwu* to another individual, a shop, or a state institution like the Shanghai Museum, after socialist transformation he was obligated to sell to the state at fixed prices. He notes that though "there was a period in which it was called joint state-private ownership, in reality it was already led by the state."[36]

[31] Zhang Ling, "Kanhua yibeizi zhiqiushi zhenwei."
[32] Qi Wenjuan, "Shanghai wenwu zhengli cangku de lishi gongji" (The historical contribution of the Shanghai cultural relics warehouses), *Shanghai wenhua shizhi tongxun* (Shanghai gazetteer of cultural history), no. 33(1994), pp. 74–75.
[33] Zheng Zhong, *Bowuguan yu shoucangjia*, pp. 168–174. Di Yin Lu refers to this process as "salvage archaeology," documenting how the museum retrieved more than ten thousand pieces during its first year of work, 1959–1960. See Lu, "Seizing Civilization," pp. 121–131.
[34] *SHWWBWGZ*, pp. 424–427.
[35] Ibid. See also Denise Y. Ho, "Reforming Connoisseurship: State and Collectors in Shanghai in the 1950s and 1960s," *Frontiers of History in China*, vol. 7, no. 4 (2012), pp. 608–637.
[36] Interview in Shanghai with Zhu Li, July 18, 2011.

The second way to build the Shanghai Museum's collections was through gifts from private collectors. By 1959 an estimated 1,011 people and 198 organizations had donated a total of 70,000 *wenwu* and 270,000 books.[37] Individuals gave for various reasons. In his oral history Ma Chengyuan, the young bronze expert who had accompanied Premier Zhou through the storehouse, remarks that "In the early years of Liberation, there were few political movements, so collectors felt no pressure to donate *wenwu* to the state ... donations were totally dependent on the abilities of the *wenwu* workers; anyone who worked in acquisitions in the 1950s knew what it was like to 'eat porridge outside of a closed door,' to be left out in the cold."[38] Although donations were actively solicited, with collectors using their cultural capital to buy political capital, donating *wenwu* during political campaigns was always portrayed as an act of patriotism. Reporting on donations in 1961, the local *Wenhui bao* described individuals as "moved by the *wenwu* policies of the Party," and collectors and their families made speeches that recapitulated with the appropriate language.[39] To accompany a 1961 donation, the sons of collector Wu Fangsheng declared that they "had realized that these ancient paintings were the creation of the nation's forebears and they belong to the nation's culture. Through our recent study of the Party and state policies for protecting the nation's cultural heritage, we have learned that the cultural relics left to us by our ancestors are properly the people's property."[40] By echoing Mao's "On New Democracy," collectors supported *wenwu* for the nation, burnishing their political credentials. In return, the Shanghai Museum recognized such gestures with certificates, small cash awards, and exhibitions of donors' collections, to illustrate both the collectors' artistic taste and their patriotic spirit.[41]

[37] "Qiannian wenwu fangshe duomu guangcai" (One thousand years of cultural relics emit a radiance to dazzle the eyes), *Wenhui bao*, September 20, 1959, p. 2.

[38] Duan Lian, Song Shijuan, and Chen Ling, eds., *Wangshi yu jiyi*, p. 2.

[39] Xu Jiren and Peng Jian'an, "Wenwu chongsheng" (Cultural relics reborn), *Wenhui bao*, May 31, 1959, p. 3; "Shanghai bowuguan xintian yipi zhengui wenwu" (The Shanghai Museum adds a new batch of precious cultural relics), *Guangming ribao* (Guangming daily), November 10, 1961, p. 1.

[40] Zheng Zhong, *Haishang shoucang shijia* (Collectors in Shanghai) (Shanghai: Shiji chuban jituan, Shanghai shudian chubanshe, 2003), p. 244.

[41] Shanghai bowuguan (Shanghai Museum), ed., *Guoyun lou shuhua jicui* (Selections from the paintings and calligraphy works of Guoyun Lou [donated by the Gu Gongxiong family]) (Shanghai: Shanghai shuhua chubanshe, 2002). Zhu Li noted that the cash awards were very small—a painting worth 1,000 yuan was rewarded with a token of 10 yuan. Interview in Shanghai with Zhu Li, July 18, 2011. Di Yin Lu quotes Zheng Zhong in describing these practices as "collector psychology," though she takes this further by suggesting a "cult of consent" or a stage on which donations were performed. See Lu, "Seizing Civilization," pp. 29, 94–107, 341.

Donations could also be prompted by financial duress—an exchange of cultural capital for economic capital. Almost all of the collectors had been capitalists before 1949 and they faced the nationalization of their businesses during the 1952 Five Antis Campaign and subsequent difficulties securing employment because of their bad class status.[42] Though the small cash awards were symbolic, the Shanghai Museum was able to offer substantial benefits, such as work assignments or university places for their children. For example, on many occasions the museum tried to persuade former capitalist Gong Xuren—featured in Shanghai's Class Education Exhibition—to reveal that he possessed a bronze measure named for the Warring States philosopher Shang Yang (390–338 BC). In addition to asking him to name his price, the Shanghai Museum suggested a place for his daughter at Jiaotong University and resolution of his housing problems, but Gong maintained that his father had sold the bronze years earlier.[43] Despite the unsuccessful acquisition, this case demonstrates the degree to which the Shanghai Museum was attuned to the collectors and their most intimate affairs; when Chen Peifen and Zhong Yinlan took turns on the museum's emergency hotline, they already had a mental catalogue of the collectors and their private possessions.

What kinds of exhibitions were made from these collections? The imagined visitor to the museum was a citizen of New China, and by 1956 the Shanghai Museum's audience consisted of at least 40 percent of those with worker backgrounds. Linking art and production, history and revolution, the docents developed special narratives aimed at inspiring interest in production. Docents might use "exhibition articles (*chenliepin*) related to [the workers'] knowledge of production," for instance showing textile workers early handwoven fabrics or explaining the development of iron and bronze to machinists.[44] Exhibitions were not, however, limited to the fine arts or to handicrafts. Ever the handmaiden to politics, the Shanghai Museum mounted special exhibitions to accompany political campaigns. During the Socialist Education Movement it displayed revolutionary relics and exhibited replicas of shantytown housing.[45] Curators also used temporary exhibitions to propagandize

---

[42] On unemployment in Shanghai after 1949, see Eddy U, "The Making of *Zhishifenzi*: The Critical Impact of the Registration of Unemployed Intellectuals in the Early PRC," *The China Quarterly*, no. 173 (March 2003), pp. 100–121.

[43] Zheng Zhong, *Haishang shoucang shijia*, pp. 52–58.

[44] Li Ming, "Shanghai bowuguan dui gongren guanzhong jinxing jiangjie de jidian jingyan" (A few experiences from the Shanghai Museum's narration for workers), *Wenwu cankao ziliao* (Cultural relics reference materials), no. 2 (1956), p. 64.

[45] "Jinxi duibi jifa jieji ganqing" (Comparing past and present stimulates class feelings), *Wenhui bao*, February 16, 1964, p. 2.

Ill.6.2. Bronzes on display in the Shanghai Museum, ca. 1960s. SMA
H1-14-3-23

the museum's own work. In 1956, for instance, the Shanghai Museum
displayed photographs and bronzes to show how *wenwu* could be rescued
from scrap metal.[46] On the ten-year anniversary of the PRC in 1959,
museum officials curated an exhibit on Shanghai's first ten years of
cultural relics work. In reviews, both major Shanghai newspapers used
the metaphor of China herself as a museum, restored and made open to
the public after 1949.[47]

This decennial exhibition took place in the Shanghai Museum's new
building, the Zhonghui Bank Building at Number 16, Henan South
Road. Within the Art Deco building, in rooms with yellow plaster walls
and wooden chevron floors, designer Fei Qinsheng was charged with
making an exhibit with the "historical period as warp and artistic category
as weft." Fei, an oil painter, joined the Shanghai Museum in 1954. In the
international context of the 1950s, Fei Qinsheng studied with a Soviet
propaganda artist at the Sino-Soviet Friendship Building and also with

[46] Xu Xiaomu, "Shanghai bowuguan juban 'Cong feitongzhong qiangjiu wenwu zhanlan'"
(Shanghai Museum puts on an "Exhibition on cultural relics rescued from scrap metal"),
Wenwu cankao ziliao, no. 4 (1957), p. 45.
[47] Gu Wei, "Zhi gu ai jin: Kan shinianlai Shanghai wenwu bowuguan shiye chengjiu
zhanlan" (Knowing the past and loving the present: Visiting an exhibition on the success
of Shanghai's cultural relics and museum work during the last ten years), *Jiefang ribao*
(Liberation daily), June 12, 1959, p. 5; Xu Jiren and Peng Jian'an, "Wenwu chongsheng"
(Cultural relics reborn), *Wenhui bao*, May 31, 1959, p. 3.

Ill.6.3. A Venezuelan women's delegation tours the Shanghai Museum,
July 21, 1963. SMA H1-13-2-84

a Japanese expert in advertising. Together with Abe Masatoshi, Fei
created an exhibition whose recognition by the State Bureau of Cultural
Relics made it a model for all of China to learn from. In his memoirs, Fei
Qinsheng writes that from today's perspective, the design appears old-
fashioned, but at that time "the style of the exhibit was pure and clean,
quiet and restrained."[48]

Asked about the docents and the Shanghai Museum's narrative script,
Li Junjie explains that docents wrote their own texts, following whatever
was on display and subject to approval by the museum's leadership.
"A truly good narration was more than just recitation of the script; it
also adapted to the audience. If you were talking to students, you were to
adopt a style that suited their ages; senior middle-school students and
junior middle-school students are very different. The key was for the

---

[48] Fei Qinsheng, *Liushinian chenlie yishu zhilu* (Sixty years of exhibition art) (Shanghai:
Shanghai guji chubanshe, 2012), pp. 1–14.

docent to have a rich variety of things to say." In addition to audiences of students and workers, the Shanghai Museum also received foreign visitors, and to reach even larger numbers, staff brought traveling exhibitions to cultural palaces and even to the countryside. Li Junjie remembers putting up pop-up exhibits following contemporary politics, using artifacts from Taiwan to make the case for its liberation. "At that time, we went to factories, to the countryside, and to the streets; we even did exhibitions on the Bund, hanging up photographs of artifacts and then talking about them."[49] Within and beyond the walls of the Zhonghui Bank Building, the Shanghai Museum used *wenwu* to illustrate historical narratives and to make political arguments.

Though the Shanghai Museum's *wenwu* provided material evidence for political movements, as an institution it was not exempt from the cycles of campaigns that buffeted Maoist China. While leaders like Shen Zhiyu had the political and artistic credentials to be both "red" and "expert," its staff included many artists and intellectuals with bourgeois family backgrounds. In 1960, for example, the majority of the employees in cultural relics work were "born of the exploitative classes," and of the 121 staff members of the Shanghai Museum, only 15 percent came from worker or peasant backgrounds. Like other work units, the museum organized monthly political meetings and Marxist-Leninist study groups, and it sent its staff to the countryside to engage in manual labor.[50] Constantly conscious of the importance of "thought work," the docents at the Shanghai Museum wrote self-criticisms in the pages of *Wenwu cankao ziliao* (Cultural relics reference materials), to be read by all of their colleagues. Using their own surveys of over two thousand workers who had toured the Shanghai Museum, the docents admitted that they had been insufficiently warm and patient toward them, even holding their noses to avoid the odor from the workers' bodies.[51] Whether or not such stock criticisms were true, the Shanghai Museum staff were particularly vulnerable to attack.

Some political campaigns hit the Shanghai Museum and Shanghai's collectors hard. During the Hundred Flowers Movement in 1957, when Director Xu Linyu of the Shanghai Cultural Relics Commission stepped forward to enumerate failures to protect *wenwu*, his voice was joined by

[49] Interview in Shanghai with Li Junjie, July 20, 2011.
[50] Shen Zhiyu, "Xuexi Mao Zedong sixiang, tigao wenwu, bowuguan gongzuo zhong de zhengcexing he sixiangxing" (Study Mao Zedong Thought and improve adherence to the policy and ideological content of cultural relics and museum work), in *SZYWBLJ*, pp. 7–8.
[51] Li Ming, "Shanghai bowuguan dui gongren guanzhong jinxing jiangjie de jidian jingyan," p. 63.

another participant who said that Party cadres had stifled open debate about scholarly questions.[52] Though these criticisms were echoed all the way up the line to Zheng Zhenduo of the State Bureau of Cultural Relics, the subsequent Anti-Rightist Campaign ended any further dissent.[53] Collectors also suffered during political campaigns. On Zhong Yinlan's first day of work in 1952, she attended a struggle session against the painter and connoisseur Xie Zhiliu for allegedly speculating in art.[54] In 1964, when the rural Four Cleanups Campaign against corruption spread to the city as part of a new Five Antis Campaign, collectors were once again caught up in accusations of illegal behavior. Attacked for a litany of crimes, including speculation, smuggling, forgery, and tax evasion, guilty verdicts forced collectors to sell their *wenwu* in order to pay the fines. Stories of patriotic donations and exhibitions celebrating collectors had their dark side: the nationalization of *wenwu* by political-campaign fiat.[55]

In the course of the political campaigns, *wenwu* became commodities. But in the museum, they also had their own political role to play. As Shen Zhiyu explained in a 1960 speech, the Shanghai Museum's collection cultivated a new, materialist way of seeing the world. First, following Mao Zedong's "On New Democracy," exhibitions should create a respect for history that would lead people to look to the future. Second, and quoting Mao's "On Practice," Shen said that perceiving an object was not enough; one also had to understand the logic of its development. Thus the work of an exhibition was to move the viewer from perception to reason, to see the *wenwu* as part of a larger system.[56] Writing in 1964, Shen further elaborated on the idea of using understanding to cultivate thinking. By observing handicrafts in a museum, workers were to see themselves—and their labor—as part of the progression that had led to the socialist revolution. By viewing art objects presented according to different stages of class society, the audiences would see how objects reflected the "birth, development, and decline of different classes." Finally, visitors were also to be critical of individual artworks, careful to weigh an object's artistic achievement with the artist's class background;

---

[52] Ma Lan, "Shi baocang ru feiwu de renmin: Minghua guwu dangzuo cipin feipin bei dajin 'lenggong'" (People watching precious collections [treated] as trash: Famous paintings and antiquities taken as defective goods and trash and put into the "frozen palace"), *Xinmin bao* (New people's daily), May 15, 1957, p. 2.

[53] Roderick MacFarquhar, *The Hundred Flowers Campaign and the Chinese Intellectuals* (New York: Frederick A. Praeger, 1960), pp. 174–176; Zheng Zhenduo, "Dang he zhengfu shi zenyang baohu wenwu de?" (How have the Party and government protected cultural relics?), *Renmin ribao*, July 22, 1957, p. 8.

[54] Zheng Zhong, *Bowuguan yu shoucangjia*, pp. 121–126.

[55] Ho, "Reforming Connoisseurship."   [56] Shen Zhiyu, "Xuexi Mao Zedong," pp. 5–7.

"artistic contribution" was not to replace criticism of his "reactionary politics." Throughout, Shen Zhiyu warned that beauty, whether in an object or in its exhibition, was secondary to politics. The audience should not "gain the impression of revering the past and not the present."[57] An exhibition should follow Mao's dictum, "use the past to serve the present."

The very presence of these prescriptions suggests that visitors' ways of seeing did not always accord with the ways the curators had intended for them to see. It is likely that some still understood *wenwu* as celebrations of the past, that others perceived beauty before understanding politics, and that few saw an artist's bad class background before admiring his ability with a brush. A central difficulty lay in what curators acknowledged was the dual nature of *wenwu*. An object could be at once a patriotic artwork made by the hands of a reactionary, or the manufacture of a worker enjoyed by a member of the exploiting classes. In "On New Democracy" Mao argued,

To clarify the process of development of this ancient culture, to throw away its feudal dross, and to absorb its democratic essence is prerequisite for the development of our new national culture ... but we should not absorb anything and everything uncritically. We must separate all the rotten things of the ancient feudal ruling class from the fine ancient popular culture that is more or less revolutionary in character.[58]

However, having defined antiquity as both feudal and democratic, Mao did not give instructions on how to separate the two. Cautioned Shen Zhiyu, "If there are *wenwu* where the [democratic] essence and the [feudal] dross are mixed ... in principle it should not be exhibited to the public."[59] Precisely how to criticize ancient culture was the dilemma presented when the Cultural Revolution's salvoes began with the "Attack on the Four Olds."

Cultural Revolution and the "Attack on the Four Olds"

When the "Attack on the Four Olds" began, workers at the Shanghai Museum defended art and antiquity as *wenwu* properly under state

---

[57] Shen Zhiyu, "Shanghai bowuguan gongzuo gangyao" (Outline of work for the Shanghai Museum), in *SZYWBLJ*, pp. 60–67.

[58] Stuart R. Schram, *The Political Thought of Mao Tse-tung* (New York, Praeger, 1963), pp. 356–367.

[59] Shen Zhiyu, "Shanghai bowuguan gongzuo gangyao," p. 64. Other objects not for display included cultural relics that "dishonor the nation ... or will have an ill effect on politics or social life." Shen Zhiyu did not give examples, but from other writings on foreign museums, it can be inferred that objects such as shoes for bound feet would fall into the former category.

protection. Holding hands in the human shield around the Longhua Pagoda, Zhong Yinlan and others argued that it was a *wenwu*, not part of the "Four Olds." Indeed, historic sites like the Longhua Pagoda had previously been designated cultural relic protection units. Together with Longhua Temple, it was categorized as part of Shanghai's ancient architecture, while the First Party Congress Site was labeled revolutionary memorial architecture.[60] In 1963, the State Council promulgated regulations for the preservation of *wenwu* with "historical, artistic, and scientific value, and also those of memorial significance."[61] State protection also extended to moveable *wenwu*, making the People's Committee in every administrative area responsible for all *wenwu* within its jurisdiction.[62] When Zhong Yinlan and her colleagues rushed to collectors' homes as they were being searched by Red Guards, she introduced herself as being from the Shanghai Museum. "They knew that *wenwu* were supposed to be protected, but they didn't differentiate between *wenwu* and the 'Four Olds.' So we would say, go ahead and attack the 'Four Olds'—gold, silver, jewelry, and whatever you want to attack. Leave the *wenwu* to us."[63]

But for many, the definition of the "Four Olds" was unclear, and the meaning of "attack" was equally ambiguous. The idea of the "Four Olds" first appeared in *Renmin ribao* (People's daily) on June 1, 1966, in an editorial that defined the Cultural Revolution as the destruction of old ideology, culture, customs, and habits, and the fostering of those proletarian in their stead. On August 8, 1966, the "Attack on the Four Olds" and creation of the "Four News" was enshrined in the Central Committee's "Decision Concerning the Great Proletarian Cultural Revolution," and on August 19, Beijing Red Guards began their campaign to attack the "Four Olds."[64] But as historian Wang Nianyi has argued, the distinction between "old" and "new" was never made clear.[65] A Beijing Red Guard manifesto entitled "One Hundred Ways to Destroy the Old and to Establish the New," for example, called on Red Guards to "open savage fire on the 'Four Olds,' and to smash to bits imperialist,

---

[60] *Quanguo gesheng, zizhiqu, zhixiashi diyipi wenwu baohu danwei mingdan huibian* (The first group of national cultural relic protection units in each province, autonomous region, and special municipality) (Beijing: Wenwu chubanshe, 1958), p. 18.

[61] Fan Jingyi et al., eds., *Wenwu baohu falü zhinan* (Guide to the cultural relics protection law) (Beijing: Zhongguo chengshi chubanshe, 2003), pp. 473–476. These regulations were replaced by the first law on cultural relics in 1982.

[62] *Wenwu shangdian gongzuo shouce* (Handbook for cultural relics stores) (Beijing: Zhongguo wenwu shangdian zongdian, 1981).

[63] Interviews in Shanghai with Zhong Yinlan, December 25, 2009, August 12, 2010.

[64] Li Kwok-sing, comp., *A Glossary of Political Terms of the People's Republic of China*, trans. by Mary Lok (Hong Kong: Chinese University Press, 1995), pp. 426–428.

[65] Wang Nianyi, *Da dongluan de niandai* (The age of great turmoil) (Zhengzhou: Henan renmin chubanshe, 1988), pp. 67–68.

revisionist, and bourgeois goods and all things not in accord with Chairman Mao's thought." The one reference to *wenwu* in the document declared, "all bookstores and libraries must be internally purified and must clear away all poisonous weeds."[66] Such an interpretation, shared by Shanghai's "Burn-the-Pagoda-Headquarters," was license for total destruction.

As the "Attack on the Four Olds" spread through Beijing and elsewhere, Red Guards eager to prove their revolutionary mettle defaced historic sites and temples and ransacked personal collections. Against this movement, some tried to preempt the destruction. Beijing's Palace Museum shut its doors days before the campaign began, and Premier Zhou Enlai sent PLA troops to guard the Palace Museum's perimeter; the only section left open was the *Rent Collection Courtyard*, a class education exhibition that used sculpture to criticize a landlord from the "old society."[67] Farther from the center of power, tensions between destruction and preservation erupted into violence. At Confucius's birthplace in Qufu, as historian Dahpon Ho has shown, residents faced off against local Mao Zedong Thought Red Guards over the Confucian Temple complex. Like the Shanghainese at Longhua, the defenders argued for *wenwu* and nation, and County Secretary Li Xiu made a speech defining the site as "the Chinese people's outstanding cultural legacy." Workers at the gate of the Confucius Mansion echoed him by using the language that was employed at the Longhua Pagoda just days before, saying, "this has been the work of my ancestors for generations."[68] In this moment such debates surrounded *wenwu* both large and small.[69]

---

[66] Mao Zedong zhuyi xuexiao hongweibing (Red Guards of Mao Zedongism School), "Pojiu lixin yibailie" (One hundred items for destroying the old and establishing the new) (August 1966), in *WDGW*. Translation of this document comes from Michael Schoenhals, ed., *China's Cultural Revolution, 1966–1969: Not a Dinner Party* (Armonk, NY: M. E. Sharpe, 1996), p. 216.

[67] Liang Dan, "Beijing bowuguan gongzuo jishi" (Chronicle of Beijing's museum work), *Zhongguo bowuguan* (Chinese museums), no. 1 (1994), pp. 88–95; Jeannette Shambaugh Elliott, with David Shambaugh, *The Odyssey of China's Imperial Art Treasures* (Seattle: University of Washington Press, 2005), pp. 129–131; *Beijing zhi: Wenwu juan: Wenwu zhi* (Beijing gazetteer: Volume on cultural relics: Cultural relics gazetteer) (Beijing: Beijing chubanshe, 2006), p. 694; " Qi Benyu zai Gugong de jianghua" (Qi Benyu's speech at the Palace Museum), December 1, 1966, in *Wuchanjieji wenhua da geming cankao ziliao*, vol. 4, in *WDGW*.

[68] Dahpon David Ho, "To Protect and Preserve: Resisting the Destroy the Four Olds Campaign, 1966–1967," in *The Chinese Cultural Revolution as History*, edited by Joseph W. Esherick, Paul G. Pickowicz, and Andrew G. Walder (Stanford, CA: Stanford University Press, 2006), pp. 84–92.

[69] Li Xiu delivered his speech on August 24, 1966. Qufu's event is known as the 8–26 Incident, when locals successfully rebuffed an attack by Qufu Normal Institute. Ho, "To Protect and Preserve," pp. 84–88.

Back in Shanghai, Red Guards streamed through the streets to "prole-tarianize" and "revolutionize" a city that was being vilified for its capitalist and imperialist past. Turning from Nanjing Road and Yong'an Department Store to the foreign architecture on the Bund, the Red Guards dismantled Western markers, including the lions that guarded the former Hong Kong and Shanghai Bank.[70] Though *Renmin ribao* reportage of Shanghai underscored the extirpation of foreign things, traditional historic sites also fell under attack. Most were not as fortunate as the Longhua Pagoda: all of the images of the gods in the City God Temple were smashed, all of the Buddhas at the Chenxiang Pavilion were destroyed, all of the *wenwu* at the Jing'an Temple were lost, thousands of volumes of scripture at the Longhua Temple were burned, and the cross at Xujiahui Cathedral was torn down and its interior was torched.[71] Reporting on the damage to *wenwu* protection units in October 1966, the Shanghai Cultural Relics Commission explained that the Red Guards and the accompanying revolutionary masses had so thoroughly destroyed some sites that they were beyond attention. The Commission thus removed the *wenwu* protection unit designation from Shanghai's historic sites.[72]

With this bureaucratic measure, it appears that the Shanghai Cultural Relics Commission was bowing to the dictates of the Red Guards. In its report to the Shanghai People's Committee, the Commission wrote that eliminating the *wenwu* protection units was in accordance with the "Great Proletarian Cultural Revolution's smash-ing of the 'Four Olds' and establishing of the 'Four News.'" But at the same time, the report also suggests the work of a quiet salvage opera-tion. Four places, including a temple, a guildhall, and two pagodas in the suburbs, were determined to have a "definite historical value," and the Commission requested that photographs and surveys be taken if any of the buildings were to be later removed, reconstructed, or demolished. Of some of the artifacts that survived, like temple deities, Confucius tablets, and grave markers, the Commission recommended

---

[70] "Shanghai Tianjin geming xiaojiang he shangye zhigong xiang boxue jieji 'sijiu' fadong zonggong: Huiqi geming tie saozhou, hengsao yiqie jiuxisu" (Revolutionary little generals and commercial workers in Shanghai and Tianjin launch a general offensive against the "Four Olds" of the exploiting classes: Raising the revolutionary iron broom, they sweep away all old customs), *Renmin ribao*, August 25, 1966, p. 2, in *WDGW*. For a detailed secondary account, see Li Xun, *Wenge zaofan niandai: Shanghai wenge yundong shigao* (The age of revolutionary rebellion: A history of Shanghai's Cultural Revolution move-ment) (Hong Kong: Oxford University Press, 2015), 2 vols., pp. 98–103.
[71] *SHWWBWGZ*, pp. 171, 174, 177. For more on historic sites, including eyewitness accounts and preemptive storage of cultural relics, see Chen Zhiqiang, *Wenbo xianqu*, pp. 193–203.
[72] SMA B172-3-5, pp. 11–14.

that they be removed and stored in local museums. Finally, the Commission stressed that if any construction or agricultural development was to take place in the vicinity of historic graves, it retained the right to coordinate excavation.[73] Thus, in the aftermath of the "Attack on the Four Olds," the Cultural Relics Commission stopped to take stock. Unable to close doors over the *wenwu* of historic sites, and hemmed in by the uncertainty of the future, the cultural bureaucracy nonetheless attempted to stand guard.

However, like Beijing's Palace Museum, the Shanghai Museum did shut its doors, ostensibly so that it too could "make revolution."[74] Director Shen Zhiyu and Vice Director Ma Chengyuan wrote a report to the Shanghai People's Government making the following three proposals: first, if collectors were to be searched, the museum should be notified and staff should be sent to handle the *wenwu*; second, *wenwu* brought to the museum should be kept on their owners' behalf (*daiguan*), with receipts issued; and third, after the political movement was over, the government was to issue regulations regarding the next steps.[75] Mayor Cao Diqiu approved the document, and the Shanghai Museum went into action. With meticulous lists that included the collectors' names, work units, addresses, and the *wenwu* in their possession, the museum telephoned all of the relevant work units and installed a hotline. Vice Director Ma also staffed the phone and preemptively had others paint revolutionary slogans on the glass cases. When museum workers were dispatched, they bore Red Guard armbands around their sleeves.[76]

[73] Ibid., pp. 12–14.

[74] Zheng Zhong, *Bowuguan yu shoucangjia*, p. 217. It appears that special visits continued to be arranged. In *Asahi Shimbun* in November 1966, art historian Miyakawa Torao, writing of his August visit, asserted that he had seen no evidence of destruction of cultural relics. See Miyakawa Torao, "Hongweibing yu wenwu" (Red Guards and cultural relics), in *Waiguoren kan wenhua da geming* (Foreigners view the Cultural Revolution), edited by Itō Takeo (Hong Kong: Dasheng chubanshe, 1969), pp. 122–123.

[75] Zheng Zhong, *Bowuguan yu shoucangjia*, p. 215. I have not seen a copy of this report in the archive, but both Li Junjie's and Zhong Yinlan's oral accounts match Zheng's report. Party Secretary Chen Pixian's memoir makes note of an order his office issued on August 24, which included regulations against searching houses, damaging public property, burning archives, and destroying documents, but it is unclear whether this order included cultural relics. Chen Pixian, *Chen Pixian huiyilu: Zai "yiyue fengbao" de zhongxin* (The memoirs of Chen Pixian: At the center of the "January Storm") (Hong Kong: Sanlian shudian, 2005), p. 58.

[76] Zheng Zhong, *Bowuguan yu shoucangjia*, pp. 215–218. In my interviews, Zhong Yinlan disputed the notion that museum workers dressed as Red Guards, but she told Di Yin Lu how the Shanghai Museum had its own Red Guard unit. See Lu, "Seizing Civilization," p. 176. Ma Chengyuan's *New York Times* obituary asserts that he ordered museum workers to dress as Red Guards. See "Ma Chengyuan, 77, President of Shanghai Museum, Dies," *The New York Times*, October 15, 2004.

With a response system in place, Shanghai Museum staff waited by the phone. Sometimes work units rang, other times individual collectors stole out of their houses to use public telephones. An anonymous caller telephoned to deliver the two somnolent lion statues, dangling from cranes, that the Red Guards had ripped off the Bund.[77] When the museum received a call from a collector, a team with at least one specialist would hasten forth, sometimes arriving in the middle of a house search. Zhong Yinlan recounts the story of Liu Jingji, a former textile manufacturer and collector of paintings,

I arrived at Liu Jingji's house and spent the entire night there, from six p.m. to eleven the next morning ... he had many paintings, about 2,000 or more ... first he was struggled by the rebels, and then he was made to stand in his garden. He stood until the rebels left and then he snuck back inside. Liu saw me writing the inventory and he came to stand next to me while I wrote out the numbers, one by one identifying the paintings and the scrolls by name. This is so-and-so artist, this is such-and-such painting. He stood there for a long time, and finally he asked: "Miss, you seem to be a *wenwu* expert ... you look at the painting and immediately know its name ... what work unit are you from?" I responded, "The Shanghai Museum. Our museum will protect them." And immediately his spirits lifted, and he showed me other things. He had a Wen Peng (1498–1573) calligraphy, a Shi Tao (1642–1707) landscape; he said, "Take them away, take them all away, don't leave a single thing behind."[78]

Liu Jingji's experience has been told and re-told as a story of the Shanghai Museum's success. After the Cultural Revolution, he was so moved to receive his collection intact that he allowed Zhong Yinlan to choose forty of the best paintings.[79]

But not all of the *wenwu* in private collections fared so well. The museum's lists included only known collectors who had significant holdings, and in the end it received *wenwu* from only about two hundred families.[80] Those not fortunate enough to be on a list may have heard rumors of protection, but to no avail.[81] Additionally, in the hands of the Red Guards the Shanghai Museum's lists could inadvertently lead to tragedy. Gong Xuren, the alleged owner of the Shang Yang bronze measure, was struggled by Red Guards in his home for twenty-eight consecutive days and nights. Having first hidden the measure from the Japanese during wartime and then from the Shanghai Museum in the 1960s, it was ferreted out from his nephew's home by Red Guards.

---

[77] Zheng Zhong, *Bowuguan yu shoucangjia*, p. 217; Duan Lian, Song Shijuan, and Chen Ling, eds., *Wangshi yu jiyi*, p. 19; SMA B3-2-199, pp. 10–14.

[78] Interview in Shanghai with Zhong Yinlan, August 12, 2010.   [79] Ibid.

[80] Chen Zhiqiang, *Wenbo xianqu*, p. 204.

[81] Nien Cheng, *Life and Death in Shanghai* (New York: Penguin Books, 1986), pp. 69–78.

As they "beat drums and gongs," carrying it aloft as a "fruit of victory," Gong Xuren had a heart attack and died on the way to the hospital.[82] The Red Guards of Shanghai's Class Education Exhibition subsequently added a display on Gong Xuren's life, never once mentioning the fact or manner of his death.[83]

Despite the Shanghai cultural bureaucracy's initiative and bottom-up response to the "Attack on the Four Olds," it remained reactive damage control at best. The Longhua Temple was smashed, but the Longhua Pagoda was saved; Red Guards seized Gong Xuren's family treasure, but Zhong Yinlan rescued Liu Jingji's collection of paintings. In Shanghai, as elsewhere in China, museum workers defended art and antiquity as *wenwu* of the nation and as the handiwork of China's working people. But these arguments were not always sufficient, and as the Shanghai Cultural Relics Commission picked up the pieces in the wake of the Red Guards and the Shanghai Museum stacked its exhibition rooms with crates of *wenwu* from private collectors, its own leadership fell under attack. Shen Zhiyu's own house was searched in October 1966, and the Shanghai Museum's Red Revolutionary Rebels struggled against the old guard.[84] With the January Revolution in 1967, both the Shanghai People's Government and the Shanghai People's Committee were over-thrown. At the museum, Shen was labeled a "capitalist roader" and removed from his position.[85] After a brief interregnum by the Shanghai People's Commune—whose placard the Shanghai Museum collected as a Cultural Revolution *wenwu*—the Shanghai Revolutionary Committee became the new municipal government. Protection of *wenwu* now required a revolutionary argument.

The Wenwu Small Group, the Shanghai Museum, and cultural preservation

In the winter of 1966–1967, the Shanghai Museum was at a turning point. The younger generation depicted below in the foyer, gathered around a luminous statue of Mao and surrounded by banners proclaiming the right to rebel, had lost its leaders. Now that the previous power

[82] *SHWWBWGZ*, p. 297; Zheng Zhong, *Haishang shoucang shijia*, pp. 52–58.
[83] SMA C4-2-8, p. 11.
[84] Chen Zhiqiang, *Wenbo xianqu*, pp. 209–212. Shen Zhiyu was searched as part of a wave of searches of artists with connections to Jiang Qing in the 1930s. From September 1966 to October 1972, in a total of 121 large struggle sessions and 109 small struggle sessions, sixty cadres from the Shanghai Museum were struggled. Shen Zhiyu was struggled fifty-two times. From December 1967 to September 1968, three people committed suicide and two attempted suicide.
[85] Chen Zhiqiang, *Wenbo xianqu*, p. 210.

Ill.6.4. A group photo of the staff of the Shanghai Museum during
acquisition of a placard from the Shanghai People's Commune,
undated. Image courtesy of the collection of Zheng Zhong, *Wenhui bao*

holders had lost their legitimacy, the argument that art and antiquity
should be protected as *wenwu* under state protection was in doubt.
The Shanghai Museum workers were not alone in this moment. From
the outbreak of the "Attack on the Four Olds," they were connected to
the central leaders in Beijing. On the day of the Longhua Pagoda inci-
dent, Mayor Cao Diqiu convened a meeting to transmit a directive from
Premier Zhou Enlai that read, "In the course of the 'Attack on the Four
Olds,' you must protect historical *wenwu* by any means necessary."
It was thus Premier Zhou's name that was invoked in defense of
Shanghai's Jade Buddha Temple, as it was elsewhere.[86] But although
Zhou's name had some resonance, it was insufficient, even in Beijing.
On December 1, 1966, Qi Benyu, a junior member of the CCRG,
went to Beijing's Palace Museum to deliver a speech. An historian and
vice editor of the journal *Red Flag* who had become Mao's secretary
in May 1966, Qi and the other members of the CCRG were charged
with directing the course of the Cultural Revolution. At the Palace
Museum, Qi suggested that the imperial grounds be turned into
a class education exhibition, a "Revolutionary Palace Museum" in

---

[86] Ibid., pp. 200–203.

which the *wenwu* would be protected as the people's property and used
to raise class consciousness.[87]

Two months later, and after Shanghai's January Revolution, Qi Benyu
convened a second Beijing meeting on January 27, 1967. This time, he
addressed a group of cultural workers assembled from Beijing libraries,
bookstores, *wenwu* protection units, museums, and paper mills. Invoking
senior members of the CCRG, such as Chen Boda and Kang Sheng, Qi
Benyu called on the audience to discuss the state of *wenwu*: why were rare
books being sold for scrap paper and how could taking care of *wenwu* be
properly understood? The participants revealed that ordinary people
were preempting the Red Guards by destroying their own collections.
As representatives of the China Bookstore and the New China Bookstore
explained, "Residents are burning their calligraphy and paintings."
Furthermore, institutions that previously purchased rare books were
afraid to intervene. Infuriated, Qi Benyu responded, "I myself will buy
them! There are some that are necessary for reading. . . . You rebel groups
also don't approve of burning books, [so] you should write a petition,
'Don't burn string-bound books!' The proletariat needs to carry out
struggle with [the books] and you also need these things as [objects] of
criticism." Arguing that preservation was the prerequisite to attack, Qi
ticked off instructions: *wenwu* protection units should write petitions,
wenwu should be centrally organized and preserved, and Red Guards
and museums should work together. No matter to which faction one
belonged, Qi stressed, all cultural workers had to adhere to the following
principles: separate out the books, protect and manage the *wenwu*, and do
not destroy.[88]

---

[87] "Qi Benyu zai Gugong de jianghua," December 1, 1966. In his 2015 memoirs published
online, Qi Benyu explains that at the urging of his secretary, Jin Yaonan, he gave a speech
forbidding the burning of books. Qi Benyu, "Huiyi Jiang Qing tongzhi" (Remembering
Comrade Jiang Qing), *Fuxing wang*, July 30, 2015, part 3, www.mzfxw.com/e/action/S
howInfo.php?classid=18&id=44595 (accessed June 2, 2016). In his full memoir published in 2016, Qi recalls reporting damage to *wenwu* to Jiang Qing, who in turn informed
Mao. See Qi Benyu, *Qi Benyu huiyilu* (Recollections of Qi Benyu) (Hong Kong:
Zhongguo wenge lishi chubanshe, 2016), p. 505.

[88] "Qi Benyu yu tushu wenwu kaogu bowuguan deng danwei geming zaofanpai daibiao
zuotan" (A discussion meeting with Qi Benyu and representatives from the revolutionary
rebel factions of work units representing libraries, cultural relics, archaeology, museums,
and so forth), January 27, 1967, *Wuchanjieji wenhua da geming shouzhang jianghua huibian*
(Collection of leaders' speeches during the Great Proletarian Cultural Revolution), April
1967, in *WGDW*. Note that the China Bookstore dealt in antiquarian and second-hand
books, whereas the New China Bookstore sold new books; both were state-run. In his
2016 memoirs, Qi reveals that he convened this meeting under Mao's orders, that Mao
was happy to have read reports of it, and that Mao approved of both his speech and the
measures it suggested. Qi Benyu, *Qi Benyu huiyilu*, p. 505.

The subsequent response was both bottom-up and top-down. In mid-February 1967, the rebels in Beijing's cultural institutions followed up with a petition that used "On New Democracy" to explain the necessity of ancient culture in the development of new democratic culture. While the petition praised the "Attack on the Four Olds," its authors argued that "If we only burn ancient books, periodicals, calligraphy, and paintings, we will lose the objects of our criticism." Instead, they offered suggestions that echoed those made at Qi Benyu's meeting, calling for the buying of rare books, the sealing of state collections, rescues from paper mills, and the purchase of private collections.[89] Though this manifesto appeared to be a revolutionary call to arms, it was backed by central power. On the day the petition was issued, the Chinese Academy of Sciences requested that the Shanghai Bureau of Culture issue a report on the state of its *wenwu*.[90] Several days later, the CCRG issued a directive to the Ministry of Culture and the Bureau of Cultural Relics, notifying all Shanghai subordinates to identify and protect metal Buddhas and other *wenwu* in metal-smelting plants.[91] In the following months, the Central Committee, the State Council, and the Shanghai Revolutionary Committee all issued orders to affirm the preservation of the old to build the new; to protect *wenwu* was revolutionary.[92]

As the petition circulated, Beijing set up a Beijing Municipal Small Group for Sorting Ancient Books and Cultural Relics (Beijingshi Gushu

---

[89] Beijing zaozhi zongchang shoudu zhigong geming zaofanzhe lianzongzhan (Beijing Paper-Making Industrial Complex Workers' Revolutionary Rebels United Station) et al., *Guanyu baohu gujiu shukan zihua de changyishu* (Proposal regarding the protection of ancient and old books, periodicals, calligraphy, and paintings), unpublished flyer, February 15, 1967.

[90] SMA B172-3-5, pp. 8–9.   [91] Ibid., p. 1.

[92] In chronological order: On March 16, the Central Committee, State Council, and Military Affairs Commission issued a notice on state property, entitled "Zhonggong zhongyang, guowuyuan, zhongyang junwei guanyu baohu guojia caichan, jieyue nao geming de tongzhi" (Notice from the Central Committee, the State Council, and the Military Affairs Commission on protecting state property and economizing when making revolution), *Wuchanjieji wenhua da geming youguan wenjian huiji*, no. 2 (June 1967), in *WDGW*. On May 14, 1967, "Zhonggong zhongyang guanyu wuchanjieji wenhua da gemingzhong baohu wenwu tushu de jidian yijian" (Several opinions of the Central Committee in regard to protecting cultural relics and books during the Great Proletarian Cultural Revolution), May 14, 1967, *Wuchanjieji wenhua da geming wenjian huibian*, April 1, 1968, in *WDGW*. On June 19, 1967, Shanghaishi geming weiyuanhui zhengzhi xuanchuanzu (Shanghai Revolutionary Committee, Political Propaganda Group), *Genju zhonggong zhongyang zhishi jingshen, Shanghaishi wenwu tushu qingli xiaozu zai shi geming wenwu weiyuanhui de zhijie lingdaoxia yijing zhenshi chengli, bing kaishi gongzuo* (According to the spirit of the directive of the Chinese Communist Party, the Shanghai Municipal Small Group for Sorting Cultural Relics and Books has already been formally established and has begun its work under the direct leadership of the Shanghai Revolutionary Committee), unpublished flyer, June 19, 1967.

Wenwu Qingli Xiaozu).[93] At the same time, in the shell of Shanghai's Xujiahui Cathedral, Zhong Yinlan went to work.[94] Shanghai's Municipal Small Group for Sorting Confiscated Cultural Relics and Books (Shanghaishi Chachao Wenwu Tushu Qingli Xiaozu) (cited hereafter as the Wenwu Small Group), eventually consisted of over one hundred workers from twelve different work units, including the Shanghai Bureau of Culture and the Shanghai Commission for Cultural Relics.[95] By September 1967, the Wenwu Small Group reported that it had received 280,000 *wenwu* and 360,000 volumes of books. Its members retrieved from scrap-metal plants 8,000 plus *jin* of bronze objects and handicrafts and from scrap-paper mills over 4,000 *jin* of books. The Wenwu Small Group compiled an index with photographs of the most valuable *wenwu* and books, including Shang and Zhou bronzes, Song, Yuan, Ming, and Qing ceramics, books, seals, currency, and modern handicrafts. The compilers highlighted particular objects in praise of the nation, describing the color and firing of a Song ceramic as indicative of China's technical achievements.[96] In describing its work, the Wenwu Small Group created a narrative for the Red Guards' Cultural Revolution actions, explaining how they had raised the great red banner of Mao Zedong Thought to return these *wenwu* to the working masses. Like the Shanghai Class Education Exhibition that made no mention of how Gong Xuren died, the Wenwu Small Group boasted that the perspicacious revolutionary masses of the Shanghai Flour Factory had seized the Shang Yang bronze measure from the "blood-sucking devil." "Now,"

[93] *Beijing zhi: Wenwu juan: Wenwu zhi*, pp. 558–559. It is interesting to note that its establishment, on February 13, 1967, preceded the petition by two days. In Beijing this group eventually employed over eighty people, and sorted 5,385,000 *wenwu*, 185,300 paintings, and 2,357,000 volumes from 8,000 households. It rescued 314 tons of books and 85 tons of metal from scrap processing plants. In my survey of present-day gazetteers on culture, only the Beijing volumes mention this institution, though the Guangzhou Municipal Gazetteer outlines the sorting and return of objects from 1984 to 1986. *Guangzhou shizhi* (Guangzhou gazetteer) (Guangzhou: Guangzhou chubanshe, 1999), vol. 16, p. 759. Cultural Revolution ephemera suggest that such work went on elsewhere, as reported in a flyer reprinted by the Nanjing Museum and the Nanjing Library, Beijingshi gushu wenwu qingli xiaozu guanyu tiaoxuan gujiu shukan biaozhun de yijian (Opinions of the Beijing Municipal Small Group for Sorting Ancient Books and Cultural Relics on the standards for selecting ancient books), June 1967.
[94] Although the archival documents and the gazetteer date the establishment of the Wenwu Small Group to April 1967, in interviews Zhong Yinlan remembered the date as February 1967. It is more likely that Shanghai and Beijing began work at the same time, even if official establishment came later. Interviews in Shanghai with Zhong Yinlan, December 25, 2009, August 12, 2010.
[95] SMA B172-3-5, p. 26.
[96] Ibid., pp. 31–33; 8,000 *jin* is equal to about 8,818 pounds, and 4,000 *jin* is equal to about 4,409 pounds.

they wrote, "it has finally been returned to the hands of the working people."[97]

Backed by all of the organs of power from the CCRG to the Shanghai Revolutionary Committee, the rhetoric of the Wenwu Small Group became increasingly self-assured. It drew from Mao's writings beyond "On New Democracy," extracting from his remarks at the Sixth Plenum of the Central Committee in 1938: "Another of our tasks is to study our historical heritage and use the Marxist method to sum it up critically ... Today's China is an outgrowth of historic China. We are Marxist historicists; we must not mutilate history. From Confucius to Sun Yat-sen, we must sum it up critically, and we must constitute ourselves as the heirs to this precious legacy."[98] Further, the Wenwu Small Group glorified the Red Guard house searches as cultural preservation for the masses:

In the course of the historically unprecedented Great Proletarian Cultural Revolution, personally started and directed by our Great Leader Chairman Mao, the little generals of the Red Guards and the revolutionary masses have from the homes of the capitalist roaders ... and the ox-demons and snake-spirits, confiscated numerous precious *wenwu* and books which are the creation of the motherland's historical laboring masses. This is an immortal contribution established by the Red Guards, this is a great victory for Mao Zedong Thought.[99]

To underscore the idea that the collection and preservation of *wenwu* had been part of the Cultural Revolution all along, in its reports the Wenwu Small Group changed the date of its founding. Never mentioning the work that Zhong Yinlan began in February nor its official establishment in April, by October 1967 the Wenwu Small Group was stating that its work had begun in August 1966.[100] In this way, it laid claim to any and all activities related to *wenwu* protection as the rightful return of art and antiquity to the masses. All were credited as the revolutionary accomplishment of the Red Guards.

The Wenwu Small Group continued to work throughout the Cultural Revolution. Between June 1967 and December 1968, it received 3,320,000 *wenwu* and handicrafts, and 5,470,000 volumes of books.[101]

---

[97] Ibid., p. 35.

[98] Ibid., p. 30. This quotation is from "The New Stage in the Development of the National War of Resistance Against Japan and the Anti-Japanese National United Front," Report to the Enlarged Sixth Plenum of the Central Committee of the Chinese Communist Party, from October 12 to October 14, 1938, in *Mao's Road to Power: Revolutionary Writings, 1912–1949, Vol. VI: The New Stage, 1937–1938*, edited by Stuart R. Schram (Armonk, NY: M. E. Sharpe, 2004), p. 538. I use Schram's translation.

[99] SMA B172-3-5, p. 30.   [100] Ibid., p. 31.

[101] *SHWWBWGZ*, p. 376. As a point of comparison, Beijing totals amounted to 1,850,000 paintings, 23,570,000 volumes, and 5,380,000 miscellaneous cultural relics. See Wang Nianyi, *Da dongluan de niandai*, pp. 70–71.

Ill.6.5. Staff of the Shanghai Museum pose in the foyer of the Shanghai Museum, September 27, 1967. Image courtesy of the collection of Zheng Zhong, *Wenhui bao*

The role of its workers was to take in *wenwu*, and for those objects whose ownership was known, receipts were issued to show that the Shanghai Museum was taking care of them on their owners' behalf. Among Cultural Revolution ephemera in Shanghai today there are receipts and inventories; those including paintings are marked with Zhong Yinlan's name.

But at the same time, many of the *wenwu* collected had no known provenance. Most were haphazardly piled in the Wenwu Small Group's collection stations, and some were about to be smelted or pulped before they were rescued. Part of the job of the workers in the Wenwu Small Group was to sort what was considered *wenwu*, or art objects dating from the period of the Qianlong Emperor (r. 1735–1796) or earlier, from handicrafts (*gongyipin*), which were to be funneled through state-run export companies and sold for foreign currency.[102] One significant

---

[102] Interviewees often alluded to China's need for foreign currency during the Mao years and explained that less important artwork could be exported for foreign exchange. I searched data on commodities exported for foreign currency, but I never found a category for cultural relics.

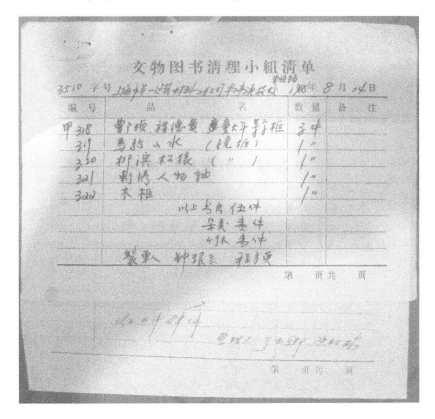

Ill.6.6. Receipt from the Wenwu Small Group, August 14, 1968. Image courtesy of the collection of Qu Yongfa, Shanghai Haiyan Tushu Wenhua Company, Ltd.

intervention by Zhong Yinlan and her colleagues was to petition the Shanghai Revolutionary Committee that such a definition was not "scientific," that one could not break off China's art historical past in such a way. Curating for the future, Zhong argued on behalf of the retention of exemplary post-Qianlong artwork; with the approval of the Shanghai Revolutionary Committee she combed the warehouses of the export companies and returned some 60,000 objects.[103] Even in revolution—or perhaps *especially* in revolution—the Shanghai Museum continued to collect.

[103] Interview in Shanghai with Zhong Yinlan, December 26, 2009.

In this way, the Shanghai Museum is linked to other collections made in revolution. The Louvre, for example, opened in 1793 during the French Revolution. Of its inaugural months, Andrew McClellan writes, "Inside the museum, the feeling of Revolutionary conquest was unequivocal. The works of art on display had been prized from their pre-Revolutionary settings and returned to their 'rightful' owners: the people." The collection of the revolutionary Louvre would expand through military exploits; returning from Italy, Napoleon paraded Italian paintings and sculpture as the spoils of war.[104] In the Soviet Union, the revolution of 1917 was followed by a mass nationalization of art in imperial, private, and church collections. In addition to creating state museums, artwork—along with other valuables—was sold by official decree and through the Museum Department of the People's Commisariat of Enlightenment to provide gold for industrialization.[105] Di Yin Lu's study of the Shanghai Museum demonstrates that within fifteen days during the "Attack on the Four Olds" in 1966, the Shanghai Museum inventoried 6,184 objects (of which 38 were top-tier *wenwu*, more than the average in a single preceding year) and that between 1966 and 1969, the Shanghai Museum acquired 106,000 objects, increasing its collection by 71 percent.[106] In the realm of collecting, the Cultural Revolution was as unprecedented for China as the Red Guards had claimed.[107]

In the later years of the Cultural Revolution, the curation of exhibitions was restored. In June 1973, Shen Zhiyu was recalled from the May 7 Cadre School to prepare the museum for its re-opening and he was

---

[104] Andrew McClellan, *Inventing the Louvre: Art, Politics, and the Origins of the Modern Museum in Eighteenth-Century Paris* (Berkeley: University of California Press, 1999), pp. 98, 116–123.

[105] See Natalya Semyonova and Nicolas V. Iljine, eds., *Selling Russia's Treasures: The Soviet Trade in Nationalized Art, 1917–1938* (New York: Abbeville Press, 2013), especially ch. 1.

[106] Lu, "Seizing Civilization," pp. 198–199, 219–225. This is especially significant when considering the top-tier (of the three) categories of cultural relics. Of the 6,184 collected during the "Attack on the Four Olds," thirty-eight were top-tier *wenwu*, more than the average for single preceding years. Of the 106,000 objects, 6,650 were top-tier *wenwu*. Lu calculates that since top-tier *wenwu* acquired between 1949–1964 numbered 539, "Cultural Revolution appropriations ... boosted the museum's finest collections by 1,234%," p. 225.

[107] Such a phenomenon is not limited to revolutions. The seizure of European art by Nazi Germany is probably the most famous example. In her study of Vichy France, Elizabeth Karlsgodt shows how collaborators used the idea of French patrimony to retain artwork confiscated from Jewish collectors and how the strength of the museum system in France—including its attendant policies and laws—was the result of the occupation. See Elizabeth Campbell Karlsgodt, *Defending National Treasures: French Art and Heritage under Vichy* (Stanford, CA: Stanford University Press, 2011).

Ill.6.7 and Ill.6.8. Denouncing the Kong family's entrance tablet and surveying the luxuries of the Kong family. Images courtesy of Thomas H. Hahn Docu-Images

appointed to the Revolutionary Committee of the Shanghai Museum. In the following year, under the direction of Ma Chengyuan, the bronze room was reinstalled under the banner, "Slaves Created History."[108] To accord with the concept that "Labor Created the World," a room on Chinese ceramics formed the second display.[109] Exhibitions were decidedly political; to accord with the 1974 political campaign to criticize Lin Biao and Confucius, the Shanghai Museum mounted an exhibit on the founding emperor of Qin.[110] It ran in parallel with a display at Qufu, Confucius's birthplace in Shandong Province, where local officials transformed the Confucius Mansion into an exhibition space, displaying the

---

[108] Chen Zhiqiang, *Wenbo xianqu*, p. 232. Feng Danfeng et al., "Cong qingtongqi kan chiren de 'lizhi': Shanghai bowuguan qingtongqi chenlieshi xunli" (Viewing the exploitation in the "Rites" from the bronzeware: Touring the bronze object room at the Shanghai Museum), *Xuexi yu pipan* (Study and criticism), no. 6 (1974), pp. 23–24.

[109] Chen Zhiqiang, *Wenbo xianqu*, p. 232.

[110] "Shanghai bowuguan wei peihe pi Lin pi Kong yundong: Juban 'Qin Shihuang tongyi Zhongguo wenwu tupian zhanlan'" (In order to follow the Criticize Lin Biao, Criticize Confucius campaign, the Shanghai Museum mounts an "Exhibition of photographs of cultural relics from Qin Shihuang's unification of China"), *Wenhui bao*, October 3, 1974, p. 3.

Ill.6.7 and Ill.6.8. (cont.)

Kong family's tablets, imperial gifts, property records, and personal possessions.[111] Photographs of visitors denouncing the tablets and docents describing the luxuries circulated as a set of images to be displayed, an exhibition of an exhibition.

As museums re-opened, cultural relics work reappeared in the national media. Articles about *wenwu* were released during Henry Kissinger's secret visit in 1971 and on the last day of President Richard Nixon's 1972 trip to China; both men toured the Palace Museum.[112] After the Nixon visit, Ma Chengyuan was tasked with preparing an exhibition to be sent to the United States.[113] Also in 1972, the Peking Foreign Languages Press published an English-language book entitled *New Archaeological*

---

[111] *Juebu yunxu kai lishi daoche* (Never allow historical regression) (Beijing: Renmin meishu jiaoyu chubanshe, 1974).

[112] This pattern is noted in *Survey of China Mainland Press*, no. 4949, p. 71 and no. 5090, p. 201. The former article appeared in a Xinhua News Agency release of July 24, 1971, and the latter article appeared in *Renmin ribao* on February 28, 1972. On the reopening of the Palace Museum, see Elliott, with Shambaugh, *The Odyssey of China's Imperial Art Treasures*, pp. 130–131.

[113] "Ma Chengyuan, 77, President of Shanghai Museum, Dies," *The New York Times*, October 15, 2004.

Finds in China: Discoveries During the Cultural Revolution, which high-lighted peasant contributions to the excavations.[114] The work of the Shanghai Museum also reappeared in local newspapers. In 1975, Shanghai's *Wenhui bao* published an article on "New Discoveries in Cultural Relics," using the examples of two Western Zhou wine vessels to explain how the Shanghai Museum had rescued them from a smelting plant. Unlike *Wenhui bao*'s coverage of *wenwu* in the previous year, the article was not ideological, explaining only the importance of historical research.[115] Even before the end of the Cultural Revolution in 1976, the museum's bronzes were going abroad as part of cultural exchanges. The Shanghai Museum became part of reform and opening-up.

During the 1980s, the Central Committee and the State Council issued regulations on the recovery of *wenwu* and books.[116] In 1984, local autho-rities were charged with returning *wenwu* to their original owners. In Shanghai, the Wenwu Small Group estimated that among the *wenwu* and books accounted for in 1986, 76 percent of the former and 50 percent of the latter were returned.[117] In the celebrated case of Liu Jingji, he was so overjoyed to see his collection again that he made a donation to the Shanghai Museum. The family of Gong Xuren, whose wife had also passed away during the Cultural Revolution, decided to sell the Shang Yang bronze measure to the museum; today it is listed as one of the museum's great treasures.[118] However, innumerable *wenwu* remained lost. Even without accounting for objects destroyed in the "Attack on the Four Olds," or the discrepancy between the amount the Wenwu Small Group collected in 1967–1968 (3,320,000 *wenwu* and handicrafts) and what remained in 1986 (810,000 *wenwu* and handicrafts), there were 1,920,000 missing *wenwu* and handicrafts for which the state made monetary restitutions.[119] A central question remains: who was the col-lecting for, after all?

---

[114] *New Archaeological Finds in China: Discoveries During the Cultural Revolution* (Peking: Foreign Languages Press, 1972), pp. 11–12, 47–54. In the same year, the Cultural Relics Press (Wenwu chubanshe) and the People's Art Press (Renmin meishu chu-banshe) issued at least three books with the same title (*Wenhua da geming shiqi chutu wenwu*). See The Chinese University of Hong Kong Library, Special Collections.

[115] "Wenwu xin faxian" (New discoveries of cultural relics), *Wenhui bao*, July 22, 1975, p. 3.

[116] "Zhonggong zhongyang, guowuyuan guanyu shouhui wenhua da geming shijian sanshi de zhengui wenwu he tushu de guiding" (Central Committee and State Council regula-tions on the retrieval of precious cultural relics and books scattered during the Cultural Revolution), June 4, 1980, *Ganshen gongzuo zhengce wenjian xuanbian* (Selected policy documents for trial work) (Beijing: Dangjian duwu chubanshe, 1993), in *WDGW*.

[117] *SHWWBWGZ*, p. 377.

[118] Zheng Zhong, *Haishang shoucang shijia*, p. 56. See also Chen Xiejun, ed., *Gems of Shanghai Museum* (Beijing: Renmin jiaoyu chubanshe, 2007), p. 47.

[119] *SHWWBWGZ*, pp. 376–377.

The Wenwu Small Group's reports presented the collection of *wenwu* as by and for the revolutionary masses. To the problem of *wenwu* where the "democratic essence and the feudal dross" were mixed, the Cultural Revolution reply was that material culture's class status came from its ownership. Returned to the masses by the Red Guards, the Wenwu Small Group asserted, *wenwu* could "serve the worker-peasant-soldiers, serve proletarian politics, and serve the creation of a glorious socialist new culture."[120] But if contemporary reports preserved in the archives tell the appropriately revolutionary story, Zhong Yinlan and Li Junjie—who also worked for the Wenwu Small Group—are adamant that the objects were being taken care of on behalf of the collectors. In Zhong Yinlan's memory, the revolutionary rhetoric simply consisted of slogans. She describes with pride her life in the countryside while sorting *wenwu*: "We had a very high consciousness, and we didn't pay any mind to our living conditions. If one day a painting from the Qianlong period would suddenly leap out at us or a painting from the Ming dynasty, a Dong Qichang (1555–1636), we were overjoyed, what a wonderful thing, a Dong Qichang painting. ... For *wenwu* to be protected by our own hands, this was a thing with great meaning, which made us very happy."[121] Similarly, Zhu Li, who was sent by the Antiquities Market to participate in the Wenwu Small Group, frames his work as serving the museum and, by extension, the state. Calculating that the Wenwu Store handed 7,000 pieces over to the Shanghai Museum, he comments, "Despite the fact that we were engaging in trade, in actuality we were protecting. So I am very proud, very happy, feeling that the work I did was a great contribution to the state."[122]

For this generation for whom museum work was truly a product of New China, working with the Wenwu Small Group was an unprecedented education. Zhong Yinlan was on her feet at dawn, appraising her quota of 1,000 paintings per day; on one side an assistant was rolling and unrolling scrolls, on her other side there was a scribe; she was only allotted half an hour for lunch. In her two years in the countryside and six years with the Wenwu Small Group, Zhong Yinlan may have seen more paintings than most collectors saw in a lifetime.[123] Zhu Li, the Antiquities Market appraiser who called Zhong Yinlan his "elder sister," remarks that

[120] SMA B172-3-5, p. 36.
[121] Interview in Shanghai with Zhong Yinlan, August 12, 2010.
[122] Interview in Shanghai with Zhu Li, July 18, 2011.
[123] Interview in Shanghai with Zhong Yinlan, August 12, 2010. For reference, the Shanghai collector Qian Jingtang (1908–1983) examined over 50,000 paintings during his lifetime. Ho, "Reforming Connoisseurship," p. 614.

"other people could go and rebel, or write big-character posters. I would go and study, study our ancient culture and art ... there were some things that one had never seen before and now one *could* see them, so it made one rejoice."[124] Perhaps the irony is that though the Cultural Revolution and its rhetoric were repudiated, collecting antiquity was for the masses after all—first to cultivate the generation that came of age in New China and then to be curated for the public in the post–Cultural Revolution era of reform.

Conclusion: Culture and nation in the era of reform

In 1996 the Shanghai Museum reopened in a grand new building on People's Square. Shaped like one of the ancient bronze vessels that workers in New China once saved from the scrap heaps of industrialization, it conferred legitimacy to the state that was then leading China in its economic miracle. Like the Shanghai Municipal Museum of Republican times which framed Shanghai City Hall, today's Shanghai Museum faces the Shanghai People's Government. If the Shanghai Municipal Museum reflected Republican China's dreams of cultural construction, the 1996 Shanghai Museum speaks for China's Four Modernizations.

Within the museum, the exhibitions have been transformed. The curation that began in 1952 with displays by dynasty, that changed in 1959 to accord with the Marxist stages of development, and that throughout the political campaigns were supplemented with temporary exhibitions, is today a collection of 120,000 rare objects presented by genre in ten permanent galleries. Museum Director Chen Xiejun writes that the task of exhibition is to allow people to "enjoy the beauty of the exhibition, raise their aesthetic temperament, and be nurtured in history and relics, art and aesthetics, and so on."[125]

With this emphasis on beauty, the Shanghai Museum may appear to bear no mark of its Mao-era past. But its socialist experience has shaped what it is today. Shen Zhiyu and Ma Chengyuan, the two who directed the response to the "Attack on the Four Olds," returned as museum directors during the reform era. For Shen, the Cultural Revolution

---

[124] Interview in Shanghai with Zhu Li, July 18, 2011.

[125] Li Rongrong, ed., *Ningjing de huihuang: Shanghai bowuguan xinguan chenlie sheji jiexi* (Quiet brilliance: Analysis of the form of the exhibitions in the new Shanghai museum) (Beijing: Wenwu chubanshe, 2005), p. 12. Its collection consists of nearly one million cultural relics, and twenty-one categories including bronzes, pottery and porcelain, calligraphy, paintings, jade, ivory, carved clay, painted bamboo and wood, bones and tortoise shells, seals, furniture, and so forth.

years were spent studying oracle bones; while the younger generation had the Wenwu Small Group as a classroom, he in political disgrace had only his study. For Ma, witnessing the dispersal of China's *wenwu* overseas galvanized his leadership of the museum. In an oral history he describes his feelings of conflict—both joy and lament—when he encountered Chinese *wenwu* on a 1980 trip to America. The consequences of the Cultural Revolution thus spurred Ma both to attempt to retrieve objects from overseas and to build a world-class museum for Shanghai. Otherwise, he declared, "I would be ashamed before our ancestors and unable to face the next generations."[126] The experience of the Mao period remains indelible in many other ways: Ma Chengyuan cultivated political patronage to secure the new, central location of the museum; the present-day organization by category began with Shen and Ma's design in 1970; and of course, many of the items in the collection were acquired by the museum as the fruits of a political campaign.[127]

Like the First Party Congress Site, the Shanghai Museum is an institution that has hosted many exhibits over time. During the Mao era, its exhibitions narrated official history, contrasted Old and New China, and critiqued class society. But above all its exhibitions were and are about antiquity, and therefore the case of the Shanghai Museum offers a way of thinking about the fate of Chinese tradition in the People's Republic. The museum workers' defense of *wenwu* in the "Attack on the Four Olds" and their collection in the name of the Cultural Revolution add a material culture perspective to recent studies of Cultural Revolution culture. Such scholarship, including Barbara Mittler's work on cultural products—from poster art to propaganda music—suggests that Cultural Revolution culture was part of a longer process of modernization that consciously integrated more of Chinese tradition than our popular image of iconoclasm suggests.[128] For the workers of the Shanghai Museum, China's antiquity was always part of the revolutionary narrative. From the very beginning, Mao's "On New Democracy" provided a raison d'être: without historic continuity, there would be no new culture.

---

[126] Duan Lian, Song Shijuan, and Chen Ling, eds., *Wangshi yu jiyi*, pp. 5–6.
[127] In the 2002 preface to Zheng Zhong's *Haishang shoucang shijia*, Wang Qingzheng of the Shanghai Museum notes that over 90 percent of the collection was collected from the people.
[128] Barbara Mittler, *A Continuous Revolution: Making Sense of Cultural Revolution Culture* (Cambridge, MA: Asia Center, Harvard University, 2012). This interpretation may be contrasted with Lin Yü-sheng's concept of "totalistic iconoclasm," a wholesale rejection of the past traced to the May Fourth Movement. See Yü-sheng Lin, *The Crisis of Chinese Consciousness: Radical Antitraditionalism in the May Fourth Era* (Madison: University of Wisconsin Press, 1979).

Beyond offering a lesson for our understanding of the Cultural Revolution, the story of the Shanghai Museum illuminates the longer period of China under Mao. Though Ma Chengyuan's oral history recalls the years of Liberation as a "blank sheet of paper" and as an opportunity to establish a "new-style socialist museum," the reality was much more complex.[129] The Shanghai Museum was established by artists from the Communist underground, its new generation was trained by the old, and its collections were built on previous connoisseurship. Its exhibitions, like those of previous regimes, were those of a state in power. The stewardship of *wenwu* lent a political legitimacy that was as acutely felt in 1949 as it was in the reform era when Ma Chengyuan—like many a Chinese intellectual before him—felt a pang of sadness when seeing Chinese *wenwu* exhibited abroad. In her analysis of the success of the early CCP, Elizabeth Perry has argued that, "cultural nationalism has always been a cornerstone and touchstone of Chinese Communism."[130] The Shanghai Museum demonstrates that this has been true even in moments of crisis like the Cultural Revolution. By collecting antiquity *in* and *for* the revolution, the Shanghai Museum continued to curate the nation.

---

[129] Duan Lian, Song Shijuan, and Chen Ling, eds., *Wangshi yu jiyi*, p. 2.
[130] Perry, *Anyuan*, p. 285.

Conclusion

A gray brick building, a begging gourd, a dissected frog, the scars on a worker's body, a luxurious fur coat, and a Song dynasty vase: in China's Mao era, the people of Shanghai encountered all of these objects as part of local exhibitions. Each object imparted a political lesson; each item was curated for revolution. The gray brick building was the First Party Congress Site, excavated from obscurity to become an icon in the CCP's founding myth. The begging gourd, a remnant of life in the "old society," became a prop to contrast past bitterness with a secure life in the workers' new village. The frog—a science experiment as display—aimed to convince children that there were no evil spirits; true revolutionary successors would love science and eliminate superstition. Curators used the worker's scars to illustrate class suffering through individual stories, class status physically embodied. During the Cultural Revolution, Red Guards mimicked previous exhibitions with their own displays; confiscated objects like the fur coat were proof of capitalist yearnings. The changing meaning of the Song vase followed the narrative arc of antiquity's role in the Mao period and after: an object of ancient democratic essence, a symbol of class society, the handiwork of historical laboring masses returned to the people, and a rarity to cultivate the aesthetic sensibility of a viewer in the post-Mao era of reform.

The curators of these objects always had a political goal in mind and often a contemporary political campaign to complement. The 1951 handbook for Shanghai neighborhood cadres explained that one needed to have "bamboo-in-the-breast," a clear vision to be materialized.[1] Like Zhong Yinlan at her brush, studying to become an appraiser of painting and calligraphy, the curator envisioned his bamboo, the truth in material phenomenon. Yet despite the seeming clarity of an exhibition's message—underscored by the presence of objects—this book has shown the contradictions in the politics of Mao-era culture. At the

---

[1] *Jiedao lilong jumin shenghuo shouce* (A handbook for neighborhood residential life) (Shanghai: Xinwen ribao guan, 1951), pp. 42–43.

First Party Congress Site, museum officials worked for historical accuracy but were bound to follow the "Red Line." In the new Fangua Lane, a curated community represented China's working class, and exceptional living conditions promised a socialist future for all. For the Young Pioneers at the anti-superstition exhibition, science educators exchanged one kind of belief for faith in science, in a time when the Mao cult was on the rise. At the class education exhibitions, curators struggled to portray a class threat that was both latent and ultimately doomed. At these exhibits and in the Red Guard showcases, narrators tried to elicit the proper emotions and to prevent unorthodox interpretations. During the Cultural Revolution, Shanghai Museum workers preserved *wenwu* for the revolution; their collection on behalf of the masses was ultimately for a state that never relinquished its cultural nationalism. In all of these case studies, to curate revolution was to grapple with the paradoxes of the Mao period.

This book uses the word "curating" to refer to all stages of putting on an exhibition, from assembling a collection of objects, to their display and narration, to the rituals of the exhibition hall. Thinking of curating as a process illuminates how propaganda was produced and consumed in Mao's China, through a medium that brought together many forms. As with textbooks and newspapers, and like radio and announcements, museums presented both script and sound. Similar to paintings and cartoons, exhibitions—which incorporated images with artifacts—were visual. Likened to a classroom, exhibition halls were places to give and receive lessons. Not unlike a meeting room or a public square, exhibits were sites where political rituals were performed. What made an exhibit unique was its premise that, based on real things, it reflected the truth of the world in a way that other media did not. Having been taught how to see an object as part of a system, a visitor was meant to view the outside world—with all of its physical things—as that system. With each stage of curating an exhibition, the revolution took material form.

Curating collections

Curating began with collection. This process is most evident in the examples of the First Party Congress Site and the Shanghai Museum, whose tasks were and continue to be the stewardship of relics, whether of the revolution or of antiquity. In the case of the First Party Congress Site, collection included amassing tens of thousands of revolutionary *wenwu*, conducting research to locate and restore sites of revolutionary significance, and interviewing thousands of old cadres to collect data on the history of the CCP. In the case of the Shanghai Museum, curating also began with the painstaking task of gathering, whether it consisted of convincing connoisseurs to donate, piecing together shattered bronzes from scrapheaps, or culling art from confiscated possessions. If revolution was continuous, so too was its collection. Witness the First Party Congress Site taking in Cultural Revolution objects and the Shanghai Museum collecting the placard of the Shanghai People's Commune. Even at times when it was too politically sensitive to display certain objects, one could still collect—hence the accumulation of research by Vice Director Ren Wuxiong of the First Party Congress Site for "when the time would be right" and Shanghai Museum curator Zhong Yinlan's understanding that all *wenwu* "were cultural heritage . . . and if you lost one, you were one down."[2]

Collection, and the research that it entailed, was not limited to museums. Exhibition workers, with a political message as "bamboo-in-the-breast," often began by analyzing the thinking of the masses. This kind of inquiry is most clearly evident in the anti-superstition exhibition, in which teachers noted examples of superstitious thinking among Young Pioneers and compiled lists of questions that the students asked about the supernatural. In addition to collecting viewpoints that were to be targeted, a curator gathered materials. As the 1961 directions on factory exhibits suggested, propaganda was "releasing an arrow" tipped with the historical materials gathered in the course of research. As the factory propagandists asked, "Where do the materials come from? They come from the masses. From which of the masses do they come? Primarily they come from old workers with a real blood lineage. These workers are, in the final analysis, our best teaching material because the character of our working class is concentrated in their bodies."[3] For the political-campaign exhibitions of the Mao period, a curator went to the masses: class education exhibition workers interviewed victims of alleged class enemies, and Red Guard docents were said to best call forth emotion when they heard bitterness recalled firsthand.

By "materials" curators meant both artifacts and the stories that supported them. For example, recall the checklist for the class education exhibition in the Shanghai countryside. The interviewer was to determine whether the peasant had preserved artifacts, but he was also there to collect a narrative. He asked questions about life before and after Liberation, listened to tales of oppression, observed the transformation

---

[2] Duan Lian, Song Shijuan, and Chen Ling, eds., *Wangshi yu jiyi: Shanghai diqu bowuguan, jinianguan koushu fangtanlu* (Past and memory: A record of oral histories and interviews from Shanghai local museums and memorial halls) (Shanghai: Shanghai cishu chubanshe, 2010), p. 66; interview in Shanghai with Zhong Yinlan, December 25, 2009.

[3] SMA C1-2-3596, pp. 46–52.

in the peasant's life, inspired his class consciousness, and recorded his denunciation. Here, collecting was doing history at the most local level, in a moment that historian Guo Wu has described as "a grassroots-level cultural movement that attempted to reconstruct the modern Chinese historical narrative and let workers and peasants tell their own life and history."[4] In this book, the most comprehensive display of artifacts and stories is the example of Fangua Lane, with materials from the rickshaw of the "old society" to the apartment block of the "new society," made complete with stories from its own residents. For what could be more authentic than real things narrated by living people?

Finally, collection took the form of gathering incriminating evidence for a political campaign. The curators of the class education exhibition, for example, had access to all manner of information from the state. The archives and the PSB provided documents from land reform to the Five Antis Campaign, and the courts lent artifacts and photographs from past cases.[5] During political campaigns, collecting revolution was collecting to accuse. This practice influenced the subsequent Cultural Revolution house searches. To discover certain objects—weapons, Nationalist flags, bars of gold—was to have proof that the owners were class enemies. The crucial role of these materials is evident in how the Red Guard factions used exhibitions against one another, whether physically defending a collection or creating dueling displays to discredit an opponent. Collection could take on a militant air, as if curation was a way to do battle. Of the lions that guarded the former Hong Kong and Shanghai Bank on the Bund, the Shanghai Bureau of Culture wrote, "In this Great Proletarian Cultural Revolution, the masses have captured this pair of lions and brought them to our [Shanghai] museum. Let them be preserved here as criminal evidence, forever declaring to our descendants how imperialism invaded China!"[6] Curating revolution gave material objects the power to speak.

Curating exhibitions, curating narratives

How to give artifacts voice? Despite the idea that objects could speak on their own, artifacts were selected and organized into exhibitions that were in turn narrated with words. As Shen Zhiyu reminded his Shanghai

---

[4] Guo Wu, "Recalling Bitterness: Historiography, Memory, and Myth in Maoist China," *Twentieth-Century China*, vol. 39, no. 3 (October 2014), p. 246.
[5] SMA C4-2-1, pp. 117–118.
[6] Zheng Zhong, *Haishang shoucang shijia* (Collectors in Shanghai) (Shanghai: Shiji chuban jituan, Shanghai shudian chubanshe, 2003), p. 217; Duan Lian, Song Shijuan, and Chen Ling, eds., *Wangshi yu jiyi*, p. 19; SMA B3-2-199, pp. 10–14.

Museum colleagues in 1960, the educational task of the museum was to raise perception to the level of reason.[7] For the first task of engaging the senses, exhibitions in Mao's China took on a variety of forms. In museums they were formal: at the First Party Congress Site visitors beheld oil paintings and examined documents, and at the Shanghai Museum visitors considered artifacts in simple glass display cases. By contrast, local and grassroots exhibitions were often little more than photographs and drawings pinned up on walls. Class education exhibitions and Red Guard displays laid out everyday objects on cloth-covered tables—the better to present materials as evidence. In each of these cases, artifacts had to be chosen with care; curators were exhorted not to send mixed messages. Of *wenwu*, Shen Zhiyu wrote in 1964 that objects should not be displayed if their artistic achievement was ambiguous, nor should anything with adverse political or social effects be exhibited.[8] Critics of the class education exhibition warned against arranging objects as if they were department store products or as if they were "Buddhas in a temple," demanding that the aura of the objects be harnessed to the display's political purpose.[9]

Indeed, objects and images could bring a narrative to life. The painter Li Bin (b. 1949) remembers being a primary-school student in Shanghai and going with his mother to attend an anti-spy exhibition at a local cultural palace. Too young to recognize all of the Chinese characters, Li was drawn to the images, which depicted a boy like himself watching a woman collect boiled water from a tiger stove. Astonished by the ease with which she lifts the water, the boy in the drawing follows her home and discovers the source of her strength. The "woman" removes her wig . . . she is a male spy! Almost sixty years later, Li recalls, "at that time, I was so scared that my hair stood on end! Now that I think about it, it was really like a movie. The Communist Party truly knew how to do things." In a glass case the spy's captured possessions were displayed: a wig, a dress, and a radio transmitter. For Li Bin, who grew up to illustrate Cultural Revolution pictorial exhibitions and is today a prominent painter, this exhibition changed how he saw the world. "I was always afraid of spies . . . I got used to looking around at women to see if any of them had an Adam's apple!"[10]

---

[7] Shen Zhiyu, "Xuexi Mao Zedong sixiang, tigao wenwu, bowuguan gongzuo zhong de zhengcexing he sixiangxing" (Study Mao Zedong Thought and improve adherence to the policy and ideological content of cultural relics and museum work), in *SZYWBLJ*, pp. 6–7.

[8] Shen Zhiyu, "Shanghai bowuguan gongzuo gangyao," in *SZYWBLJ*, p. 64.

[9] SMA B123-6-1534, p. 9.

[10] Interview in Shanghai with Li Bin, July 10, 2013. A photograph of an anti-spy exhibition appears in fig. 11 of Michael Schoenhals, *Spying for the People: Mao's Secret Agents, 1949–1967* (Cambridge: Cambridge University Press, 2013).

By the standard of the neighborhood cadre handbook—to give viewers new eyes—the exhibit was a success.

Mao-era exhibitions imparted many local stories and linked them to a primary narrative of revolution. The First Party Congress Site was literally "the place where our Party was born," the first stop on a pilgrimage—real or imagined—of CCP history. Curators made the "Red Line," or Chinese history according to Mao's own writings on the subject, their guiding principle. Although techniques of display have changed since Mao's death, the "Red Line" still guides historical narrative. As the example of the First Party Congress Site shows, narrative also served to localize the revolution, highlighting Shanghai's place in Party history. Down to the level of the neighborhood, as the showcase of Fangua Lane demonstrates, personal narratives were linked to the revolution. An individual like Wang Lanhua could trace her family's history from the *gundilong* of the shantytown to her role as Party secretary, then to her children's promising futures in New China. Interviewing people who were with Mao in the Yan'an base area, a place and time often seen as the crucible of Maoism, political scientists David Apter and Tony Saich suggest that Mao crafted a revolutionary discourse, interpreting the world to change it.[11] In a similar way, local exhibitions like Fangua Lane's encouraged individuals to write their own life histories using the revolution's vocabulary: before and after Liberation, standing up, "old" and "new" society. Exhibition is one way to understand how revolutionary discourse trickled down to the most grassroots level.

The Mao-era narrative of antiquity was inseparable from that of revolution. Since its founding in 1952, the Shanghai Museum presented *wenwu* as part of national history and as inspiration for the socialist present. The display of historical *wenwu*, curators wrote, would allow the masses to assimilate "the quintessence of ancient culture, raise the nation's self-respect, and develop the nation's new culture."[12] It was the revolution, after all, that preserved the cultural relics of the nation; a 1959 Shanghai Museum exhibition on "ten years of cultural relics work" argued that it was only in New China that *wenwu* were protected and displayed to the masses. Though today we think of the Shanghai Museum as an art museum, during the Mao period it held all manner of exhibitions: on Party history, on the second Sino-Japanese War, and on

---

[11] David E. Apter and Tony Saich, *Revolutionary Discourse in Mao's Republic* (Cambridge, MA: Harvard University Press, 1994).

[12] *Shanghai bowuguan chenliepin shuomingshu* (Guide to Shanghai Museum exhibits) (Shanghai: Shanghai bowuguan, November 1952), p. 4.

Shanghai before and after 1949.[13] That all of these narratives—of locality and nation, of war and revolution, of past and present—could be housed in one institution suggests the broad base on which the CCP staked its legitimacy. In this context, the activities of the Shanghai Museum during the Cultural Revolution do not seem out of place; antiquity was part of the revolution from its inception. This does not mean that the relationship between antiquity and revolution was not fraught. *Wenwu* were both the products of the historical working classes and the luxury items of the class oppressors; a painting could reflect cultural essence while its brushstrokes were done by an artist from the ruling class; and a curator might be the best expert but his class background could be insufficiently red. In New China contradictions were to produce a new synthesis, and a new culture was to be built on the old.

Joining the narratives of revolution and nation was a third one of class. Even the Communist Youth League exhibition, "Love Science and Eliminate Superstition," was foregrounded with a history of class: in antiquity, people did not understand nature and therefore made up superstitions; in class society, the ruling classes exploited such super-stitions to oppress the people; but with Liberation, the people could use science to conquer nature, exceeding the ancients' wildest dreams. This book's case studies of the class education exhibition and the Red Guard exhibition show how narratives about class were made during the Mao era's continuous revolution. These narratives were arguments for the persistence of class in socialist society: the former supported Mao's call for continuous class struggle against a capitalist restoration and the latter proved that hidden class enemies had been found, a justification for the Red Guard attacks. Exhibitions in Mao's China therefore made and reinforced class narratives old and new.

All of these narratives had to be voiced, usually through docents, though on rare occasions—as at the First Party Congress Site during the Cultural Revolution years—through tape recordings. This book has shown how the docent scripts were meticulously constructed; at the First Party Congress Site there were domestic and foreign texts, lists of prescribed questions and answers, and instructions on what to emphasize and when to deflect. The memories of retired Shanghai Museum officials show how they wrote their own scripts, and how they adapted their narration depending on the audience. The class status of the docents always mattered; at Fangua Lane only the most exemplary of its chosen people could be expected to host a delegation of foreign visitors, and at

---

[13] "Jinxi duibi qifa jieji ganqing" (Comparing past and present stimulates class feelings), *Wenhui bao* (Wenhui daily), February 16, 1964, p. 2.

the class education exhibition and the Red Guard display, docents had to have the right backgrounds. At Shanghai's Class Education Exhibition the best docents spoke "as if they [were] speaking their own hatred and bitterness, so much so that they themselves shed tears."[14] As a Red Guard narrator from The East is Red Department Store wrote, the mastery of a text came when "it became the words one's own heart wanted to say."[15] In the process of raising perception to reason, emotion also played an important role.

Missing are alternative narratives, as each exhibition was official history and politics, and every narrative text was checked for its political content. This book has suggested that unofficial narratives existed at the margins. The First Party Congress's revolutionary narrative privileged Mao and the importance of Party founding; the role of others was suppressed or erased outright. Fangua Lane was exemplary but exceptional; most others in Shanghai—including the great majority of Fangua Lane's original inhabitants—did not enjoy its conditions. Children, even Young Pioneers, might have had different understandings of religion at school and at home. While class education exhibitions and Red Guard displays seemingly brooked no opposition, contemporary critiques and memories today suggest that some had been dazzled rather than outraged. And if the Shanghai Museum's Cultural Revolution is in its own account a heroic tale of *wenwu* rescued, the story of destroyed or missing objects has vanished along with their material traces.

If there is an alternate exhibition narrative to be written, some of its contents may be held in the closed archives of the Bureau of Public Security. In one 1960 example far from Shanghai, a visitor to a People's Commune Exhibition Hall under Chongqing Municipality wrote,

Thank you for your warm narration, but this exhibition still cannot cover up the people's calamities, my grandfather eating hemp leaves or my mother weeping by his side. It is lucky that Grandfather starved to death this year, otherwise who knows how much more living punishment he would have had to endure.[16]

Guo Wu and others have argued that *yiku sitian*, and the historical practices of the early 1960s writ large, were intended to obscure the failures of the Great Leap Forward.[17] Such a visitor's comment, logged as "reactionary writing," confirms not only that exhibitions were

---

[14] SMA C4-2-1, p. 93.   [15] SMA B123-6-1536, p. 15.
[16] "Renmin gongshe zhanlanguan yijianbushang faxian fandong ziju" (Reactionary writings in the comments book are discovered in the People's Commune Exhibition Hall), *Disheqing jianbao*, no. 10 (April 7, 1960), p. 1. Ephemera in the collection of the Jianchuan Museum Cluster, Anren Township, Sichuan Province.
[17] Wu, "Recalling Bitterness, p. 250.

complicit as well, but also that some attendees understood them as such. However, as Kirk Denton rightly warns in his study of present-day museums, we should not assume that all—or even many—visitors were skeptical, that "we fail to understand China in its fullness if we neglect these official narratives and their power to persuade."[18] Likewise, for many people involved in exhibitions during Mao's China—from Wang Lanhua when speaking with Félix Pita Rodríguez to Zhong Yinlan rushing to collectors' homes—the narratives rang true.

Curating rituals

Visiting an exhibition in Mao's China was a ritual: visitors proceeded through space and time, they listened to scripts and participated on cue, and sometimes they expressed emotion or shouted slogans as suggested. Museums and exhibition halls were a kind of ritual space. Though the level of formality depended on the size and the scope of the display, visitors followed a prescribed path—literally and metaphorically— beginning with a prefatory space, perhaps with a Mao Zedong quotation or a bust of Mao, winding through rooms and listening to a docent narrate the objects and illustrations, and ending with a conclusion that could include slogans to be shouted in unison or a second Mao statue to admire. The ritual of moving through the exhibition in a group, following a docent or listening to one stationed in a room, was bolstered by already familiar rituals from a broader political culture. Photographs from this period illustrate what postures the visitor would take. At Beijing's Museum of the Chinese Revolution, for example, Young Pioneers pledge to the national flag, children sit with their arms wrapped around their knees as they listen to narrators, upturned faces follow a docent's white pointer, and the eyes of people gathered around the scaffold where Li Dazhao was hanged drop to the floor.[19] Such official portrayals are reflected in the examples in this book: the meetings that followed the Shanghai Class Education Exhibition show how carefully participation was constructed and observed, archival photographs from the Red Guard exhibition show groups reciting Mao quotations, and Shanghai students remember marching to Fangua Lane as part of their military training—a pilgrimage to the past.[20]

---

[18] Kirk A. Denton, *Exhibiting the Past: Historical Memory and the Politics of Museums in Postsocialist China* (Honolulu: University of Hawai'i Press, 2014), p. 267.

[19] "Zai Zhongguo geming bowuguanli" (In the Museum of the Chinese Revolution), *Wenwu* (Cultural relics), no. 10 (1964), pp. 3–20.

[20] SMA C4-2-1, p. 80; SMA B123-6-1540, p. 3; interview in Shanghai, July 24, 2013.

The presentation of curated narratives was also a ritual, part of exhibition's participatory propaganda. Artifacts and stories, at least for local exhibitions, were collected from the people. During a visit, docents worked to cultivate emotions, both their own and those of the audience. Sometimes the ritual of *yiku sitian* was performed by an individual who had experienced the old society, like the elderly workers of Fangua Lane who volunteered to tell of their past bitterness with the *gundilong* houses at their backs. At other times docents retold the stories that they had gathered through interviews, channeling the emotions they had witnessed and experienced firsthand. To stir such emotions was perhaps the ultimate way of participating in propaganda; as Red Guard reports claimed, the verb *"gandong"* (to move, to touch) is made up of two characters, one for the feelings of the speaker, *"gan"* (feelings, emotions) and the other for the listener being moved, *"dong"* (to move, to change).[21] The best evidence for the success of a class education exhibition was if a visitor was so moved that he leapt forward to *yiku sitian* himself. In such an environment there was pressure to participate in the exhibition as prescribed. With others shouting Red Guard slogans, or reenacting the ritual of the house search, who would dare not raise his fist?

Curating rituals extended to activities that took place after a visit concluded. Sometimes a visit culminated with a meeting in which the visitors could publicly examine their reactions or even make self-criticisms. The display was meant to make teachers of its viewers: a Young Pioneer instructed his elders to discard superstitious incense burners, a worker father used his old employment contract to give his son a class lesson, a visitor to a class education exhibition copied out its text to teach his work unit. Beyond teaching, curating revolution created both a vocabulary and a repertoire of political action. The class education exhibitions and the subsequent Red Guard showcases demonstrate this most clearly. Strophe and antistrophe, the former taught that class enemies could be identified by their hidden possessions and the latter put them on display; class struggle was indeed continuous, and it was right to rebel. The political-campaign exhibits not only cultivated visitors to see the world with new eyes, but they also gave them scripts to accuse and denounce. An exhibition was more than revolution's textbook—it could also be revolution's handbook.

To what degree did people in Mao's China wish to partake in its exhibitionary culture? Some, especially in the early years, may have simply attended as something to do. A retired cadre (b. 1950), with

---

[21] SMA B123-6-1534, p. 8. The original word actually implies that only one person, not two, was moved.

vivid childhood memories of a dark church basement with guns, gold bars, and American dollars, explained that his mother's relatives lived nearby; after eating dinner together, "we just went next door to take a look."[22] Visitors to the Red Guard exhibitions may also have gone for the spectacle. But most exhibitions beyond those ad hoc and at the most grassroots required reservations and tickets, and one attended with one's school or work unit. However, even if participation at an exhibition was mandatory, it was in the visitor's interest to learn its content. Some attendees at Shanghai's Class Education Exhibition spent hours copying its contents, taught it back to their work units later, and used it as a model for carrying out the Socialist Education Movement. In an era of swiftly changing politics, an exhibition's content was particularly valuable: it was the latest Party-approved text, written in a language tailored for a popular audience. That in the summer of 1966 individuals asked to visit the Shanghai Class Education Exhibition—which by then had added a Cultural Revolution tail—suggests a genuine desire to understand a bewildering political campaign. Visiting an exhibition was a way to learn the script.

Socialist museums and new exhibitions

The curators of New China called its museums "socialist museums" (*shehuizhuyi bowuguan*), stressing their unprecedented nature, their ideological function, and their role in social transformation: the socialist museum mounted more exhibitions and brought them to more people than its predecessors. Describing its collection in 1952, the Shanghai Museum explained that with the various political movements of the early 1950s, the people had a higher political consciousness, stronger enthusiasm for production, and a greater need for education and culture.[23] Throughout the Mao period, the socialist museum continued to represent antiquity, nation, revolution, and new culture. Even during the Cultural Revolution, propaganda materials highlighted the protection of *wenwu*; one booklet issued in 1972 included state documents praising *wenwu* work since 1949, declaring that "the cultural quintessence created by the historical working masses" would create a new culture.[24] The same themes were emphasized in handbooks for cultural workers into the post-Mao era of reform. In a socialist museum, exhibitions had to be

---

[22] Interview in Shanghai, July 2, 2013.

[23] *Shanghai bowuguan chenliepin shuomingshu*, p. 4.

[24] *Wenwu baohu guanli xuanchuan ziliao* (Propaganda materials for the protection and management of cultural relics) (Shanghai: Shanghaishi wenwu baoguan weiyuanhui, 1972), pp. 1–4.

ideological, scientific, and aesthetic, reflecting developmental laws and "allowing the people to understand their own historical and creative strength."[25]

But despite these pioneering claims, the socialist museum had more in common with museums from the pre-1949 Republican era than its founders would have admitted. The museums of Republican China also framed antiquities as national treasures.[26] The Nationalist government also exhibited the revolution, establishing memorial monuments, displaying the possessions of martyrs, and celebrating a founding father. Local governments used museums for public education. The Shanghai Municipal Museum, for example, focused on artifacts from Shanghai and of the nation.[27] Museums of nation, revolution, and locality all aimed to shape the Republican citizen; just as nineteenth-century European museums sought to tutor the crowd, the Shanghai Municipal Museum required its visitors to register, to speak respectfully, and to follow the prescribed route in single file.[28] Both Republican-era museums and socialist museums partook in the exhibitionary culture of the state in power, but the CCP was able to go even further. Its military victory, consolidation of control, and permeation of local society allowed the CCP to make culture a key element in its post-1949 construction: it absorbed the collections of preexisting museums, took control of customs and the market, and directed all cultural professions. If New China did not yet have wealth, it had power, and such power was necessary to harness culture for its own purposes. And if nation and revolution were the two pillars of political legitimacy, the Communist Party—facing its rival across the Taiwan Straits—put both on display.

New China's socialist museums were different from Republican-period institutions in their ideology. Though ideological valences would change over time, a socialist museum was to apply Marxism, Leninism, and Mao Zedong Thought to the objects of nation and of revolution. In many

[25] *Wenwu gongzuo shouce* (Handbook for cultural relics work) (Shanghai: Shanghaishi wenwu guanli weiyuanhui, n.d.), p. 164. This quotation comes from a 1979 document; the handbook includes documents up until the early 1990s.

[26] Cheng-hua Wang, "The Qing Imperial Collection, Circa 1905–1925: National Humiliation, Heritage Preservation, and Exhibition Culture," in *Reinventing the Past: Archaism and Antiquarianism in Chinese Art and Visual Culture*, edited by Hung Wu (Chicago: Center for the Art of East Asia, University of Chicago, 2010), pp. 320–341.

[27] *Shanghaishi bowuguan zhangze* (Shanghai Municipal Museum rules and regulations) (Shanghai: Shi bowuguan, 1936), pp. 1–2.

[28] See Tony Bennett, "The Exhibitionary Complex," in *Culture/Power/History: A Reader in Contemporary Social Theory*, edited by Nicholas B. Dirks, Geoff Eley, and Sherry B. Ortner (Princeton, NJ: Princeton University Press, 1994), pp. 133–139; *Shanghai shili bowuguan yaolan* (Shanghai Municipal Museum exhibition), August 1948, p. 16.

respects, exhibitionary culture in Mao's China followed the Soviet example. Like the Soviet Union, which credited the Red Army with protecting
historic sites and which moved swiftly to protect museums, New China
employed the PLA and established Cultural Relics Commissions as it
took over new jurisdictions. Socialist China's cultural bureaucracy
mirrored the Soviet one; although museums came under the jurisdiction
of a Bureau of Culture, they were always controlled by the Party's
Department of Propaganda. In format and display, China's revolutionary
museums traced Soviet revolutionary museums in lockstep, most notably
in that Mao's "New Democracy" and Stalin's *History of the Communist
Party of the Soviet Union (Bolsheviks): Short Course* literally provided the
outline for their respective exhibition rooms. Like others in the socialist
bloc, China adopted the principles and techniques of Soviet exhibitionary
culture. For example, the Museum for German History was directly
inspired by the Soviets and presented as a *Volksmuseum* with artifacts
from the people; it opened in 1952, the same year as the Shanghai
Museum.[29] The National Museum of the Vietnamese Revolution was
established in 1959, concurrent with the opening of Beijing's Museum of
the Chinese Revolution, and to this day its presentation of narrative and
artifacts maintains the style of the period.[30]

Mao-era museums thus followed the Soviet Union as the exhibitionary
culture of a socialist state in power. This common museology not only
exhibited similar things in similar ways, but it also displayed historical
processes as the inevitable result of socialist principles. Linking China to
other examples of state socialism, Rubie Watson explains that Mao
"justified his own leadership and that of his party by writing himself into
history—by making himself, his followers, and his 'line' the inevitable
result of historical forces."[31] Such a historical narrative was the Chinese
socialist museum's narrative, whether it was a revolutionary history
museum like the First Party Congress Site or an art museum like
the Shanghai Museum. As the present was also a product of historical
development, the socialist museum—like Fangua Lane—celebrated

[29] Jon Berndt Olsen, *Tailoring Truth: Politicizing the Past and Negotiating Memory in East Germany, 1945–1990* (New York: Berghahn Books, 2015). The collection of the Museum for German History (Museum für Deutsche Geschichte) was transferred to the German Historical Museum (Deutsches Historisches Museum) with reunification.
[30] Tiến Dũng Lê, ed., *Guidebook: Vietnam National Museum of History* (Hanoi: National Museum of Vietnamese History, 2014), pp. 70–194. In 2011 the museum was integrated into the Vietnam National Museum of History, in the same way that Beijing's Museum of the Chinese Revolution is now the National Museum of China.
[31] Rubie S. Watson, ed., *Memory, History, and Opposition under State Socialism* (Santa Fe: School of American Research Press, 1994), p. 2.

contemporary achievements. In this way, China also followed the Soviet Union's exhibitions of agricultural or infrastructural development.[32] Indeed, at a time when "the Soviet Union's today [was] China's tomorrow," exhibitions of Soviet achievements went on display in Beijing.[33] However, there was one aspect of Soviet exhibitionary culture that socialist China did not follow: while China held anti-superstition exhibitions that sometimes attacked religious figures, it did not create anti-religion museums.[34]

Where socialist China departed from both the Republican-era precedent and the Soviet model was in the second mode of exhibitionary culture, that of a revolutionary movement. This mode originated in the land reform movement's "new exhibitions" (*xin zhanlanhui*), which did more than exhibit class struggle—they were part of class struggle. New exhibitions curated revolution by modeling the rituals of class struggle; the class education exhibitions that became Red Guard exhibitions were vehicles for accusation and exposure, linking material possessions to class in a way that no other propaganda medium suggested. With Mao's claim that class persisted in socialist society and that class struggle would be long term, new exhibitions became part of continuous revolution. That the Soviet Union did not have similar exhibitions is due to this divergence in class rhetoric and a different culture of denunciation. Writing of denunciation in modern European history, Sheila Fitzpatrick and Robert Gellately distinguish between the collective, public outcasting of enemies during a revolution and spontaneous accusation by an individual to the totalitarian state.[35] With China's continuous revolution, struggle sessions remained collective and public, seemingly spontaneous but often organized. In the Soviet case, a privately mailed letter of denunciation was followed by a state investigation; in the Chinese case, an individual's own personal letters could be laid bare on display—for the revolutionary masses to attack and condemn.

[32] Sheila Fitzpatrick, *Everyday Stalinism: Ordinary Life in Extraordinary Times: Soviet Russia in the 1930s* (New York: Oxford University Press, 1999), p. 71; Karen Petrone, *Life Has Become More Joyous, Comrades: Celebrations in the Time of Stalin* (Bloomington: Indiana University Press, 2000), pp. 155–156.

[33] *Sulian jingji ji wenhua jianshe chengjiu zhanlanhui tupian jieshao* (Pictorial introduction to the exhibition of Soviet achievements in economic and cultural construction) (Beijing: Zhaohua meishu chubanshe, 1955).

[34] S. A. Smith, "Contentious Heritage: The Preservation of Churches and Temples in Communist and Post-Communist Russia and China," *Past and Present*, vol. 226, supplement 10 (2015), pp. 194, 196.

[35] Sheila Fitzpatrick and Robert Gellately, eds., *Accusatory Practices: Denunciation in Modern European History, 1789–1989* (Chicago: University of Chicago Press, 1997), pp. 1–2.

Exhibitionary culture's revolutionary mode drew from traditional Chinese cultural repertoire, most evident in China's display of class.[36] Whereas in Soviet museums tools and documents illustrated in Marxist terms who owned the means of production, Chinese curators chose to exhibit class by illustrating suffering and counting grievances to settle accounts.[37] On display were scars and wounded bodies, and the riches of the exploiting classes were explained by equating them with the necessities that peasants and workers required for survival: the price of one fur coat could feed 120 workers for a year. These techniques reflect temple portrayals of sins and enumerate crimes like Buddhist ledgers of merit and demerit, showing how Mao-era political culture was indebted to traditional forms.[38] Likewise, as Ann Anagnost suggests, the ritual of speaking bitterness may have originated in Chinese village culture, in which a victim airs grievances in public to be either affirmed or contested by the crowd.[39] Sharing a bitterness meal resembles lineage ceremonies in which all the participants eat symbolic food together.[40] Even the idea of putting people on display calls to mind scenes from the county magistrate's office in imperial times, when convicts were made to wear heavy wooden boards around their necks or were left to starve in cages for all to see.[41] The behavior of some visitors to the Shanghai Class Education Exhibition further suggests its similarity to a temple; there the capitalist trembled as if before the statue of the city god, feeling that the docents and the models were pointing fingers at him.[42] In its revolutionary mode, Mao-era exhibitionary culture was at its most Chinese.

Exhibitionary culture in Mao's China thus operated in two modes, the socialist museum and the new exhibition reflecting the practices of the state in power and the state in revolution. These modes of legitimation and mobilization could and did overlap: consider the First Party Congress

[36] For an analysis of the role of tradition in Chinese political theater, see Joseph W. Esherick and Jeffrey N. Wasserstrom, "Acting Out Democracy: Political Theater in Modern China," *Journal of Asian Studies*, vol. 49, no. 4 (November 1990), pp. 835–865.

[37] *Sulian bowuguanxue jichu* (Fundamentals of Soviet museology) (Beijing: Wenwu chubanshe, 1957), pp. 307–308. The comparison between bourgeois luxury and peasant poverty was observed at the Ho Chi Minh Museum in Hanoi, April 5, 2015.

[38] See Anne Swann Goodrich, *The Peking Temple of the Eastern Peak* (Nagoya: Monumenta Serica, 1964), p. 248. One part of the temple depicts a "court of ill-gotten wealth," with the guilty carrying objects such as pieces of coral and ingots of precious metals.

[39] Ann Anagnost, *National Past-Times: Narrative, Representation, and Power in Modern China* (Durham, NC: Duke University Press, 1997), p. 31.

[40] See Jun Jing, *The Temple of Memories: History, Power, and Morality in a Chinese Village* (Stanford, CA: Stanford University Press, 1996), pp. 155–157.

[41] For these and other punishments, see Philip A. Kuhn, *Soulstealers: The Chinese Sorcery Scare of 1768* (Cambridge, MA: Harvard University Press, 1990), pp. 7–22.

[42] SMA C4-2-1, p. 92.

Site turning into a Cultural Revolution broadside or the disappearance of the Red Guard exhibition in favor of one on the January Revolution. And while their political functions differed, both forms shared a mass nature. Exhibitions in Mao's China were grassroots in a way that exhibits in Republican China were not. Stories came from the people, and though they were curated by officials and told by docents, the authenticity of their telling came from hearing the narratives from their source. Artifacts came from the masses, whether in a neighborhood display or in a class education exhibition, and they could be extremely humble: a begging gourd, an identification card, even a bodily scar. That exhibits were Party-directed does not diminish the participatory nature of the propaganda—that it was a former beggar called Wang Lanhua who proposed the preservation of part of Fangua Lane's shantytown, or that two young women of modest background, Chen Peifen and Zhong Yinlan, could rise to the leadership of the Shanghai Museum. If history was made by the masses, revolution was curated by the people.

Legacies of Mao's exhibitionary culture

In our times, it is difficult to find traces of the Mao-era exhibitions described in this book. The First Party Congress Site and the Shanghai Museum, whose curators devoted the early reform years to restoring the exhibitions to history, are still extant as institutions. The exhibition of Fangua Lane continued to host schoolchildren until it was torn down in 1996, and with it, its vision of a socialist future that never came to be.[43] The displays most explicitly tied to contemporary political campaigns have left few footprints outside of the archives, though ephemera from class education exhibitions can be bought online and some memories of Red Guard exhibits are recorded on Internet blogs. Asked about the fate of Guo Linshuang of Yong'an Department Store, who was featured in its Red Guard exhibition, the official in charge of company history denied knowing of Guo's whereabouts in the years after socialist transformation. These objects and histories, once so assiduously preserved to curate revolution, have mostly disappeared or have been deliberately elided. Their material cultures—whether of the old society or the new society— are increasingly scarce.

If Mao's exhibitionary culture had two modes, today's China primarily employs the exhibitionary culture of a state in power, using museums to

---

[43] On the removal of Fangua Lane's shantytown exhibition, see Wing-Chung Ho, "Building Up Modernity? The Changing Spatial Representations of State Power in a Chinese Socialist 'Model Community,'" *Modern Asian Studies*, vol. 42, no. 6 (2008), p. 1146.

make and reflect official narratives. At the First Party Congress Site, the permanent exhibition is still framed by Party historiography and its claim that the founding of the Chinese Communist Party was the inevitable outcome of China's historical development. In its wax-works tableau, Mao remains at the center. The Shanghai Museum has gained world renown, fulfilling the reform era's goal of using exhibitions abroad to propagandize China's "splendid history and national culture."[44] China's exhibitions continue to chart narratives of modernization and development. As in Fangua Lane, visitors to the China Pavilion at the 2010 Shanghai Expo were shown domestic spaces and their material improvements over time. Museums persist as the ritual spaces of political legitimacy. In 1990, President Jiang Zemin chose Beijing's Museum of the Chinese Revolution as a backdrop for his speech on "patriotic education" and "socialist education," calling on museums to take responsibility.[45] In 2012, President Xi Jinping introduced his regime's hallmark slogan, the "China Dream," at the National Museum of China.[46]

The exhibitionary culture of a revolutionary movement reemerges when China is in political-campaign mode. For example, two months after the 1989 Tiananmen student movement, Beijing's Military Museum of the Chinese People's Revolution mounted an exhibition on the "Suppression of the Beijing Counterrevolutionary Riot," which received over 30,000 visitors daily.[47] The anti-superstition exhibitions reappeared in 2000, when displays warned of the dangers of Falungong, a *qigong* practice that went from a registered organization to a heretical cult.[48] In the cases of both Tiananmen and Falungong, exhibitions were deployed to control the script and to identify and attack enemies. More recently, Xi Jinping's crackdown on corruption has revived the Mao-era class education exhibition. These anti-corruption exhibits showcase confiscated liquor and scenes of banqueting, letters of repentance, and

[44] See a 1984 Ministry of Culture circular, in *Wenwu gongzuo shouce*, p. 168.
[45] "Jiang Zemin tongzhi canguan 'Zhongguo gemingshi chenlie' jieshushi de jianghua" (Speech by Comrade Jiang Zemin upon viewing the conclusion of the "Exhibition of Chinese revolutionary history"), *Dangshi yanjiu ziliao*, no. 9 (1990), pp. 2–3.
[46] See Kirk A. Denton, "China Dreams and the 'Road to Revival,'" *Origins: Current Events in Historical Perspective*, vol. 8, no. 3 (December 2014), http://origins.osu.edu/article/china-dreams-and-road-revival (accessed September 30, 2016); Denton, *Exhibiting the Past*, pp. 73–74.
[47] Xu Yunping, "Xuexie de jiaokeshu: Pingxi Beijing fangeming baoluan zhanlan ceji" (A textbook written in blood: Sidelights of the exhibition on the suppression of the Beijing counterrevolutionary riot), *Renmin ribao* (People's daily), September 1, 1989, p. 1.
[48] Jian Ping, Shao Zhen, and Dong Hui, "Rang kexue de guanghui qusan 'yinmai'" (Let science's glory dispel the "haze"), *Dangjian zazhi*, no. 5 (2000), pp. 37–38.

confessions copied onto display boards. Visitors encounter not only the crime but also the punishment, in the form of handcuffs and prison dioramas. Anti-corruption exhibits also show real people, both through videos and actual officials recounting their stories live. Like the capitalists who confessed after attending Shanghai's Class Education Exhibition, some officials have reportedly turned in bribes after a visit stirs their guilt.[49] But these similarities to revolutionary exhibitionary culture remain limited. Today's exhibitions aim not at revolution; on display are opponents of the state, not enemies of the revolution.

Perhaps the most conspicuous difference between Mao's exhibitionary culture and that of China's today is the absence of displays about the Mao years themselves. In contrast to the 1950s and 1960s, when contemporary history was either central to the topic on display or foremost in the curators' minds—using the past to serve the present—exhibitions today treat the revolution with caution. Curated by the Shanghai History Museum, an exhibit at the base of the Pearl Tower in Shanghai showcases the social and cultural life of the Republican era, with no mention of its labor movements or the Chinese Communist Party founding.[50] At the Shanghai Expo in 2010, recent history began only in 1978, the beginning of China's era of reform and opening-up. In Beijing, the new National Museum of China covers the achievements of the Mao period as "socialist construction," but it does not address the political campaigns from land reform to the Cultural Revolution, movements once made material by "new exhibitions."[51] With the exception of memorial museums to Party leaders or to socialist icons like Lei Feng, no official museum focuses on the Mao period; in recent years a few private museums have made such an attempt, but these exist only by successfully anticipating local censors.[52] Exhibitions *of* Mao's China remain taboo for a host of reasons: they would reveal the tragedies and violence of its campaigns, they might raise questions about the responsibility of individuals as well as of the state, and they

[49] See "The Emerging Business of Anti-Corruption Shows," *Xinhua News*, July 28, 2015, http://news.xinhuanet.com/english/2015-07/28/c_134455958.htm (accessed October 3, 2016); "Anti-Corruption Exhibition a Spectacle of Shame, Confiscated *Baijiu*," *Global Times*, December 21, 2015, http://www.globaltimes.cn/content/959732.shtml (accessed October 3, 2016).

[50] Interview in Shanghai with Fang Yunfang, vice curator of the Shanghai History Museum, May 11, 2007; Elizabeth J. Perry, "Shanghai's Politicized Skyline," in *Shanghai: Architecture and Urbanism for Modern China*, edited by Peter G. Rowe and Seng Kuan (Munich: Prestel, 2004), p. 107.

[51] Denton, *Exhibiting the Past*, pp. 72–73.

[52] See Denise Y. Ho and Jie Li, "From Landlord Manor to Red Memorabilia: Reincarnations of a Chinese Museum Town," *Modern China*, vol. 42, no. 1 (2016), pp. 30–31.

could challenge the Party's ideology as well as its system of power. Exhibitions *in* Mao's China, after all, created narratives and arguments, mobilized memory and emotion, made of its viewers revolutionary participants, and enlivened objects at once to celebrate revolution and to accuse its discontents. Such displays of politics curated China's Communist revolution, in all its power and its fragility.

Bibliography

A Li 阿励, ed. *Shanghai de gushi* 上海的故事 (Stories of Shanghai). Hong Kong: Zhonghua shuju, Xianggang fenju, 1973.

Anagnost, Ann. *National Past-Times: Narrative, Representation, and Power in Modern China.* Durham: Duke University Press, 1997.

Antonioni, Michelangelo. *Cina.* Rome: Rai Trade, 2007.

Apter, David E., and Tony Saich. *Revolutionary Discourse in Mao's Republic.* Cambridge, MA: Harvard University Press, 1994.

Ba Jin. "A Cultrev Museum." In *Seeds of Fire: Chinese Voices of Conscience*, edited by Geremie Barmé and John Minford, pp. 381–384. New York: Hill and Wang, 1988.

Baum, Richard. *Prelude to Revolution: Mao, the Party, and the Peasant Question, 1962–66.* New York: Columbia University Press, 1975.

Baum, Richard, and Frederick C. Teiwes. *Ssu-Ch'ing: The Socialist Education Movement of 1962–1966.* Berkeley: Center for Chinese Studies, University of California, 1968.

Beijing zaozhi zongchang shoudu zhigong geming zaofanzhe lianzongzhan 北京造纸总厂首都职工革命造反者连总站 (Beijing Paper-Making Industrial Complex Workers' Revolutionary Rebels United Station) et al. *Guanyu baohu gujiu shukan zihua de changyishu* 关于保护古旧书刊字画的倡议书 (Proposal regarding the protection of ancient and old books, periodicals, calligraphy, and paintings). Unpublished flyer, February 15, 1967.

Beijing zhi: Wenwu juan, wenwu zhi 北京志: 文物卷, 文物志 (Beijing gazetteer: Volume on cultural relics, cultural relics gazetteer). Beijing: Beijing chubanshe, 2006.

"Beijingshi gushu wenwu qingli xiaozu guanyu tiaoxuan gujiu shukan biaozhun de yijian" 北京市古书文物清理小组关于挑选古旧书刊标准的意见 (Opinions of the Beijing Municipal Small Group for Sorting Ancient Books and Cultural Relics on the standards for selecting ancient books). June 1967.

Bennett, Tony. "The Exhibitionary Complex." In *Culture/Power/History: A Reader in Contemporary Social Theory*, edited by Nicholas B. Dirks, Geoff Eley, and Sherry B. Ortner, pp. 123–154. Princeton, NJ: Princeton University Press, 1994.

Bergère, Marie-Claire. *Shanghai: China's Gateway to Modernity*, translated by Janet Lloyd. Stanford, CA: Stanford University Press, 2009.

Blake, C. Fred. *Burning Money: The Material Spirit of the Chinese Lifeworld.* Honolulu: University of Hawai'i Press, 2011.

Brady, Anne-Marie. *Making the Foreign Serve China: Managing Foreigners in the People's Republic.* Lanham, MD: Rowman & Littlefield, 2003.

Braester, Yomi. *Painting the City Red: Chinese Cinema and the Urban Contract.* Durham, NC: Duke University Press, 2010.

Brown, Jeremy. *City versus Countryside in Mao's China: Negotiating the Divide.* Cambridge: Cambridge University Press, 2012.

"Moving Targets: Changing Class Labels in Rural Hebei and Henan, 1960–1979." In *Maoism at the Grassroots: Everyday Life in China's Era of High Socialism*, edited by Jeremy Brown and Matthew D. Johnson, pp. 51–76. Cambridge, MA: Harvard University Press, 2015.

Brown, Jeremy, and Matthew D. Johnson, eds. *Maoism at the Grassroots: Everyday Life in China's Era of High Socialism.* Cambridge, MA: Harvard University Press, 2015.

Brown, Jeremy, and Paul G. Pickowicz, eds. *Dilemmas of Victory: The Early Years of the People's Republic of China.* Cambridge, MA: Harvard University Press, 2007.

Buke wangji jieji douzheng: Jieshao Shandongsheng jieji jiaoyu zhanlanhui 不可忘记阶级斗争: 介绍山东省阶级教育展览会 (Never forget class struggle: Introducing Shandong Province's class education exhibition). Cai Fengming 蔡丰明, and Zhang Lili 张丽丽, eds. *Minsu Shanghai: Zhabei juan* 民俗上海：闸北卷 (Folk customs of Shanghai: Zhabei volume). Shanghai: Shanghai wenhua chubanshe, 2007.

Chan, Anita, Richard Madsen, and Jonathan Unger. *Chen Village: The Recent History of a Peasant Community in Mao's China.* Berkeley: University of California Press, 1984.

Chen Duanzhi 陈端志. *Bowuguan* 博物馆 (Museums). Shanghai: Shangwu yinshuguan, 1937.

Bowuguanxue tonglun 博物馆学通论 (General survey of museum studies). Shanghai: Shanghai bowuguan, 1936.

Chen, Janet Y. *Guilty of Indigence: The Urban Poor in China, 1900–1953.* Princeton, NJ: Princeton University Press, 2012.

Chen Peicun 陈沛存, and Ren Rui 任锐. "Jianguan sishinian zhi huigu" 建馆四十年之回顾 (Looking back on forty years since the establishment of the museum). In *Shanghai geming shi ziliao yu yanjiu* 上海革命史资料与研究 (Materials and research on Shanghai's revolutionary history), vol. 1, pp. 236–266. Beijing: Kaiming chubanshe, 1992.

Chen Pengju 陈鹏举, ed. *Shoucang lishi* 收藏历史 (Collecting history). Shanghai: Shanghai shudian chubanshe, 1998.

Chen Pixian 陈丕显. *Chen Pixian huiyilu: Zai "yiyue fengbao" de zhongxin* 陈丕显回忆录:在 "一月风暴"的中心 (The memoirs of Chen Pixian: At the center of the "January Storm"). Hong Kong: Sanlian shudian, 2005.

Chen Qiuhui 陈秋辉, ed. *Shen Zhiyu wenbo lunji* 沈之瑜文博论集 (Collected writings by Shen Zhiyu on cultural relics and museums). Shanghai: Shanghai guji chubanshe, 2003.

Chen, Ruoxi. *The Execution of Mayor Yin and Other Stories from the Great Proletarian Cultural Revolution*, translated by Nancy Ing and Howard Goldblatt. Bloomington: Indiana University Press, rvsd. ed., 2004.

Chen, Xiaomei. "Performing the 'Red Classics': From The East is Red to The Road to Revival." In *Red Legacies in China: Cultural Afterlives of the Communist Revolution*, edited by Jie Li and Enhua Zhang, pp. 151–183. Cambridge, MA: Asia Center, Harvard University, 2016.

Chen, Xiejun 陈燮君, ed. *Gems of Shanghai Museum*. Beijing: People's Education Press, 2007.

Chen Yingfang 陈映芳, ed. *Penghuqu: Jiyi zhong de shenghuo shi* 棚户区: 记忆中的生活史 (Shantytown districts: Memories of life histories). Shanghai: Shanghai guji chubanshe, 2006.

"Shehui kongjian jiegou yu chengshi pinkun: 1949 nian hou de Shanghai penghuqu" 社会空间结构与城市贫困: 1949年后的上海棚户区 (The structure of social space and urban poverty: Shanghai's shantytowns after 1949). Hong Kong: Centre for China Urban and Regional Studies, Hong Kong Baptist University, Occasional Paper no. 80 (February 2008).

Chen Yunqian. "Local Exhibitions and the Molding of Revolutionary Memory (1927–1949)." *Chinese Studies in History*, vol. 47, no. 1 (Fall 2013), pp. 29–52.

Chen Zhiqiang 陈志强. *Wenbo xianqu: Shen Zhiyu zhuan* 文博先驱:沈之瑜传 (Museum pioneer: A biography of Shen Zhiyu). Shanghai: Shanghai wenhua chubanshe, 2011.

Cheng, Nien. *Life and Death in Shanghai*. New York: Penguin Books, 1988.

Clark, Paul. *The Chinese Cultural Revolution: A History*. Cambridge: Cambridge University Press, 2008.

Clunas, Craig. *Superfluous Things: Material Culture and Social Status in Early Modern China*. Cambridge: Polity Press, 1991.

Coble, Parks M., Jr. *Chinese Capitalists in Japan's New Order: The Occupied Lower Yangzi, 1937–1945*. Berkeley: University of California Press, 2003.

The Shanghai Capitalists and the Nationalist Government, 1927–1937. Cambridge, MA: Council on East Asian Studies, Harvard University, 1980.

Commission of the Central Committee of the C.P.S.U. (B.), ed. *History of the Communist Party of the Soviet Union (Bolsheviks): Short Course*. New York: International Publishers, 1939.

Compton, Boyd, trans. *Mao's China: Party Reform Documents, 1942–44*. Seattle: University of Washington Press, 1952.

Corney, Frederick C. *Telling October: Memory and the Making of the Bolshevik Revolution*. Ithaca, NY: Cornell University Press, 2004.

Cultural Revolution Video Collection. DVD (VHS Tape Transfer) (Decade in the Great Cultural Revolution, ca. 1978). Available in the Fairbank Collection, Fung Library, Harvard University.

Dangde xuanchuan gongzuo wenjian xuanbian 党的宣传工作文件选编 (Selected documents on Party propaganda work), 4 vols. Beijing: Zhonggong zhongyang dangxiao chubanshe, 1994.

David-Fox, Michael. *Showcasing the Great Experiment: Cultural Diplomacy and Western Visitors to the Soviet Union, 1921–1941*. Oxford: Oxford University Press, 2011.

DeMare, Brian James. *Mao's Cultural Army: Drama Troupes in China's Rural Revolution*. Cambridge: Cambridge University Press, 2015.

Denton, Kirk A. "China Dreams and the 'Road to Revival.'" *Origins: Current Events in Historical Perspective*, vol. 8, no. 3 (December 2014). http://origins.osu.edu/ article/china-dreams-and-road-revival (accessed September 30, 2016).

——— *Exhibiting the Past: Historical Memory and the Politics of Museums in Postsocialist China*. Honolulu: University of Hawai'i Press, 2014.

Diamond, Norma. "Model Villages and Village Realities." *Modern China*, vol. 9, no. 2 (April 1983), pp. 163–181.

Ding Dahua 丁大华. "Shisuo hanjian de hongweibing chaojia zhanguo zhanlan-hui" 世所罕见的红卫兵抄家战果展览会 (A sight seldom seen: The Red Guards' house search fruits of battle exhibition). *Wenshi jinghua* 文史精华 (Essentials of literature and history), no. 1 (January 2008), pp. 25–31.

Ding Yuguo 丁裕国. "Shanghai pinfu chaju diaocha baogao" 上海贫富差距调查报告 (Report on Shanghai's disparities between the rich and poor). August 29, 2011. http://blog.sciencenet.cn/blog-3100-480892.html (accessed March 9, 2014).

Dong, Guoqiang, and Andrew G. Walder. "Local Politics in the Chinese Cultural Revolution: Nanjing Under Military Control." *Journal of Asian Studies*. vol. 70, no. 2 (May 2011), pp. 425–447.

Dong Tingzhi 董庭芝 and Zhang Zurong 章祖蓉. "Guanyu zhonggong 'yida' daibiao renshu de jizhong shuofa" 关于中共"一大"代表人数的几种说法 (Several ways of explaining the number of delegates to the "First Party Congress"). In *Dangshi yanjiu ziliao* 党史研究资料 (Party history research materials), edited by Zhongguo geming bowuguan dangshi yanjiushi 中国革命博物馆党史研究室 (Party history research office of the Museum of the Chinese Revolution). Chengdu: Sichuan renmin chubanshe, no. 1, 1980. pp. 157–162.

Dongbei ribao 东北日报 (Northwest daily news).

Dongbei renmin zhengfu weishengbu 东北人民政府卫生部 (Health Department of the Northeast People's Government), ed. *Dapo mixin* 打破迷信 (Smash superstition). September 1950.

Du Xing 杜兴. "'Posijiu' zhanlan ji" "破四旧"展览记 (A record of an attack on the Four Olds exhibition). *Shidai jiaoyu* 时代教育 (January 2010). http://news .ifeng.com/history/zhiqing/xiaohua/detail_192012_07/04/15759320_0.shtml (accessed September 30, 2016).

Du Xuefeng 杜学峰. "'Wenge' de 'huoren zhanlan'" "文革"的"活人展览" ("Living exhibitions" during the "Cultural Revolution"). *Zhongshan fengyu* 钟山风雨 (Zhongshan wind and rain), no. 2 (2010), p. 49.

Duan Lian 锻炼, Song Shijuan 宋时娟, and Chen Ling 陈凌, eds. *Wangshi yu jiyi: Shanghai diqu bowuguan, jinianguan koushu fangtan lu* 往事与记忆: 上海地区博物馆，纪念馆口述访谈录 (Past and memory: A record of oral histories and interviews from Shanghai local museums and memorial halls). Shanghai: Shanghai cishu chubanshe, 2010.

Elleman, Bruce A. *Diplomacy and Deception: The Secret History of Sino-Soviet Diplomatic Relations, 1917–1927*. Armonk, NY: M. E. Sharpe, 1997.

——— *Moscow and the Emergence of Communist Power in China, 1925–30: The Nanchang Uprising and the Birth of the Red Army*. London: Routledge, 2009.

Elliott, Jeannette Shambaugh, with David Shambaugh. *The Odyssey of China's Imperial Art Treasures*. Seattle: University of Washington Press, 2005.

Esherick, Joseph W., Paul G. Pickowicz, and Andrew G. Walder, eds. *The Chinese Cultural Revolution as History*. Stanford, CA: Stanford University Press, 2006.

Esherick, Joseph W., and Jeffrey N. Wasserstrom. "Acting Out Democracy: Political Theater in Modern China." *Journal of Asian Studies*, vol. 49, no. 4 (November 1990), pp. 835–865.

Eustace, Nicole et al. "AHR Conversation: The Historical Study of Emotions." *American Historical Review*, vol. 117, no. 5 (December 2012), pp. 1487–1531.

Fan Jingyi 范敬宜 et al., eds. *Wenwu baohu falü zhinan* 文物保护法律指南 (Guide to the cultural relics protection law). Beijing: Zhongguo chengshi chubanshe, 2003.

Fei Qinsheng 费钦生. *Liushinian chenlie yishu zhi lu* 六十年陈列艺术之路 (Sixty years of exhibition art). Shanghai: Shanghai guji chubanshe, 2012.

Feng Danfeng 冯丹枫 et al. "Cong qingtongqi kan chiren de 'lizhi': Shanghai bowuguan qingtongqi chenlieshi xunli" 从青铜器看吃人的 "礼治": 上海博物馆青铜器陈列室巡礼 (Viewing the exploitation in the "Rites" from the bronzeware: Touring the bronze object room at the Shanghai Museum). *Xuexi yu pipan* 学习与批判 (Study and criticism), no. 6 (1974), pp. 23–24.

Feng Meichun 冯梅春. "Fangualong de bianqian" 蕃瓜弄的变迁 (Historical changes in Fangua Lane). In *Shanghai wenshi ziliao xuanji: Zhabei juan* 上海文史资料选辑:闸北卷 (Collection of Shanghai historical materials: Zhabei volume). Shanghai: Shanghaishi zhengxie wenshi ziliao bianjibu, 2004.

Feng, Xiaocai. "Rushing Toward Socialism: The Transformation and Death of Private Business Enterprises in Shanghai, 1949–1956." In *The People's Republic of China at 60: An International Assessment*, edited by William C. Kirby, pp. 240–258. Cambridge, MA: Asia Center, Harvard University, 2011.

Fernsebner, Susan R. "Objects, Spectacle, and a Nation on Display at the Nanyang Exposition of 1910." *Late Imperial China*, vol. 27, no. 2 (December 2006), pp. 99–124.

Fitzpatrick, Sheila. *Everyday Stalinism: Ordinary Life in Extraordinary Times: Soviet Russia in the 1930s*. Oxford: Oxford University Press, 1999.

Fitzpatrick, Sheila, and Robert Gellately, eds. *Accusatory Practices: Denunciation in Modern European History, 1789–1989*. Chicago: University of Chicago Press, 1997.

Foucault, Michel. *Discipline and Punish: The Birth of the Prison*, translated by Alan Sheridan. New York: Vintage Books, 2nd ed., 1995.

Gao, Mobo. *The Battle for China's Past: Mao and the Cultural Revolution*. London: Pluto Press, 2008.

Gao, Yuan. *Born Red: A Chronicle of the Cultural Revolution*. Stanford, CA: Stanford University Press, 1987.

Gerth, Karl. "Wu Yunchu and the Fate of the Bourgeoisie and Bourgeois Lifestyles under Communism." In *The Capitalist Dilemma in China's Communist Revolution*, edited by Sherman Cochran, pp. 175–201. Ithaca, NY: East Asia Program, Cornell University, 2014.

Gongren zaofan bao 工人造反报 (Workers' rebel news).

Gongzuo tongxun 工作通讯 ([People's Liberation Army] work bulletin). Edited by Zhongguo renmin jiefangjun zong zhengzhibu 中国人民解放军总政治部 (General Political Department of the PLA).

Goodrich, Anne Swann. *The Peking Temple of the Eastern Peak.* Nagoya: Monumenta Serica, 1964.

Goossaert, Vincent, and David A. Palmer. *The Religious Question in Modern China.* Chicago: University of Chicago Press, 2011.

Gross, Miriam. *Farewell to the God of Plague: Chairman Mao's Campaign to Deworm China.* Berkeley: University of California Press, 2016.

Gu Bingquan 顾炳权, ed. *Shanghai fengsu guji kao* 上海风俗古迹考 (A study of customs and historic sites in Shanghai). Shanghai: Huadong shifan daxue chubanshe, 1993.

Gu Guanying 顾冠英, comp. *Zhonghua quanguo mingsheng guji daguan* 中华全国名胜古迹大观 (China's famous places, historic sites, and grand vistas). Shanghai: Dalu tushu gongsi, 1921.

Guang Qin 光勤. "Xihou wangzeng wo yi zhang" 洗后望赠我一张 (After you develop it, I hope you will give me a copy). *Lu Xun yanjiu dongtai* 鲁迅研究动态 (Lu Xun research trends), no. 1 (1989), pp. 24–31.

Guangming ribao 光明日报 (Guangming daily).

Guangzhou diqu hongweibing geming zaofan zhanguo zhanlanhui. 广州地区红卫兵革命造反战果展览会 (Guangzhou area Red Guards' fruits of rebellion exhibition). December 1966.

Guangzhou shizhi 广州市志 (Guangzhou gazetteer). Guangzhou: Guangzhou chubanshe, 1999.

Guide to the City of Moscow, a Handbook for Tourists. Moscow: Co-operative Publishing Society of Foreign Workers in the U.S.S.R., 1937.

Guo Tiancheng 郭天成, Cao Yiding 曹一丁, and Qian Xuezhong 钱学忠, eds. *Zhabei quzhi* 闸北区志 (Zhabei District gazetteer). Shanghai: Shanghai shehui kexueyuan chubanshe, 1998.

Guy, R. Kent. *The Emperor's Four Treasures: Scholars and the State in the Late Ch'ien-Lung Era.* Cambridge, MA: Council on East Asian Studies, Harvard University, 1987.

Haifeng 海枫. *Guangzhou diqu wen'ge licheng shulüe* 广州地区文革历程述略 (An account of the Cultural Revolution in the Canton area). Hong Kong: Youlian yanjiusuo, 1971.

Han Yingjie 韩英杰. "Shanghai lao chenghuang miao" 上海老城隍庙 (Shanghai's old City God Temple). *Lüxing jia*, no. 11 (1959), pp. 34–36.

Harrison, Henrietta. *The Making of the Republican Citizen: Political Ceremonies and Symbols in China, 1911–1929.* Oxford: Oxford University Press, 2000.

   "A Penny for the Little Chinese: The French Holy Childhood Association in China, 1843–1951." *American Historical Review*, vol. 113, no. 1 (February 2008), pp. 72–92.

He Xiaoqian 何晓情. "Women zou zai Nanjing lushang" 我们走在南京路上 (Let's go for a walk on Nanjing Road). In *Xin Shanghai gushi* 新上海故事 (Stories of new Shanghai). Shanghai: Shaonian ertong chubanshe, 1964.

Henriot, Christian. "A Neighbourhood under Storm: Zhabei and Shanghai Wars." *European Journal of East Asian Studies*, vol. 9, no. 2 (2010), pp. 291–319.

"Slums, Squats, or Hutments? Constructing and Deconstructing an In-Between Space in Modern Shanghai (1926–65)." *Frontiers of History in China*, vol. 7, no. 4 (2012), pp. 499–528.

Hershatter, Gail. *The Gender of Memory: Rural Women and China's Collective Past.* Berkeley: University of California Press, 2011.

Hess, Christian. "Revolutionary Real Estate: Envisioning Space in Communist Dalian." In *Visualizing Modern China: Image, History, and Memory, 1750–Present*, edited by James A. Cook, Joshua Goldstein, Matthew D. Johnson, and Sigrid Schmalzer, pp. 185–202. Lanham, MD: Lexington Books, 2014.

Hinton, William. *Fanshen: A Documentary of Revolution in a Chinese Village.* New York: Vintage Books, 1966.

Ho, Dahpon David. "To Protect and Preserve: Resisting the Destroy the Four Olds Campaign, 1966–1967." In *The Chinese Cultural Revolution as History*, edited by Joseph W. Esherick, Paul G. Pickowicz, and Andrew G. Walder, pp. 64–95. Stanford, CA: Stanford University Press, 2006.

Ho, Denise Y. "The Old Society and the New Society: Towards a Material Culture of China's Cultural Revolution." In *The Oxford Handbook of History and Material Culture*, edited by Sarah Carter and Ivan Gaskell. Oxford: Oxford University Press, 2017.

"Reforming Connoisseurship: State and Collectors in Shanghai in the 1950s and 1960s." *Frontiers of History in China*, vol. 7, no. 4 (2012), pp. 608–637.

"Revolutionizing Antiquity: The Shanghai Bureaucracy in the Cultural Revolution, 1966–1968." *The China Quarterly*, no. 207 (September 2011), pp. 687–705.

Ho, Denise Y., and Jie Li. "From Landlord Manor to Red Memorabilia: Reincarnations of a Chinese Museum Town." *Modern China*, vol. 42, no. 1 (2016), pp. 3–37.

Ho, Wing-Chung. "Building Up Modernity? The Changing Spatial Representations of State Power in a Chinese Socialist 'Model Community.'" *Modern Asian Studies*, vol. 42, no. 6 (2008), pp. 1137–1171.

The Transition Study of Postsocialist China: An Ethnographic Study of a Model Community. Singapore: World Scientific, 2010.

Ho, Wing-Chung, and Petrus Ng. "Public Amnesia and Multiple Modernities in Shanghai: Narrating the Socialist Future in a Former Socialist 'Model Community.'" *Journal of Contemporary Ethnography*, vol. 27, no. 4 (August 2008), pp. 383–416.

Hong Hong 洪宏. "Guo Linshuang he Shanghai Yong'an gongsi" 郭琳爽和上海永安公司 (Guo Linshuang and Shanghai's Yong'an Company). In *Zhongguo bainian shangye juzi* 中国百年商业巨子 (A hundred years of China's business magnates), edited by Liu Yu 柳渝. Changchun: Dongbei shifan daxue chubanshe, 1997.

Hongweibing dianying zhipianchang yi geming qunzhong 红卫兵电影制片厂一革命群众 (One member of the revolutionary masses of the film studio Red Guards). "Shanghai hongweibing geming zaofan zhanlanhui zhengji wenhua da geming zhongyao wenxian" 上海红卫兵革命造反展览会征集文化大革命重要文献 (The Shanghai Red Guards Revolutionary Rebels Exhibition is seeking important documents from the Cultural Revolution). *Wenyi zhanbao* 文艺战报 (Newsletter from the cultural and artistic front), no. 36 (December 3, 1967), p. 4.

Honig, Emily. *Sisters and Strangers: Women in the Shanghai Cotton Mills, 1919–1949.* Stanford, CA: Stanford University Press, 1986.

Hu Jie 胡杰. *Though I am Gone* (我虽死去). DVD. New York: dGenerate Films, 2007.

Hua Xing 华幸. "Mao Zedong he Zhongguo gongchandang de chuangli" 毛泽东和中国共产党的创立 (Mao Zedong and the founding of the Chinese Communist Party). In *Mao Zedong zai Shanghai* 毛泽东在上海 (Mao Zedong in Shanghai), edited by Zhonggong Shanghai shiwei dangshi yanjiushi 上海市委党史研究室 (Party history office of the Shanghai Party Committee of the Chinese Communist Party), pp. 244–256. Beijing: Zhonggong dangshi chubanshe, 1993.

Huang Bi 黄碧. "Longhua guta de qingchun" 龙华古塔的青春 (Spring at Longhua Pagoda). *Lüxing jia* 旅行家 (Traveler), no. 3 (1956), pp. 20–21.

Huang Longbao 黄龙保, and Yan Xiaofeng 颜晓峰, eds. *Zhongguo lidai fandui mixin zongheng tan* 中国历代反对迷信纵横谈 (A survey of opposition to superstition in Chinese history). Beijing: Xuexi chubanshe, 1999.

Hunansheng shehuizhuyi jieji jiaoyu zhanlanhui jianjie 湖南省社会主义阶级教育展览会简介 (Introduction to Hunan Province's socialist class education exhibition). March 1964.

Hung, Chang-tai. *Mao's New World: Political Culture in the Early People's Republic.* Ithaca, NY: Cornell University Press, 2011.

Jian Ping 建平, Shao Zhen 少真, and Dong Hui 东辉. "Rang kexue de guanghui qusan 'yinmai'" 让科学的光辉驱散"阴霾" (Let science's glory dispel the "haze"). *Dangjian zazhi* 党建杂志 (Party construction magazine), no. 5 (2000), pp. 37–38.

Jiang Yi 江怡, and Shao Youmin 邵有民, eds. *Zhonggong Shanghai dangzhi* 中共上海党志 (Gazetteer of the Shanghai Chinese Communist Party). Shanghai: Shanghai shehui kexueyuan chubanshe, 2001.

"Jiang Zemin tongzhi canguan 'Zhongguo gemingshi chenlie' jieshushi de jianghua" 江泽民同志参观"中国革命史陈列"结束时的讲话 (Speech by Comrade Jiang Zemin upon viewing the conclusion of the "Exhibition of Chinese revolutionary history"). *Dangshi yanjiu ziliao* 党史研究资料 (Party history research materials), no. 9 (1990), pp. 2–3.

"Jiangsu geming bowuguan choubeichu zhengji xize" 江苏革命博物馆筹备处征集细则 (Collection of regulations for the Jiangsu Revolutionary Museum Preparatory Committee), *Shanghai tebieshi jiaoyuju jiaoyu zhoubao* 上海特别市教育局教育周报 (Shanghai Municipal Bureau of Education education weekly), no. 4 (1929), pp. 7–8.

Jiangsusheng jieji jiaoyu zhanlanhui shuomingshu 江苏省阶级教育展览会说明书 (Guide to Jiangsu Province's class education exhibition). 1965.

Jiaqiang dui qingshaonian de jieji jiaoyu 加强对青少年的阶级教育 (Strengthen class education among the youth). Shanghai: Shanghai jiaoyu chubanshe, 1963.

Jiedao lilong jumin shenghuo shouce 街道里弄居民生活手册 (A handbook for neigh-borhood residential life). Shanghai: Xinwen ribao guan, 1951.

Jiefang ribao 解放日报 (Liberation daily).

Jiefangjun huabao 解放军画报 (PLA pictorial).

Jin Bian 靳边. "Fangualong de jinxi" 蕃瓜弄的今昔 (Past and present in Fangua Lane). In *Shanghai de gushi* 上海的故事 (Stories of Shanghai). Shanghai: Shanghai renmin chubanshe, 1965.

Jin Dalu 金大陆. *Feichang yu zhengchang: Shanghai "wenge" shiqi de shehui sheng-huo* 非常与正常: 上海"文革"时期的社会生活 (Extraordinary and ordinary: Social life during Shanghai's "Cultural Revolution" period), 2 vols. Shanghai: Shanghai cishu chubanshe, 2011.

Jin Ding 金鼎. "Budao de Longhua ta" 不倒的龙华塔 (The Longhua Pagoda that did not fall). In *Shoucang lishi* 收藏历史 (Collecting history), edited by Chen Pengju 陈鹏举, pp. 235–237. Shanghai: Shanghai shudian chubanshe, 1998.

Jing, Jun. *The Temple of Memories: History, Power, and Morality in a Chinese Village.* Stanford, CA: Stanford University Press, 1996.

Jiu Shanghai shiliao huibian 旧上海史料汇编 (Compilation of historical materials on old Shanghai), 2 vols. Beijing: Beijing tushuguan chubanshe, 1998. Reprint of *Shanghai yanjiu ziliao* 上海研究资料 (Materials on Shanghai research). Shanghai: Zhonghua shuju, 1936, 1939.

Jolles, Adam. "Stalin's Talking Museums." *Oxford Art Journal*, vol. 28. no. 3 (October 2005), pp. 429–455.

Juebu yunxu kai lishi daoche 决不允许开历史倒车 (Never allow historical regres-sion). Beijing: Renmin meishu jiaoyu chubanshe, 1974.

Kamm, John. "Shanghaied at the Feather and Down Minifair." In *My First Trip to China: Scholars, Diplomats, and Journalists Reflect on their First Encounters with China*, edited by Kin-ming Liu, pp. 220–227. Hong Kong: East Slope Publishing Limited, 2012.

Kan geming wenwu, xue geming chuantong 看革命文物, 学革命传统 (Look at revolutionary relics, study the revolutionary tradition). Shanghai: Shanghai renmin chubanshe, 1976.

Karlsgodt, Elizabeth Campbell. *Defending National Treasures: French Art and Heritage under Vichy.* Stanford, CA: Stanford University Press, 2011.

Knight, Sophia. *Window on Shanghai: Letters from China, 1965–67.* London: Deutsch, 1967.

Koloskvoa, T. G. "Central Museum of V. I. Lenin." In *Museums in Revolution: Four Historical Museums in Moscow*, edited by Marien van de Heijden, pp. 28–41. Amsterdam: IISG, 1998.

Kotkin, Stephen. *Magnetic Mountain: Stalinism as a Civilization.* Berkeley: University of California Press, 1995.

Kraus, Richard Curt. *Class Conflict in Chinese Socialism.* New York: Columbia University Press, 1981.

Kuhn, Philip A. *Soulstealers: The Chinese Sorcery Scare of 1768.* Cambridge, MA: Harvard University Press, 1990.

Lai, Delin. "Searching for a Modern Chinese Monument: The Design of the Sun Yat-sen Mausoleum in Nanjing." *Journal of the Society of Architectural Historians*, vol. 64, no. 1 (March 2005), pp. 22–54.

Lao Sheh. *Dragon Beard Ditch: A Play in Three Acts*, translated by Liao Hung-ying. Peking: Foreign Languages Press, 1956.

Lê, Tiến Dũng, ed. *Guidebook: Vietnam National Museum of History*. Hanoi: National Museum of Vietnamese History, 2014.

Lee, Haiyan. *The Stranger and the Chinese Moral Imagination*. Stanford, CA: Stanford University Press, 2014.

Leese, Daniel. *Mao Cult: Rhetoric and Ritual in China's Cultural Revolution*. Cambridge: Cambridge University Press, 2011.

Leighton, Christopher R. *The Revolutionary Rich: Political Fortune and Red Capitalism in China, 1949–1979*. Forthcoming.

Leonova, O. *Museums of the U.S.S.R.* Moscow: Foreign Languages Publishing House, 1939.

Leys, Simon. *Chinese Shadows*. New York: Penguin Books, 1974.

Li Chunkang 李纯康. "Shanghai de bowuguan" 上海的博物馆 (Shanghai's museums). *Lüxing zazhi*旅行杂志(Travel magazine), vol. 22, no. 7 (1948), pp. 23–24.

Li Guohe 李果河. "Wo chengle 'huoren zhanlan' de zhanpin" 我成了"活人展览"的展品(I became an artifact in a "living exhibition"). *Yanhuang chunqiu* 淡黄春秋, no. 1 (2012), pp. 58–60.

Li, Jie. *Shanghai Homes: Palimpsests of Private Life*. New York: Columbia University Press, 2015.

Li, Kwok-sing, comp. *A Glossary of Political Terms of the People's Republic of China*, translated by Mary Lok. Hong Kong: Chinese University Press, 1995.

Li Ming 黎明. "Shanghai bowuguan dui gongren guanzhong jinxing jiangjie de jidian jingyan" 上海博物馆对工人观众进行讲解的几点经验 (A few experiences from the Shanghai Museum's narration for workers). *Wenwu cankao ziliao*文物参考资料 (Cultural relics reference materials), no. 2 (1956), pp. 63–64.

Li Rongrong 李蓉蓉, ed. *Ningjing de huihuang: Shanghai bowuguan xinguan chenlie sheji jiexi* 宁静的辉煌: 上海博物馆新馆陈列设计解析 (Quiet brilliance: Analysis of the form of the exhibitions in the new Shanghai museum). Beijing: Wenwu chubanshe, 2005.

Li Xun 李逊. *Wenge zaofan niandai: Shanghai wenge yundong shigao* 文革造反年代: 上海文革运动史稿 (The age of revolutionary rebellion: A history of Shanghai's Cultural Revolution movement), 2 vols. Hong Kong: Oxford University Press, 2015.

Li, Zhensheng. *Red-Color News Soldier: A Chinese Photographer's Odyssey Through the Cultural Revolution*. New York: Phaidon Press, 2003.

Liang Dan 梁丹. "Beijing bowuguan gongzuo jishi" 北京博物馆工作纪事 (Chronicle of Beijing's museum work), *Zhongguo bowuguan* 中国博物馆 (Chinese museums), no. 1 (1994), pp. 88–95.

Liang, Samuel Y. "Amnesiac Monument, Nostalgic Fashion: Shanghai's New Heaven and Earth." *Wasafiri*, vol. 23, no. 3 (2008), pp. 47–55.

Lifton, Robert Jay. *Thought Reform and the Psychology of Totalism: A Study of "Brainwashing" in China*. New York: W. W. Norton, 1963.

Lin, Yü-sheng. *The Crisis of Chinese Consciousness: Radical Antitraditionalism in the May Fourth Era*. Madison: University of Wisconsin Press, 1979.

Loh, Robert. "How the Chinese Reds Hoodwink Visiting Foreigners." U.S. Congress. House of Representatives. Committee on Un-American Activities. Eighty-Sixth Congress. Second Session. April 21, 1960.

Lu, Di Yin. "Seizing Civilization: Antiquities in Shanghai's Custody, 1949–1996." PhD diss., Harvard University, 2012.

Lu, Hanchao. *Beyond the Neon Lights: Everyday Shanghai in the Early Twentieth Century.* Berkeley: University of California Press, 1999.

Lu, Tracey L-D. *Museums in China: Materialized Power and Objectified Identities.* London: Routledge, 2014.

Ludden, Yawen. "Making Politics Serve Music: Yu Huiyong, Composer and Minister of Culture." *TDR: The Drama Review*, vol. 56, no. 2 (Summer 2012) (T214), pp. 152–168.

Luo Dingjiang 罗定江. "Jieshao yueliang zhanlanhui" 介绍月亮展览会 (An exhibition to explain the moon). *Kexue dazhong* 科学大众 (Mass science), no. 6 (1952), pp. 172–175.

Ma Chengyuan 马承源, Huang Xuanpei 黄宣佩, and Li Junjie 李俊杰, eds. *Shanghai wenwu bowuguan zhi* 上海文物博物馆志 (Gazetteer of Shanghai's cultural relics and museums). Shanghai: Shanghai shehui kexueyuan chubanshe, 1997.

MacFarquhar, Roderick. *The Hundred Flowers Campaign and the Chinese Intellectuals.* New York: Frederick A. Praeger, 1960.

The Origins of the Cultural Revolution Vol. 3: The Coming of the Cataclysm, 1961–1966. Oxford: Oxford University Press, 1997.

MacFarquhar, Roderick, and Michael Schoenhals. *Mao's Last Revolution.* Cambridge, MA: Belknap Press of Harvard University Press, 2006.

Mao Zedong. *Quotations from Chairman Mao Tsetung.* Peking: Foreign Languages Press, 1972.

Mariani, Paul P. *Church Militant: Bishop Kung and Catholic Resistance in Communist Shanghai.* Cambridge, MA: Harvard University Press, 2011.

Matten, Marc Andre, ed. *Places of Memory in Modern China: History, Politics, and Identity.* Leiden: Brill, 2012.

McClellan, Andrew. *Inventing the Louvre: Art, Politics, and the Origins of the Museum in Eighteenth-Century Paris.* Berkeley: University of California Press, 1999.

McDougall, Bonnie S. *Mao Zedong's "Talks at the Yan'an Conference on Literature and Art": A Translation of the 1943 Text with Commentary.* Ann Arbor: Center for Chinese Studies, University of Michigan, 1980.

Meng Xing 孟醒. *Shui zhu chenfu: Zhonggong yida daibiao chenfulu* 谁主沉浮：中共一大代表沉浮录 (Who is in control: The rise and fall of the delegates to the First Party Congress). Beijing: Renmin chubanshe, 2009.

Meyer-Fong, Tobie. *Building Culture in Early Qing Yangzhou.* Stanford, CA: Stanford University Press, 2003.

Mitchell, Timothy. *Colonising Egypt.* Berkeley: University of California Press, 1988.

Mitter, Rana. "Behind the Scenes at the Museum: Nationalism, History, and Memory in the Beijing War of Resistance Museum, 1987–1997." *The China Quarterly*, no. 161 (March 2000), pp. 279–293.

Mittler, Barbara. *A Continuous Revolution: Making Sense of Cultural Revolution Culture*. Cambridge, MA: Asia Center, Harvard University, 2012.

Miyakawa Torao. "Hongweibing yu wenwu" 红卫兵与文物 (Red Guards and cultural relics). In *Waiguoren kan wenhua da geming* 外国人看文化大革命 (Foreigners view the Cultural Revolution), edited by Itō Takeo, pp. 122–123. Hong Kong: Dasheng chubanshe, 1969.

Munro, Donald J. *The Concept of Man in Contemporary China*. Ann Arbor: University of Michigan Press, 2000.

"Egalitarian Ideal and Educational Fact in Communist China." In *China: Management of a Revolutionary Society*, edited by John M. H. Lindbeck, pp. 256–301. Seattle: University of Washington Press, 1971.

Naquin, Susan. "True Confessions: Criminal Interrogations as Sources for Ch'ing History." *National Palace Museum Bulletin* (Taibei), vol. 11, no. 1 (March–April 1976), pp. 1–17.

Nedostup, Rebecca. *Superstitious Regimes: Religion and the Politics of Chinese Modernity*. Cambridge, MA: Asia Center, Harvard University, 2009.

Neibu cankao 内部参考 (Internal reference).

Neican xuanbian 内参选编 (Selections from internal reference).

New Archaeological Finds in China: Discoveries During the Cultural Revolution. Peking: Foreign Languages Press, 1972.

Ni Xingxiang 倪兴祥. "Chedi 'yiwu daishi' chenlie zhidao sixiang de tihui" 贯彻"以物带史"陈列指导思想的体会 (The experience of thoroughly carrying out the exhibition principle of "using objects to represent history"). *Zhongguo bowuguan tongxun* 中国博物馆通讯 (Chinese museums newsletter), no. 9 (2000), pp. 6–8.

Niu Weiping 钮卫平, ed. *Bainian huiwei: Shanghai chengshi lishi fazhan chenlieguan xunli* 百年回味: 上海城市历史发展陈列馆巡礼 (Recalling one hundred years: The exhibition hall on the history of Shanghai's urban development). Shanghai: Shanghai yuandong chubanshe, 2003.

Nongcun meishu shouce 农村美术手册 (Handbook for rural art). Shijiazhuang: Hebei renmin chubanshe, 1975.

Nora, Pierre. "Between Memory and History: *Les Lieux de Mémoire*." *Representations*, no. 26 (Spring 1989), pp. 7–24.

Olsen, Jon Berndt. *Tailoring Truth: Politicizing the Past and Negotiating Memory in East Germany, 1945–1990*. New York: Berghahn Books, 2015.

Pantsov, Alexander V., with Steven I. Levine. *Mao: The Real Story*. New York: Simon & Schuster, 2012.

Perry, Elizabeth J. *Anyuan: Mining China's Revolutionary Tradition*. Berkeley: University of California Press, 2012.

"Moving the Masses: Emotion Work in the Chinese Revolution." *Mobilization*, vol. 7, no. 2 (June 2002), pp. 111–128.

Shanghai on Strike: The Politics of Chinese Labor. Stanford, CA: Stanford University Press, 1993.

"Shanghai's Politicized Skyline." In *Shanghai: Architecture and Urbanism for Modern China*, edited by Peter G. Rowe and Seng Kuan, pp. 104–109. Munich: Prestel, 2004.

Perry, Elizabeth J., and Li Xun. *Proletarian Power: Shanghai in the Cultural Revolution*. Boulder, CO: Westview Press, 1997.

Petrone, Karen. *Life Has Become More Joyous, Comrades: Celebrations in the Time of Stalin.* Bloomington: Indiana University Press, 2000.

Pita Rodríguez, Félix. *Zhongguo renmin de shou* 中国人民的手 (Manos del pueblo Chino y otros poemas), translated by Zhao Jinping 赵金平. Beijing: Zuojia chubanshe, 1964.

Pochu Lin Biao "Siren bang" de xiandai mixin 破除林彪 "四人帮"的现代迷信 (Eliminate the modern superstition of Lin Biao and the "Gang of Four"). Beijing: Renmin chubanshe, 1978.

Pochu mixin guatu 破除迷信挂图 (Posters from the exhibition "Eliminate superstition"). Beijing: Kexue puji chubanshe, 1965.

Pochu mixin wenda 破除迷信问答 (Questions and answers for eliminating superstition). Shanghai: Shanghai renmin chubanshe, 1963.

Qi Benyu 戚本禹. "Huiyi Jiang Qing tongzhi" 回忆江青同志 (Remembering Comrade Jiang Qing). *Fuxing wang*, July 30, 2015. www.mzfxw.com/e/action/ShowInfo.php?classid=18&id=44595 (accessed June 2, 2016).

Qi Benyu huiyilu 戚本禹回忆录 (Recollections of Qi Benyu). Hong Kong: Zhongguo wenge lishi chubanshe, 2016.

Qi Wenjuan 戚文娟. "Shanghai wenwu zhengli cangku de lishi gongji" 上海文物整理仓库的历史功绩 (The historical contribution of the Shanghai cultural relics warehouses). *Shanghai wenhua shizhi tongxun* 上海文化史志通讯 (Shanghai gazetteer of cultural history), no. 33 (1994), pp. 74–75.

Qianwan buyao wangji jieji douzheng: Tianjinshi Hongqiaoqu Santiaoshi lishi bowuguan/jieji jiaoyu zhanlan: Xueleishi bufen jianjie 千万不要忘记阶级斗争: 天津市红桥区三条石历史博物馆/阶级展览: 血泪史部分简介(Never forget class struggle: History museum and class education exhibition of Santiaoshi, Hongqiao District of Tianjin Municipality: Introduction to a blood-and-tears history). n.d.

Qianwan buyao wangji jieji he jieji douzheng: Yunnansheng jieji jiaoyu zhanlanguan neirong jianjie 千万不要忘记阶级和阶级斗争: 云南省阶级教育展览馆内容简介 (Never forget class and class struggle: An introduction to the contents of Yunnan Province's Class Education Exhibition Hall). January 1966.

Quanguo gesheng, zizhiqu, zhixiashi diyipi wenwu baohu danwei mingdan huibian 全国各省，自治区，直辖市第一批文物保护单位名单汇编 (The first group of national cultural relic protection units in each province, autonomous region, and special municipality). Beijing: Wenwu chubanshe, 1958.

"Renmin gongshe zhanlanguan yijianbushang faxian fandong ziju" 人民公社展览馆意见簿上发现反动字句 (Reactionary writings in the comments book are discovered in the People's Commune Exhibition Hall). *Disheqing jianbao* 敌社情简报 (Bulletin on social enemies), no. 10 (April 7, 1960), p. 1.

Renmin ribao 人民日报 (People's daily).

Robson, James. "Faith in Museums: On the Confluence of Museums and Religious Sites in Asia." *PMLA*, vol. 125, no. 1 (January 2010), pp. 121–128.

Rong Geng 容庚. *Jinwen bian* 金文编 (A compilation of bronze characters). Beijing: Zhonghua shuju, 1985.

Sang, Ye. *China Candid: The People on the People's Republic*, edited by Geremie R. Barmé, with Miriam Lang. Berkeley: University of California Press, 2006.

Scarlett, Zachary A. "China after the Sino-Soviet Split: Maoist Politics, Global Narratives, and the Imagination of the World." PhD diss., Northeastern University, 2013.

Schmalzer, Sigrid. *The People's Peking Man: Popular Science and Human Identity in Twentieth-Century China*. Chicago: University of Chicago Press, 2008.

Red Revolution, Green Revolution: Scientific Farming in Socialist China. Chicago: University of Chicago Press, 2016.

"Speaking about China, Learning from China: Amateur China Experts in 1970s America." *Journal of American–East Asian Relations*, vol. 16, no. 4 (Winter 2009), pp. 313–352.

Schoenhals, Michael, ed. *China's Cultural Revolution, 1966–1969: Not a Dinner Party*. Armonk, NY: M. E. Sharpe, 1996.

Doing Things with Words in Chinese Politics. Berkeley: Institute of East Asian Studies, University of California, 1992.

Spying for the People: Mao's Secret Agents, 1949–1967. Cambridge: Cambridge University Press, 2013.

Schram, Stuart R., ed. *Chairman Mao Talks to the People: Talks and Letters, 1956–1971*. New York: Pantheon Books, 1974.

Mao's Road to Power: Revolutionary Writings, 1912–1949, Vol. VI: The New Stage, August 1937–1938. Armonk, NY: M. E. Sharpe, 2004.

Mao's Road to Power: Revolutionary Writings, 1912–1949, Vol. VII: New Democracy, 1939–1941. Armonk, NY: M. E. Sharpe, 2005.

The Political Thought of Mao Tse-tung. New York: Praeger, 1963.

Schwarcz, Vera. *Time for Telling Truth is Running Out: Conversations with Zhang Shenfu*. New Haven: Yale University Press, 1992.

Semyonova, Natalya, and Nicolas V. Iljine, eds. *Selling Russia's Treasures: The Soviet Trade in Nationalized Art, 1917–1938*, translated by Andrew Bromfield and Howard M. Goldfinger. New York: Abbeville Press, 2013.

Shandongsheng jieji jiaoyu zhanlanhui huikan 山东省阶级教育展览会会刊 (Proceedings of the Shandong provincial class education exhibition). October 1964.

Shanghai bowuguan 上海博物馆 (Shanghai Museum), ed. *Guoyun lou shuhua jicui* 过云楼书画集萃 (Selections from the paintings and calligraphy works of Guoyun Lou [donated by the Gu Gongxiong family]). Shanghai: Shanghai shuhua chubanshe, 2002.

Shanghai bowuguan chenliepin shuomingshu 上海博物馆陈列品说明书 (Guide to Shanghai Museum exhibits). Shanghai: Shanghai bowuguan, 1952.

Shanghai gaige kaifang ershinian: Zhabei juan 上海改革开放二十年: 闸北卷 (Twenty years of Shanghai's reform and opening: Zhabei volume). Shanghai: Shanghai yuandong chubanshe, 1998.

Shanghai geming shi yanjiu ziliao: Jinian jiandang 70 zhou nian 上海革命史研究资料: 纪念建 党70周年 (Research materials on Shanghai's revolutionary history: Commemorating the 70th anniversary of the founding of the Party). Shanghai: Shanghai sanlian shudian, 1991.

Shanghai jiaoyu 上海教育 (Shanghai education).

Shanghai jingjutuan "Haigang" juzu 上海京剧团"海港"剧组 ("On the Docks" crew of the Shanghai Opera Troupe), ed. *Haigang* 海港 (On the docks). Beijing: Renmin wenxue chubanshe, 1974.

Shanghai Municipal Archive 上海市档案馆.

Shanghai shehui kexueyuan jingji yanjiusuo 上海社会科学院经济研究所 (Economics Institute of the Shanghai Academy of Social Sciences), ed. *Shanghai Yong'an gongsi de chansheng, fazhan, he gaizao* 上海永安公司的产生, 发展, 和改造 (The emergence, development, and reform of Shanghai's Yong'an Company). Shanghai: Shanghai renmin chubanshe, 1981.

Shanghai shili bowuguan yaolan 上海市立博物馆要览 (Shanghai Municipal Museum exhibition). August 1948.

Shanghai tushuguan 上海图书馆 (Shanghai Library), ed. *Lao Shanghai fengqing lu: Jianzhu xunmengjuan* 老上海风情录: 建筑寻梦卷 (Old Shanghai's vistas: Architectural volume). Shanghai: Shanghai wenhua chubanshe, 1998.

Zhongguo yu shibo: Lishi jilu, 1851–1940 中国与世博: 历史记录, 1851–1940 (China and the world exposition: Historical records, 1851–1940). Shanghai: Shanghai kexue jishu wenxian chubanshe, 2002.

"Shanghaishi daojiao xiehui di'erjie di'erci lishihui jueyi" 上海市道教协会第二届第二次理事会决议 (Resolution of the board of directors of the Shanghai Municipality Daoist Association at the second meeting of the second session). In *Shanghai daojiao* 上海道教 (Daoism in Shanghai), no. 2 (1991), pp. 1–2.

Shanghaishi geming weiyuanhui zhengzhi xuanchuanzu 上海市革命委员会政治宣传组 (Shanghai Revolutionary Committee, Political Propaganda Group). *Genju zhonggong zhongyang zhishi jingshen, Shanghaishi wenwu tushu qingli xiaozu zai shi geming wenwu weiyuanhui de zhijie lingdaoxia yijing zhenshi chengli, bing kaishi gongzuo* 根据中共中央指示精神, 上海市文物图书清理小组在市革命文物委员会的直接领导下已经真实成立, 并开始工作 (According to the spirit of the directive of the Chinese Communist Party, the Shanghai Municipal Small Group for Sorting Cultural Relics and Books has already been formally established and has begun its work under the direct leadership of the Shanghai Revolutionary Committee). Unpublished flyer, June 19, 1967.

Shanghaishi wenwu baowuguan weiyuanhui 上海市文物博物馆委员会 (Shanghai Cultural Relics Commission), ed. *Shanghai de guanghui geming shiji* 上海的光辉革命史迹 (Shanghai's glorious revolutionary traces). Shanghai: Shanghai jiaoyu chubanshe, 1978.

Shanghaishi Xuhuiqu zuzhi renmin jingji shenghuo gongzuozu 上海市徐汇区组织人民经济生活工作组 (Work group on the economic life of the people in Xuhui District of Shanghai Municipality), ed. *Jumin shenghuo fuwu shouce* 居民生活服务手册 (Handbook for serving residential life). Shanghai: Shanghai wenhua chubanshe, 1960.

Shao, Qin. "Exhibiting the Modern: The Creation of the First Chinese Museum, 1905– 1930." *The China Quarterly*, no. 179 (September 2004), pp. 684–702.

Shapiro, Judith. *Mao's War Against Nature: Politics and the Environment in Revolutionary China*. Cambridge: Cambridge University Press, 2001.

Shen Yi 沈怡. "Gongchengshi yu difang guji" 工程师与地方古迹 (Engineers and local historical sites). *Gongcheng: Zhongguo gongchengshi xuehui huikan* 工程：中国工程师 学会会刊 (Chinese Engineering Society Journal), vol. 16, no. 2 (1943), pp. 23–24.

Shenbao 申报 (Shanghai news).

Shilin 史林 (Historical review).

Shiwange weishenme 十万个为什么 (10,000 "Whys?"). Shanghai: Shaonian ertong chubanshe, 1962.

Shoudu hongweibing geming zaofan zhanlanhui 首都红卫兵革命造反展览会 (Capital Red Guards revolutionary rebel exhibition). Beijing: Shoudu dazhuan yuanxiao hongdaihui, 1967.

Smith, S. A. "Contentious Heritage: The Preservation of Churches and Temples in Communist and Post-Communist Russia and China." *Past and Present*, vol. 226, supplement 10 (2015), pp. 178–213.

 Like Cattle and Horses: Nationalism and Labor in Shanghai, 1895–1927. Durham, NC: Duke University Press, 2002.

 "Redemptive Religious Societies and the Communist State, 1949 to the 1980s." In *Maoism at the Grassroots: Everyday Life in China's Era of High Socialism*, edited by Jeremy Brown and Matthew D. Johnson, pp. 340–364. Cambridge, MA: Harvard University Press, 2015.

Smith, Steve A. "Local Cadres Confront the Supernatural: The Politics of Holy Water (*Shenshui*) in the PRC, 1949–1966." In *The History of the PRC (1949–1976)*, edited by Julia Strauss, pp. 145–168. Cambridge: Cambridge University Press, 2007.

Snow, Edgar. *Red China Today: The Other Side of the River*. Harmondsworth: Penguin Books, 1970.

Song Yongyi 宋永毅, ed. *Zhongguo wenhua da geming wenku* 中国文化大革命文库 (Chinese Cultural Revolution database). Hong Kong: Xianggang Zhongwen daxue, Zhongguo yanjiu fuwu zhongxin, 2002. CD-ROM.

Sowerby, Arthur de Carle. "The History of the Shanghai Museum (R.A.S.)." *Journal of the North Branch of the Royal Asiatic Society*, vol. 65 (1934), pp. 3–10.

Stites, Richard. "Iconoclastic Currents in the Russian Revolution: Destroying and Preserving the Past." In *Bolshevik Culture: Experiment and Order in the Russian Revolution*, edited by Abbott Gleason, Peter Kenez, and Richard Stites, pp. 1–24. Bloomington: Indiana University Press, 1985.

Su, Yang. *Collective Killings in Rural China During the Cultural Revolution*. Cambridge: Cambridge University Press, 2011.

Sulian bowuguanxue jichu 苏联博物馆学基础 (Fundamentals of Soviet museology). Beijing: Wenwu chubanshe, 1957.

Sulian jingji ji wenhua jianshe chengjiu zhanlanhui tupian jieshao 苏联经济及文化建 设成就展览会图片介绍 (Pictorial introduction to the exhibition of Soviet achievements in economic and cultural construction). Beijing: Zhaohua meishu chubanshe, 1955.

Sun Wu 孙武, ed. *Tantian shuodi po mixin* 谈天说地破迷信 (Talk of everything and smash superstition). Tianjin: Tianjin renmin chubanshe, 1964.

Survey of China Mainland Press (Hong Kong: U.S. Consulate, 1950–1977).

Tang Zhijun 汤志钧. *Wuxu shiqi de xuehui he baokan* 戊戌时期的学会和报刊 (Study societies and periodicals during the 1898 period). Taibei: Taiwan shangwu yinshuguan, 1993.

Tian, Xiaofei. "The Making of a Hero: Lei Feng and Some Issues of Historiography." In *The People's Republic of China at 60: An International Assessment*, edited by William C. Kirby, pp. 293–305. Cambridge, MA: Asia Center, Harvard University, 2011.

U, Eddy. "The Making of *Zhishifenzi*: The Critical Impact of the Registration of Unemployed Intellectuals in the Early PRC." *The China Quarterly*, no. 173 (March 2003), pp. 100–121.

van de Ven, Hans J. *From Friend to Comrade: The Founding of the Chinese Communist Party, 1920–1927*. Berkeley: University of California Press, 1991.

van der Heijden, Marien, ed. *Museums in Revolution: Four Historical Museums in Moscow*. Amsterdam: IISG, 1998.

Vogel, Ezra F. *Canton Under Communism: Programs and Politics in a Provincial Capital, 1949–1968*. Cambridge, MA: Harvard University Press, 1969.

Wagner, Rudolf G. "Reading the Chairman Mao Memorial Hall in Peking: The Tribulations of the Implied Pilgrim." In *Pilgrims and Sacred Sites in China*, edited by Susan Naquin and Chün-fang Yü, pp. 378–423. Berkeley: University of California Press, 1992.

Wakeman, Frederic, Jr. "'Cleanup': The New Order in Shanghai." In *Dilemmas of Victory: The Early Years of the People's Republic of China*, edited by Jeremy Brown and Paul G. Pickowicz, pp. 21–58. Cambridge, MA: Harvard University Press, 2007.

Walder, Andrew G. *Fractured Rebellion: The Beijing Red Guard Movement*. Cambridge, MA: Harvard University Press, 2009.

Wang, Cheng-hua. "The Qing Imperial Collection, Circa 1905–1925: National Humiliation, Heritage Preservation, and Exhibition Culture." In *Reinventing the Past: Archaism and Antiquarianism in Chinese Art and Visual Culture*, edited by Hung Wu, pp. 320–341. Chicago: Center for the Art of East Asia, University of Chicago, 2010.

Wang Nianyi 王年一. *Da dongluan de niandai* 大动乱的年代 (The age of great turmoil). Zhengzhou: Henan renmin chubanshe, 1988.

Wang, Xiaoxuan. "The Dilemma of Implementation: The State and Religion in the People's Republic of China, 1949–1990." In *Maoism at the Grassroots: Everyday Life in China's Era of High Socialism*, edited by Jeremy Brown and Matthew D. Johnson, pp. 259–278. Cambridge, MA: Harvard University Press, 2015.

Wang Yeqiu 王冶秋. "Sulian guoli geming bowuguan" 苏联国立革命博物馆 (The Soviet Museum of the Revolution). *Wenwu cankao ziliao* 文物参考资料 (Cultural relics reference materials), no. 10 (1950), pp. 66–77.

Watson, Rubie S., ed. *Memory, History, and Opposition under State Socialism*. Santa Fe: School of American Research Press, 1994.

Wei Dongfeng 卫东风. "Linglei de zhanshi: Wenge shiqi zhanlan huodong anlie fenxi" 另类的展示：文革时期展览活动案例分析 (Another kind of exhibition: An analysis of Cultural Revolution exhibition activities). *Dazhong wenyi* 大众文艺 (Popular literature and art), no. 9 (2009), pp. 98–100.

Weida de yiyue geming shengli wansui zhanlanhui 伟大的一月革命胜利万岁展览会 (Exhibition wishing long life to the victory of the great January Revolution). Shanghai: Shanghai wuchanjieji gemingpai, August 1968.

Weigelin-Schwiedrzik, Susanne. "Party Historiography." In *Using the Past to Serve the Present: Historiography and Politics in Contemporary China*, edited by Jonathan Unger, pp. 151–173. Armonk, NY: M. E. Sharpe, 1993.

Wenhui bao 文汇报 (Wenhui daily).

Wenwu baohu guanli xuanchuan ziliao 文物保护管理宣传资料 (Propaganda materials for the protection and management of cultural relics). Shanghai: Shanghaishi wenwu baoguan weiyuanhui, 1972.

Wenwu gongzuo shouce 文物工作手册 (Handbook for cultural relics work). Shanghai: Shanghaishi wenwu guanli weiyuanhui, n.d.

Wenwu shangdian gongzuo shouce 文物商店工作手册 (Handbook for cultural relics stores). Beijing: Zhongguo wenwu shangdian zongdian, October 1981.

Wu, Guo. "Recalling Bitterness: Historiography, Memory, and Myth in Maoist China." *Twentieth-Century China*, vol. 39, no. 3 (October 2014), pp. 245–268.

Wu, Hung. *The Wu Liang Shrine: The Ideology of Early Chinese Pictorial Art*. Stanford, CA: Stanford University Press, 1989.

Wu, Yiching. *The Cultural Revolution at the Margins: Chinese Socialism in Crisis*. Cambridge, MA: Harvard University Press, 2014.

Wuhan shehuizhuyi jieji jiaoyu zhanlanhui huikan 武汉社会主义阶级教育展览会会刊 (Proceedings of the Wuhan socialist class education exhibition). June 1, 1964.

Xiang Da 向达. "Wei wenwu qingming" 为文物请命 (A plea on behalf of cultural relics), *Zhongjian* 中建 (China constructs), vol. 3, no. 6 (1948), p. 8.

Xiao Ming 肖鸣, Xin De 心得, and Bao Yuan 葆元, eds. *Jiang kexue po mixin* 讲科学破迷信 (Discussing science and smashing superstition). Jinan: Shandong renmin chubanshe, 1963.

Xinmin wanbao 新民晚报 (New people's evening news).

Xinwen ribao 新闻日报 (News daily).

Xu Hanhui 许汉辉, Huang Fuxiang 黄富厢, and Hong Birong 洪碧荣. "Shanghaishi Zhabeiqu Fangualong gaijian guihua sheji jieshao" 上海市闸北区蕃瓜弄改建规划设计介绍 (An introduction to the reconstruction plan for Fangua Lane in Zhabei District of Shanghai). *Jianzhu xuebao* 建筑学报 (Journal of architecture), no. 2 (1964), pp. 20–22.

Xu Xiaomu 徐孝穆. "Shanghai bowuguan juban 'Cong feitongzhong qiangjiu wenwu zhanlan'" 上海博物馆举办 "从废铜中抢救文物展览" (Shanghai Museum puts on the "Exhibition on cultural relics rescued from scrap metal"). *Wenwu cankao ziliao* 文物参考资料 (Cultural relics reference materials), no. 4 (1957), p. 45.

Xuanchuan dongtai (xuanbian): 1980 宣传动态 (选编):1980 (Propaganda trends [Selections]: 1980). Beijing: Zhongguo shehui kexue chubanshe, 1981.

Xuanchuan dongtai 1983 宣传动态1983 (Propaganda trends 1983). Beijing: Zhongguo shehui kexue chubanshe, 1984.

Yang Yaojian 杨耀健. "Shouwei zaofan zhanlan" 守卫造反展览 (Guarding the rebels' exhibition). *Hongyan chunqiu* 红岩春秋, no. 1 (1998), pp. 40–42.

Yeh, Wen-hsin. *Shanghai Splendor: Economic Sentiments and the Making of Modern China, 1843–1949*. Berkeley: University of California Press, 2007.

*Yiguan hairen dao*一贯害人道. (The Way of Persistently Harming People). Directed by Li Enjie 李恩杰 and Wang Guangyan 王光彦. Beijing: Zhongyang dianyingju Beijing dianying zhipianchang, 1952.

Yuan Tongli 袁同礼. "Kangzhan qizhong woguo bowuguan zhi dongtai yu qiantu" 抗战期 中我国博物馆之动态与前途 (The situation and future of our nation's museums during wartime). *Zhongguo bowuguan xiehui huibao* 中国博物馆协会会报 (Journal of the Chinese Museum Association), no. 1 (1941), pp. 2–4.

Yue, Daiyun, and Carolyn Wakeman. *To the Storm: The Odyssey of a Revolutionary Chinese Woman*. Berkeley: University of California Press, 1985.

"Zai Zhongguo geming bowuguanli" 在中国革命博物馆里 (In the Museum of the Chinese Revolution). *Wenwu* 文物 (Cultural relics), no. 10 (1964), pp. 3–20.

Zhai, Qiang. "Mao Zedong and Dulles's 'Peaceful Evolution' Strategy: Revelations from Bo Yibo's Memoirs." *Cold War International History Bulletin*, nos. 6/7 (Winter 1995/1996), pp. 228–331.

Zhang Geng 长庚. *Jiang kexue po mixin* 讲科学破迷信 (Discussing science and smashing superstition). Shanghai: Shanghai keji chubanshe, 1964.

Zhang Wenqing 张文清 et al. *Mao Zedong zai Shanghai* 毛泽东在上海 (Mao Zedong in Shanghai). Shanghai: Shanghai shudian chubanshe, 2003.

Zhang Xiaochuan 张笑川. *Jindai Shanghai Zhabei jumin shehui shenghuo* 近代上海闸北居民 社会生活 (Social life in modern Shanghai's Zhabei District). Shanghai: Shanghai cishu chubanshe, 2009.

Zhang Xing 张行. "Bowuguan kepu jiaoyu gongneng tantao" 博物馆科普教育功能探讨 (An exploration into the functions of museums in science dissemination education). *Sichou zhi lu* 丝绸之路 (The silk road), no. 6 (December 1995), pp. 54–55.

Zhejiang ribao 浙江日报 (Zhejiang daily).

Zheng Zhong 郑重. *Bowuguan yu shoucangjia* 博物馆与收藏家 (Museum and collectors). Shanghai: Shanghai wenyi chubanshe, 2000.

  Haishang shoucang shijia 海上收藏世家 (Collectors in Shanghai). Shanghai: Shiji chuban jituan, Shanghai shudian chubanshe, 2003.

  "Zhong Yinlan de shuhua jianding shengya" 钟银兰的书画鉴定生涯 (Zhong Yinlan's career in painting appraisal), *Wenwu tiandi* 文物天地(Cultural relics heaven-and-earth) (March 2006), pp. 48–53.

Zhonggong Shanghai shiwei dangshi yanjiushi 中共上海市委党史研究室 and Shanghaishi wenwuju 上海市文物局 (Research Office of the Shanghai Communist Party Committee and the Shanghai Municipal Bureau of Cultural Relics), eds. *Zhongguo gongchandang zaoqi zai Shanghai shiji* 中国共产党早期在上海史迹 (Historical relics in Shanghai from the Chinese Communist Party's early period). Shanghai: Tongji daxue chubanshe, 2013.

Zhongguo geming bowuguan 中国革命博物馆 (Museum of the Chinese Revolution), ed. *Jiefangqu zhanlanhui ziliao* 解放区展览会资料 (Materials on exhibitions in the liberated areas). Beijing: Wenwu chubanshe, 1988.

Zhongguo geming bowuguan dangshi chenlie bu 中国革命博物馆党史陈列部 (Party History Exhibition Department of the Museum of the Chinese

Revolution). "Dangshi chenlie de jige wenti" 党史陈列的几个问题 (Several issues regarding exhibiting Party history). *Dangshi yanjiu ziliao* 党史研究资料 (Party history research materials), no. 6 (1979), pp. 122–129.

Zhongguo gongchandang diyici quanguo daibiao dahui huizhi jinianguan 中国共产党第一次全国代表大会会址纪念馆 (Memorial hall of the Chinese Communist Party's First Party Congress Site), ed. *Zhongguo gongchandang diyici quanguo daibiao dahui huizhi* 中国共产党第一次全国代表大会会址 (The Chinese Communist Party's First Party Congress Site). Shanghai: Shanghai renmin meishu chubanshe, 2001.

Zhongguo gongchandang xuanchuan gongzuo wenxian xuanbian 中国共产党宣传工作文献选编 (Selected documents on the propaganda work of the Chinese Communist Party), 4 vols. Beijing: Xuexi chubanshe, 1996.

Zhongyang guwu baoguan weiyuanhui 中央古物保管委员会 (Committee to Promote the Preservation of Antiquities), ed. *Zhongyang guwu baoguan weiyuanhui shilu* 中央古物保管委员会实录 (Proceedings of the Central Commission on the Preservation of Antiquities). Nanjing: Zhongyang guwu baoguan weiyuanhui, June 1935.

Zhou, Xun, ed. *The Great Famine in China, 1958–1962: A Documentary History.* New Haven: Yale University Press, 2012.

Zhu Minyi 诸民谊. Xingzhengyuan wenwu baoguan weiyuanhui niankan 行政院文物保管委员会年刊 (Annual of the Cultural Relics Commission of the Administrative Yuan). Nanjing, 1941.

Chinese Character List

bangyang: 榜样 — model

biantiantu: 变天图 — map saved for a "change in the sky"

biantianzhang: 变天账 — ledger saved for a "change in the sky"

bolanguan: 博览馆 — museum-library; museum

bowuguan: 博物馆 — museum

bowuyuan: 博物院 — museum-garden

chachao: 查抄 — to search and confiscate

chaojia: 抄家 — house search

chenlie: 陈列 — display

chenlieguan: 陈列馆 — display hall

chenliepin: 陈列品 — exhibition articles

daiguan: 代管 — to manage on another's behalf

dazibao: 大字报 — big-character poster

dianxing: 典型 — model

douzheng guoshi: 斗争果实 — fruits of struggle

duixiang: 对象 — target

Fangualong: 蕃瓜弄 — Fangua Lane

fanshen: 翻身 — to stand up

gandong: 感动 — to move, to touch

ganxing zhishi: 感性知识 — perceptual knowledge

geming shiji: 革命史迹 — revolutionary trace or vestige

geming wenwu: 革命文物 — revolutionary cultural relic

geming yizhi: 革命遗址 — revolutionary site

gongren xincun: 工人新村 — workers' new village

gongxun: 功勋 — achievement

gongyipin: 工艺品 — handicraft

gundilong: 滚地龙 — makeshift dwelling, literally "earth-rolling dragon"

hongxian: 红线 — "Red Line"

huiyi duibi: 回忆对比 — comparing past and present

huizhi: 会址 — meeting site

huoren zhanlan: 活人展览 — living exhibition

jiangjie: 讲解 — to narrate; narration

jieji ganqing: 阶级感情 — class feeling

jieji jiaoyu zhanlan: 阶级教育展览 — class education exhibition

jiezhan: 阶展 — class education exhibition

jinianguan: 纪念馆 — memorial hall or museum

jinxiandai wenwu: 今现代文物 — modern cultural relic

jiu shehui: 旧社会 — old society

kepu: 科普 — science dissemination

liangyi sancha: 两忆三查 — two remembrances, three investigations

lixing zhishi: 理性知识 — rational knowledge

mixin: 迷信 — superstition

mofan: 模范 — model

niugui sheshen: 牛鬼蛇神 — ox-demons and snake-spirits

penghuqu: 棚户区 — shantytown

po sijiu: 破四旧 — Attack on the Four Olds

qinshou zhanlan: 禽兽展览 — display of beasts

re'ai kexue, po mixin: 热爱科学，破迷信 — "Love Science and Eliminate Superstition"

shehuizhuyi bowuguan: 社会主义博物馆 — socialist museum

shengli guoshi: 胜利果实 — fruits of victory

shiwu: 实物 — material artifact

siqing: 四清 — Four Cleanups

suku: 诉苦 — speaking bitterness

wenwu: 文物 — cultural relic

wenwu baohu danwei: 文物保护单位 — cultural relic protection unit

wufan: 五反 — Five Antis

xiazhijiao: 下之角 — "lower corner"

xin shehui: 新社会 — new society

xin zhanlanhui: 新展览会 — new exhibition

xinjiu duibi: 新旧对比 — compare the old and new

xuanchuan: 宣传 — propaganda

yida huizhi: 一大会址 — First Party Congress Site

Yiguandao: 一贯道 — Way of Pervading Unity

yiku sitian: 忆苦思甜 — recalling bitterness and reflecting on sweetness

yikufan: 忆苦饭 — bitterness meal

Yong'an gongsi: 永安公司 — Wing On Company; Yong'an Company

zhanguo: 战果 — fruits of battle
zhanlan: 展览 — exhibition
zhanlanguan: 展览馆 — exhibition hall
zhanlanhui: 展览会 — exhibition
zhanpin: 展品 — display objects
zhuanti: 专题 — topic
zuizheng: 罪证 — criminal evidence

Index

Note: Page numbers in *italic* type indicate illustrations.

Abe Masatoshi, 223
accusation. *See* denunciation
All-China Federation of Labor, 158
Anagnost, Ann, 16, 75, 262
ancestral graves, 131
Anhui Province, 129
Anting Incident, 53n92, 53
antiques, 168, 207, 259
Antiquities Market, 218, 219, 244
antiquity, 2, 9, 13, 248, 258, 259; beliefs
   about natural phenomena, 117, 254;
   Mao-era narratives of, 253–254; Mao's
   definition of, 226; and natural
   phenomena, 117, 254; preservation of
   artifacts of, 5, 19, 213, 214, 215, 254. *See
   also wenwu*
Anti-Rightist Campaign, 47, 225
anti-superstition campaign, 18, 22,
   106–125, *113*, 137, 249, 261, 262, 264;
   and class education exhibits, 153, 171,
   248; and handbooks, 135; limitations of,
   130–133; and students' questions, 250.
   See also Love Science and Eliminate
   Superstition Exhibition
Antonioni, Michelangelo, 88, 92
Anyuan, 15, 55, 56
Apter, David E., 253
archives, 21–22, 33–34, 47, 48, 49, 64n15,
   100, 251, 255
art, 252; and correct interpretation of,
   42–43; market for, 219; preservation of,
   9; as propaganda, 15; Red Guard seizure
   of, 168, 213, 213n8; relationship with
   politics, 5, 14, 15, 16, 42n65, 42; and
   revolutionary narrative, 23
art collections, 213, 213n8, 221, 227,
   231–232, 234. *See also* Shanghai
   Museum
artifacts. *See wenwu*

artifacts of everyday life. *See* objects
atheism, 108, 132
"Attack on the Four Olds," 19, 137, 168,
   172, 179–180, 181, 183, 190, 210,
   211–214, 215, 226–235; definition and
   meaning of, 227–228; Shanghai Museum
   response to, 240, 245, 246
authenticity, 17, 58, 263

bacteria, 107, 108n13
Ba Jin, 208
Bao Huiseng, 30
Baum, Richard, 143, 144n12
begging, 3, 81, 83, 175, 248, 263
Beijing, 27, 30; house searches, 180n29;
   Red Guards (*see* Beijing Red Guards);
   Tiananmen Square, 5, 12, 50, 57, 176,
   264; and *wenwu* protection, 232–235. *See
   also* Dragon Whisker Creek; Museum of
   the Chinese Revolution; National
   Museum of China; Palace Museum
Beijing Municipal Small Group for Sorting
   Ancient Books and Cultural Relics,
   235–236
Beijing Normal University, 183
Beijing Red Guards, 23, 169–170, 176,
   194; exhibition of, 182–183, 184–186,
   191n66, 206n129; and exhibition
   disbanding, 205; manifesto of, 227–228
Bennett, Tony, 6, 83, 259n28
Bentham, Jeremy, 151
Bergère, Marie-Claire, 61–62n7
biantiantu/biantianzhang (maps and
   ledgers), 153, 161, 168, 173, 191,
   191n66, 193, 195
big-character posters, 18, 172, 180,
   186, 199
bitterness meal. *See yikufan*
Blake, C. Fred, 103n2

boat children, 125, 126, 127, 128
books: burning of, 234; preservation of, 9, 236, 243
bourgeoisie, 144, 156, 158, 161, 169; national, 207n132
Bowen Girls' School, 28, 29, 33, 37
Bo Yibo, 158
Braester, Yomi, 15, 23n62, 76
bronzes, 218, 219, 222, *222*, 245, 250; Shang Yang measure, 221, 231–232, 236–237, 243; Mandate of Heaven, 5
Brown, Jeremy, 4n8, 90, 106n10, 144
Buddha, 127, 128; statues, 210, 211, 229
Buddhism, 109, 112, 129, 134–135; ledgers of merit and demerit, 262
Bund, 24, 229, 231, 251

cadres, 9, 12, 16, 21, 75, 91, 249; and class education exhibitions, 153, 154; handbooks for, 1–4, 14, 64, 81n78, 248, 253; purging of, 143–144; and religious practice, 130–131, 133, 133n95; and Socialist Education Movement, 112, 143–144, 151
calligraphy, 218, 234
Cao Diqiu, 69, 181, 230, 233
Caoyang New Village, 61–62n7
capitalists, 23, 24, 67, 151, 179, 190, 262; accusations against, 162, 174, 182; art collections of, 213, 221; class education exhibition focus on, 156–169, 193, 221; and class status, 142, 143, 145, 156; exploitation by, 151, 165; and nationalization, 221; objects symbolizing, 248; "peaceful evolution" to restore, 158, 163–164; and Shanghai Museum, 221; Shanghai associated with, 67, 146, 156, 159, 175, 179–180, 229; socialism's struggle with, 144; victims of, 199
Capital Red Guards Revolutionary Rebel Exhibition, 184–186, 206
Catholicism, 109, 118, 129, 133n92
"cattle and horses" trope, 75–76n59, 79, 87, 138
CCP. *See* Chinese Communist Party
CCRG. *See* Central Cultural Revolution Group
Central Commission on Antiquities, 214
Central Committee, 29, 30, 168, 227, 243; Mao as member of, 47, 48–49; Sixth Plenum, 237; Tenth Plenum, 142–143, 158
Central Cultural Revolution Group, 184, 206, 232–235, 237
ceramics, 236, 241

Chan, Anita, 143n9
Changsha, 151
Chen, Xiaomei, 42
Chen Boda, 150, 185, 206n128, 234
Chen Duanzhi, 8, 9n32, 214n10
Chen Duxiu, 28, 40, 48n78, 52, 55
Cheng, Nien, 231n81
Chen Liansheng, Abbot, 135
Chen Peicun, 30n16, 31, 33n18, 33n20, 33–34, 37, 37n41, 38n44, 46
Chen Peifen, 8, 213, 214, 217, 218, 218n28, 221, 263
Chen Pixian, 142, 158, 163, 164–165, 171, 181, 181n33, 230n75
Chen Ruoxi, 84
Chen Tanqiu, 43
Chenxian Pavilion, 229
Chen Xiejun, 243n118, 245
Chen Yi, 5, 6, 9, 25, 91, 185, 216–217
Chen Yingfang, 69n42, 93
Chen Zhiqiang, *85*, 109, 211n2, 211n3, 213n7, 229n71, 231n80, 232n84, 241n108
Chiang Kai-shek, 66, 98, 161, 191, 194, 214; hidden portrait of, 195, 200, 203
children: and anti-superstition campaign, 18, 22, 114, 121, 124n63, 125, 126, 127; belief in ghost stories, 128; and museum rituals, 256; and religion, 255. *See also* students; youth
China Bookstore, 234
"China Dream" (slogan), 264
China Pavilion, 99–100, *100*, *101*, 264
Chinese Academy of Sciences, 235
Chinese Civil War, 9, 12, 62, 67, 215
Chinese Communist Party, 12–15, 33, 41; anti-superstition campaigns, 106–125, 127; and class consciousness, 142–143, 145; and collections, 9, 12, 13; and cultural products, 7, 13–15, 35, 247, 249, 259; failures of, 133–134; founding of, 17, 23, 24, 25, 26n2, 27, 38, 40, 42, 46–47, 49, 253, 255, 264, 265; founding date, 26, 58–59; founding myth, 34–39, 49–50, 248, 253; historical materials about, 41, 46–50, 56, 58–59, 249; icon of founding (*see* First Party Congress Site); legitimization of, 36; Mao's role in (*see* Mao Zedong); membership expansion, 49; military victory, 259; and museums, 2, 3, 4, 8, 9, 12; official history, 4, 16, 38–39, 47, 264; organization, 49; Propaganda Department, 260; propaganda tools, 12, 14, 28, 30, 38, 109, 198, 260; religion policy, 109, 130, 136–137; and science, 108–109, 112,

122–125; Secretariat members, 48n78; as state in power, 259; and *wenwu* protection, 2, 5–6, 9, 12–13, 17, 19, 25, 33, 56, 214–216, 227, 228, 232, 235, 243, 260. *See also* Central Committee; Mao era; reform era

Chinese Communist revolution. *See* curating revolution; Museum of the Chinese Revolution; revolution

Chinese Museum Association, 7

Chongqing, 183, 184, 255

Christianity, 104n5, 109, 129, 130, 132, 133

churches, 104n5, 109, 111, 119, 136, 183, 240, 258

Cina (documentary film), 88

cinema, 15, 19, *20*, 23, 24

city god, 109, 262

City God Temple, 109–112, 128, 129–130, 131, 133–135, 216; attendance, 134; Red Guard damage to, 229

civil war. *See* Chinese Civil War

Clark, Paul, 14–15

class: art objects as reflection of, 225–226; crimes of, 195, 196, 199 (*see also* class enemies); and Cultural Revolution, 196, 204–205; of docents, 156, 254–255; exhibitions about (*see* class education exhibition); Fangua Lane distinctions of, 94–95; of Fangua Lane hosts, 83; fears of restoration, 151; ideology of, 141, 142–144, 145, 153; land reform definition of, 152; language of, 205; models of, 90; narratives of, 83, 198–205, 254; negative labels of, 143; objects as markers of, 15, 17, 18, 24, 83, 138, 139, 141, 143, 144, 147, 152, 153, 180, 195–196, 198, 205, 209, 210, 248, 251, 253, 257, 261, 262; pre-1949 definition of, 143; propaganda about, 104, 144, 250; reassigning labels of, 143, 144; rhetoric of, 147–148; and status determination, 143, 144; and superstitions, 107, 108, 115, 124, 126, 136, 137; and symbols of suffering, 23, 138, 248; victims of, 163; and *wenwu*, 225–226, 254; *yiku sitian* and understanding of, 16. *See also* bourgeoisie; capitalists; masses; peasants; proletariat; workers

class bitterness, 146, 154

class conflict, 115–116. *See also* class enemies; class struggle

class consciousness, 3, 21, 64, 73, 74n55, 141, 142–143, 144, 145n15, 148, 158, 188, 251, 258

class education exhibition, 4–5, 8, 19, 22, 137, 138–173, 199, 228, 248, 263, 265; and Central Cultural Revolution Group, 233–235; Cultural Revolution prerogative vs., 168–172; curatorial techniques, 152–153, 154, 158–164, 171, 193, 251, 257, 262; display of objects, 151, 152, *155*, *160*, 195, 252; docents, 255; effectiveness of, 141; elements of, 145–151; and emblematic objects, 153; as exposé, 197; as famine response, 149; and Fangua Lane, 64, 65, 71; ideological core of, 143; length of visits, 157; origins of, 73–74; prop design, *139*; provincial, 150–161; purpose of, 169; and Red Guards, 14, 18, 142, 164, 168, 169–172, 175, 183, 198, 199, 202, 204, 208, 254; responses to, 74, 87, 142, 152–153, 154, 156, 175, 257; success of, 152; techniques of, 141–142, 145–147, 159–160, 197, 251; workers at, *149*. *See also* Shanghai Class Education Exhibition

class enemies, 137, 143, 144, 163, 169, 171, 183, 197, 205; exhibition of, 188–189, 191, 192, 193–198, 208, 250, 262; exposure of, 18, 137, 174, 181, 254, 257; hidden, 152–153, 175, 210, 254; linking old with new, 152, 153, 163; objects signifying, 153, 194–196, 198, 210, 251, 257; portrayal of, 163, 175. *See also* class struggle; counterrevolutionary/counterrevolutionaries

class feeling, 144, 146, 154, 175, 198, 199, 201, 202, 203; and hatred, 20, 188–189, 205

class status. *See* class

class struggle, 43, 74n55, 108, 112, 115–116, 127, 142–146, 151, 254, 261, 267; and Cultural Revolution, 142, 143, 173, 197; exhibitions depicting, 152, 153, 156, 168, 170, 171, 172; narration as, 198; past and present, 151–152, 153; Red Guard exhibition of, *20*, 176, 183, 200–201, 204, 208. *See also* exploitation

class suffering, objects as symbols of, 23, 138, 248

Clunas, Craig, 5n14

Coble, Parks M., Jr., 194n71

collections, 21, 34, 249–251; of Chinese Communist Party, 9, 12, 13; curating

process, 249–250; during Cultural Revolution, 13, 19, 52, 227, 240; as house search targets, 213, 213n8, 227; in imperial China, 5, 6, 7; political threats to, 225; present-day maintenance of, 22; preservation of, 243; purpose of, 4; Red Guards' destruction of, 228. *See also* art collections; document collections; Shanghai Museum; *wenwu*
collective identity, 5–6
collective memory, 74n55
collectivization, 36–37, 130, 143
collectors. *See* collections
colonialism. *See* imperialism
Comintern, 44, 45–46, 48, 49
communism, 4, 8, 14, 145, 157–158
Communist China. *See* Chinese Communist Party; People's Republic of China
comparing past and present. *See huiyi duibi*; Old and New China; *yiku sitian*
computers, 124, 136
confessions, 162, 163, 167–168; display of, 265
confiscated possessions. *See* house search; objects
Confucius, 52, 89, 92, 237; display of birthplace, 241; Mansion, 228, *241*; tablets and grave markers, 229; temples, 136n107, 228. *See also* Criticize Confucius, Criticize Lin Biao Campaign
consumer goods, 99–100, 145, 178
continuous revolution, 4, 41, 210, 250, 254, 257, 261
Corney, Frederick, 33n19, 39
corruption, 144, 161, 163, 225; exhibits of, 264–265
counterrevolutionary/counterrevolutionaries, 2, 43, 68, 74, 88, 106, 118, 119–120, 121; crimes of, 200; intent as, 190; objects seized as, 173, 176, 180, 181, 192, 195; religion as, 127; superstition as tool of, 106, 118, 119–120, 121, 124, 125, 137, 153. *See also* class enemies
countryside: and class status, 144; famine, 148, 149; "Four Cleanups" campaign, 143–144; Red Guard exhibitions, 184; religious revival, 130, 133; resettlement to, 104, 111; sent-down youth, 205, 224, 244
Criticize Confucius, Criticize Lin Biao Campaign, 52, 92
Cuba, 60
cultural nationalism, 7, 13, 15, 35, 247, 249

cultural production, 14–17, 220–226
cultural relic. *See wenwu*
Cultural Relics Bureau, 29
Cultural Relics Commission, 260
Cultural Revolution, 14–15, 39, 87, 150, 174–210, 258, 265; and big-character posters, 18, 172, 180, 186, 199; Central Cultural Revolution Group, 184, 206, 233–234, 235, 237; and class struggle, 142, 143, 173, 197; collective killings during, 208; cultural products of, 14, 246; curating of, 13, 197–198; definition of, 227; end of, 134; and exhibitions, 4–5, 13, 18–19, 137, 176–189, 197, 208–209, 248, 263; and factionalism, 204–205; Fangua Lane during, 64n14, 83–85, 92, 95, 97, 202; fiftieth anniversary of, 208; and First Party Congress Site, 13, 27, 50–56, 52n90, 250, 263; inception of, 168, 176, 227; and Mao Zedong Thought, 197; and markers of class, 15, 17, 18, 24, 83, 138, 141, 144, 147, 152, 153, 180, 195–196, 198, 205, 209, 210, 248, 251, 253, 262; open struggle prerogative of, 169; proposed museum of, 208, 233–234; rehabilitation of victims of, 207; and Shanghai Museum, 19, 211–247, 249, 250, 253, 255; slogans of, 191; Socialist Education Movement as precursor to, 18, 142, 164, 172, 258; studies of, 246; and treatment of intellectuals, 183; *wenwu* of, 52, 215, 232, 234, 237, 243; and Wenwu Small Group, 236–239, 243, 244; and workers, 163; years preceding, 39–41, 42. *See also* "Attack on the Four Olds"; Gang of Four; Red Guards; struggle sessions
culture: politics of, 14–17; traditional, 2, 19, 262. *See also* exhibitionary culture; political culture
curating, 249–258; definition of, 248; juxtaposition method, 192–193; and socialist museums, 258–263; stages of, 21–22, 249; tools of, 159, 250–251. *See also* narratives; rituals
curating revolution, 1, 19, 21, 23, 39–56, 263; aspects of, 13–16; and class education exhibitions, 172; and exemplary objects, 248; and incriminating evidence, 251; initiation of, 24; and juxtaposition, 64, 192–193; in Mao's China, 1–6, 13, 17, 27, 38–39, 49–50, 88, 266; museum's function in, 3, 4, 13, 15–17, 34–35; and narrative, 3, 8, 19, 23, 36, 40, 253, 254, 255, 260; and

paradoxes of Mao era, 249; people's role in, 263; political goal of, 248; process of, 21–22, 39–42, 249–258; Red Guards' approach to, 23, 176, 187, 189–193, 197–205; and "Red Line," 40–42; Soviet model of, 8, 12, 36–37, 39, 261. *See also* class education exhibition; Fangua Lane; First Party Congress Site

Daoism, 109, 135
David-Fox, Michael, 92–93
Dazhai, 89
death, 115, 128; funerals, 131n86; graves, 131. *See also* ghosts
DeMare, Brian, 15
Deng Enming, 43n66
Deng Tuo, 82
Deng Yingchao, 55n104
Denton, Kirk, 8, 35, 39, 57n108, 59n117, 106n10, 256, 264n46, 265n51
denunciation, 74, 164, 172–173, 183; collective vs. spontaneous, 261
department stores, 18, 23, 263. *See also* Yong'an Department Store
Diamond, Norma, 89n104, 90n106
diamonds, 192
dianxing. See model
diaries, 161–162, 163, 173, 182
Ding Dahua, 185n48, 185n51, 186, 187, 205n125
display: of class enemy, 188–189, 191, 192, 193–198, 262; importance in exhibition work, 21; narrative support for, 3, 251–256; of objects (*see under* objects); reactions to, 204; sites of, 17–19; and state in power mode, 58; of wounded bodies, 146, 152, *155*, 199, 248, 262, 263. *See also* exhibitionary culture; exhibitions
display boards, 132, 172, 265
docents: class status of, 156, 254–255; emotions elicited by, 15, 257; explanation of Cultural Revolution by, 51; handbooks for, 22; ideological correctness of, 156; narratives of, 21, 41, 196, 254–255; of neighborhood exhibitions, 3, 52–54; and participatory propaganda, 13; Red Guards as, 19, 175, 176, 182, 189, 196, 197, 198–205, 255; scripts for, 40, 43–48, 51, 187, 201, 223, 254, 256, 258; Shanghai Museum, 221, 223–224; tape-recording replacement of, 52, 254; and visitor questions, 46
documents, 13, 176, 180, 181, 186, 191n66, 192, 252; historical, 8, 34, 41, 55–56

Dong Guoqiang, 204–205, 205n121
Dongbei ribao (Northeast daily news), 188
Dong Biwu, 28, 30, 30n16, 43, 46, 47, 48, 49
Dong Xiwen, *Founding Ceremony of the Nation* (painting), 42, 42n65
dragon god, 102, 117, 130
Dragon Whisker Creek (Beijing), 76, 87
Dragon Whisker Creek (play and film), 76
drama, 15, 16
dream premonitions, 108, 109
Dulles, John Foster, 157

East is Red, The (song-and-dance epic), 42
East is Red Department Store (formerly Yong'an Department Store), 18, 175, 180, 181, 194, 197, 198, 200, 202, 209, 255; renaming of, 207
education: class ideology incorporated into, 142, 145; mass, 1, 2, 8; models, 90; museum role, 3, 8, 12, 34, 259; patriotic, 3, 26, 264; socialist, 14, 16, 18, 258, 264. *See also* anti-superstition campaign; class education exhibition; Socialist Education Movement
Eisenhower, Dwight D., 158
Elizabeth II, 135
Elleman, Bruce A., 49n80
Elliott, Jeanette Shambaugh, 5n13, 228n67
emotions: and Chinese Communist revolution, 197–198; elicitation of, 15, 19, 199–200, 201, 202, 249, 254, 257, 265. *See also* class feeling; class hatred
employment contract, 138, 141, 257
Esherick, Joseph W., 262n36
everyday life: cultural practice as central to, 14–15; materials of, 100; narratives of, 17; objects of (*see* objects); symbols of, 1, 3
evidence: curation of, 163, 251; objects equated with, 196; scars as, 248, 262, 263; scientific, 115
exhibitionary culture: Chinese history of, 2, 5–17, 262; of Cultural Revolution, 176; definition of, 6; and definition of display, 21; of Mao-era, 2, 4, 8, 13, 21, 58, 64, 83, 87, 88, 98, 252–254, 260, 262–266; and militancy, 251; and modernization, 7; and nationalism, 7; participation in, 257–258; power of, 17, 83; as propaganda, 14, 18; Red Guards' use of, 18–19, 174–176, 190–192, 198, 251; of reform era, 263–265; of a revolutionary movement, 4, 13, 18–19, 92, 189, 261, 262, 264, 265; and ritual, 16, 256–258;

Soviet model of, 36, 260, 261, 262; of a state in power, 13, 58, 92–93, 259, 261, 262, 263–264. *See also* exhibitions; museums; new exhibitions; *specific exhibitions and museums*

Exhibition of Red Guard Achievements, 18–19, 22, 23, 174–176, 179–210, 254–258; aims and accomplishments of, 204–205; assessment of, 205–210; in Beijing, 182–183, 184–186, 191n66, 205, 206n129; class narratives, 193–198, 202, 254; continuous revolution as lesson of, 210; curatorial technique of, 187, 192–193; different forms of, 185; display of class enemies, 188–189, 191, 192, 193–198, 208, 250, 262; display of confiscated objects, 9, 18, 174–175, 180, 182n37, 182–183, 184, 186, 188, 190–192, 191n66, *192*, 203–204, 209, 248, 250, 252; and disposition of confiscated objects, 206; docent preparation, 196, 198–205, 250; in Guangzhou, 183, 191n66, 205; house search reenactment, 200; idea for, 181–182; and land reform, 188–189, 261; lessons of, 210; and Mao Zedong Thought, 197; materiality of, 202; mixed memories of, 203–204, 263; narration of, 199–202, 249, 255; and "Red Line," 201; replaced by January Revolution exhibit, 263; as ritual, 256; visitor numbers, 175; visitor procedure, 191–192, 256; visitor reactions, 197, 202, 203, 249, 257; visitor rituals, 256, 258

exhibitions: ad hoc, 18, 105; of Chinese Communist Party founding, 25; class hatred cultivated by, 188–189; class narrative reinforced by, 254; comparison to other media, 249; as cultural products, 15; curating process (*see* curating); elements of, 1–2, 3, 13, 16–17, 21; factory, 4, 75, 250; forms of, 252; goal of, 2; grassroots, 1–3, 4, 17, 257, 263; as handbooks, 1, 4, 13, 172, 257; living, 64–65, 83–102, 147, 204, 208–209, 262; local, 17, 105, 252, 253; as mass education tool, 8; modernization of, 264; multi-media, 14, 150–151; narrative accompaniment, 21, 251–256; personal impact of, 251; pictorial, 16; political uses of, 1, 4, 6, 13, 16, 18, 82–83, 92, 171, 187, 241, 248, 250, 251, 252, 257–258, 263, 264; preparation process (*see* curating); purposes of, 4 (*see also* propaganda); question-and-answer format of, 82–83;

traveling, 2, 37, 53–54, 105, 112, 224; words referring to, 7, 8. *See also* display; docents; museums; new exhibitions; visitors; *specific exhibitions*

exorcist, *118*

exploitation, 73, 145, 152, 158, 159–160, 165, 194; possessions seen as evidence of, 189–190, 195–197, 253, 262

factories, 66, 74, 144; exhibits, 4, 75, 250; surveillance, 151–152

Falungong, 136, 264

famine, 38, 87, 104, 130, 131, 148, 149, 250, 254

Fangua Lane, 22, 23, 59, 60–102, 171, 253, 256, 260, 262, 264; apartment blocks, 17, 60, 61–62, 69–71, *86*, 89, 91–95, *96*; cost of renovation, 93; cultural relic status of, 97; and Cultural Revolution, *84–85*, 92, 95, 97; demolition of shantytown exhibit, 263; designation for renewal, 69–70, 74–75; deterioration of, 96–97, 102; as emblematic of Shanghai, 83; foreign visitors to, 17, 61, 63–64, 64n14, 83–*85*, *85*, *86*, 87–88, 93, 94, 254; history of, 65–76; materials from, 251; media images of, 71, 72–73, 83; as microcosm of New China, 17, 18, 59, 60–63, 75–76, 87–88, 89, 91, 92, 97, 171; model residents of, 81–82, 83, 91; narratives of, 73–74, 97, 98, 255; panorama of, *69*; as participatory propaganda, 64–65, 84, 86–88, 92–93; "Past and Present" exhibit, 64–65, 76–83, 84, 87, 94, 102, 192; poster of, *62*; residents' return to, 69–70, *70*, 71, 75, 81; residents' stories of, 88–89, 253; and shantytown exhibit, 67, 91, 213, 263; Spring Festival, 71, *72*; student visits to, 17, 64, 64n14, 84, 87, 92, 94, 262; vista of, *62*; wartime devastation of, 66–67, 91; and *yiku sitian*, 16, 18, 73, 74, 75, 76, 81, 84, 87, 92, 250, 257

Fangua Lane Elementary School, 92, 97

Fang Yunfang, 265n50

fanshen (to stand up), 2, 73; Fangua Lane as embodiment of, 64, 82, 83, 89

farming, 36–37, 143, 144

Fei Qinsheng, 222–223

Feng, Xiaocai, 177n14

fengshui, 112

feudalism, 112, 117n50, 130, 169, 192; examples of, 193–194

First Party Congress: dating of, 25, 26, 26n2, 43, 58; delegates to, 43, 44, 45–50;

documentation of, 48–50; and "Red Line," 40; as turning point, 44, 49

First Party Congress Site, 8, 26–59, *51*, 170, 171, 201; ambiguity and contradictions of, 40, 48, 248; authentication of, 29–30, 33, 34; collection, 13, 22, 24, 26, 252; as cultural relic, 8, 17, 22, 23, 25, 33, 45–47, 57, 227; and Cultural Revolution, 13, 27, 50–55, 175, 250, 263; curating process, 249, 250; display layout, 37–39, 57–59; docent scripts, 40, 43–48, 49, 51, 187, 254; excavation and authentication of, 26–30; and exhibitionary culture of a state in power, 58, 84, 201; exterior of, *31*; foreign visitors to, 39, 44–46, *45*, 47–48, 50, 83; and founding myth, 17, 64, 253; and historical research, 46–50; as icon, 22, 24, 26, 248; Mao-era importance of, 23; as Mao monument, 50; marker for, 26; master narrative of, 36, 39, 41, 84, 255; multiple functions of, 8, 37; new exhibition, 55–56; paintings, 42–43; pilgrimages to, 23; and portable displays, 53–54; present-day, 22–23, 27, 54, 56–59, 262, 263; and rectification of names, 55; "Red Line" adherence to, 40, 41, 42–43, 44, 49–50, 75, 201, 249; and reform era, 27, 55–57, 263; restoration of, 25, 27, 29, 31, *32*, 36, 43; revisions to, 42n65, 42–43, 157; Ryckmans' critique of, 39; search for, 17, 25, 26, 213; status today of, 22–23, 26, 55–59, 263; tape recording, 52, 254; visitor questions, 47–49

Firth, Clifton, 77n65, *78*, 84, 88

Fitzpatrick, Sheila, 261

Five Antis Campaign, 131n86, 143, 144, 144n9, 161, 221, 225, 251

flags, 191, 251

foreign exchange, 238

foreign visitors, 17, 23, 60, 254; to China in 1970s, 93, 242; and Cultural Revolution, 52; to exhibitions, 17, 23, *44*, 254; to Fangua Lane, 17, 61, 63–64, 64n14, 75–76, *82*, 83–85, *85*, *86*, 87–88, 93, 94, 96, 254; to First Party Congress Site, 39, 44–46, *45*, 47–48, 50, 52n90, 83; to Shanghai Museum, 224; to Soviet Union, 92–93

Foreign Languages Publishing House, 36

fortune-telling, 109, 112, 114, 117, *118*, 124, 128, 129, 179; "scientific," 136

Founding Ceremony of the Nation (painting), 42; alterations to, 42n65

Four Cleanups Campaign, 143–144, 157, 161, 162, 225

Four Modernizations, 245

"Four Olds," 19, 137, 168, 172, 179, 210, 211, 214, 229; unclear definition of, 227–228. *See also* "Attack on the Four Olds"

France, 240, 240n107

French Concession, 28, 43, 44, 104

French Revolution, 240

fur coats, 183, 192, *192*, 193, 248, 262

Fuxing Middle School, 145, 146, 147, 148, 203–204

Gang of Four, 52, 54, 136, 142, 154. *See also* Jiang Qing; Yao Wenyuan; Zhang Chunqiao

Gao, Mobo, 215n16

Gao, Yuan, 184, 204

Gao Gang, 42n65

Gellately, Robert, 261

geming wenwu (revolutionary cultural relics), 12, 31, 34

Gerth, Karl, 179n23

ghosts, 103, 104, 108, 111, 114, 119–120, 126; belief in, 128, 129; refutations of, 116

gods: belief in, 108, 111, 114, 129; refutations of, 116, 117

gold, 168, 173, 180, 182, 191, 191n66, 196, 203, 207, 240, 251, 258; hidden, 189–190, 200

Gong Pinmei, Bishop, 118–119, 137

Gong Xuren, 168, 221, 231–232, 236, 243

Gong Zhaodi, 81, 82, 83, 84

Good Eighth Company Campaign, 23n62

Goodrich, Anne Swann, 262n38

Goossaert, Vincent, 108

Great Britain, 6, 135

Greater Shanghai Municipal Center, 8–9

Great Exhibition (London), 6

Great Leap Forward, 37, 71, 91, 141, 144, 148, 150, 178n22; religion during, 110–111; failures of, 133–134, 255. *See also* famine

Gross, Miriam, 105

Guangdong Province, 66, 131, 208

Guangzhou, 175, 183, 191n66, 205, 208n138, 236n93

Guangzhou Red Guard exhibition, 183, 191n66, 205

Guangxi University, 208

Gu Jingqing, 108

gundilong (makeshift dwelling), 65–66, 66n23, 68, 73, 75, 83, 84, 96–98, 127n74, 175, 253, 257, 262
guns. *See* weapons
Guo Linshuang (Leon Kwok), 174, 176–179, 194, 208–210, 263; charges against, 178; death of, 207; former life of, 177, 178, 194–195, 209; overseas descendants of, 207–208; Red Guards' treatment of, 174–175, 180–181, 181n31, 191, 193, 194–195, 196, 197, 198, 200, 210
Guomindang. *See* Nationalist Party
Guo Quan, 194
Guo Zhikai, 207
Guy, R. Kent, 5n13

handbooks, 14, 227n62, 248, 258; anti-superstition, 124n63, 135–136; for cadres, 1–4, 14, 64, 81n78, 248, 253; exhibitions as, 1, 4, 13, 172, 257; for museum workers, 21, 22, 258; Soviet museology, 36, 36n35; for rural artists, 1n1
handicrafts, 238, 243
Hangzhou, 46, 112
Han Xiaoqiang (fictional character), 19, 21, 24, 138, 140–141
Harbin, 175, 182n37
Hardoon, Silas, 98
Harrison, Henrietta, 35, 121n55
Hebei Province, 183
Heilongjiang Province, 150n35, 182n37, 199
Henan Province, 151n39
Henriot, Christian, 62n9, 66, 67n29, 93–94
Hershatter, Gail, 4n9, 62, 73–74, 90
He Shuheng, 43
Hess, Christian, 70n45
Heude, Pierre, 6
Hinton, William, 187
historical research, 46–47, 55–56, 249
historic sites, 2, 27, 260; preserved temples as, 109; Red Guard defacing of, 228, 229; restoration and touring of, 5–6, 36. *See also* First Party Congress Site
history: Chinese Communist Party, 4, 16, 38–39, 264; and displays, 3, 4, 8, 9, 19, 253; elisions from, 254, 262, 264; grassroots, 13, 251, 263; and material objects (*see wenwu*); official interpretation of, 4, 16, 17, 39, 41, 42–43, 48–50, 255; oral, 22, 47, 73, 250; and propaganda, 14; and "Red Line," 46–47, 49; writing of, 16

Ho, Dahpon, 228
Ho, Wing-Chung, 21, 60n2, 65n20, 68, 74, 89, 91, 92n115, 94n130, 263n43
Ho Chi Minh Museum, 262n37
holy water, 107, 117, 121, 130, 133
Hong Kong, 63, 80, 94, 208
Hong Kong and Shanghai Bank, 24, 229, 251
Hongkou Park, 146
Honig, Emily, 80n71, 91n113
house search, 13, 18, 19, 173, 174–175, 180–183, 186–187, 198, 200, 204, 205, 208, 227; art collectors as targets of, 213, 213n8, 221, 227, 231–232, 234; confiscations, 9, 18, 173, 174–175, 180, 182, 183, 186, 191, 194–198, 200, 206–210, *241*, 248, 250; as cultural preservation for the masses, 237; films of, 186, *187*, *188*; and hidden objects, 189–192, 195, 196, 197, 200, 203; and informants, 190, 195; memoirs relating, 206n128; reenactment of, 257; and Shanghai Museum, 231. *See also* objects
housing: dioramas at Shanghai Expo, 99–100. *See also* Fangua Lane; *gundilong*; shantytowns
Hu Jie, 205n122
Hufei School for Children of Boat People, 125, 126, 127, 128
huiyi duibi (comparing past and present), 163, 249; and class education exhibitions, 65; as display, 2, 16, 34; by Fangua Lane residents, 74–75, 77; and Five Antis Campaign, 144; by old workers, 87, 152, 159; and Shanghai Museum, 150. *See also yiku sitian*
Hunan Province, 151, 153; workers' movement, 40, 45
Hundred Flowers Movement, 130, 224–225
Hung, Chang-tai, 16, 36, 39, 42n65
Hu Qiaomu, 112n36
Hu Shi, 42

iconoclasm, 246, 246n128
icons, 22, 23, 24, 26, 112, 248, 265. *See also* First Party Congress Site
identity cards, 138, 141, 151, 263
ideology: aesthetics serving, 3; of class, 142; correctness, 15, 19, 112, 156, 157; science serving, 108–109, 124–125; socialist museums and, 258, 259–260
imperialism, 19, 23, 24, 87, 98, 194, 251; and class education exhibits, 146, 151,

159; cultural, 2; opposition to, 41; and superstition, 118
incense, 109, 110, 111, 127, 130, 133, 134
intellectuals, 8, 43, 183, 208, 215, 224
International Settlement, 38, 66, 79
Iskra (Soviet magazine), 178
Islam, 109

jade, 192, 210
Jade Buddha Temple, 134, 233
January Revolution, 206, 232, 234, 263
Japanese Occupation, 9, 66–67, 91n113, 214–215
jewels, 168, 181, 203
jewelry, 191, 192, 195
Jiang Dayi, 218
Jiang Qing, 90, 184, 205n122, 206n128, 232n84
Jiangsu Province, 7, 153, 157
Jiang Wenhuan, 169
Jiang Zemin, 57, 264
Jianzhu xuebao (Journal of architecture), 69–70
Jiefang ribao (Liberation daily), 51, 54, 69, 71, 100, 135
jiezhan. See class education exhibition
Jilin Province, 129, 131, 188
Jin Dalu, 53n92, 181
Jing, Jun, 262n40
Jing'an Temple, 229
Johnson, Matthew D., 4n8, 106n10
journalists, 167

Kang Sheng, 234
Kang Youwei, 7, 194
Karlsgodt, Elizabeth Campbell, 240n107
Kexue dazhong (Mass science), 105
keys, 174, 175, 195
Kissinger, Henry, 242
Knight, Sophia, 182
knowledge: authorized, 4; perceptual, 3, 21, 252, 255; power projected by, 6; rational, 3, 21, 251, 255
Koloskvoa, T. G., 38
Kong Xiangxi, 194
Korean War (Resist America and Support Korea), 1–2, 72
Kotkin, Stephen, 67
Kraus, Richard, 142
Kuhn, Philip A., 262n41

land deeds, 153, 191–192. *See also bian-tiantu/biantianzhang*
landlords, 9, 143, 144, 183, 193, 199; on display, 151, 152, 153; house searches of,

189–190, 195; property redistribution, 187, 188
land reform, 9, 13, 74, 187, 199, 204, 261, 262, 265; and definition of class, 152; and "new exhibitions," 188–189, 261; and "settling accounts," 148, 187–189; and "speaking bitterness," 16
Lao She, *Dragon Whisker Creek* (play), 76
ledgers. *See biantiantu/biantianzhang*
Lee, Haiyan, 89
Leese, Daniel, 16, 74, 176
Lei Feng, 89, 150, 162n75, 265
Leighton, Christopher R., 179n25
Lenin, Vladimir, 30, 42, 43
Leninism, 49
Lenin Museum, 36–37
Leonova, Olga, 36–37
letters, 74, 148–149, 182, 261, 264
Levine, Steven I., 46n69
Leys, Simon, 40n53
Li, Jie, 142n4, 207, 265n52
Liang, Samuel, 57–58
Liang Qichao, 108
Liang Sicheng, 37
Liberation (1949), 2, 4, 66, 68, 74, 76, 177, 178–179; possessions from before, 152; and Shanghai Museum, 216, 247; as temporal frame, 62. *See also* Old and New China
Li Bin, 252
Li Da, 28, 46, 48n78
Li Dazhao, 40–41, 55, 256; "On Question and Theory," 42
Li Enjie, 106n18
Lifton, Robert Jay, 125
Li Gancheng, 69
Li Hanjun, 27, 28, 44
Li Helin, 183
Li Hongyan, 138, 140–141, 144, 147
Li Junjie, 216, 217, 218n27, 224, 230n75, 244
Lin, Yüsheng, 246n128
Lin Biao, 52, 83, 92, 184, 185
Lin Boqu, 42n65
Li Rongrong, 245n125
Li Shucheng, 28
Li, Zhensheng, 150n35
literacy, 4, 91; and illiteracy, 3, 80n74
Little Red Book, 51, 191
Liu Jingji, 231, 232, 243
Liu Shaoqi, 42n65, 53n92, 55, 92
Liu Wencai, 141–142
living exhibition, 64–65, 83–102, 204, 208–209, 262; and class education,

146–150; as participatory propaganda, 86–87, 147

living textbooks, 37, 42, 151

Li Xun, 53n92, 163, 180n30, 181, 191n66, 206n128, 207n131, 229n70

Li Yanong, 216

Loh, Robert, 93n120

Long Bow Village (Shanxi), 187

Longhua Pagoda, 211–213, *212*; and Red Guards, 211–212, 214, 229; renovation of, 2, 109, 215; and Shanghai Museum staff, 211–212, 227, 229, 232, 233

Longhua Temple, 232

Louvre, 240

Love Science and Eliminate Superstition Exhibition, 18, 23, 104–105, 108, *110*, 111, 114–137, *117*, *118*, 254; beliefs post-exhibition, 125–137; rhetoric and narrative of, 114–125, 136–137, 254; text of, 127–128, 132–133. *See also* anti-superstition campaign

Lu, Di Yin, 213n8, 218n27, 220n41, 230n76, 240, 240n106

Lu, Hanchao, 67

Lu, Tracey L.-D., 9, 11, 35

Luo Genmei, 103–104, 105, 109, 114, 128, 134

Lu Xun, 60, 61n4, 120, 158, 183, 204; Memorial Hall, 55, 55n104; tomb, 33n21

luxury items, 174, 176, 178, 183, 192, *192*, 193, 248, 262; as symbols of exploitation, 195, 196, 254

Macau, 63

MacFarquhar, Roderick, 143n8, 144, 144n10, 176, 186n53, 205n124, 225n53

Ma Chengyuan, 217–218, 220, 230, 241–242, 245–247

Magnitogorsk, 67

Malawi, *45*

Mao era: cultural bureaucracy of, 260; and curating revolution, 1–6, 17, 27, 38–39, 49–50, 88, 249, 266; exhibitionary culture of, 4, 8, 13, 21, 64, 83, 87, 88, 98, 99, 252–266; and Fangua Lane's significance, 65, 98; and importance of First Party Congress Site, 23, 28, 49–50, 59; models in, 89, 90; as "new society," 4, 6n15, 62, 77; paradoxes of, 249; political culture of, 14–17, 248–249; and religious practice, 131–134, 136–137; and Shanghai Museum, 213, 246–247; and Sino-Soviet split, 38, 48; as taboo in China today, 265–266; tragedies, 265–266

Maoism. *See* Mao Zedong Thought; "Red Line"

Mao Zedong, 12, 90; analysis of revolution, 40; and Central Committee, 47, 48–49; and Chinese Communist Party founding, 17, 42, 47–48, 49–50n82, 55, 58–59; class ideology of, 141, 142–143, 153; cult of, 16, 74, 249; death of, 4, 54, 92, 134; and First Party Congress Site, 17, 30, 37, 40, 44, 46, 47, 48–49, 50, 55, 58–59, 255, 264; and founding date, 26, 58–59; and founding myth, 17, 49–50; and founding role, 17, 40, 47; gratitude toward, 74, 82, 106; historical narrative of, 260; on model-emulator dialectic, 89; and nature, 122; and "peaceful evolution," 158, 163; and Pita Rodríguez, 61n4; portraits of, 41, 71, 73, 100, 102, 178; and PRC founding declaration, 12; quotations of, 38, 55, 56, 140, 157, 191, 226, 256; and Red Guards, 176, 185, 186, 191; and "Red Line," 17, 27, 37, 39, 40, 41, 51–52, 75, 248, 253, 260; and religious belief, 133; representations of, 43, 265; and revolutionary discourse, 253, 255; and revolutionary sites, 33–34; and science, 122; sculpture of, 191, 256; writings of, 17, 19, 40, 138, 214, 253; "On New Democracy," 2, 14, 37, 38, 41, 214, 220, 225, 226, 235, 237, 246, 260; "On Practice," 3, 225; *Quotations of Chairman Mao*, 51; *Selected Works*, 124, 138; "Talks at the Yan'an Conference on Literature and Art," 14; "Three Great Revolutionary Movements," 112

Mao Zedong Thought, 17, 21, 41, 51, 56, 145n15, 208, 253, 259; and Red Guards, 169, 170, 183, 196–197, 198, 200, 201, 202, 211, 228, 236, 237

maps. *See biantiantu/biantianzhang*

Mariani, Paul P., 118

Maring (Hendricus Sneevliet), 45–46, 45–46n69

Marx, Karl, 30, 43, 127

Marxism, 17, 43, 44, 262; Chinese interpretation of, 89, 237

Marxism-Leninism, 3, 38, 40, 47, 224

Marxism-Leninism-Mao Zedong Thought, 17, 40, 136, 259

mass culture, 14. *See also* political culture

mass education, 1, 2, 8

masses: class education exhibitions for, 141; and class enemies, 174; Communist Party as voice of, 75; education of, 1, 2; historical role of, 263; mobilization of,

41, 262; models for, 91; and participation in exhibition, 261, 263; and patriotism, 2; and propaganda, 104, 250; and religious practices, 131–132; and Shanghai Museum, 2; and socialist education, 151; *wenwu* confiscated for, 236–237, 243, 245, 249, 253
mass mobilization, 1–2, 262
"mass work," museum role in, 21
material culture. *See* objects
materialism, 3, 13, 17, 108, 225
Matten, Marc Andre, 5, 6n15
May Fourth Movement, 38, 40, 42, 214, 246n128
May Thirtieth Movement, 49
McClellan, Andrew, 240
McDougall, Bonnie S., 14n42
memoirs, 22, 26, 27, 28, 33, 47, 48, 55, 88, 158, 181n33, 206, 206n128, 223, 230n75, 234n87
memory, 34, 62, 266; collective, 74n55. *See also* memoirs; oral histories
Mencius, 52
Meyer-Fong, Tobie, 5n14
military, 15. *See also* People's Liberation Army; soldiers
Military Museum of the Chinese People's Revolution, 264
Minhang District, 88, 165
Ministry of Culture, 37, 235
missionaries, 121, 151
Mitchell, Timothy, 6n20
Mittler, Barbara, 15, 156, 246
Miyakawa Torao, 230n74
mobilization, 1, 262; exhibition as tool of, 4, 13, 16
model, 17, 18, 19, 81–82, 83; dialectic of, 89, 90; Fangua Lane as, 89–97; sites, 92–93; Shanghai Museum as, 23; villages, 90
modernization, 7, 13, 15, 98, 108, 264
monks, 110, 114, 131n86, 211
monuments, 8, 29. *See also* First Party Congress Site
moon, 106–107
Munro, Donald J., 89, 90
Museum of German History, 260
Museum of the Chinese Revolution, 13, 39, 47, 48, 59, 260; founding of, 12, 35–36, 259; and historical documents, 55–56; and Jiang Zemin speech, 57, 264; and "Red Line," 40, 41, 42, 52, 56; renamed National Museum of China, 59; visitor rituals, 256
Museum of the Cultural Revolution, 208

museums, 1–9; anti-religion, 136, 136n107; characteristics and exhibitionary modes of, 13, 21; Chinese Communist transformation of, 2, 3, 4, 8, 9, 12; in Chinese history, 5–8, 9, 12, 34–38, 217, 219, 245, 258–261; educative role of, 3, 8, 12, 34, 259; grassroots nature of, 1–2; as ideological tool, 8; as living textbooks, 37; modernization role of, 7; and Nationalists, 34–35, 217, 259, 261; and political legitimacy, 6, 264; private, 265; purpose of, 21; of revolution, 8, 17, 240, 258–263; as ritual space, 256; socialist, 258–263; Soviet model of, 8, 12, 36–37, 38, 260, 261; terms for, 7; types of, 4. *See also* curating; docents; exhibitionary culture; exhibitions; visitors; *specific museums*

Nanjing Road, 18, 23–24, 177, 180, 207, 229
Nanshi District, 34n24, 105, 110, 134, 162
Nanshi District People's Committee, 111
Nanshi People's Government, 135
Nantong Museum, 7
Napoleon, 240
narratives, 1, 2–3, 41, 196, 249, 251–256, 266; alternative, 255; of antiquity, 253–254; authenticity of, 263; of class, 83, 198–205, 254; docent, 21, 41, 196, 254–255; of everyday life, 17; of Fangua Lane, 73–74, 98; of future prosperity, 99; historical, 4, 17, 52, 251, 260–261; as "making revolution," 19; master, 36; model, 90; of nation, 13, 254, 260; official, 255, 256; personal, 13, 16, 17, 73, 250, 253; Red Guard exhibition, 193–202, 249, 254, 255; of revolution, 3, 8, 19, 23, 36, 48–50, 57, 253, 254, 255, 260; ritualization of, 257; tape-recorded, 52, 254; of transformation, 73. *See also* scripts; *yiku sitian*
nationalism, 5, 7, 9, 14, 253; cultural, 247, 249; narratives of, 13, 254, 260
Nationalist Party (Guomindang), 5, 49, 66, 68, 152, 251; anti-superstition campaigns of, 108, 125; and cultural relics, 214, 215; and museums, 34–35, 217, 259, 261; Northern Expedition, 8, 66; and Red Guard denunciations, 174, 191, 194; and religion, 136n107
National Museum of China, 59, 265; Xi Jinping speech, 264
National Museum of the Vietnamese Revolution, 260

natural disasters, as euphemism for famine, 38, 130, 134, 148, 149, 193; as natural phenomenon, 115–117, *117*

natural phenomena, 115–117, *117*, 125, 126, 136; personification of, 122, 254

Nazi Germany, 240n107

Nedostup, Rebecca, 108, 125

Neibu cankao (Internal reference), 75, 94, 129, 130, 132, 152

Neiman, Vladimir, 44–46, 45n69

New China. *See* Old and New China; *yiku sitian*

New China Bookstore, 234

New Culture Movement, 8

new democracy. *See* Mao Zedong, "On New Democracy"

new exhibitions, 188–189, 262, 265; definition of, 261

new society. *See* Old and New China; *yiku sitian*

New Youth: magazine, 28, 29; office, 37

Ng, Petrus, 89

Nie Yuanzi, 183, 186

Nikolsky (Vladimir Neiman), 45–46, 45–46n69

1911 Revolution, 8, 38

Ni Xingxiang, 56, 56n107, 58, 58n113

Nixon, Richard, 242

Nora, Pierre, 5

Northern Expedition, 8, 66

object lessons, 3, 16, 141, 248

objects: and class, 15, 17, 18, 24, 77, 83, 138, 139, 141, 143, 144, 147, 151, 152, 153, *155*, 171, 173, 175, 176, 180, 181, 192–196, 198, 202, 205, 209–210, 248, 251, 254, 257, 261, 262; for comparing past and present, 150, 152, 248; display of, 1–5, 9, 16–17, 18, 21, 22, 53, 151, 152, *155*, 158–163, 165, 168, 173–176, 180–184, 182n37, 186, 188, 190–192, 191n66, *192*, 194–198, 200, 202–204, 206, 209, 210, *241*, 242, 248, 250, 252, 259, 263; disposition of, 206–207; as evidence, 5, 115, 132, 163, 175, 194–197, 250, 252; of Fangua Lane residents, 64, 87; from First Party Congress Site, 25; hiding of, 17, 189–192, 195, 196, 197, 200, 203; political lesson from, 248; of religious rituals, 109; searches for (*see* house search); of workers, 138, 140, *140*, 141, 151, 168. *See also wenwu*

October Revolution, 36, 39, 52, 240

Old and New China, 2–4, 6, 6n15, 23, 24, 27, 68, 180, 245, 254, 263; ambiguity between, 163; in class education, 141–142, 146, 150, 152, 159, 162–163, 171; and class struggle, 143, 151–152, 153; and definitions of class, 143; Fangua Lane as metonym for, 17, 59, 60–65, 71, 73, 76–83, 87, 89–97, 102, 171, 192, 251, 257; and Guo Linshuang, 177–178; and labor practices, 163; and Liberation as temporal frame, 2, 4, 62; and Mao-era exhibitionary complex, 83, 98; objects comparing, 150, 152, 248; and recalling bitterness, 74, 87, 154; and revolutionary discourse, 253; and Shanghai Museum, 213, 216–226, 244; and superstition, 104, 108, 115, 129. *See also yiku sitian*

Olsen, Jon Berndt, 260n29

On the Docks (opera and film), 19, *20*, 21, 24, 138, *139*, 139–140

opera, 19, 21, 138, 146, 209

Opium War, 38, 52

Oppose Feudal Superstition Exhibition, 112, 126

oral histories, 22, 47, 73, 250

overseas Chinese, 90, 178, 207

ox-pen imprisonment, 181, 215

Palace Museum, 7, 228, 230, 233–234; Nixon and Kissinger tour of, 242

Palmer, David, 108

panopticon, 151–152

Pantsov, Alexander V., 46n69

paper money, 103, 109, 121, 126

participatory propaganda, 198, 257–258, 263, 266; class education exhibition as, 142; definition of, 13; Fangua Lane as, 64–65, 83, 86–88, 92–93; Red Guard exhibition as, 198

patriotism, 2, 3, 26, 57, 220, 264

"peaceful evolution," 142, 157–158, 159–161, 166; premise of, 163–164; and Red Guard accusations, 170

Pearl TV Tower, 98, 265

peasants, 40, 41, 142, 144, 153, 187, 242; and Chinese Communist revolution, 23, 42; and class education exhibitions, 154, 193, 262; and class feeling, 154–155; clothing of, 146; as museum visitors, 50; narratives of, 251; and Red Guard exhibitions, 175, 183; and religious revival, 130, 131–132, 133; and shantytown housing, 23; and "speaking bitterness," 73–74, 188

Peking Man, 58n113

Peking University, 182–183
Peng Dehuai, 52
People's Liberation Army, 23, 56, 175; and cultural relics, 9, 216, 228, 260; Political Department, 148; "two remembrances, three investigations" campaign, 74. *See also* soldiers
People's Republic of China: Cuban goodwill tour of, 60; and economic miracle, 207, 245; fifteenth anniversary of, 72–73; founding of, 1, 4, 12, 25, 62; new elite of, 143; tenth anniversary of, 36, 50. *See also* Chinese Communist Party; Cultural Revolution; Mao era; reform era
perceptual knowledge, 3, 21, 252, 255
Perry, Elizabeth J., 15, 41, 53n92, 98–99n144, 159n70, 163, 180n30, 181, 198–199, 217, 247, 265n50
Petrone, Karen, 71n46
pharmaceuticals, 192, 193
photographs, 1, 152, 174, 252, 256; alteration of, 55; of confiscated objects, 18; Red Guards' use of, 183, 193, 194–195; of workers, 156, 175
pilgrimage, 23, 25, 253, 256
Pinghu County, 155–156
Pita Rodríguez, Félix, 60–61, 61n4, 63, 96–97, 256
PLA. *See* People's Liberation Army
political campaigns: and cultural production, 14–17, 220–226; and curating revolution, 248; and exhibitions, 1, 4, 6, 13, 18, 82–83, 92, 171, 187, 241, 248, 250, 251, 252, 257–258, 263, 264; and *wenwu*, 220–225. *See also specific campaigns*
political consciousness. *See* class consciousness
political culture, 14–19
political legitimacy, 6, 13–16, 35, 254, 262, 264; and cultural and military power, 15; and nation and revolution, 259
possessions. *See* objects
post-socialist/post-socialism. *See* reform era
Potemkin villages, 92–93
proletariat, 43, 74, 145; and bourgeoisie, 144, 156, 158. *See also* workers
propaganda: anti-superstition, 111–112, *113*, 114, 133; art as, 15; Chinese Communist use of, 12, 14, 29, 30, 38, 109, 198, 260; of class, 104, 144, 250; and class education, 144, 148–149, 154, 171, 172; and curating process, 249; exhibits as (*see* exhibitionary culture; *specific exhibitions*); forms of, 14, 22, 148,

249; grassroots, 1, 2–3, 4, 15, 17, 18; on protection of *wenwu*, 258–259. *See also* participatory propaganda
Pushkin, Alexander, 36
Putuo District, 61n7, 166

Qiang Zhai, 158, 158n63
Qian Jingtang, 244n123
Qianlong Emperor, 238
Qi Benyu, 206, 206n128, 233, 234, 235
qigong, 136, 264
Qin Emperor, 241
Qing dynasty, 6, 7, 8, 66, 108, 204
Qin Shao, 7n24
Qufu, 241. *See also* Confucius

radio transmitters, 195, 252
recalling bitterness. *See yiku sitian*
"red and expert," 224, 254
Red Army (Soviet), 36, 260
Red Flag (journal), 233
Red Guards, 174–210; Beijing manifesto of, 227–228; and big-character posters, 18, 172, 180, 186, 199; and class education exhibitions, 14, 18, 142, 164, 168, 169–172, 175, 183, 198, 199, 202, 204, 208, 254; curating exhibits, 13, 18–19, 23, 137, 174, 176, 181, 187, 189–193, 197–205, 251, 254, 257; conclusion of movement, 205–207, 250; destruction of collections by, 210, 228; as docents, 19, 175, 176, 182, 189, 196, 197, 198–205, 250, 255; exhibitions as revolutionary, 201; and factional fighting, 181, 251; and house searches (*see* house search); inception of movement, 168; justification of rebellion, 197, 236, 237; and Mao Zedong Thought, 169, 170, 183, 196–197, 198; and Shanghai Museum, 19, 211–212, 230–232; slogans, 257; targets, 211–213, 214; violence, 172n124, 176, 180, 181, 211; and *wenwu* for the masses, 244. *See also* "Attack on the Four Olds"; Beijing Red Guards; Exhibition of Red Guard Achievements; struggle sessions
"Red Line," 17, 27, 39, 75, 248, 253, 260; ambiguity and contradictions of, 40, 47, 249; components of, 40–42; and Cultural Revolution, 50–55; and curating revolution, 40–42; different connotations of, 201; and First Party Congress, 41, 44, 49–50, 75, 201; as guiding principle, 39; and Mao, 17, 26, 38, 39, 40, 41, 51–52, 75, 248, 253, 260; overturning of, 56; and

Red Guard exhibitions, 201; visual representation of, 42–43
Red Terror, 195
Red Tourism, 57
reform era: anti-superstition handbooks, 135–136; exhibitionary culture of, 263–265; and Fangua Lane, 64n14, 95–96, 102; and First Party Congress Site, 27, 56–57, 263; and Four Modernizations, 245; and patriotic education, 57; narrative of prosperity, 99, 245; and Red Tourism, 57; and religiosity among youth, 134–135; and Shanghai Museum, 243, 245–246, 247, 263, 264
refugees, 62, 67, 91
religion, 15, 129–137, 255; campaigns against, 104, 107, 108, 110–112, 117–121, 127, 132, 136, 229, 261; and exhibition texts, 18; five official, 109; and Great Leap Forward, 136; and missionaries, 121, 151; persistence of practice, 110, 114, 129–134; restoration of legitimacy, 135; scientific experiments vs., 115; and secularization, 109; and superstition, 108, 121, 127, 137. *See also* temples; *specific religions*
Renmin ribao (People's daily), 23, 24, 66, 87–88, 179–180, 181–182, 186, 229; "Four Olds" editorial, 227; list of confiscations, 191
Rent Collection Courtyard (sculpture), *141*, 141–142, 150
Ren Wuxiong, 40, 46–47, 49, 53, 250
Republican era, 6, 7, 176–177; and civil war, 9, 12, 62, 67, 215; exhibitions during, 263, 265; and Japanese Occupation, 9, 66–67, 91n113, 214–215; and museum development, 7, 8, 9, 12, 34–35, 36–37, 38, 217, 219, 245, 258–261; socialist museums compared with, 259–260
revisionism, 42, 42n65, 92, 142, 143, 157, 158
revolution: class-based, 17; and class education exhibition, 172; and collection, 239–240; and collective denunciation, 261; continuous, 4, 41, 210, 250, 254, 257, 261; and emotion, 198–199; icons of, 22; legitimization of, 13; Mao's analysis of, 40, 112; master narrative of, 36; museums of, 8, 12–13, 17, 19, 34–37, 240, 258, 259–260, 264; narratives of, 3, 8, 19, 23, 36, 48–49, 57, 253, 254, 255, 260; and political legitimacy, 259; and "Red Line," 41, 75; relics of, 3, 12, 33,

37, 58, 63, 227; rhetoric of, 244; sites of, 23, 33–34, 38, 50, 84; stages of, 41; vocabulary of, 4; *wenwu* of, 5–6, 8, 12, 17, 19, 33, 34, 35, 36, 57, 58, 59, 198, 225, 243, 249, 253; world, 24. *See also* continuous revolution; counterrevolutionary/ counterrevolutionaries; Cultural Revolution; curating revolution; *specific revolutions*
revolutionary history museum, 259–260; changed view of, 56; definition of, 13; display techniques, 34; and Mao Zedong Thought, 41, 51; and Nationalist Party, 8, 35; Shanghai plan for, 25–26
rituals, 15, 19, 21, 84, 249, 256–258, 261, 264; as legitimizing, 16, 35; and museum visitors, 4, 8, 141, 256–258
Rong Geng, 218, 218n28
Rong Shuren, 166–167
Rong Yiren, 170
Rong Zongjing, 159, 159n70, 167, 171
Rowe, Peter B., 265n50
Royal Asiatic Society, 6, 219
Ryckmans, Pierre, 39–40, 44, 46

Saich, Tony, 253
Sang Ye, 59n115
Santiaoshi History Museum, 150
Scarlett, Zachary A., 54n100, 82n80
scars, on display, 146, 152, *155*, 199, 248, 262, 263
Schmalzer, Sigrid, 58n113, 93, 103n1, 108, 112n35, 122
Schoenhals, Michael, 176, 186n53, 197, 198n85, 205n124, 252n10
Schram, Stuart R., 2n4, 3n5, 143n6, 226n58, 237n98
Schwarcz, Vera, 41n56
science, 102, 103–109, 114–127, 134–137; experiments, 112, 114–115, 248; ideological use of, 108–109, 112, 122, 136; Mao-era teaching of, 23, 105, 116–117, 125, 132, 248; and new democratic culture, 14; and socialist museums, 259. *See also* Love Science and Eliminate Superstition Exhibition
self-criticism, 167, 224, 257
Seng, Kuan, 265n50
"settling accounts," 148, 187–189
Shandong Province, 23, 241; class education exhibition, 150–151, 151n41, 152–153, 154, 157; Red Guards, 170, 171, 203
Shanghai, 23, 33, 46, 65, 76, 83, 87–88; art market, 216, 219, 236; Communist

takeover of, 9, 23–24, 74; early museums, 6; eight vistas of, 211; Five Antis Campaign, 131n86, 143, 144, 251; French Concession, 28, 43, 44, 65, 104; historic sites, 26, 34, 35, 109, 229; history of foreign presence, 2, 6, 24, 146, 219; house searches, 180, 180n29, 190; and January Revolution, 206, 234, 263; Longhua Pagoda, 211–213, *212*; past vs. present, 19, 87, 146, 229; Pearl TV Tower, 98, 265; and Red Guards, 169, 170, 171, 181, 185, 211, 229; Republican-era municipal center, 8–9; shantytowns, 17, 22, 23, 67, 93, 97–98, *99*, 253, 263; Socialist Education Movement, 112; as symbol for capitalism, 67, 146, 156, 159, 175, 179–180, 229; as symbol for revolution, 23–24, 31, 34, 35; wartime destruction, 8, 66–67; Wenwu Small Group, 236–239, 243; *yiku sitian* exhibitions, 75; Yong'an Department Store, 176–177. *See also* City God Temple; Exhibition of Red Guard Achievements; Fangua Lane; First Party Congress Site; Shanghai Class Education Exhibition; *specific districts*
Shanghai Bureau of Commerce, 174n3, 175, 198
Shanghai Bureau of Construction, 167, 211n1
Shanghai Bureau of Culture, 22, 34, 37, 54, 109, 154, 213, 235, 236, 251, 260; Anti-Rightist Campaign attacks on, 47; relationship with Cultural Relics Commission, 216
Shanghai Class Education Exhibition, 18, 64, 75, 142, 154–173, *160*, 175, 179, 199, 236; anti-capitalist focus of, 156, 221; criticism of, 165–166, 203; Cultural Revolution revisions to, 172; curation of, 158, 159–164, 171, 172, 250; docents, 255; measure of success, 164–165; as political campaign, 171; and Red Guards, 168–172, 232; rituals of, 256; scale of, 156, 157, 164; stated purpose of, 158; display layout, 159–160; visitors to, 157, 164–168, 258, 262
Shanghai Cultural Relics Commission, 5, 63, 109, 111, 212n4, 213, 214, 216, 217, 224–225; institutional history, 216n19; response to Red Guards, 229–230, 231, 232
Shanghai Expo, 99–100, *100*, *101*, 264, 265
Shanghai History Museum, 265
Shanghai jiaoyu (Shanghai education), 145

Shanghai Municipal Government, 28, 216
Shanghai Municipal Museum (Republican era), 8–9, *10*, *11*, *12*, 35, 245, 259
Shanghai Museum, 2, 5–8, 60, 86, 211–247, 232n84; catalogue, 214; collection, 3, 13, 22, 23, 210, 216–221, *222*, 225, 239–241, 243, 250, 252–253, 258; and Cultural Revolution, 13, 19, 52, 226–233, 245–246, 249, 250, 254, 255; curating process, 249–250; docent scripts, 223–224, 254; donations to, 220–221; educational task of, 251–252; exhibitions, 38, 150, 221–222, 245, 247, 252, 253; founding of, 19, 213, 247, 259; mission of, 213–214; as a model, 23; new building, 222–223, 245; "Past and Present" exhibit, 150; and political campaigns, 220–226; protection of Longhua Pagoda, 211–212, 227; as reflection of state in power, 247; in reform era, 243, 245–246, 247, 263, 264; re-opening of, 240–241; and Red Guards, 19, 211–212, 213, 230–232; Revolutionary Committee, 241; and Shen Zhiyu as director, 245–246; staff, 217–219, 224, 230–231, *233*, *238*; stature of, 23, 245–246, 263; visitors to, 221, *223*, 223–224, 226; and *wenwu*, 19, 23, 24, 210–211, 213, 214, 225, 226–227, 230, 232–245, 246, 247, 249, 253, 255; Wenwu Small Group, 236–239, 243, 244, 246
Shanghai Party Committee, 30, 37, 74–75, 144, 154, 163, 168–169; Propaganda Department, 22, 25, 27, 29, 42–43, 154, 156, 169; and Socialist Education Movement, 171–172
Shanghai People's Committee, 77, 84n85, 111, 229, 232; Cultural and Education Office, 22
Shanghai People's Commune, 232, *233*, 250
Shanghai People's Congress, 166, 167, 177, 208
Shanghai People's Government, 230, 232, 245
Shanghai Revolutionary Committee, 50, 52, 63, 180, 185n50, 206, 232, 237, 239
Shanghai Revolutionary History Memorial Museum, 37, *44*, 50n83
Shanghai University, 169
Shanghai Workers' Palace, 38, 149–150

shantytowns, 17, 22, 23, 64n15, 69, 221, 253; and class education exhibition, 150, 159, 175; conditions of, 65–68, 87, 88n98, 91; descriptions today, 97–98; diorama of, 98, 99; Fangua Lane apartments contrasted with, 60, 64, 71, 87; 1960s growth, 93–94; and "Past and Present" exhibit, 77, 150; preservation for exhibition, 63–64, 88, 213, 263; and Red Guard exhibition, 175; visitors to, 77, 85, 87, 94. *See also* Fangua Lane

Shao, Qin, 7n24
Shapiro, Judith, 122, 134n96
Shen Jianzhi, 218
Shenxin Mills, 159, 166–167
Shen Zhiyu, 6, 7n24, 60, 215, 216n18, 217, 224, 232n84; on exhibition work, 21, 225–226, 252; and First Party Congress site search, 17, 25–29, 33, 34, 213; on museum's educative role, 2–3, 251–252; and protection of Shanghai Museum, 230; and Red Guards, 232, 232n84; return to Shanghai Museum, 240–241; as Shanghai Museum director, 245–246

Sheshan Cathedral, 146
Siccawei (Xujiahui) Museum, 6
Sichuan Province, 132, 133n92; *Rent Collection Courtyard* exhibition, 141, 141–142, 150

silver, 191, 196, 203, 207; dollars, 180
Sino-Japanese War, 9, 66–67, 91, 177, 214–215, 253
Sino-Soviet Friendship: Building, 222; palaces, 151
Sino-Soviet split, 38, 48
slogans, 146, 191, 244, 256, 257
slums. *See* shantytowns
Smith, Stephen, 75–76n59, 106n10, 107–108n13, 117n50, 133, 136n107, 261n34
Sneevliet, Hendricus, 45–46n69
Snow, Edgar, 63, 67, 69
socialism, 4n8, 87, 143, 145, 260; and capitalism, 144; icons of, 265; visual culture of, 15. *See also* communism
socialist construction, 2, 3–4, 14–16, 259; role of science in, 108; Soviet display of, 36–37; today's display of, 265
Socialist Education Movement, 16, 112, 132, 143–149, 161, 221; and class education exhibition, 139, 142, 150, 153, 154, 157, 165, 171, 197, 199, 258; and Cultural Revolution, 18, 142, 164, 172, 258; origins of, 143, 143n8; purpose of,

170–172; scope of, 143–148; targets of, 160; Twenty-Three Articles, 144
socialist museums, 258–263; characteristics of, 257–259; narrative of, 260; Republican-era museums vs., 259–260, 261
socialist transformation, 143, 177–179, 209, 219, 221, 258, 263
soldiers, 50, 74, 94–95, 148–150, 165, 175
Song dynasty: basins, 184; pagoda, 109, 211; vase, 248
Song Meiling, 98
Soviet Museum of the Revolution, 13, 17, 34, 36–37, 240
Soviet Union, 67, 71n46, 109, 215, 222; as anti-religion, 136; archival documents, 47; cultural bureaucracy, 260; as curatorial model, 8, 12, 36–37, 39, 261; and denunciation, 261; exhibitionary culture of, 36, 260, 261, 262; as museum model, 8, 12, 36–37, 38, 260, 261; October Revolution, 36, 39, 240; revolutionary museums, 260; split with China, 38, 48; Western visitors to, 92–93. *See also* Soviet Museum of the Revolution
space exploration, 123, 124
speaking bitterness, 16, 73–74, 75, 92, 144, 148, 156, 188, 250, 257; origins in Chinese tradition, 262
spirit: medium, 117, 118, 121; world, 108, 114, 117, 248
Spring Festival, 71, 72, 73, 81, 101–102, 111–112, 129, 134, 150, 177, 211, 217
Stalin, Joseph, 36, 37, 260
State Cultural Relics Bureau, 12–13, 34, 223, 225
state in power: and anti-superstition exhibition, 136; exhibitionary culture of, 13, 92–93, 259, 260, 261, 262, 263–264; and First Congress Site, 58, 84, 201; revolutionary movement vs., 13, 58, 201, 262–263; and Shanghai Museum exhibitions, 247
state in revolution: exhibitionary culture of, 4, 13, 18–19, 92, 189, 261, 262, 264, 265. *See also* revolution
storytelling, 16, 18, 251
struggle sessions, 150n35, 159, 174, 181, 185, 186, 199, 200, 210, 211, 232n84, 261; as collective, 261; exhibition accompanying, 182n37; against Xie Zhiliu, 225
students: and class education, 18, 138, 142, 144, 145–148; competitive system, 128–129n80; and Longhua Pagoda,

211–212; and religious practice, 132; and science dissemination, 103–107, 114–134; and superstition, 114, 128, 137, 150, 250; and traditional beliefs, 18, 114; visits to Fangua Lane, 17, 64, 64n14, 84, 87, 92, 94, 263. *See also* Red Guards; Young Pioneers

Su, Yang, 208

Sun Yat-sen, 8, 9, 237, 257; residence, 33n21, 35; mausoleum, 5, 35; Three Principles of the People, 35

supernatural, 102, 114, 130, 250

superstitions, 18, 102–104, 114–118, 124–128, 179, 248–250, 254; appeal to children, 128; articles of, 109, 257; class associated with, 107, 108, 115, 124, 126, 136, 137; dangers of, 117–118, 121–122, 126; as deep-rooted, 127–129, 132; definition of, 114. *See also* anti-superstition campaign

Suzhou Creek, 66, 79, 79n68

Taiping Rebellion, 38

Taiwan, 224, 259

Tang, Xiaobing, 15

Teiwes, Frederick C., 144n12

temples, 109, 110, *110*, 136n107, 262; increased attendance, 130; Red Guards' destruction of, 228, 229; restricted access to, 111, 112, 136n107

Ten Great Buildings, 36

textbooks, 4, 37, 42, 151

Though I am Gone (documentary film), 205n122

"thought work," 111–112, 145n15, 224, 250

Tiananmen, 5, 12, 50, 176; student movement, 57, 264

Tianjin, 90, 133, 150, 151

Tibet, 175

tin mines, 150

Tolstoy, Leo, 36

Tongji University, 182

"two remembrances, three investigations," 74, 148

U, Eddy, 221n42

Unger, Jonathan, 143n9

united front, 41, 48, 216

United States, 1–2, 82, 246, 258; imperialism, 118; McCarthy era, 93; military, 151, 152; Nixon visit, 242; "peaceful evolution," 157–158

Université l'Aurore, 219

van de Ven, Hans J., 48n78, 49

Vietnam, 82, 84, 260, 262n37

visitors, *12*, 15, 21–22, 254, 264; to class education exhibitions, 157, 164–172, 262; to Fangua Lane, 17, 64n14, 83–*85*; to First Party Congress Site, 40–41, 50, 52; mobilization of, 13; participation, 19, 83; and participatory propaganda, 13; questions, 46; to Red Guard exhibitions, 175, 183, 186, 190, 191–192, 197, 203, 258; response, 2, 16, 18, 21, 152, 202–203, 226, 251, 254–256, 257, 262; rituals of, 4, 8, 141, 256–258; to Shanghai Municipal Museum, 259; workers as, 3, 50, 83, 221, 224, 225; world view, 3, 4. *See also* foreign visitors; students

visual culture, 14, 15, 42, 170, 171

Vogel, Ezra F., 144n9

Walder, Andrew G., 128–129n80, 204–205, 205n121

Wang Chaowen, 43, 43n66

Wang Fuqing, 88–89

Wang Guangyan, 106n10

Wang Jingwei, 27, 194, 214

Wang Jinmei, 43

Wang Lanhua, 60, 61, 61n5, 62, 63, 63n12, 65–66, 67, 68, 70n45, 72, 73, 75, 96–97, 178, 253, 256; as critic, 92; and Fangua Lane exhibition, 76, 81n79, *86*, 88–89, 253, 263; on *gundilong*, 65–66; as organizer, 94; reform era self-portrayal, 97

Wang Nianyi, 180n29, 191n66, 227, 237n101

Wang Qingzheng, 246n127

Wang, Xiaoxuan, 134n96

Wang Yanchun, 151

Wang Yeqiu, 12–13, 30, 33, 34, 36–37

Wasserstrom, Jeffrey N., 262n36

water goblins, 114, 125, 128

Watson, Rubie, 260

weapons, 168, 180, 181, 182, 186, 188, 195, 251; display of, 152, 191, 191n66, 192, 257

Weigelin-Schwiedrzik, Susanne, 41, 48n77

Wenhui bao (Wenhui daily), 24, 71, 73, 86–87, 96, 138, 213n8, 243

wenwu (cultural relic): abroad, 246, 247; and class, 225–226, 254; of Cultural Revolution, 52, 215, 232, 234, 237, 243; destruction of, 227, 234, 243; display, *241*, 241–243, 252; dual nature of, 226, 254; First Party Congress Site as, 8, 17, 22, 23, 25, 26, 27, 33, 46–47, 57; and

Hundred Flowers Movement, 224–225; integrity of, 56; lost in Cultural Revolution, 243; in media, 243; and memory, 34; nationalization of, 225; as national treasures, 3, 5, 9, 23, 184, 253; place in revolution, 210; and political campaigns, 221–222; pre and post-1949 museum treatment of, 257–259; preservation of, 214–215, 216; private trade in, 219, 220, 225, 244; propaganda about, 258–259; protection units (*wenwu baohu danwei*), 33, 234, 235–238, 244; Red Guard threat to, 19, 210, 211, 213, 215, 227, 228, 229–232; of revolution, 5–6, 8, 12, 17, 19, 31, 34, 35, 37, 57, 58, 59, 198, 225, 243, 249, 253; salvage of, 229–234, 242–245; Shanghai Museum early collection of, 2–3, 216, 219, 220, 222, 224, 240; Shanghai Museum rescue of, 19, 23, 24, 210–211, 213, 214, 225, 226–227, 232–245, 246, 247, 249, 253, 255; of state in power, 58; state protection of, 2, 5–6, 9, 12–13, 17, 19, 25, 29, 33, 34, 55, 214–216, 223, 225, 227, 228, 260; temples and churches as, 109; top-tier, 240, 240n106; Wenwu Small Group index, 236; and *yiku sitian* narratives, 16, 76, 92

Wenwu cankao ziliao (Cultural relics reference materials), 12, 36, 224

Wenwu Small Group, 236–239, 243, 244, 246; founding date, 237; receipt from, *239*

West Lake Exposition, Revolutionary Memorial Hall, 8, 35

will-o'-wisp, 116, 125, 126

Wing On (Yong'an) Company, 176

workers, 19, 24, 38, 97, 171, 250, 254, 258; Anyuan movement, 56; bodies of, 250; "cattle and horses" trope, 75–76n59, 138; children of, 138, 145; and class education exhibitions, 142, *149*, 149–150, 154–155, 159, 161, 165, 193, 257; clothing of, 193, 194; comparing past and present lives of, 87, 152, 159; diorama of, 140; displays of confiscated objects, 197; exploitation of, 156, 159–160, 166; family origins, 138; Fangua Lane as new village for, 17, 18, 23, 61, 73, 74, 75, 81, 83, 87, 88, 91n113, 92, 248; Fangua Lane exhibit vs. class education exhibit on, 159; Fangua Lane visits by, 64n14, 86–87; Hunan movement, 40, 44; injuries of, 152, 156, 159, *160*, 175, 193, 248; as museum

visitors, 3, 50, 83, 221, 224, 225; narratives of, 251; 1960s layoffs of, 163; objects owned by, 138, 140, *140*, 141, 151, 165; scars of, 146, 152, *155*, 156, 199, 248, 262, 263; and Shanghai Museum, 221; and shantytown conditions, 65–66, 68, 77; and symbols of oppression, 108, 151; and *wenwu*, 238, 254. *See also* class struggle; proletariat

work teams, 107, 155, 165, 168, 171, 184

World's Fairs, 6

Wu Fangsheng, 220

Wu, Guo, 16, 74n55, 151n38, 172n124, 251, 255

Wu, Hung, 5n12

Wu, Yiching, 143, 178n20

Xiang Da, 215, 215n14

Xiaojinzhuang, 90

Xie Fuzhi, 205n122

Xie Zhiliu, 225

Xi Jinping: anti-corruption campaign, 264; "China Dream," 264

Xinhua News Agency, 134

Xinjiang Province, 81, 148

Xinmin wanbao (New people's evening news), 166

Xintiandi, 26, 37, 57

Xinwen ribao (News daily), 177

Xue Wenchu (Mrs. Li Shucheng), 30, 53

Xuhui District, 65, 104n5, 121, 127, 129

Xujiahui, 6; Cathedral, 109, 129, 229, 236; Orphanage, 121

Xu Linyu, 217, 224–225

Xu Yao, *Fangua Lane Has Changed*, 62

Yan'an, 14, 253

Yang Kuan, 217

Yangpu District, 9, 128

Yang Shuhui, 27, 28–29

Yang Xiguang, 163

Yang Yaojian, 183, 184n42, 207n132

Yang Zhongguang, 25, 28

Yan Jichang, fur coat, *192*, 193

Yao Qingxiong, 55, 55n194

Yao Shifeng, 189, 191, 193, 197, 200

Yaoshui Lane, 76, 150

Yao Wenyuan, 52, 168

Yao Zhen, 25, 26

Yeh, Wen-hsin, 176–177, 177n13, 194n72

Ye Jianying, 206n128

Yiguandao (Way of Pervading Unity), 106, 136

Yiguan hairen dao (film), 106, *107*, 112

yikufan (bitterness meal), 65, 87, 146–147, 148, 262

yiku sitian (recalling bitterness/reflecting on sweetness), 18, 92, 101–102, 138, 145, 146, 155, 172n124, 250, 257, 262; and class education exhibition, 74, 87, 152–153, 154, 156, 175; and Fangua Lane, 16, 18, 73–76, 81, 83, 87, 92, 257; goals of, 74; and Great Leap Forward famine, 255; origins of, 73–74; "Past and Present" exhibit, 64–65, 76–83, 84, 87, 94, 102, 192; repertoire of, 148, 159; and Shanghai Class Education Exhibition, 162–163, 167; Shanghai exhibitions of, 75, 138, 141, *149*; Socialist Education Movement, 16. *See also* Old and New China

Yong'an Department Store, 146, 174–179, 263; international licenses of, 194; Red Guard takeover of, 18, 179–180, 194, 209, 229; restoration of name, 207–208; socialist transformation of, 177, 178, 179

Young Pioneers: and Love Science and Eliminate Superstition Exhibition, 18, 114, 115, 122, 125–128, 130, 249, 250; and religious belief, 133, 134, 255

youth: discontent among, 147–148; increased religiosity of, 134–135; sent to countryside, 205, 224, 244. *See also* children; students

Youth League, 130, 132–133, 145, 254

youth palaces, 38

Yue, Daiyun, 182–183, 183n38

Yu Gardens, 2, 216

Yu Huiyong, 138

Yunnan Province, 150, 151, 153

Zhabei District, 61, 62–63, 71, 91, 95; gazetteer, 98; People's Committee, 63; wartime devastation, 66–67; Workers' Palace, 64. *See also* Fangua Lane

Zhang Chunqiao, 52, 142, 154, 157, 158n66, 163–164, 170

Zhang Guotao, 48n78

Zhang Jian, 7

Zhang Ruiheng, *Take a shuttle and explore outer space, 123*

Zhaojiabang Road, 76, 87

Zhejiang Province, 23n61, 112, 126

Zhejiang University, 46

Zheng Zhenduo, 225

Zheng Zhong, 213n8, 220n41, 230n75

Zhong Yinlan, 76, 211–212, 213, 214, 216, 217, 221, 225, 230n75, 250, 256, 263; and protection of *wenwu*, 23, 227, 231, 232, 236, 237, 239, 243, 244; training of, 218–219, 248

Zhou Enlai, 55n104, 206, 212n5, 228; calligraphy for Santiaoshi History Museum, 150; death of, 53–54; directive protecting *wenwu*, 233; and Shanghai Museum, 217

Zhou Fohai, 27, 27n4, 28, 33

Zhou, Xun, 110

Zhou Zhiyou, 27

Zhu Li, 218n27, 219, 220n41, 244–245

Zhu Minyi, 214n12

Zhu Rongji, 98

For EU product safety concerns, contact us at Calle de José Abascal, 56–1°, 28003 Madrid, Spain or eugpsr@cambridge.org.

 www.ingramcontent.com/pod-product-compliance
Ingram Content Group UK Ltd.
Pitfield, Milton Keynes, MK11 3LW, UK
UKHW010249140625
459647UK00013BA/1750